AT THE TABLE OF POWER

AT THE TABLE OF POWER

Food and Cuisine in

the African American Struggle

for Freedom, Justice, and Equality

DIANE M. SPIVEY

University of Pittsburgh Press

Published by the University of Pittsburgh Press, Pittsburgh, Pa., 15260

Manufactured in the United States of America
Printed on acid-free paper
10 9 8 7 6 5 4 3 2 1

Cataloging-in-Publication data is available from the Library of Congress

ISBN 13: 978-0-8229-4731-8
ISBN 10: 0-8229-4731-5

Cover illustrations: Olexandra Kolyadina, Courtesy Depositphotos, Inc.
Cover design: Joel W. Coggins

CONTENTS

ACKNOWLEDGMENTS

My deepest gratitude is extended to Mrs. Freida Wormley, Mr. Stanton L. Wormley Jr., Mr. Peter Shelton, Professor Vincent Thompson, Ms. Edna Jordan Smith, Chef Joe Randall, and my husband, Donald Spivey, for their time and graciousness afforded me. I also wish to thank the following individuals and institutions.

In Washington, DC: Dr. Matthew Wasniewski, Historian, US House of Representatives; Benjamin Hayes, Office of the Historian, US House of Representatives; Dr. Katherine Scott and Mary Baumann, US Senate Historical Office, US Senate; Ms. Felicia Wivchar, Office of History and Preservation, Office of the Clerk, US House of Representatives; Mr. Bryant Stukes, Commission on Art, Office of Senate Curator, US Senate; Ms. Theresa Malanum, Collections Specialist, Office of Senate Curator; Dr. Donald A. Ritchie, Senate Historian, US Senate; Mr. William R. Ellis Jr., Federal Judicial Records, Archives 1, Textual Reference Section, Textual Archives Services Division, National Archives and Records Administration; Mr. Bruce Kirby, Jennifer Brathovde, Joseph D. Jackson, and Patrick Kerwin, Manuscript Division, Library of Congress; Mr. Frank Herch, Law Library of Congress; Ms. Joellen Elbashir, Manuscript Division, Moorland Spingarn Research Center, Howard University; and Mr. Kamal McClarin, Interpretative Ranger, Frederick Douglass National Historic Site, in Anacostia, DC.

In Massachusetts, thanks go to Ms. Elizabeth Bovier, Archives and Records Preservation, Massachusetts Supreme Judicial Court, Suffolk County Courthouse, Boston; Ms. Irene Axelrod, Peabody Library / Essex Museum, Salem; Houghton Library, Harvard University, Cambridge; Ms. Tracy Potter, Massachusetts Historical Society, Boston; Mr. Sean

Casey in Rare Books and Manuscripts, John J. Devine Jr. in the Social Science/Government Documents Department, and James Lipp, Boston Public Library, Boston; Ms. Connie Mendes, Fall River Historical Society, Fall River; Ms. Marilyn Schachter, Museum of African American History, Boston; Ms. Sara Goldberg, Historic Newton, Jackson Homestead and Museum, Newton; Mr. Brian Sullivan, Mount Auburn Cemetery, Cambridge; Ms. Susan Greendyke, Art Collections Manager, Bureau of State Office Buildings, Boston.

In New York: Ms. G. McLaurin in the Manuscripts, Archives and Rare Books Division, and Ms. Sharon Howard in the Jean Blackwell Hutson General Research and Reference Division, Arthur A. Schomburg Center for Research in Black Culture, New York; Ms. Tara C. Craig, Rare Book and Manuscript Library, Butler Library, Columbia University, New York; Mr. Ted O'Reilly, Manuscript Department, New York Historical Society, New York; Mr. David M. Ment, Municipal Archives, City of New York; Ms. Rosemary Switzer, Rare Books and Special Collections, Rush Rhees Library, University of Rochester, Rochester; Jamie, Saratoga Springs Historical Society, Saratoga Springs.

In Pennsylvania: the State Library of Pennsylvania, Harrisburg; Mr. Jack Gumbrecht, at the Historical Society of Pennsylvania, Philadelphia; Ms. Cornelia S. King and Phil Lapsansky, the Library Company of Philadelphia, Philadelphia; Ms. Brenda Galloway-Wright and John Pettit, Department of Urban Archives, Samuel L. Paley Library, Temple University, Philadelphia; Ms. Nancy R. Miller, University of Pennsylvania Archives, North Arcade/Franklin Field, Philadelphia.

In Baltimore, Maryland, I am grateful to Mr. Francis O'Neill, Reference, Maryland Historical Society, and Ms. Lisa Crawley, Reginald F. Lewis Museum of Maryland African American History & Culture. In Virginia, many thanks go to the Library of Virginia, Richmond; Ms. Sarah Myers, Fred W. Smith National Library for the Study of George Washington, Mount Vernon; and Ms. Anna Berkes, Jefferson Library, Thomas Jefferson Foundation, Inc., Charlottesville. I would also like to express my gratitude to the State Historical Society of Wisconsin, Madison, as well as to Ms. Lee Campinha-Schenck, Rhode Island Black Heritage Society, Providence; Mr. Bert Lippincott, Newport Historical Society, Newport; and Ms. Ann Amaral, Newport Public Library, Reference Department, Newport. In Connecticut, I am grateful to Ms. Heather Dean, Yale Collection of American Literature, Beinecke Rare Book and Man-

Acknowledgments

uscript Library, Yale University, New Haven, and Ms. Diana McCain, Connecticut Historical Society, Hartford. I also wish to thank Mr. Josh Larkin Rowley, Rare Book, Manuscript, and Special Collections Library, William R. Perkins Library, Duke University, Durham, North Carolina; Mr. Ronald Figueroa, Mr. Jorge Fiterre, and Clarissa Arguello, Inter-Library Loan Department, Otto Richter Library, University of Miami, Coral Gables, Florida; Ms. Chloe Raub, Archives and Special Collections, Newcomb Institute, Tulane University, New Orleans, Louisiana; and Ms. Jan Longone, American Culinary History at Special Collections, Hatcher Library, University of Michigan, Ann Arbor, Michigan.

Last, but certainly not least, I wish to praise and thank Abby Collier, Amy Sherman, Pippa Letsky, and the entire team at the University of Pittsburgh Press for their professionalism, hard work, and for believing in my work.

PROLOGUE

Long before cooking and cuisine evolved into an arm of the entertainment industry, when the United States still considered cooking a type of labor suitable only for society's bottom rung, the foundation of America's national cuisine was formulated in the pots and cauldrons of America's southern Black cooks. However, judging by nineteenth and twentieth centuries' and many of today's culinary historical accounts of the foundation of America's cuisine, you would never know that Africans and their descendants were the dominating presence in American kitchens from this country's inception. They stood at the helm as creative head chefs of farms and plantations, restaurants, hotels, steamboats, lodges and private clubs, trains, and homes of the elites. The prevailing accounts, or *culinary master narratives*, have not only erased the true contributions of Africans and African Americans to American cuisine, they also represent and reinforce *culinary apartheid*—that is, the theft of African and African American creativity and contributions in American food and cooking by assigning Black culinary achievements to others. These accounts continue to deliberately pigeonhole African American cuisine in the category of *soul food*, used as a type of cultural and culinary shackle.[1]

The fact is, by erasing or minimizing the depth and value of the African American presence in American culinary history, the culinary master narrative also erases the history of conflict and brutality perpetrated against Blacks in America, brutality wholly caused and sanctioned by America's statutes, laws, and legislation. The same enactments that established the precept of inferiority—and thereby powerlessness—of Blacks in America during slavery, and the third-class status of Blacks beyond the end of formal slavery, are the same laws and legislation that today support and maintain White supremacy with regard to the history of cooking in America.

At the Table of Power offers a unique insight into the historical experience and cultural values of African America, and America in general, by way of the kitchen. Within these pages lies a powerful story beckoning you, daring you, to witness this culinary, cultural, and political journey taken hand in hand with the fight and uphill battle of Africans in America from colonial slavery through the Reconstruction era and beyond. Pushed into the few narrow avenues of livelihood presumed suitable for those whom society deemed inferior to Whites, some Black cooks became successful in the field of the culinary arts. In doing so, African American culinary artists more than earned a rightful place at the table of culinary power and contribution. They and their struggle must be fully recognized if the culinary history of America is to step over the color line.

From the beginning, all Africans in America were presumed to be slaves, whether they were or not, and as such, anything created, produced, or conceived by Africans and their descendants, including their culinary contributions, was considered to be the property of Whites. Slavery jurisprudence—that is, laws created and enforced and court decisions handed down during the era of slavery, such as Supreme Court Judge Thomas Ruffin's decision in *State v. John Mann*—mandated that Africans in America were *"doomed in [their] own person and [their] posterity, to live without knowledge and without the capacity to make anything [their] own, and to toil that another may reap the fruits"* (italics added).[2]

From the rural country kitchen and steamboat floating palaces to marketplace street vendors and restaurants in urban hubs of business and finance, Africans in America cooked their way to positions of distinct superiority, and thereby became indispensable. Despite their many culinary accomplishments, the vast majority of Black culinary artists have been rendered invisible. They do not share in the accolades and notoriety as either the founders or the creators of American cuisine, nor are they represented in the moneymaking echelons of today's celebrity chefs. Slavery jurisprudence legitimizes culinary apartheid and upholds now, as it did during slavery, the interrelationship between the American judicial system and institutionalized racism.

Food and politics have always formed a strong, inextricable relationship. One venue where the African culinary presence was deeply entrenched was in the White House, where presidential personal preferences for Black cooks during numerous administrations were a serious matter and not open to debate. African cooks such as Hannah Till and her husband, Isaac, were featured in all of George Washington's kitchens, including Valley Forge, where the Tills cooked for the Continental Army encamped there from December 1777 to June 1778. Washington's favorite restaurant and hangout was "Black Sam" Fraunces's Tavern, an eating place where plans began that resulted in the formation of the United States of America. Enslaved though they were, head chefs Hercules and James Hemings were responsible for building the culinary reputations of George Washington and Thomas Jefferson, respectively. They not only contributed tremendously to the evolution of American cuisine, they were also instrumental in sowing the seeds for the development of what America refers to as "fine dining."

The African culinary presence was found everywhere cooking and cuisine were offered. Rhode Island boasted its culinary experts. Beginning in 1700 and for the next seventy years, the city of Newport attained phenomenal maritime commercial success through the trade in commodities such as rum, which was produced by Africans in slavery.

Culinary excellence, however, was not just the domain of persons in bondage. Free and freed persons of African descent—Samuel Fraunces in New York, Edith Fosset and members of her family in Ohio, to name a few—established businesses offering fine dining during the era of slavery, and beyond. Such was found in Salem, Massachusetts, between 1805 and 1857 where the John and Nancy Remond family of caterers wined and dined Supreme Court judges, presidents, and foreign dignitaries. Thomas Downing and his son George T. were free Blacks who established culinary legacies that began in 1830 with the sale of oysters in an upscale establishment on New York City's Wall Street. George T's businesses and his legacy grew, spanning three states, from New York to Rhode Island, and to Washington, DC.

Africans established their culinary presence in Philadelphia by way of marketplace and street-corner vendors and by accomplished chefs such as James Prosser, St. John Appo, and Robert Bogle, all of whom catered lunch and dinner meetings for libraries and literary societies as well as important social functions. Even though Africans brought national and international acclaim to Philadelphia, as the center of epicurean delights, current food writers claim that Blacks were lacking in culinary and business skills until they were taught cooking and catering by French immigrants. In a later era, members of the clergy of Philadelphia's Catholic Church—drinking and partying their way through Prohibition and the Great Depression—were no strangers to the African cook, as they were among hundreds of clients who did not look to the French to cater their affairs. Their preference was for Black cooking.

Those who persevered to become caterers, restaurateurs, chefs, and private cooks constituted a minute percentage of the Black population, but they endeavored to make a difference. Denied the right to vote, allowed to pay for first-class accommodations but denied the right to occupy them, denied livelihoods defined as anything other than menial or service oriented, these culinary artists challenged the inferior status of Africans in America that was made into law and thereby institutionalized by the *Dred Scott* decision of 1857. Although slaves without masters themselves, several wore the badge of culinary activist. They constantly rallied to aid their sisters and brothers in bondage as agents of the Underground Railroad, or as soldiers in or as financial supporters of Black regiments raised for the purpose of fighting in the Civil War, and in other aspects of the struggle, believing that freedom, justice, and equality for *all* Africans were close at hand.

Considered useless and dangerous by White America, free African culinary artists also threatened the institution of slavery by their being free, and precisely because they were self-sufficient. With the end of the Civil War in 1865, more culinary artists such as James Wormley of Washington, DC, established themselves in business as hoteliers, caterers, and restaurant owners. A few of these purveyors of cuisine—Joshua Bowen Smith, in Massachusetts, and Tunis Campbell, in Georgia, along with other Blacks—entered the world of politics after the granting of "full" citizenship, during the Reconstruction era, from 1865 to 1877, as politics was considered a battleground for overall racial progress as well as a tool of recognition for African American business people and professionals. Nevertheless, despite concerted and diligent efforts to be productive and take care of their own, many African American individuals and their communities in America were the targets of organized terrorist attacks and massacres throughout the nineteenth century and first few decades of the twentieth century. Fueled by Whites' political rivalry and labor competition with Blacks and by the desire of Whites to curtail Black freedoms and advancement of any kind and by any means necessary, a proliferation of Jim Crow laws was put in place, including the ultimate bulwark against Black equality and advancement in post–Civil War America—and clearly the reincarnation of the precept of African inferiority—the Supreme Court decision *Plessy v. Ferguson* in 1896.[3]

The story presented here is character driven, as well as thematic, within a chronological framework. I do "step back," or digress in some instances, to provide background information, or a base on which to present material. Drawing on primary research from over fifty archives in the United States, oral testimony, and a plethora of popular and secondary sources, this is not only a cookbook but also a reference work and a biographical dictionary. Intertwining social issues, personal stories, and political commentary, I provide a historical analysis and contribution to an in-depth understanding that exposes the politics of the day— as well as the politics of today—together with recipes from nineteenth- and twentieth-century manuscripts, personal papers, and cookbooks, twentieth-century recipes from the African continent, as well as some of my own creation. The recipes, as in music, represent the "pregnant pause"; not a constant feature, they punctuate, appearing just enough at certain intervals to make the combination of the story and the recipes interesting.

I should mention that throughout my discourse I refer to African Americans (Africans brought to the Americas as slaves) as "Africans," "Africans in America," "African Americans," "Blacks," and "Black Americans." I use all of these interchangeably, and the term "African" is used frequently because it is the correct racial/geographical heritage of Blacks in America, and because, based on their treatment, there was never a time in the history of this country when Africans, brought to the Americas in chains, were allowed to forget that they were exactly that. Also, African women have been the dominant figures as cooks in private homes. They have also run restaurant and hotel kitchens. Although I focus on a number of these females, the majority of the caterers, chefs, and restaurateurs under discussion in this treatise are African males, culinarians and heads of households who sometimes skillfully maneuvered both their livelihoods and their politics around the powerful individuals with whom they came in contact.

If you were Black and the family breadwinner, you had few choices in choosing an occupation during the seventeenth through early twentieth centuries in this country's history. Many Black men chose to work in food because during these eras there was usually no repression in Blacks "overseeing" what was considered a menial or domestic service oriented task. There was money to be made performing this task since, as everyone knows, everybody has to eat. Many of these men, and their wives, had to wear many hats. Not only did husband and wife work together diligently as a team to make the business successful (family members were always integral to the team), they also involved themselves in the struggle for justice and equality. The stories of the men and women showcased here are among many who are historically significant; they stand out and deserve attention for their contributions at the table of power.

AT THE TABLE OF POWER

FROM THE BEGINNING

The Struggle against Culinary Apartheid

For far too long there has been an attempt to focus, relegate, pigeonhole, and confine African Americans as merely purveyors of "soul food." Consequently, the myriad creations of rich and delectable soups and stews, exotically spiced meats, side dishes, and vegetables, and irresistible desserts and drinks of every variety by African female and male cooks, and the African origin of the creative process of many of these creations served on American tables from this country's inception, are still almost never acknowledged. The usual discourse relative to the African contribution to food history in America describes that contribution as "a touch of African spicing," but after such phrases are added on, "like appliqués to a jacket," the foundation of the dish or cuisine is described as purely European. In presenting Europe's supposed culinary methods as the foundation of American cuisine, and in leaving out the true creative role of the African and Native American cook, the writers present a "master narrative"—that is, a formula or script written for, about, and usually by Europeans that is intended to serve as providing the only true account.

The late University of California–Berkeley historian Professor Ronald Takaki, for example, has taken this script (this "master narrative," as he called it) to task, with reference to the way in which American history has traditionally been taught in US schools. The same Eurocentrism, the same marginalization of Africans and Native Americans, is prevalent in the traditional master narrative of American culinary history, which states that cooking and cuisine were founded by Americans of European ancestry and are rooted in so-called Western civilization. Where Africans and other people of color are included, Europeans are hailed as having *improved* their cuisine. America's culinary master narrative has trained the average person's perspective to support, maintain, and reinforce the belief in the master narrative and thereby ensure that its content, though lacking an informed and honest story, is passed down.[1]

Unfortunately, the severity of the problem runs deep and can be compared to the era of apartheid in South Africa. When the South African government decided it wanted a particular area of African land for Whites, an area already occupied by Native Africans, the apartheid government simply came in with bulldozers and leveled the African community. With their bulldozers they obliterated Africans and their homes from the land, they then claimed the land, rebuilt it, renamed it, and designated the area as "Whites Only" territory. Africans were physically erased from the land and never allowed on it again, unless they were in some servant capacity to Whites. This happened repeatedly in South Africa in areas such as Cape Town's District Six.

The same scenario, culinary apartheid, applies to the African cook in American culinary history. Many of us are aware that numerous cookbooks were compiled and published by southern White women after the end of the Civil War. The recipes in these cookbooks were hailed as the creations of the White women who had them published. The recipes were actually collections of the creations of the African women and men who served the Whites, creations that the White women wrote down and then had published in their own names as authors. Some of these books contained a rare reference to a Black cook. They were easy to spot; these cooks were always called by their first names or the first name was preceded by the term "Aunt," "Uncle," or "Mammy."

The identities of the actual enslaved African cooks who created these recipes and all references to them were, in this way, marginalized and effectively erased from history. This was the means to an end because the end of the Civil War (White society blamed the war itself primarily on Africans in America) fostered the attempt to forge White southern nationalism, and in this case southern nationalism centered around food. Africans were to play no part in this nationalism, so that in promoting southern White culture, the concept of "southern cooking" started out as *Whites Only Cuisine*. With an imperialist mindset steeped in colonialist values, Whites have taken recipes and cooking methods of African and African American creation and creativity, claimed the recipes and the creativity, renamed them, and bulldozed into oblivion the names of and all reference to the originators.[2]

I am reminded of one such example of the bulldozing in more modern times when, in 1963, Republican Senator J. Glenn Beall from Maryland rose on the Senate floor "to defend the fair name of the great Free State of Maryland against an insult." Beall explained, "Just as the distinguished Senators from Georgia would resent a knotty little peach being called 'a Georgia peach,' just as the Senators from Idaho would resent a puny little spud being called 'an Idaho potato,' just as the distinguished Senators from Maine would resent a crawfish being called 'a Maine lobster,' and just as the distinguished Senators from Kentucky would resent cheap bootleg being called 'Kentucky bourbon[,]' I resent the crabcakes being served in the Senate dining room being called 'Maryland crabcakes.'" The Senate restaurant menu, Beall reported, offered "fried fresh 'Maryland crabcakes'" with tartar sauce, macaroni au gratin, and old-fashioned coleslaw. However, Beall states, "no Marylander would recognize what is served. . . . I simply say they fall far short of the high standard of 'Maryland crabcakes,' that tasty dish which has helped to make the name 'Maryland' loved throughout the Nation. Patrons of our dining room should be protected from deception." When Alabama Senator Hill suggested that the Senate would like to be able to compare the superiority of Maryland crab cakes to those of the Senate dining room, by demonstration, Beall promised to arrange it.[3]

A few days later, on January 21, 1963, Senator Beall appeared on the Senate floor armed with a letter and recipes from Helen Avalynne Tawes, wife of the governor of Maryland, J. Millard Tawes, a conservative Democrat who never actively pushed for the enactment of civil rights laws and a native, as was his wife, of the conservative Eastern Shore of Maryland. Among the recipes sent by Mrs. Tawes was one for crab cakes, which she suggested be given to the chef of the Senate restaurant to replace the one being used, because, she said, "hers" "is the best crabcake recipe [she] know[s] of."[4]

———————

The following recipe sent by Helen Avalynne Tawes was printed in the *Congressional Record*.

Crabcakes, As Submitted to the Senate, by Avalynne Tawes

- One pound crab claw meat
- Two eggs
- Two tablespoons mayonnaise
- One tablespoon Kraft's horse-radish mustard
- 1/4 teaspoon salt
- 1/8 teaspoon pepper
- Dash of tabasco sauce
- One tablespoon parsley chopped

Combine all above ingredients including the unbeaten eggs and mix lightly together. Form mixture into desired size of cake or croquette. Do not pack firmly, but allow the mixture to be light and spongy. Roll out a package of crackers into fine crumbs. Then pat the crumbs lightly on the crab cake and fry in deep fat just until golden brown. Remove from hot fat just as soon as golden brown.

Drain on absorbent paper and serve hot.[5]

Tawes fails to mention that it was African American men and women, some who worked for her and her husband's families, who created and made famous these delicacies in the eighteenth through twentieth centuries. It is also notable to mention that some of these delicacies might well have been lost to Maryland in the nineteenth century because of C. W. Jacobs and the members of Maryland's Committee on Colored Population. Many White households in Maryland were about to be ruined. Jacobs and his committee were the ones who suggested that all free Africans in the state be reenslaved, a ploy to force free Africans to leave the state. The only reason why Maryland did not go through with this was that neither the economy of the state nor the "nonslaveholding farmers, tradesmen, and householders who depended upon their [African] labor" could do without them. The question became, "Who is to supply the places of the free colored women who are hired by the week, month or year as cooks or house servants, in thousands of families throughout the state?" Whether slave or free, African cooks were the base on which Maryland's culinary heritage stood.[6]

The crab cake recipe presented on the Senate floor was included in a pamphlet composed of recipes handed out with campaign literature that would help elect Tawes's husband to the governor's seat in 1958. African Americans, however, were bulldozed out of Tawes's collection of recipes in both her culinary pamphlet and her cookbook. With Tawes's version of Maryland recipes bestowing credit to her mother and mother-in-law, a new reinforcement of culinary apartheid and the culinary master narrative was thereby created, one that certain lawmakers were happy to help her disseminate.[7]

When it comes to overlooking and shortchanging African American culinary artists, one of the major areas of this country where the shortchanging has always taken place is in the state of Louisiana, often described as some sort of melting pot, where various ethnicities and races came together to forge a so-called Creole society. According to writers on the subject, the foundation of this Creole society—and therefore the foundation of Louisiana's cuisine, which has also been termed "Creole"—is European, specifically French. The master narrative is alive and well, entrenched in Louisiana, even though it is the one state where you will hear the African contribution to its cuisine and culture mentioned slightly more often. And the only reason it is mentioned slightly more often is because, as in Brazil, its culture and cuisine are so deeply Africanized one would look insane to try to leave it out.

A description of the French population in colonial Louisiana around which the culinary master narrative is written is crucial. It is imperative to mention that, in 1719, Louisiana was colonized by the rejects and worst dregs of French society. French colonization turned Louisiana into a penal colony. Prisoners condemned to the galleys who had their sentences commuted, soldiers guilty of desertion, vagabonds, murderers, those arrested for debauchery, acts of violence, drunkards, and beggars, as well as neighbors and family members considered troublesome, were all prime candidates for deportation to Louisiana. Many French women had even worse reputations than the men. Some had been removed from dungeons. One was a serial killer and had murdered fifteen people. The majority of the women were in their thirties and accused of theft, prostitution, assassination, blasphemy, debauchery (usually with married men), irreligion, and repeated lying.[8]

As reported in numerous volumes, it was Native Americans who saved the Europeans, particularly in the realm of food. Native Americans taught the French everything there was to know about the topography of the land, its flora and fauna, the building of boats and the navigation of the network of treacherous waterways that facilitated communication among French settlements. Native American expertise in agriculture was passed on to White colonists in various regions of early America. Whites were also taught how to hunt, fish, build houses, make clothes and how to dress, the uses of herbal medicines, and preparation and preservation of food. The Chitimacha peoples, who occupied the delta area south and west of New Orleans and whose diet relied heavily on shellfish and seafood, taught the early French colonists techniques of crop cultivation that included corn, squash, potatoes, tobacco, and other indigenous foods.[9]

African culinary and cultural infusions into Louisiana appeared in different stages. Africans were brought to Louisiana as slaves in 1719. The slave ships carried rice seed and Africans knowledgeable in rice cultivation. African expertise in rice production made rice a reliable food crop for local consumption in Louisiana. Gwendolyn Midlo Hall writes that two-thirds of the Africans brought to Louisiana by the French were from the Senegambia region. This region, between the Senegal and Gambia Rivers, is more than a geographical area, it contains homogenous culture and a common historical and social legacy. Also noteworthy is that most of the Africans brought into Louisiana by the French came directly from Port Lorient in Africa. Most slave trade voyages made stops at various Caribbean islands and left Africans there to be "seasoned," but Louisiana slaveholders and slave traders received ships arriving "nonstop" from Africa. This certainly suggests that African cultural traits that have permeated and persisted throughout Louisiana's history did so undiluted by other environments.[10]

For this reason it is essential to compare agricultural production in the ancestral home of these West Africans during the early eighteenth century to agriculture in eighteenth-century France. The Senegal Valley, made extremely fertile by the flooding of the river, has been compared to the Nile Valley. Farming in West Africa always took into account, among other things, the ecological setting: indigenous crops (borrowed or replaced), the nature of households in various farming societies, the kinds of tools used, how production is organized and carried out, and how farming communities interact socially and economically within larger agricultural networks. With an understanding of their own ecological settings, farmers in West Africa employed complex land use combinations that allowed them to differentiate categories of farming. Within combinations of upland (shifting) cultivation, valley bottom flood retreat cultivation, and hunting and gathering over fallow and uncultivated land, they have been adept at creating or conserving just the right conditions for plant growth on forest and grassland fields or varieties of valley, and homestead or non-homestead farms.[11]

West African farmers were therefore aware of the importance of the condition and characteristics of the soil in different regions. They used a variety of approaches designed to improve yields and fertility that are dependent upon social and environmental factors. For plant growth under intense rainfall, the methods used included heaping, ridging, mulching, terracing, minimum tillage, and vegetation cover to minimize erosion. Nevertheless, most literature dealing with African agriculture fails to acknowledge that agriculture was independently developed in Africa and not a foreign skill brought in from Europe or Asia.

The procedures developed to cultivate fruits, vegetables, herbs, and spices—evolving them from African wild species—were innovations that were indigenous to Africa, "uniquely African-invented techniques concerned with the proper management of the physical and ecological properties of African soils." The Diola of Guinea-Bissau, for example, transformed most of the mangrove swamps lining a number of river estuaries into a network of paddy fields. Their techniques of dyking, desalinating, ridging, and transplanting antedate all European contact, and linguistic evidence has shown that ancient West, Central, and East African agricultural practices, especially those in Tanzania, and terms used to describe those practices, migrated to the Americas long before its so-called discovery. The Yoruba and Bini and other Nigerian societies have lived in settled communities on the same sites for several hundred years and have evolved agricultural systems that allow continuous cultivation of their soils without loss of fertility.[12]

In addition, African rice (*oryza glabberima*) was domesticated in West Africa thousands of years ago (thirty-five hundred years is one estimate, but it was probably much earlier), long before Asian rice (*oryza sativa*) was known on the continent. Paddy rice was grown along the Upper Guinea coast. Both wet and dry rices were well developed and cultivated throughout the Senegal Valley. Corn, called *Mil* in Senegal, was of two kinds, *gros* and *petit*, and was widely cultivated. Several varieties of peas, as well as huge fields of "excellent tobacco" were grown. Abundant crops of indigo and cotton, which "grew almost without cultivation," could be found. Salt was produced at the mouth of the Senegal River and traded on a number of inland routes. The Senegal River was also the site of deep-sea-fishing-vessel building. There were natural prairies along the Senegal River that fed cows, sheep, goats, all "with a marvelous flavor," in addition to fowl of just about every kind. The fowl were fed with corn (or pearl millet) and grew "very fat, and consequently very tender." Africans were famous as expert hunters "and one sees regiments rather than companies of partridges, guinea fowl, wood pigeons, sea birds and migratory birds." Referred to as *lougans*, the fields in which corn, peas, melons, rice, and other vegetables were grown were also planted in abundance.[13]

Rice with shrimp and fruit combine to produce marvelous flavors for stuffing game hens. Plentiful in Africa, the hens are served on many West, East, and Southern African tables.

Cornish Hens with Shrimp, Rice, and Mango Stuffing

- 4 cornish hens
- Season birds to taste with garlic salt with parsley, seasoned salt, black pepper, cilantro, and parsley flakes. Coat birds generously with paprika
- 12 tablespoons butter
- For stuffing:
- About three tablespoons dende,* or peanut, or olive oil
- 1 tablespoons finely grated ginger
- 1 medium onion, chopped
- A heaping 1/2 cup chopped green or red bell pepper
- 2 "bird"** chili peppers, seeds removed and finely chopped
- 1/4 rounded teaspoon ground allspice
- 1 teaspoon EACH, or more to taste, black pepper and garlic salt with parsley
- 1 medium tomato, chopped
- 10 fresh shrimp (31–40 per pound size), shelled and deveined
- 1/2 cup cooked rice
- 1 cup peeled and cubed mango

After seasoning, place 3 tablespoons of butter in each hen cavity. Bake, tightly covered, in a preheated 350 degree oven 1 hour to 1 hour and 20 minutes, depending on the size of the birds. Baste hens with pan juices when done. Use pan juices as sauce for hens.

Heat oil in skillet. Add remaining ingredients, except shrimp, rice, and mango. Cook, stirring often, until onions and peppers are tender. Stir in shrimp, rice, and mangoes. Continue cooking and stirring often, just long enough to cook shrimp (approximately 7 minutes).

Stuff equal amounts of mixture in each bird cavity and serve.[14]

*Dende oil, or palm oil, is thick and reddish-orange in color, and is the cooking oil of choice of many Africans in the Motherland, as well as in the Diaspora.
**Bird chili peppers are small, elongated chilies, available fresh in red, green, purple, and orange from specialty (African, Asian, and Indian) food grocers.

West Africans, such as the Wolof of the Senegal/Gambia region, were known to grind one of their abundant crops, "maize of the white variety," into flour, which was then added to oil and liquid. This basic batter was sometimes baked, and imaginative variations on the basic batter would turn out cakes, breads, and dumplings. Soups and stews using corn as the main ingredient were common. Palm wine was consumed in West Africa, but in some regions both wine and beer brewed specifically from corn were the only types consumed.[15]

One multipurpose indigenous food crop in Africa is sorghum, known as guinea corn in West Africa (presumably because for a long time botanists confused it with maize). The grains of certain varieties were popped like popcorn. Sorghum grain is made into flour for a thick pancake batter that is fried in groundnut or palm oil. Sorghum beer is a favorite beverage consumed at wrestling matches either as burkutu, an alcoholic gruel, or as pito, with the sediment removed. At any rate, West Africans were familiar with maize, corn, sorghum, and rice long before Columbus mistakenly ran into what is now called the Americas.[16]

Any discussion of Africa's culinary and agricultural civilizations has to include mention of its highly skilled and multitalented metallurgists. Besides blacksmiths, coppersmiths, and horseshoe makers, there were the goldsmiths, silversmiths, and the arms makers who made knives, hatchets, axes, and blades of iron. Africa's iron mining industries—not just on the West Coast but throughout the continent—produced new mining tools and made possible an industrial advancement that had a great impact on an already superior agricultural production, as well as on household and kitchen utensils. Superior crops provided a larger collection of revenue on land and trade. The technology of the West African iron industry evolved to master agriculture and provided the basis for other specialized societies to develop. These were crucial skills needed in the founding of Louisiana and America in general. These were skills

11

put to great use in New Orleans and surrounding areas, as the skills of African iron forgers can be seen in the ornate grill work prevalent in the architecture of the city's homes and businesses.[17]

West Africans who were not dependent on agriculture were pastoralists or expert in the art of catching fish. Favorite methods of preparing fish were pickled, raw, fried, boiled, and what we have come to call gumboing. Dried shrimp and crayfish are still must-have ingredients in stews and sauces, some of which combine different types of fish with coconut milk and other ingredients. Crab, lobster, cod, mackerel, sole, alligator, pike, prawn, gilthead, eel, shrimp, sprat, flounder, carp, and many other varieties of catch were obtained from oceans, rivers, streams, and lagoons and always provided "fisher folk" such as the Twi of Ghana and the Muslim Bozo, who depended heavily on fishing and boat trade on the Niger and Bani Rivers, with enormous quantities of fish that were dried and salted or smoked to keep for long periods of time for sale at markets located well into the interior of the continent.

Many West African cities had open air retail markets, which were principally in the hands of women. The market streets were filled with stalls selling calabashes, palm oil, palm wine, ducks, chickens of many colors, fresh beef, mutton and other meats, yams and yam fritters, guinea corn (sorghum) and millet beers, groundnuts, raw and cooked beans, thin brown cakes (which were said to smell like gingerbread), bean cakes (*akara*), meal dumplings, and oblong-shaped bean buns called *jenkaraga*, and soups and stews. Some of the ready-made dishes included *enjibotchi* (rice with sauce), *eko* (durra porridge), *killishi* (roasted meat, marinated and basted with oil), herbs and spices, and *atchia-kara* (a yam and vegetable sauce ladled over a combination of chunks of beef, goat, and lamb).

West Africa's ancient Mali Empire—one of the largest empires in West African history, and in the world—was known for its trained male and female physicians and surgeons. The roots of its wealth, however, were in food surplus and gold. It is especially important to note West Africa's highly developed organization of trade, commerce, and industry since current writers on the culinary history of Philadelphia's nineteenth-century Black restaurateurs and caterers assign the success of these Blacks to America's French immigrants, who are credited with teaching Blacks everything they knew about cooking and business acumen. During West Africa's early iron age, however, Mali's old city of Djenne (or Jenne) developed as an important center of interregional trade, long before the influence of the trans-Saharan trade. Djenne linked forestlands to the south with those of the savannas, and by way of Timbuktu, with the caravans of the trans-Saharan trade. During the Middle Ages, Djenne was the capital of Mali and controlled the largest trading center in the world, with arms stretching to India and China. Travelers and merchants visiting Djenne referred to the town as a great flourishing market of the Muslim world and marveled at the prosperity, in terms of foods and other goods, of all Mali's citizens.[18]

It was Africans from this wealthy culinary, cultural, and economic heritage who were brought as slaves to Louisiana's colonial capital, New Orleans, founded in 1718. It was here that crops and buildings were often destroyed by floods and hurricanes. Even though skilled workers arrived from France to help maintain the colony, few of them survived. Death, disease, and famine disrupted and suspended most operations in the colony. French colonized Louisiana survived only because of African labor and African technology. African knowledge of rice production supported and maintained a reliable food crop that could be grown in the swamplands in and around New Orleans. In fact, all of the major crops of eighteenth-century Louisiana were foods brought over with Africans from the Senegambia region.

Rice, however, was the most successful. Complex technology was involved in converting swamps and tidal wetlands into rice paddies, with which Africans were thoroughly familiar. Sixteenth-century residents along the Gambia River grew rice in the alluvial soil, using a system of dikes that harnessed the tides. Most households had a rice nursery nearby by 1685. Once rice for seeding reached Louisiana, along with Africans who knew what to do with it, by 1720 rice was "growing in great abundance all along the Mississippi River; within a few years, rice was exported to the French colonized West Indies. By 1721, the Kolly concession on the Chapitoulas coast just north of New Orleans produced six hundred quarters of rice from fourteen quarters that had been sown." Rice production expanded to such an extent that soon it relatively guaranteed that no matter what catastrophe Louisiana experienced, it could always count on having rice.[19]

Africans could also be counted on for their skills in herbal medicine. They were commonly used as medical doctors and surgeons in eighteenth-century Louisiana. Often considered better therapists than French doctors, slave doctors cured various ills. One apparently specialized in ailments specific to women; he also practiced an effective cure for scurvy before 1734.[20]

Europeans, to be sure, were looking to attain a better life, and the American colonies seemed to offer that promise. There were a few groups still arriving and by 1770 one thousand Acadians immigrated to Louisiana, having been forcibly removed from Nova Scotia by the British. Between twenty-six hundred and three thousand Acadians arrived in Louisiana between 1765 and 1785. The largest group was said to arrive from France aboard Spanish ships in 1785. They had returned to France from Nova Scotia and were subsequently sent on to Louisiana. Acadians, or Cajuns, were among the "poverty stricken immigrants [who] survived only where they could build upon the economy of the swamps that had been developed by runaway slave communities."[21]

Because the Acadians are rooted in France and are therefore European, much literature abounds extolling the qualities, creativity, and inventiveness of "Cajun" cooking. Just as important is that such literature also extolls the inherent superior culinary heritage of the French. The Acadians' roots are in Brittany, Normandy, Picardy, Poitou, and other rural peasant regions of France. With regard to cooking and cuisine, it is crucial that we take a serious look at these rural peasants in seventeenth- and eighteenth-century France in order to compare their true agricultural and culinary legacy not only with that of West Africa but also with what current food writers have offered as the master narrative.

First, cultivation was in the hands of poor peasants, and rural peasants found it especially difficult to feed themselves during the seventeenth and eighteenth centuries because "French agriculture was at this time quite backward." Henri Eugene Sée tells us in his *Economic and Social Conditions in France during the Eighteenth Century* that there was a great deal of uncultivated lands and wastelands, and "methods of cultivation remained very primitive, and progress was very slow."[22]

Uncultivated lands were important in the rural economy of the era because peasants without pasturage were allowed to graze their cattle on the common wastelands and used the produce of these lands as litter for their animals; that produce was also used as fertilizer for their fields. Sée states: "The farm-buildings were poorly arranged, and the implements were unsatisfactory and quite primitive, being hardly superior to those employed during the Middle Ages. Intensive cultivation was practically unknown almost everywhere. The system of fallow land was used universally, except in Flanders, Alsace, and a part of Normandy. Even in Picardy the land lay idle one year in three. In Brittany it was left idle every other year, sometimes for two years out of three, and certain 'cold' lands were cultivated only every seven or eight years, or even every twenty years. The artificial meadow was hardly ever used." Sée goes on to say:

> The peasants, prompted by the spirit of routine and having but little capital, devoted no great care to cultivation. They did not plow deeply, they weeded their grain negligently, sowed too late, and used poor seed. Almost everywhere there was lack of good manure. Since the farm itself furnished very little manure, leaves and ferns, allowed to rot, were used instead. This explains the small crops. . . . [Still another characteristic] was that in almost all France wheat was considered a luxury crop and rye predominated, except in Toulouse, Angoumois, and the coastal region of Brittany. Poor land was used particularly for buckwheat, and this furnished the peasants their principal nourishment in the form of cakes. In the central and southern sections maize played an important part. . . . The government, fearing that wines might take the place of grains, restricted the cultivation of the former in the eighteenth century. . . . Cattle-raising and horse-breeding remained very mediocre, although the second half of the eighteenth century witnessed a certain amount of improvement.[23]

Beaten down by the carelessness of the "great proprietors," overwhelming taxes, inadequate means of communication, and continuous obstacles blocking free cultivation and trade in agricultural commodities, France found itself enveloped in the slow development of agriculture. It did not help that in some regions such as eastern Normandy and Picardy, peasants abandoned soil cultivation to take up spinning and weaving. Such decisions had profoundly negative consequences for agriculture.[24]

The peasants' material existence in most regions of France "was still quite miserable. . . . Their dwelling-places were altogether inadequate. Most of them were built of mud, covered with thatch, and having only a single low room without a ceiling. The windows were small and had no glass. In Brittany, and especially in Lower Brittany, it has been said that the peasants lived 'in the water and in the mud.' This is one of the principal causes for the epidemics that were still so frequent." Peasants' homes in northern France, however, were a little more comfortable. In addition, peasant clothes "were often wretched." The poor peasants' clothing, "and they were almost all poor—was even more pitiful, for they had only one outfit for winter and summer, regardless of the quality of the material. And their single pair of shoes, very thin and cleated with nails, which they procured at the time of their marriage, had to serve them the rest of their lives, or at least as long as the shoes lasted."[25]

Peasants' meals, if their job was as servant, consisted of bread, butter, cakes, and sometimes bacon. It was rare to receive any other meat. The usual beverage was water, although in wine-growing areas sour wine made from grapes or apples was provided. Generally speaking:

> The food of the peasants . . . was always coarse, and often insufficient. Meat appeared on the table but rarely. In Brittany cider was drunk only in years of abundance. The basic foods were bread, soup, dairy products, and butter. Wheat bread was quite rare; only bread of rye and oats, and that frequently of poor quality, was known. In the poorest regions the peasants ate biscuits and porridge of buckwheat, or even of chestnuts or maize. Wheat and even rye served largely to pay the taxes and farm-rent, or were sold for export when this was permitted. Potatoes, which later became a staple food-product among the farmers, were grown only in a few particularly fertile regions.

In the seventeenth century there was great suffering in the rural sections of every part of France. The governor of Dauphine, Lesdiguières, wrote in 1675, "It is a fact, and I assure you that I know whereof I speak, that the great majority of the inhabitants of this province lived during the winter only from acorns and roots, and that now they can be seen eating the grass of the fields and the bark of the trees." Misery increased after 1685:

> There are practically no peasants in comfortable circumstances. There are only poor cooperative farmers who have nothing. The landlords have to furnish them with cattle, lend them food, pay their *taille* [a direct land tax on the peasantry], and take their crops in payment, and often even this does not cancel the debt. . . . The peasants live from buckwheat bread. Others, who have no buckwheat, live from roots of ferns boiled with the flour of barley or oats, and salt. . . . One finds them sleeping on straw. They have no clothing except what they wear, and that is very poor. They are destitute of furnishings and provisions. Everything in their huts points to dire need.[26]

Apparently, eighteenth-century France fared no better than seventeenth-century France. Misery grew more serious. Famine hit France in the winter of 1709, and there were great crises in 1725, 1740, 1759, from 1766 to 1768, from 1772 to 1776, and 1784. The great drought in 1785 forced farmers to sell a portion of their cattle stock. There was an enormous increase in food prices. In 1774 and 1789 farmers had to live on turnips, milk, and even grass. Day laborers, who formed an important part of the agricultural population especially in Flanders, Picardy, eastern Normandy, and Brittany were most affected by the crises. They accounted for the majority of beggars and vagabonds up to the French Revolution. The epidemic outbreaks were more frequent and devastating in rural sections than in cities; rural inhabitants had no medical care. Many sought refuge in cities, but cities were no better in opportunities to secure aid than rural areas.[27]

It can truly be said that "the real wealth of a kingdom lies in the abundance of its supply of food, which is so necessary for human life." French resources were said to be too limited to allow the French to implement real agricultural improvements, thereby rendering French agriculture retarded in development until at least 1840. They adhered to the old methods. Clearings and uncultivated lands could be used only with partial success.[28]

By 1870 the initiation of the Franco-Prussian War did not help France's situation, as the prices of foods rose by 25–75 percent. Some items, such as potatoes, cost twenty times as much as in the preceding year. In October 1870, meat rationing began, with a day's allotted portion gradually becoming smaller and smaller. Supplies ran out, and when there was not one shred of any type of regular meat left, horsemeat was substituted. No breed was spared, and thoroughbreds, cavalry horses, and mules were included in the diet of soldiers and civilians. When horsemeat became scarce, dogs, cats, and especially rats were frequent victims. Pet owners had to keep constant vigil, as regular hunts were undertaken to snatch domestic animals. Loose animals could be seen running for their lives down streets and alleys, as French matrons and their children prowled to catch that night's supper. Rats were on sale at markets for one franc each, or one franc fifty centimes for a big one. Unfortunately, the price continued to spiral upward so that not everyone could afford them, which is strange because rats occupied Paris in abundance. The multitude of rodents allowed a new industry to develop in France—the ratcatcher, who supplied both the housewife and the restaurant chef. Diners could order a *salmi* (ragout) of rats at most of the restaurants. Zoo animals were added to the menu, as Paris could no longer afford to feed them. Castor and Pollux, two elephants considered "the pride of Paris," were killed to provide food. Since there were no choices, one restaurant invested in a number of the "exotic" meats, serving elephant with *sauce chasseur*. Another restaurant became famous for its bear steaks. *Consommé d'éléphant* (elephant broth), *le civet de kangouru* (kangaroo stew), zebra, hippopotamus, giraffe, as well as saddle of cocker spaniel, camel, wolf, donkey, ostrich, antelope with truffles, and "cat delicately embellished with rats," were the objects of culinary affection in restaurants and homes in 1870 Paris. A high incidence of dysentery was blamed on the "bad rye bread" and the lack of salt, but clearly, numerous conditions prevailed, culinary and otherwise, that set the stage for widespread illness.[29]

The French chef Auguste Escoffier was an army cook during the Franco-Prussian War in 1870 and seemed to take pride in the tremendously small portions he was forced to serve. Lacking food supplies, the cavalry's horses eventually provided the meat ration. Once, Escoffier caught a rabbit, one rabbit, which he cooked and served to the officers. Needless to say, one rabbit provided very small portions for each man. Escoffier, considered the king of chefs, whom the world has placed on a culinary pedestal and thereby emulated down through the decades, prepared many menus and meals (and most other French cafés and restaurants are included in this) during times when food was rationed, when there were severe food restrictions in France and in England. These portions that he and the French served up have set the standards for the portions served in French and other restaurants all over America. Interestingly, America and the world lauds and applauds everything about French culinary "technique" and "presentation." Part of that "presentation" (the portions, for example) is based on and represents the scarcity of food and the poverty of culinary resources endemic in France during these eras. Clearly, a large part of what is lauded is in fact a defect that has been purposefully redefined as a virtue, a commendable quality or trait.[30]

With all of its problems in agriculture and food production, it is easy to see why France, along with the rest of Europe in the nineteenth and twentieth centuries, embarked on a poverty reduction program by sending its people to colonize areas outside of their borders, in addition to jumping headlong into colonialism and imperialistic endeavors in wealthier nations. Clearly, the difference between what Africans brought to Louisiana and America in general, compared to the French, speaks volumes. Africa is not only the home of humankind and important technological innovations developed in the ancient world of early human prehistory, it is also home to one of the major agricultural complexes to have evolved in the entire course of human history.

Many regions of Africa were considered bread baskets, which bountifully supplied not only the continent itself but also numerous regions of the ancient world such as Rome. Wealth in West Africa, as in any country or continent, was always defined by its agricultural production and the ability to feed its people. Currently, there are two thousand known crops that are indigenous to Africa, and there are many more that once flourished on the continent in ancient times but which have since died out. The abundance of food dictates the quality of life, and with this abundance was centered diverse culinary creativity.

It is, therefore, not far-fetched to state that people who were highly industrialized iron miners, fisherfolk, and agriculturalists (the mining of iron and other metals alone indicates their high level of civilization) would not have had problems producing rice dishes, sauces, or crab cakes. It has been written that colonial and antebellum plantation nobility brought their recipes from France to Louisiana. Even if they did, noteworthy is the fact that by this time the cuisine of France, particularly that of the elites, had already been Africanized by way of the French colonies—and especially by its most lucrative colony, St. Domingue (Haiti), in the Caribbean.[31]

Once in Louisiana, and by way of direct contact with African cooks in plantation kitchens, "French" cooking was re-Africanized, because "the skill and imaginative hands of plantation cooks—almost invariably of African origin or descent—gave a value to the cooking that exceeded the excellence of the original dish." Gwendolyn Hall suggests that "it is relevant, therefore, to look to Senegambia for the African roots of Louisiana's Afro-Creole culture." She also states that "African nations present in early Louisiana and the conditions in Africa, as well as in Louisiana, molded the formation of Afro-Creole culture."[32]

Every effort was put forth to develop New Orleans as a colony. Within a twelve-year period Africans brought to Louisiana by the French would comprise a substantial majority of the population, and that population would thoroughly Africanize Louisiana, including its cooking and cuisine, during the early years of colonization. Noteworthy, too, is that Caribbean and American cuisine continued to be re-Africanized by culinary infusions from Jamaica and Haiti after the Haitian Revolution.[33]

Many Acadians (or Cajuns, as they came to be called in Louisiana) came to Louisiana from Nova Scotia, a rocky terrain where agriculture was difficult because of the short growing seasons and harsh winters, and a land not noted for its cuisine. Much of their diet consisted of salted or dried fish and root vegetables that stored well, such as potatoes and parsnips. It has been written that Acadian fishermen traded a portion of their salt fish in the West Indies for molasses, which indicates a relationship with maintenance and support of slavery and the slave trade. But after all, slavery was the primary business to be in during that era.

Acadian potato dishes were plentiful. There was sometimes chicken or other meat, but most meals were prepared with grated potatoes as the main ingredient. Ragged and starving when they arrived in Louisiana, Acadians were taught by Native Americans and African Americans where, what, and how various plants, crops, and spices could be utilized. Cajuns were also taught medicinal remedies through herbs and spices.

In no way am I stating that Cajuns did not add their own individual touches to the cuisine they found in Louisiana. I am sure that they did, but let us not forget that the French and every other European group who came to Louisiana, as well as to all of the southern and eastern seaboard colonies, survived only as the result of help and influence from Native Americans and the African cooks whose creativity ran the kitchens. You cannot come from a history and heritage with no knowledge of spices and herbs, no varieties of fruits and vegetables, no seafood, and different meats, of not even having enough food, and then magically become purveyors of "the most unique American cuisine ever developed." A unique and distinctive cuisine was already present when the Cajuns arrived.[34]

Clearly, Cajuns are merely one of multiple examples of how everybody but Africans are credited with bringing, creating, and developing cuisine here in America (accompanying okra to America on the slave ship does not constitute the sole culinary contribution). Unquestionably, the culinary master narrative we have all been accustomed to reading and listening to is a lie, and those who extol the current master narrative are liars. European peoples may have added their touches to the cuisine they found upon reaching American shores; but, according to local chefs and culinary historians such as Edna Jordan Smith, in areas in and around New Orleans much so-called American food, like Cajun cooking, "is food done by Blacks. It's just wrapped up with other peoples' labels on it." The African and Native American components and methods of preparation, however, are the very foundation, not only of Louisiana's but of America's cuisine in general.[35]

Marcel Giraud's five-volume treatise titled *Histoire de la Louisiane française* (*A History of French Louisiana*), which many writers on the subject refer to and consider a virtual bible on early Louisiana, mentions Blacks only sparingly, in volume 2, as slaves confined to "household tasks and gardening." But Giraud also concludes that "black slaves, when available in sufficient numbers, would alone ensure the development of the country," because "upon the blacks would depend not only the cultivation of the land but also all the numberless chores inseparable from the task of building a colony." Giraud believed that, "without this contribution by workers used to living in a hot country, Louisiana would remain . . . doomed to an existence without prospect of progress." Indeed, the French did import Africans as slaves in sufficient numbers to build Louisiana.[36]

One of the areas defined by the African presence was, and is, Louisiana cookery. "The black woman," Giraud states, "was regarded as having a more open and expansive temperament than the Indian woman, and also as being harder-working and readier to spend her time in the burdensome kitchen tasks that the white woman, supposedly enervated by the climate, declined to perform." In his typical racist fashion, Giraud describes Africans as slave laborers who expressed discontent with harsh treatment by "compensation through stealing," and who took to alcohol whenever the opportunity arose. He fails to mention, however, the strong and steady African input in and imprint on *any* category of Louisiana's development, which makes his one of many master narratives unworthy of consideration as an honest and accurate story.[37]

It comes as no surprise, then, that the same racism that saturates the pages of a written history of Louisiana permeates every story regarding Blacks' input and imprint, not only in the culinary arena but also in every other field where Blacks endeavored to make a living, following the Civil War and on into the 1880s and 1890s. Following the "Wormley

Agreement," or the "Compromise of 1877," the period known as the Great Nadir saw the flourishing of the Ku Klux Klan and other terrorist groups "dedicated to the preservation of white supremacy and to keeping blacks subordinated."[38]

Although subordination of Africans by way of segregation and Jim Crow were well entrenched, there were one or two arenas in which they were included on the rosters. One was sports. There were more than sixty African ballplayers on nineteenth-century White professional baseball teams and in White leagues before *Plessy* was decided. Another arena was horse racing, which saw record-breaking Black jockeys, such as Oliver Lewis, James Winkfield, and especially Isaac Burns Murphy. But as professional baseball became a moneymaker and the size of the horse-racing purses increased, the rise of Jim Crow and the jealousy and envy of the White ballplayers and White jockey competitors pushed Blacks out of both businesses and were successful in purging the Black presence "from that point forward until 1947 when Jackie Robinson took the field with the Brooklyn Dodgers."[39]

Sports was not the only field where Africans were replaced when the job became lucrative and attractive to Whites. Throughout the 1800s, steam engines propelled locomotives in the early days of railroad travel, and Africans were usually employed to perform the filthy backbreaking work of shoveling and stoking coal into the engine's boilers. In 1940, when steam engines were replaced with diesel engines, all that needed to be done was to flip a switch. Whites now wanted those jobs, and the Brotherhood of Locomotive Firemen and Enginemen moved to ban Africans from having them. A lawsuit was brought against the Louisville & Nashville Railroad (L&N) in 1944 by African fireman William Steele and his famed African attorney Charles Hamilton Houston. He lost the case, but the US Supreme Court, in one of its most significant decisions regarding employment and labor, overturned the lower court. Also significant was that African chefs continued to propel the dining cars on the L&N Railroad. During the same month that the Steele lawsuit was heard in the courts, the L&N Railroad lost its well-known chef, James H. "Jim" Jones. Before his death, Jones had served for almost fifty years as "road chef" of the business car for four "Old Reliable" presidents: Milton H. Smith, Wible L. Mapother, Whitefoord R. Cole, and James B. Hill. He was also the president's office messenger. Jones was described as an excellent chef who prepared many appetizing meals, and no doubt many of these repasts were both served and savored during discussions of firing African employees, lawsuits, and other business matters.[40]

The modus operandi is consistent. The elimination of the African American in sports and in economic labor arenas can certainly be linked to the ongoing effort to replace the African caterer during the earlier era and the African American chef during the more modern period. The earlier era coincided with French cooking coming into vogue, around the turn of the twentieth century, leaving African caterers with fewer and fewer clients. Now, cooking was always a labor intensive endeavor, one that Whites were always willing to leave for those "on the lower rungs" of society. But just as sports was becoming big business and a money-maker in the late nineteenth and early twentieth centuries, cooking for those who do not cook for themselves was becoming lucrative as well.

The foremost criteria for anyone to be recognized as worthy of becoming a chef—that is, if you really want to be taken seriously—you have to attend a cooking school, and in this country and all of Europe the foundation of your learning experience was, and still is, to adopt "French cuisine and technique." And that is yet another issue all by itself because what they are telling you is that European cuisine, French cuisine, is the foundation of the culinary arts and is thereby so complex and superior to everyone else's that it requires a formal education to master it. This is curious because the fact is, and this has not changed, that Whites entering the culinary business here in America never hesitated to approach African cooks in private homes and private clubs and African stewards of lodge and hotel kitchens to ask these chefs and cooks to teach them about ingredients and different foods, so that they might learn "the best methods for preparing things."[41]

Today cooking is no longer seen as menial labor. The Department of Labor reclassified chefs in 1976. Today the culinary arena has evolved into an arm of the entertainment industry, and with this connection, it is no longer seen as work for the bottom rungs of society. Those who are chosen to be a part of it are paid well, and for this reason, with Cuisinart and Kitchen Aid labor saving appliances in tow, Whites now want it, and you can be certain that White pockets dominate those who are chosen.

Look at today's celebrity chefs and cookbook authors who gain all the prestige, accolades, television publicity, and the big money. With the exception of a few (until a couple of years ago there were only one or two), all of the rest are White. Are we to believe that in this country

there are only a few excellent Black chefs? Add the fact that the success-
ful White chefs and restaurateurs love to claim "their" cuisine as "New
World" and "fusion"—Caribbean/Latin American, Latin American/
Asian, Mexican/Italian, sometimes claiming North African influence
(many Whites consider North Africa as White, and not really a part of
Africa), and so forth—but with the French technique.[42]

Why don't these chefs stick with French or Spanish or Italian cuisine? Why don't they simply offer European fare, since it is supposed to
be superior? Why has the cuisine of people of color been claimed and
renamed as *their* specialty? There is even one chef in Miami and Key
West, Florida, who not only claims to be "known internationally as the
founding father of 'New World Cuisine'" but claims also to be "known
for introducing [the] concept of 'fusion' to the culinary world."[43]

First, the term "New World" is an insult to Native Americans, the indigenous Americans. Using the terminology "New World" is idiotic and
senseless because the only people new to the territories now known as
the Americas were Europeans. Second, America's first "fusion" cuisine
was African and Native American—that is, the incorporation of African
indigenous traditional methods and agricultural products with those
of all of Native America (mainland America, Mexico, Central America,
the Caribbean, and South America) and this contact took place in stages,
long before and also after the European invasion of the Americas.

Why are the same cooks and chefs who actually laid the foundation
and built the culinary repertoire of this country not better represented in
the moneymaking echelons of culinary notoriety? The answer: Culinary
Apartheid. Africans aspiring to become chefs in today's restaurants are
oftentimes met with restaurateurs' blatant racism, in that they are told
by the owners that they "couldn't have a black . . . or Latin . . . back there,
because it would make my customers uncomfortable." Other times the
first comment restaurant owners utter to a Black applicant is "the only
thing you know about is fried chicken and collard greens." Most of this
is sheer racism; however, cookbooks and articles share the blame because most written material has relegated African American cooking to
fried chicken, chitlins, and barbeque.[44]

Pigeonholing Black folks in the "soul food" corner tells you that Africans in America have never been given credit for, and have been clearly
defined out of, their own complex and diverse culinary creations. There
is an irony as well. When applicants are denied employment in restau-

rants serving foods in the traditional European, or French technique (after having been fooled into paying money to attend cooking school to learn the French technique), the only jobs they may be able to get—that is, the only experience that will be on their resumé—will include restaurants preparing barbequed spareribs and macaroni and cheese—that is, "soul food." "Soul food" has always been considered the lowest rung of cuisine, and therefore anyone who prepares it, commercially or otherwise, operates in the menial category of cooking.

Chef Joe Randall, founder of Chef Joe Randall's Cooking School in Savannah, Georgia, and a fifty-year veteran in the culinary industry, is well respected and noted for his capacity to teach, guide, and advise others on all aspects of food quality and food service operations. "Unfortunately," states Chef Randall, "in my opinion, when people refer to African American chefs [in the category of] 'soul food' they diminish the contributions from African American chefs in America. You think [an African American chef is] limited in his [or her] skills and that's not necessarily the case. The terminology sometimes pigeonholes African American chefs." When asked why she felt there is an underrepresentation of African Americans in the food industry, Chef Tanya Holland, cookbook author and founder of award-winning restaurants Brown Sugar Kitchen and B-Side BBQ, both in Oakland, California, responded, "I think there is a lot of representation in lower tier restaurants and I think a lot of it is because of politics. . . . Here [in the United States] they say, 'We don't get the [African American] applicants,' but I know that's not the truth. It starts in management. It doesn't happen in my restaurant because I make the decisions. . . . I think it's just racism."[45]

America has had an untold number of African American cooks and chefs, both male and female, throughout the nineteenth and twentieth centuries, who were the creative geniuses at the helm of nationally and world renowned kitchens. The majority were unknown, anonymous, and often purposefully made invisible. One of the most important contributions to the recognition of Black cooking talent is an online website titled the African American Chefs Hall of Fame. Another contribution is assuredly Chef Nathaniel Burton and Rudy Lombard's work titled *Creole Feast: Fifteen Master Chefs of New Orleans Reveal Their Secrets*, which presents profiles of male and female African American chefs, in addition to recipes for some of their creations served in "the most renowned and widely acclaimed restaurants in New Orleans." *Creole Feast* was first published in 1978, but these chefs' creations have long placed White--owned restaurants in New Orleans on the map, and they continue as culinary legends today. As *Creole Feast* points out, the cooking styles of these chefs "encompasses a creative improvisation not unlike that found among traditional New Orleans Black jazz musicians. Their genius relies largely on experience, combined with the full use and development of all five senses. . . . They do measure ingredients; not only with equipment but also with the cupped hands and the pinch of their fingertips." Another important aspect of describing this prestigious circle of chefs is that they *"are all primarily self-taught rather than formally trained. . . . Along the way they received help, guidance and assistance . . . from other professionals who, like them, also lacked formal training.* In this sense, they are proud heirs to the rich legacy of Creole cuisine they have inherited from *Black professional cooks"* (italics added).[46]

African American females have of course been the majority of cooks in private homes, but they have also run restaurant and hotel kitchens. *Creole Feast* profiles Annie Laura Squalls, chef of the Caribbean Room at the Hotel Pontchartrain; Rosa Barganier, of Corinne Dunbar's; Louise Joshua and Letitia Parker, chefs of the Bon Ton Restaurant; and Leah Chase of Dooky Chase's Restaurant. Mention is also made of Leona Victor, private cook at the home of Corinne Dunbar, "who opened her famous restaurant on the strength of Mrs. Victor's ingenious cooking skills. Mrs. Victor created the famous Oysters and Artichokes Dunbar and Dunbar's Banana Beignet, as well as most of the other original recipes for which Dunbar's became noted. She . . . cooked without benefit of written recipes or formal training." Mrs. Clara Mathus was Mrs. Victor's successor, cooking at Dunbar's for twenty-five years.[47]

Burton and Lombard, in *Creole Feast*, assign the term "culinary giant of her era" to one highly acclaimed Black female chef in Louisiana in the 1940s whose cookbook, *New Orleans Cook Book,* and television cooking show catapulted her to local star status. A renowned chef, caterer, restaurateur, and founder of her own cooking school in 1937, Lena Richard and her television show, "Lena Richard's New Orleans Cook Book," graced local TV twice a week on Tuesday and Thursday at 5 p.m. (occasionally at 3 p.m.). The show first appeared in 1947 (although one or two sources have her first appearance in 1949).[48]

The recipes prepared on the show were from her cookbook, *Lena*

Richard's Cook Book, self-published in 1939. This edition features Mrs. Richard's photograph and a short preface offering culinary credit for her recipes to those who have cooked "for generations in the South." Interestingly, a new edition of her book was published by Houghton, Mifflin in 1940, retitled *New Orleans Cook Book.* Houghton, Mifflin kept the dedication page, no doubt because it praises one of Mrs. Richard's former employers, Mrs. Nugent B. Vairin. What is fascinating is that Mrs. Richard's photograph, preface, and foreword are gone, replaced by an introduction authored by "an American author and journalist." A new preface appears, apparently authored by Lena Richard, this time extolling credit for the recipes "herein revealed" by "the old French chef," as the keeper of "the secrets of Creole cooking." The new preface also states, "Creole Gumbo, Court Bouillon, Crawfish Bisque, Grillade à la Creole, are no longer dishes prepared in secrecy by French chefs, to be eaten by the rich."[49]

Whose idea was this? Did Lena Richard actually write the new preface? Was she made to write it as part of a mandate to whiten and thereby appropriate these recipes (after all, they removed her photograph and tribute to undoubtedly other Black cooks and chefs), and in order to sell the book to a White audience? Did Houghton editors, or Gwen Bristow, the White "American author and journalist," write it and insist Richard go along with it? At any rate, Richard's cookbook has been written up as a landmark of Louisiana cuisine, and she has also been referred to, along with the cookbook author Mary Land, as defining New Orleans and Louisiana cuisine in the twentieth century.[50]

Lena Richard was born in New Roads, Louisiana, in 1892; her parents were Frances Laurence and John Peter Paul. She moved to New Orleans at an early age. After her mother and aunt were hired as domestics for Alice and Nugent Vairin, Lena assisted in the kitchen. She attended cooking school in New Orleans and then graduated from the Fannie Farmer Cooking School in Boston in 1918. Interestingly, she did not feel the cooking school could teach her more than she already knew. She began catering in the 1920s and then opened a sweetshop. Her 1940 cookbook was sold wherever she cooked, in addition to New Orleans department stores D. H. Holmes and Maison Blanche. Meeting Father Divine, founder of Harlem's Peace Mission Movement, helped her sales tremendously. Father Divine agreed to promote her book with his followers by selling them for two dollars each, which was a 66 percent cut in price. Father Divine sold one thousand copies of a book that "stands as a record of African American cooking in New Orleans."[51]

Around the time the 1940 edition was published, Lena Richard left New Orleans and took the position of head chef at the Bird and Bottle Inn in Garrison, New York, about fifty-five miles north of Manhattan. Her most famous dish was Shrimp Soup Louisiane. Bird and Bottle Inn later canned the bisque and sold it by mail order. Richard returned to New Orleans and opened Lena's Eatery in November 1941. Her reputation came to the attention of Charles Rockefeller of the John D. Rockefeller Foundation, and she was hired as chef of the foundation's Travis House restaurant in Colonial Williamsburg during World War II, from 1943 to 1945. In May 1943 she prepared "one of the most elaborate of dinners that had ever been served" at Travis House—for the British High command during a break from meetings with American military staff in Washington. Later that year Richard cooked for Winston Churchill's wife and daughter, Clementine and Mary Churchill. Her scalloped oysters, shrimp Creole, stuffed eggplant, and other dishes were in such demand that Travis House opened a takeout service.[52]

In 1945 she returned to New Orleans and reopened her catering business with her daughter. While her cooking show ran on TV, she also opened a new restaurant on February 19, 1949, called Lena Richard's Gumbo House. Located at 1936 Louisiana Avenue, it was a family-run establishment. Her son-in-law, Leroy Rhodes, was the manager; upkeep of the property was overseen by her husband, Percival; her daughter, Marie, was in charge of the restaurant's finances. Lena Richard also produced frozen dishes in the late 1940s at a plant that was said to employ mostly women. Her turtle soup, okra gumbo, grillades, chicken fricassee, and beef stew were distributed by Bordelon Fine Foods and shipped across the country in five- and ten-gallon containers. She died unexpectedly in 1950, but her family kept her Gumbo House going until 1958.[53]

No disrespect to Lena Richard, but there have been a number of other skilled African American chefs whose creations have defined Louisiana's cuisine. Leah Chase (also profiled in *Creole Feast*), the executive chef of Dooky Chase's Restaurant in New Orleans, may not have had her own cooking show on TV, but numerous accolades have embraced her, and her restaurant has been a New Orleans landmark for well over half a century. The oldest of fourteen children, Leah Lange Chase, from Madisonville, Louisiana, was married to musician Edgar "Dooky" Chase. When African Americans were barred from New Orleans restaurants in the 1950s and 1960s, Leah Chase cooked for civil rights workers. She even delivered meals to struggling artists and catered their openings before they became known. She still ships her famous gumbo all over the world, and her customers have included Quincy Jones and Sidney Poitier.[54]

The Black male chefs profiled in *Creole Feast* are no less distinguished. Nathaniel Burton and Charles Kirkland of Broussard's, Raymond Thomas Sr. of the French Market Seafood House, Louis Evans (author of *Louis Evans' Creole Cookbook*) and Rochester Anderson of the Caribbean Room in the Hotel Pontchartrain, Malcom Ross and Larry Williamson of Galatoire's, Austin Leslie of Chez Helene (which he opened himself), Sherman Crayton of Vieux Carre Restaurant, Charles Bailey of Braniff Place at the Grand Hotel, and Henry Carr of Manale's are merely a few of those who brought versatility and legendary tastes to the profession.[55]

Many African American females were private cooks for White families or went directly into catering. Mrs. Christine Warren was a successful caterer, whose business thrived for over thirty-five years. Ms. Lucy Ater also catered. Born in 1893, she cooked in various homes and taught herself how to cook, learning her art on the job. Friends, as well as reading cookbooks, helped her to learn cookery, and eventually she created numerous recipes herself. She began to excel in decorating cakes and other items. Salaries, however, were low; starting out she received eight dollars a week. The market and the wagons that came through the neighborhoods carrying fresh fish and other foods were venues for Ms. Ater's food supplies.[56]

Working for the Hardies for ten years, Mrs. Christine Warren accompanied them every summer by train or barge to Parish Christien. When Mr. Hardie died, she went to work for the Rittenbergs, where she stayed for eighteen or nineteen years. During that time, according to Ater's granddaughter Shirley Bateman, all of the Rittenberg's friends would call on her to cater their parties. Mrs. Rittenberg was of the opinion that Ms. Ater was too fine a cook to be confined in her kitchen. She suggested to Ater that she set up a business so that everyone would know how good she was. When one of the Rittenbergs died, Ater received a little money, which enabled her to start her catering business. During her catering years she made gumbo for the famed entertainer Jack Benny and his entourage at one of her clients' home. The next night she catered another party where Benny was in attendance. It was Ms. Ater's cooking Benny savored "all the time he was there in New Orleans."[57]

Delivering food by taxi and on foot was difficult, although the inconvenience did not deter her or hamper her business. Ms. Ater's granddaughter Shirley Bateman took over her catering business, having learned everything about catering from her grandmother, who never advertised. When this interview was conducted, Ms. Bateman was in her twenty-third year as a caterer, whose partially inherited clientele was built by word of mouth.[58]

Originally intending to become a dietitian, Ms. Bateman was thrown into the business when she had to cover for her Grandmother Ater one day when she was very ill. Grandmother Ater, however, would never tell her how to prepare dishes. Bateman learned by watching her. When she finished watching, she would go and write down what she saw and then memorize the recipe. The day Grandmother Ater became ill was the day Ms. Bateman learned how to make pie crust. She read the pie crust recipe ingredients in a few books and then made pie crust her own way. Everything was cooked from scratch, even during the busiest season, from March to January. Bateman catered parties attended by Zsa Zsa Gabor, Charleston Heston, Bob Hope, as well as George Bush when he ran for governor of Texas. At one time there were only three Black caterers in the city—Carrie Shaw (whose specialties were deboned and stuffed chicken legs and thighs and homemade ice cream) and Grandmother Ater were two of the three. There were not many caterers who did dinner parties. Bateman states that White caterers preferred cocktail parties; they liked "moving with the debutantes." Bateman also mentioned that one of the White caterers "couldn't stand to do 'tomato windows' and watercress sandwiches, so she had [Grandmother] Lucy do them for her."[59]

Shirley Bateman began doing a lot of bar mitzvahs. A rabbi explained to her all of the do's and don'ts of cooking for bar mitzvahs. Ms. Bateman says she created a recipe for quiche hors d'oeuvres. She says that after she started serving cocktail quiche, it came out on the market within three years.

Now, how often has this occurred? How many times have Black cooks and caterers served their personal creations to the rich and famous at cocktail and dinner parties, only to see these creations wind up either on the market or in food columns of newspapers, or cookbooks, with other people's names on them? In addition, Bateman mentions that one of the Rittenbergs worked with restaurateur Paul Prudhomme at one time. Was this after constant exposure to Bateman's or Grandmother Ater's culinary talent?

When asked whether any part of her culinary repertoire included special dishes, Bateman responded, "No," because everything you cook has to be a specialty. All of Ms. Bateman's specialties, too, were transported in pots by taxi, until she learned how to drive and bought a station wagon. Bateman has cooked for eighteen hundred at a single gathering for the New Orleans Saints. In fact, through Ben Wiener, she cooked for events for the Saints for eighteen years. She credits her success not to formal education as a dietitian but to what she learned on her own and from watching Grandmother Ater, who died on Christmas Day, 1980.[60]

There are numerous chefs who deserve a place on the roster, and they are not all in New Orleans. Robert W. Lee was "one of those worthy heirs to a great tradition of southern cooking." From the Biltmore Hotel in Atlanta to the King and Prince Beach Club on Saint Simons Island, Georgia, to the Harrisburger Hotel in Harrisburg, Pennsylvania, in 1939, Chef Lee helped to establish great cuisine. Lee joined the army in 1942, and during his World War II service, where he became a mess sergeant and cooking instructor, he received a medal from President Franklin D. Roosevelt for the extraordinary number of cooks he trained. He returned to the Harrisburger Hotel as a cook in 1946 after his army discharge.[61]

The hotel went through a rapid turnover of executive chefs during the next year, but finally Lee was recommended for the position of executive chef, which he accepted and held for the next twenty-seven years. Chef Lee managed the Harrisburger's kitchens with an all African American crew. This allowed him to train numerous young men and women for careers in the culinary field. For over two decades Chef Lee made the menus, hired and fired and trained hundreds of African American chefs. He also lectured and gave culinary demonstrations at Pennsylvania State University School of Hotel Management. When the owner of the Harrisburger Hotel died in 1966, Chef Lee moved on to become executive chef at the Blue Ridge Country Club until 1969. He then became executive chef at the Sheraton Hotel in Harrisburg for the Archris Hotel Corporation of Boston. During Chef Lee's tenure cooking at the Harrisburger Hotel, "lines stretched for blocks from its doors. No other menu in town offered crab cakes, chicken pot pies and chopped chicken livers prepared in classic Southern style by the city's first African-American executive chef." And over the years he did garner an award-winning reputation for his crab cakes, stuffings, hors d'oeuvres, and salads. "We didn't use cans like the chefs do today," Lee commented. "I'm about the last person who would know about preparation from the bottom." Fresh and from scratch was his credo, and he made all of the food for the hotel that way, including mayonnaise and dressings.[62]

Chef Lee won his first cooking competition at twenty-three years of age. However, he was not allowed to receive the prize in front of an audience. "At that time, the blacks could not go to the front to get their recognition," Lee said. Later in his career, Lee was asked to do a cooking demonstration at a York, Pennsylvania, hotel but was greeted by a sign directing Blacks to the rear entrance. Chef Lee threatened to leave until management agreed to let him walk through the front door. More recognition was to come, as Chef Lee was recognized for outstanding achievements in the culinary arts when he was named Chef of the Year from 1970 through 1979. He retired in 1979 and lived with his wife, Geneva, in Harrisburg until his death on November 24, 1999.[63]

The African American Chefs Hall of Fame also includes Leon West, born into a family of eight children in Boston, Massachusetts, in 1946. In 1978 Chef West joined the staff of ARAMARK. After being promoted, he was transferred to the Ernest N. Morial Convention Center in New Orleans, where he assumed the responsibility of executive chef in 1983. West is known locally and internationally as one of the most talented chefs in New Orleans. There is also Chef Stanley Jackson Sr., one of ten siblings, and a New Orleans native. His first job in New Orleans was as cook at D. H. Holmes Potpourri Restaurant on Canal Street. He was shortly promoted to chef and put in charge of the menus. Several years later, Chef Jackson met Paul Prudhomme, who at the time was head chef at Commander's Palace. Prudhomme was a fan of Jackson's work at D. H. Holmes, so much so that Jackson was one of the chefs Prudhomme asked to join him to open K-Paul's. Jackson went with him as his executive chef.[64]

The late Chef Patrick Clark was also well known in culinary circles for his creations and presentations at master cooking classes. He was a friend of Chef Joe Randall who was born in McKeesport, Pennsylvania, and raised in Harrisburg, Pennsylvania. Chef Randall served as a cook at Turner Air Force Base (a SAC installation in Albany, Georgia, that has since been shut down) while enlisted in the US Air Force in the early 1960s. He has since gone on to become the executive chef at a dozen restaurants including the award-winning Cloister Restaurant in Buffalo, New York, and the Fishmarket in Baltimore, Maryland. A catering firm was at one time under his ownership and management, and he has provided consultant services to restaurant operators and served on the faculty of four schools.

Chef Randall's uncle Richard L. Ross was a Pittsburgh, Pennsylvania, restaurateur and caterer, who early on gave his nephew a taste of what a career in the culinary field was all about. Chef Randall later completed apprenticeships with Chefs Robert W. Lee at the Harrisburger Hotel and Frank E. Castelli at the Penn Harris Hotel in Harrisburg, Pennsylvania. A founding board member of the Southern Food Alliance and Culinary Wonders, Inc., Randall is also the author of *A Taste of Heritage*. From 2000 to 2016 he owned and operated the Chef Joe Randall's Cooking School in Savannah, Georgia, which he used as a "vehicle . . . that preaches the gospel of authentic southern cuisine to all comers. The success of the school is a credit to his undying devotion to his heritage and the cuisine of the South, and his love of sharing it with others."[65]

All of these cooks and chefs should be household names, whom we should look to as culinary role models. Historically speaking, we certainly have quite a selection from which to choose. Unfortunately, most of the names of African American culinary greats have been lost or purposefully deleted from the records. Since George Washington was the first president of the United States and handed down a small record of his African culinary staff (if only because the possibility of losing one of them threw him into a panic and caused him to write letters), it is fitting to take a look not only at his kitchen and the contributions of the African chefs and cooks responsible for establishing the high culinary reputation of his homes but also at their development of an eternally influential culinary legacy for fine dining in America.

2

SUSTENANCE FOR SUSTAINING AMERICAN LIBERTY

George Washington's kitchens always featured African cooks, and he was perfectly willing to devise strategies and even circumvent the law to keep those cooks close at hand. One of Washington's most valuable assets was in the form of his chief chef, Hercules, and another, who became his chief house steward and favorite restaurateur, Samuel Fraunces. It would come as no surprise then that the tasty delicacies prepared for George and Martha Washington by African hands would fix the boundaries and decide the location of this nation's capital.

Washington's hearth at Valley Forge was no exception to his rule. Hannah Till and her husband, Isaac, were cooks in Washington's Continental Army and prepared the meals for him and his troops during the grueling winter at Valley Forge. Mrs. Till was also said to cook for General Lafayette during his campaigns in the War of Independence. After seven years with the Continental Army, Mrs. Till eventually freed herself and moved to Philadelphia where she died at the age of 102. As for all other African bondsmen who served in the Revolutionary Army, they were technically freed in 1781 but all had to wait until 1785 for legislative enactment.

New York's General Assembly enacted legislation in 1684 to bar the growing number of Africans from a long list of occupations. Although serving in every capacity of agricultural, culinary, and general labor production, slaves and servants were prohibited from engaging in trade of any commodity whatsoever, whether food products or otherwise. By 1712 Africans were significantly impeded from becoming economically self-sufficient. One such impediment was a May 9, 1715, act making it illegal for Africans or Indians to sell oysters in New York, which was a significant loss for these two groups because of the popularity of oysters in the city.[1]

African cooks, however, were "enlisted" to play a role in the revolution long before 1781. Cyrus Bustill, a baker, supplied the Patriot troops. The most prominent of the Bustill family, Cyrus was born in Burlington, New Jersey, on February 2, 1732. His father was Samuel Bustill, an eminent White Quaker lawyer of Allentown, New Jersey, who became a friend of Benjamin Franklin and is mentioned in a published work of Franklin's. Cyrus's mother, Parthenia, was an African who had been sold into slavery. As soon as he was old enough to understand his position as a slave, he steadily grew to abhor slavery. When his owner died in 1762 the plan was to sell Bustill's services for a certain number of years. Bustill, seeing a way to eventually take control of his own life, went to see Thomas Prior, a Quaker he had learned of, and asked him if he would be willing to purchase his time. Prior agreed, and Bustill worked for him for seven years, later becoming a free man.

Prior was a bread and biscuit maker, and it has been written that Bustill served as an apprentice. While at Prior's, Bustill not only learned how to read, he also developed his own methods of bread making. He began attending Quaker meetings and soon became convinced of the correctness of Quaker principles. Bustill later established his own bakeshop and built up a profitable trade. His bread was described as good bread, light, sweet, hearty, and delicious. Many of the most prominent families sent their flour to his bakery to be turned into well-baked breads and loaves.

Bustill sold biscuits, cakes, and breads for many years on credit and for profit. After the outbreak of the American Revolution, he was the supplier for the American forces for his area. Thomas Falconer, contractor for supplying troops at the port of Burlington, issued a certificate, stating that:

> I hereby certify that Cyrus Bustill has been employed in the baking of all the flour used at the port of Burlington and that he has behaved himself as a faithful, honest man and has given satisfaction such as should recommend him to every good inhabitant.
>
> Given under my hand at Burlington, May 1st 1782
> (Signed)
> Thomas Falconer.

The reverse side of the certificate from Thomas Falconer has another endorsement. It reads:

> Burlington, June 1st, 1782.
>
> I hereby certify that the within named, Cyrus Bustill, has baked
> all the bread for the Troops at this Port for the month of
> May and has in all respects answered the within character.
> Per Thos. Ives,
> Agent for the Contractors.[2]

Bustill was a businessman as well as a Patriot who wanted to contribute his services to the struggle of the Continental forces for independence. A member of his family still preserves a silver piece given to him as a souvenir from George Washington.

Patriot Cyrus Bustill displayed his loyalty to the Revolution by providing the "staff of life" wherever needed. A good recipe providing heavenly aromas for a hearty and nourishing loaf of oatmeal bread might have been one of many demonstrations.

Oatmeal Bread

- 1 pint rolled oats
- 1 quart boiling water
- 1 tablespoon lard
- 1 tablespoon salt
- 3/4 cup molasses
- Half of a yeast cake, dissolved in 1/2 cup warm water
- 2 quarts flour

Combine oats and boiling water. Let it stand until lukewarm. Stir in molasses and yeast mixture. Stir flour in gradually. Allow to rise overnight. In the morning stir and transfer dough to a baking pan. Allow to rise again and bake.[3]

Bustill satisfactorily supplying "the staff of life" for the American forces indicated that there was one position neither the British nor the American side would ever take away from Africans, and that was the job in front of the stove (or behind the pots, whichever you prefer), which bestowed upon Africans the "right" to be creative in the kitchen. The job of cooking for Whites was always open. Africans were considered eminently qualified for the labor-intensive job of cooking for and feeding Whites, and no contrary opinions from working-class Whites held sway.

Against the backdrop of slavery, the deferment or abandonment of human rights for freedmen, and revolutionary war, New York received its small share of free Black immigrants from the Caribbean islands, which at this time sweltered in their own slaveholding and slave-trading environment. One Caribbean immigrant was Samuel Fraunces, "a cook and caterer of talent, if not genius." A dark complexioned mulatto popularly known as Black Sam, Fraunces bought the building on the southeast corner of Pearl and Broad Streets from Oliver DeLancy, Beverly Robinson, and James Parker on January 15, 1762, for two thousand pounds sterling. Before long, what used to be called the Queen's Head Tavern (named after Queen Charlotte, the young wife of George III of England) became Fraunces Tavern, the social center of the city.[4]

Fraunces Tavern was a restaurant opened as an inn by the forty-year-old caterer, and it was at Fraunces Tavern that the New York Chamber of Commerce was organized in 1768. Meetings of the chamber of commerce were held in the tavern's Long Room. The tavern was frequented by the most famous men of the time, making it the scene of many notable gatherings of historical and patriotic significance. Frederic J. Haskin states that according to the City History Club of New York, which quotes Woodrow Wilson, Fraunces Tavern hosted the famous Committee of Correspondence, which "was the [real] beginning and origin of the Continental Congress, and so the seed from which our great and glorious republic sprang." Haskin continues, "here under Black Sam's roof and over Black Sam's canvasback duck and venison haunch and Canary and Madeira and musty ale, were discussed and fomented the plans which ultimately resulted in the U. S. of A. It was the excellent eating and drinking at this Queen's Head Tavern as the population called it, that [brought our] . . . forefathers together. . . . It becomes apparent that Black Sam's cookery was at once the starting point and the sustaining pabulum of American liberty."[5]

Most taverns offered meals that were totally predictable and monotonous, as well as far from delectable. Fraunces was said to be one of few "tavern keepers" known for his palate-pleasing dishes. Frederic J. Haskin understood the relationship between good food and politics when he wrote, "A consideration of the story of Fraunces Tavern shows that the place of cooks in history has been overlooked and underestimated. It is they who bring great men together and cause great events to be planned and set on foot."[6]

This, no doubt, accounts for the fact that George Washington frequently dined at Fraunces Tavern, as did "everyone of any consequence in New York," and it was Fraunces Tavern that hosted the scene of Washington's and his officers' farewell banquet on December 4, 1783. Sam Fraunces was asked by Governor Clinton to organize the first public dinner for Washington following the victory march in New York. Washington was already lodging at Fraunces Tavern from November 26 to December 4, 1783, and gave "An Entertainment" there on November 30. On Thursday, December 4, 1783, about forty-four military leaders, considered America's greatest, were present at Fraunces for the farewell dinner. Held in the Long Room and paid for by Governor Clinton, the dinner's festivities included liquor sales amounting to ninety-seven pounds, twelve shillings.[7]

Samuel Fraunces's daughter Phoebe was Washington's housekeeper at the mansion he occupied in New York in 1776. The tale about Phoebe saving the life of the slave-owning first president has been told many times. While serving as housekeeper at Washington's Richmond Hill headquarters, Phoebe fell in love with Thomas Hickey, a member of Washington's Personal Guard. One day, as she was about to serve Washington his lunch, she found Hickey lacing one of Washington's favorite vegetables (spring peas) with poison. Although sworn to loyalty to her sweetheart, she brought the peas to Washington, and as she sat the dish on the table she whispered to him the contents. The peas were tossed out of the window into the garden where chickens ate the poisoned peas and promptly fell dead.[8]

On April 23, 1785, Fraunces and his wife, Elizabeth, sold the tavern to a Brooklyn butcher, George Powers. As Fraunces had proved that he was highly qualified to run a house and business, it came as no surprise that in September 1785 George Washington wrote to Fraunces, asking him if he could recommend a good housekeeper. "As no person can judge better, of the qualifications necessary to constitute a good Housekeeper, or Household steward, than yourself, for a family which has a good deal of company and wishes to entertain them in a plain, but genteel style." Washington wrote, "I take the liberty of asking you if there is any such an one within your reach . . . if they can . . . relieve Mrs. Washington from the drudgery of ordering and seeing the Table properly covered."[9]

It came as even less of a surprise that, when Washington became president, he appointed Fraunces as his house steward and superintendent of the kitchen of what was then the White House, in New York, located at 3 Cherry Street. Fraunces kept this position until February 1790, when he was succeeded briefly by John Hyde. Washington shared his feelings regarding Fraunces's worth with his secretary, Tobias Lear: "Fra[u]nces, besides being an excellent Cook, knowing how to provide genteel Dinners, and giving aid in dressing them, prepared the Desert, made the Cake, and did every thing that Hyde and [his] wife conjointly do; consequently the Services of Hyde alone is not to be compared with those of Fraunc[e]s's." In 1791 Fraunces returned to Washington's household to work in the same capacity as steward, and as Washington stated: "If Fraunc[e]s should be employed, it ought to be made known to him, that his services in the Kitchen as usual, will be expected."[10]

Fraunces continued to work for Washington after the executive home moved to Philadelphia, until June 1794. Described as "a very excellent fellow" with regard to his cooking, in that "he tosses up such a number of fine dishes that we are distracted in our choice when we set down to table, and obliged to hold a long consultation upon the subject before we can determine what to attack. Oysters & Lobsters make a very conspicuous figure upon the ta[ble] and never go off untouched."[11]

Fraunces was paid approximately fifteen hundred dollars a year and given all provisions and supplies for the White House in Philadelphia. Always meticulously dressed, he was, in today's terms, an elegant, "dazzling urbanite." He was a man of taste and a connoisseur of wines. Fraunces opened a restaurant in Philadelphia, more elegant than his tavern in New York. The Tavern Keeper was located at 166 South Street. The next year he moved his establishment to South Water Street, naming it The Golden Tun Tavern. Washington and other dignitaries dined there, which in turn attracted foreign diplomats, merchants, and sea captains. Aristocrats and all of high society dined and banqueted there. Fraunces catered small and large social functions in the private dining and large assembly rooms.

A legend during his lifetime, Fraunces died a few months after the opening of his new restaurant in 1795. His New York eatery is memorialized with a Pennsylvania State Historical Marker located at 310 South Second Street. Interestingly, Fraunces's will stated that the federal government and several states owed him money for housing and feeding soldiers during the Revolutionary War. Back in 1783 George Washington did acknowledge Fraunces's friendship to the cause of freedom and his having "suffered in our Cause." One communication from Washington to Fraunces states: "I am happy to find, by the Concurrent Testimony of many of our suffering Brethren, and others, that you have invariably through the most trying Times, maintained a constant friendship and Attention to the Cause of our Country and its Independence and Freedom, and this Testimony is also strengthened by my own Observation. . . . I do therefore hereby recommend you to the several Executives and to all the good People of these States, as a warm Friend, . . . One who is deserving the favor and attention of these U States." Above all, Fraunces was a "sworn revolutionary," and it has been suggested that Fraunces's "friendship to the cause" took the form of spying for the Patriots, who sent secret intelligence under an alias.[12]

Fraunces was well known to cook for and feed, at his own expense, Patriot troops who would stop by his tavern. It is easy to see why he was serious about trying to retrieve some of the money he felt he was owed. Fraunces wrote to Washington and to Alexander White (member of the Virginia House of Delegates from 1782 to 1786 and from 1799 to 1801, member of Congress from 1789 to 1793, and one of the board of commissioners for the District of Columbia from 1795 to 1802) concerning a demand against the estate of a General Lee. Washington assures White that Fraunces "was remarkably attentive to our prisoners in the City of New York; supporting them, as far as his means would allow, in the hour of their greatest distress," but as far as his claim goes, Washington states he knows nothing about it. Washington goes on to tell White that General Lee, in fact, owed *him* money. Fraunces died without receiving recompense.[13]

Unfortunately, Samuel Fraunces would not be the only free African who would provide culinary maintenance and support for the US government during war times and never receive full payment or compensation. Free Africans were considered merely "slaves without masters" and were treated as such. In seventeenth-century Virginia, the home state of both George Washington and Thomas Jefferson, the first major slave codes were enacted between 1680 and 1682. An act was previously passed in 1670 clarifying the African's status in the colony. The act fixed the status of the non-Christian African as that of slave for life; later judicial and legislative moves would ensure that all Africans were presumed to be slaves. It is this presumption—or precept—that has defined African and African American culinary history, by way of the "status" of African Americans, all the way into the twenty-first century.[14]

It should be noted that Virginia's 1680 slave code statute pioneered the legal process that guaranteed, by law, the debasement and dehumanization of Africans through the institutionalization of slavery, and Virginia's policies regarding slavery law would thereby become the model of repression throughout the South for the next 180 years. With Africans in the role of slaves, Virginia was the ideal example of culinary, agricultural, and economic success for all of the colonies.[15]

It was in this legalized oppressive atmosphere and dehumanized environment that African bondspeople prepared sumptuous meals day in and day out for George Washington and all of the guests received at his plantation home at Mount Vernon (near Alexandria), Virginia. One of Washington's enslaved cooks, Hercules, first appears in the historic record for the Mount Vernon estate in George Washington's list of tithables (persons for whom taxes had to be paid) in 1770. Particularly valued for his culinary masterpieces, Hercules became chief chef at Mount Vernon and was listed as such in the 1786 Mount Vernon slave census. Hercules was a widower; his seamstress wife, Lame Alice, left him with three children. Before the District of Columbia became the nation's capital, Hercules—also known as Uncle Harkless, and whose skills in the kitchen were considered unmatched—often accompanied Washington to the presidential mansion in Philadelphia. George Washington Parke Custis, Martha Washington's grandson, spoke of Hercules as a culinary "celebrated *artiste*," who, "trained in the mysteries of his part from early youth, and in the palmy days of Virginia, when her thousand chimneys smoked to indicate the generous hospitality that reigned throughout the whole length and breadth of her wide domain, . . . was, at the period of the first presidency, as highly accomplished a proficient in the culinary art as could be found in the United States."[16]

Hercules, with his particular set of skills and energies, also *managed* Washington's kitchen, which at one point contained a German cook, Jacob Jonus, and two French cooks, Peter Gilling and a man named La-muir. Dissatisfied with the cooking in one of his presidential residences, in November 1790 Washington brought Hercules to his Philadelphia residence on a permanent basis, where the kitchen was considered by Washington as one of "the principal entertaining rooms" in the Philadelphia home.[17] In Hercules's kitchen it was noted that:

> Under his iron discipline wo[e] to his underlings if speck or spot could be discovered on the tables or dressers, or if the utensils did not shine like polished silver. With the luckless wights who had offended in these particulars there was no arrest of punishment, for judgement and execution went hand in hand. The steward, and indeed the whole household, treated the chief cook with much respect, as well for his valuable services as for his general good character and pleasing manners. . . . It was surprising the order and discipline that was observed in so bustling a scene. His underlings flew in all directions to execute his orders, while he, the great master-spirit, seemed to possess the power of ubiquity, and to be everywhere at the same moment.[18]

Hercules was said to have been given "special privileges," which included being allowed to sell leftovers from the kitchen. It has been written that these sales garnered for him from one to two hundred dollars a year. But the fact remained that Hercules understood his status was that of a slave, and in February or March 1797, at the end of Washington's presidency, Hercules, in the vernacular of inner-city America, "got into the wind"—he escaped to freedom.[19]

Even though head chef Hercules, the assistant head chef, Nathan, and other enslaved Africans were undoubtedly the persons literally slaving over the hot cauldrons in George and Martha's kitchens, and despite the unrivaled talents of Hercules and Fraunces so often lauded and applauded by Washington and members of his family, current authors of the culinary master narrative award White women—including Martha Washington herself—the credit for the dinners prepared at their homes. One twenty-first-century edited volume, titled *Dining with the Washingtons: Historic Recipes, Entertainment, and Hospitality from Mount*

Vernon, does mention Hercules and the enslaved culinary staff. However, throughout this work, and especially throughout the book's recipe chapter, which was composed by one of the contributors to the book, credit for the recipes for the foods prepared at the Washingtons' homes is given to Martha Washington, Eliza Leslie, Hannah Glasse, Elizabeth Raffald, Mary Randolph, and other eighteenth- and nineteenth-century White women, who have cookbook titles in their names. Mary Randolph's cookbook, *The Virginia Housewife*, has been called by some the most influential cookbook of the nineteenth century. If it is influential, it has African cooks to thank for that. Considering the fact that Randolph was born into plantation aristocracy in Virginia and was always surrounded by Black cooks of no ill repute, you would expect her to have garnered a great deal of information. Apparently she did.

Some of the recipes in Randolph's *The Virginia Housewife* include okra soup, catfish soup, gumbo, pepper pot, oyster soup, mock turtle soup of calf's head, boiled turnips with bacon, sweet potato buns, sweet potato pudding, cornmeal bread, hot cakes, batter cakes, and breads. Many of the recipes call for spices such as nutmeg, cloves, mace, and thyme, and slices of ham, bacon, salt pork, or ham hocks for seasoning, as well as cayenne pepper and liquor, the uses of which are standard culinary practices of Black cooks in the Americas. For one such description, see J. B. Moreton's observation, published in 1793 and titled, *West India Customs and Manners: Containing Strictures on the Soil, Cultivation, Produce, Trade, Officers, and Inhabitants, With the Method of Establishing and Conducting a Sugar Plantation*. Mary Randolph's "contribution" is noted in *Dining with the Washingtons*, but neither Hercules nor any other African cook who actually did the cooking in Washington's kitchens is ever associated with or given credit for any of the recipes or the actual culinary creative processes described in this book. According to *Dining with the Washingtons*, and this is not the first time such a stance has been taken in print, the aforementioned White women provided the culinary creativity. The enslaved cooks merely stirred the pots and served the food when done, per instructions read to them. Further, a great deal is made in this and other volumes about Martha Washington "supervising" the myriad household chores, especially the cooking, performed by the enslaved Africans. Allow this and other books to tell it, Martha was struggling, she was about to pass out, she had to work so hard because, apparently, "supervising," or telling her servants what she wanted done, was the same as performing all of the work. The idea, which has become standard culinary master narrative procedure, is to define the African cook out of and away from the culinary expertise and creation in the kitchen.[20]

Barbecued Salmon

It would be hard to define the African hand away from its own culinary heritage. Bird and cayenne peppers were grown in Washington's Mount Vernon garden, as they were a necessary ingredient in barbecue sauce and other preparations served by enslaved cooks in the 1780s. Since Europe in general does not have a culinary legacy which includes hot peppers and spices, and Africa does (one that reaches back into ancient history), common sense would attribute their use in Washington's kitchen to the Africans who cooked there.[21]

By all accounts, Washington adored seafood. Fraunces, on one occasion, graced Washington's table with shad, which Washington was said to have refused to eat because he felt that Fraunces had paid too much for it. Well, if Washington had tasted the following spicy, lip-smacking sauce on his fish, he would have never thought of telling Fraunces to "take it away."[22]

- 4–6 one-half pound Salmon fillets
- 1/4 cup Worcestershire sauce
- 2 tablespoons ketchup
- 1 teaspoon yellow mustard
- 1 tablespoon, plus 1 teaspoon molasses
- 1/8 teaspoon (or more, to taste) ground cayenne pepper
- 1/8 teaspoon garlic salt with parsley

Bake salmon fillets in a baking pan, one layer deep, in a preheated 375 degree oven for approximately 14 to 17 minutes, depending on thickness of the fillets.

While salmon is baking:

Combine remaining ingredients in a saucepan and mix well. Bring to a boil, lower heat, and simmer for 3 minutes.

Baste salmon fillets with sauce and serve. Refrigerate remaining sauce in a covered container.

Double ingredients for larger jobs, if needed, such as for chicken or ribs.

It was just as impossible to define Hercules away from stellar performances that took place in the kitchen, which is why his unexpected exit angered and frustrated Washington. Washington saw Hercules as ungrateful. And since he and other slaveholders would experience other "ungrateful" slaves, by the stroke of Washington's pen, the Fugitive Slave Act of 1793 was enacted, which empowered slaveowners to seize runaway slaves and ordered state and federal authorities to assist in their capture and return. In an overwhelming vote Congress passed the act in February of that year, and President George Washington signed it into law a short time later on February 12. One unfortunate consequence of this law was that the widespread and increasing number of kidnapped free Africans (since all Blacks were considered slaves) put the lives of all persons of African descent in jeopardy more than ever.[23]

Although known for his relentless pursuit of runaways, Washington supposedly would not advertise for an escaped bondsperson "north of Virginia." John Cline escaped from the presidential mansion in Philadelphia, but Washington did not try to find him. He did, however, spend considerable effort to reclaim Hercules, as well as Oney (Opey) Judge, a bright young seamstress, and one of Mrs. Washington's most valued servants. Washington gave a government agent—specifically, his secretary of the Treasury, Alexander Hamilton—the task of alerting port officials to be on the lookout for Oney and to board and bound her by ship, as quietly as possible so as not to cause a public commotion. An agent sent a message to Washington that she had been seen in Portsmouth but that she had support from the local antislavery forces and therefore could not be secretly retrieved. In a letter dated August 20, 1797, Martha Washington wrote to her sister, Elizabeth Dandridge Henley, expressing her frustrations: "am obliged to be my one [own] Housekeeper which takes up the greatest part of my time,—our cook Hercules went away so that I am as much at a loss for a cook as for a house keeper.—altogether I am sadly plaiged."[24]

Never mind that the status of the African culinary artist and that of the seamstress was that of slaves. Noticeably, the Washingtons saw their status as natural and felt within their rights to be upset and displeased that their slaves were not satisfied and grateful. Perhaps Ms. Judge, in her slave existence, found no comfort, no difference, in being "treated like a *child*," as Washington described it. At any rate, the Washingtons eventually gave up hope for her return.

His chef, Hercules, however, was a different matter. The loss of the chef was considered as nothing short of a disaster, a household spiraling into hell. The value of his command in the kitchen, the delicacies that Washington's table would have to do without, was not a bearable concept. Hercules had, after all, been responsible for the superior level of cuisine and hospitality afforded not only to Martha and George but to visitors to the Washingtons' homes as well. Hercules's tasty delicacies made the Washingtons' dinner table well renowned in political circles and were responsible for one of the first examples of culinary diplomacy.

In a letter dated January 10, 1798, to Frederick Kitt, Washington's household steward in Philadelphia, Washington let Kitt know that Hercules was irreplaceable:

> Mr. Kitt: We have never heard of Herculas [Washington's spelling of his name] our Cook since he left this; but little doubt remains in my mind of his having gone to Philadelphia, and may yet be found there, if proper measures were employed to discover (unsuspectedly, so as not to alarm him) where his haunts are. If you could accomplish this for me, it would render me an acceptable service as I neither have, nor can get a good Cook to hire, and am disinclined to hold another slave by purchase. If by indirect enquiries of those who know Herculas, you should learn that he is in the City, inform Colo. Clemt. Biddle . . . and will pay any expence which may be incurred in the execution of this business.[25]

Desperate and in despair, Washington wrote Kitt again later on in January and begged Kitt to continue looking for Hercules, and that if he found him, "not to give him an opportunity of escaping." Washington added that the price of his recapture was no object: "Whatever cost shall attend this business Colo. Biddle will pay."[26]

Obviously, another of Hercules's skills was in remaining elusive; he was never recaptured. Philadelphia may have been Hercules's choice to establish new roots. The city was considered "a bad neighborhood" for slaveholders. By the 1790s Philadelphia had passed a law automatically freeing any slave brought into the city and held there longer than six months. Attorney General Edmund Randolph alerted George Washington to this "problem." In order to keep his favorite foods on the table, the chief officer of the realm schemed to circumvent the law by any means necessary. So as not to take any chances, Washington had his secretary, Tobias Lear, send his bondspeople out of the city, on some phony pretense, as the six-month timeline drew near. On April 12, 1791, while on a presidential tour of the South he sent Lear an urgent letter from Richmond, Virginia, in which he states: "If upon taking good advi[c]e it is found expedient to send them [Hercules and the others] back to Virginia, I wish to have it accomplished under pretext that may deceive both them and the Public. . . . This would naturally bring . . . Hercules under the idea of coming home to *Cook*."[27]

George Washington's efforts to beat the system that existed in Philadelphia is interesting on all counts because when the Potomac area became home to the nation's capital, over one-fifth of the area's population was enslaved, many of whom were undoubtedly the property of public officials. Assuredly, if the seat of government was located in a part of the country unfriendly to slavery, slaveholders "problems" would be compounded.

In order to guarantee uninterrupted culinary bliss, the capital of the United States had to be purposefully situated in the South, in slaveholding territory, because the president who drew up the plans for the site of the capital, as well as most of the people he knew, were slaveholders, and as such, he was not about to give up (or cause others to give up) those big, fluffy biscuits, and luscious cakes and pies. Remember how Frederic J. Haskin described Samuel Fraunces's cookery as "the sustaining pabulum of American liberty," and how he defined the relationship between food and politicians: cooks "cause great events to be planned and set on foot." It was African folks cooking that determined the location of the capital of the United States. Clearly, the District of Columbia is the capital of the United States thanks to Hercules, James Hemings (Thomas Jefferson's African chef), and a host of other culinary artists held in bondage. Perhaps their names and likenesses should accompany any literature on the history of the formation of Washington, DC, as the capital.[28]

3

SUSTENANCE FOR MAINTAINING
THE LEGALITY OF SLAVERY

S laveholder Thomas Jefferson also found Philadelphia problematic while he served as secretary of state, as the law would set his bondspeople free if he held them in the city longer than six months. Like every slaveholder, he considered his cooks and chefs as prized and precious possessions. Jefferson's culinary staff made Monticello dinners legendary. Dinner guests were said to eat Jefferson out of house and home. That would certainly explain how one of the president's enslaved cooks—and other members of her family—later became best known in Cincinnati as purveyors of fine foods. And just like this family of former slaves, fellow African caterers in Massachusetts were particularly successful at producing delicious delicacies for special affairs and at making mealtime the right time to combine good cooking with strong political and social consciousness.

One of Thomas Jefferson's most prized possessions was in the person of James Hemings. Hemings accompanied Jefferson to Paris as his chef while he served as minister to the court of Louis XVI to negotiate treaties of commerce for the new republic. Staying in a country that had been absorbing African cooking since the 1600s from their colony of Saint Domingue (Haiti), Jefferson is said to have wanted Hemings to learn the French style of cooking, so he placed Hemings under an apprenticeship with the caterer Monsieur Combeaux and with a pastry chef in the house of the prince de Condé. Hemings soon became the chef de cuisine in Jefferson's kitchen on the Champs-Elysées, supposedly earning 288 livres ($48) annually. According to James's nephew Madison Hemings, James had wanted to run away. Under the new legislation of the French revolutionary government, he was already free.

Hemings returned with Jefferson to New York and then went on to Philadelphia in 1790 when Jefferson became the first US secretary of state. If the Pennsylvania Abolition Society had learned of Hemings's stay in France, it could legally have demanded his immediate freedom. Wanting to head off any action that might take his prized cook away from him, Jefferson drew up an affidavit, which promised to free Hemings if he stayed with Jefferson in Philadelphia and at Monticello:

> Having been at great expense in having James Hemings taught the art of cookery, desiring to befriend him, and to require from him as little in return as possible, I do hereby promise and declare that, if the said James shall go with me to Monticello in the course of the ensuing winter, when I go to reside there myself, and shall there continue until he shall have taught such person as I shall place under him for the purpose to be a good cook, this previous condition being performed, he shall be thereupon made free, and I will thereupon execute all proper instruments to make him free. Given under my hand and seal in the county of Philadelphia and state of Pennsylvania this 15th. day of September one thousand seven hundred and ninety three.
>
> Th: Jefferson.
> Witness
> Adrian Petit.[1]

After successfully fulfilling the condition that he pass on to his brother Peter all of his culinary expertise, James Hemings was freed. On February 5, 1796, Thomas Jefferson signed a document that "discharged of all duties and claims of servitude" thirty-year-old James Hemings. This writ of manumission continued, "[Hemings] . . . shall have all the rights and privileges of a freedman."[2]

Unfortunately, the rights and privileges of an African in America, free or not, were slight to none. James Hemings, a literate slave, left Monticello but some of his handwritten recipes remained. These recipes were put to constant use, as were the bondswomen who cooked at Monticello. One such cook was Nancy, who delighted Lafayette with her special pie of sweetbreads and oysters. The slave-owning third president relished the reputation his African cooks were building for him as being particularly fond and a purveyor of fine dining. Writers have stated that it was Thomas Jefferson who forged the enduring pattern between African Americans, haute cuisine, and the White House—that it was Thomas Jefferson who made it all happen. When Jefferson became the third president of the United States, it was Hemings's creations that his culinary tastes sorely missed. Hemings was offered the position of White House chief chef, which he turned down. French chef Honoré Julien was finally hired for the post, but Julien was no match for either James or Peter Hemings in the culinary arts. Jefferson wrote to his daughter Martha at Monticello, begging and pleading, "pray enable yourself to direct us here how to make muffins in Peter's method. . . . My cook here cannot succeed at all in them and they are a great luxury to me."[3]

The following "original receipt" was prepared (and no doubt conceived) by the cook. The results were apparently tasty and fulfilling enough to be recorded in the manuscript cookbook of Thomas Jefferson's granddaughter Septimia Anne Randolph Meikleham.

Monticello Muffins

To a quart of flour put two table spoons full of yeast. Mix . . . the flour up with water so thin that the dough will stick to the table. Our cook takes it up and throws it down until it will no longer stick [to the table?] she puts it to rise until morning. In the morning she works the dough over . . . the first thing and makes it into little cakes like biscuit and sets them aside until it is time to back them. You know muffins are backed in a grid[d]le [before?] in the [fire?] hearth of the stove not inside. They bake very quickly. The second plate full is put on the fire when breakfast is sent in and they are ready by the time the first are eaten.[4]

Here is a more modern recipe, and sure to please, as a tasty rendition for breakfast, lunch, or dinner buttermilk biscuits.

Butter Biscuits

- 3 cups all-purpose flour
- 2 tablespoons baking powder
- 1 teaspoon baking soda
- 1½ teaspoons salt
- 1/2 cup sugar
- 1 cup buttermilk or sour cream
- 8 tablespoons softened butter or shortening

Combine dry ingredients in a medium-large bowl and mix well. Work butter or shortening into dry ingredients until mixture resembles coarse meal.

Make a well in the middle of the dry ingredients and pour buttermilk into well. Gradually mix milk into dry ingredients.

Turn dough onto a floured surface. With lightly floured hands, knead dough for a few minutes. Flatten dough to about a 1/2 inch thickness. Cut dough into rounds with a floured cookie cutter or glass. Place rounds on a nonstick baking sheet and bake, in a preheated 375 degree oven, for 15 to 20 minutes.

What this tells us is that James Hemings may very well have provided some tutoring of his own while he was in France. He Africanized the dishes he prepared in Jefferson's kitchens before, during, and after his trip to France. Jefferson was obviously pleased with the results.

Jefferson's plantation kitchen was actually a gold mine of culinary talent, and some of those skilled artisans of the Monticello stove would migrate to the Midwest. One such gentleman was William B. Fossett, "one of the best known colored caterers" of Cincinnati, Ohio. William B., his father, Joseph, his mother, Edith, his brothers Peter Farley, Jesse, and Daniel, and his four sisters were all once enslaved on Thomas Jefferson's Monticello plantation. Patriarch Joseph Fossett had been an ironworker at Monticello. It was said that he "could do any thing it was necessary to do with steel or iron." William's mother, Edith, along with another bondswoman, Fanny Hern, followed the Hemings brothers as cooks at Monticello.[5]

Prevailing literature relating to Thomas Jefferson's kitchen forces a discussion of certain issues. In most of the literature on "Thomas Jefferson's" kitchen and the enslaved Africans responsible for the foods grown and consumed on his plantation the Africans are described as having learned everything they knew from the French—during Jefferson's visit to France—and from those French and Italians whom Jefferson imported to his plantations as well as from Whites with whom Jefferson did business. "Everything" includes, according to this discourse, how to grow food, the food culture developed at Monticello that planned and maintained food production, and most certainly the food preparation. Accordingly, we are told that "Monticello cooks . . . were French trained. . . . Brothers James and Peter Hemings and sisters-in-law Edith Hern Fossett and Fanny Gillette Hern . . . both relied on their training." Furthermore: "In freedom, Peter Fossett was one of Cincinnati's most prominent caterers, likely using skills and recipes gleaned from his mother, Edith Fossett, who cooked both at the President's House and Monticello." The claim in certain literature is that Edith Fossett mastered her culinary skills as a slave in training and then "passed them on to her children." If she was in training she was being trained by other bondswomen already knowledgeable in the culinary arts. Also, since the White plantation women in Jefferson's family considered cooking and housework "time-consuming" and work best left for the servants because they had better things to do, it is inconceivable that dishes created at Monticello were done "through collaboration between the skilled enslaved workers and the *white female housekeepers* of the Jefferson family" (italics added). Yet, these same lies are told in even the most recent twenty-first-century publications.[6]

Even the pots and pans Jefferson was said to have brought home from France are given credit before credit is given the cooks Fossett and Hern. According to the same wisdom, by using French utensils, "the two women transformed . . . 'plantation fare' into 'choice' meals." This would all be fine and dandy except that if all it took was French cooking and cookware, Jefferson would not have gone crazy when his French cook could not make muffins like Peter Hemings. Additionally, when Jefferson's granddaughter Ellen moved off to Boston after her marriage, she asked her mother to send Mrs. Fossett's and Mrs. Hern's recipes. Notice, she did not ask for the Frenchman's advice. The French, White female housekeepers (White female elites as housekeepers is a contradiction in terms), and French skillets, if we let some "food historians" and their literature tell it, were all responsible and given credit for creating all that was good (and tasty) in Jefferson's house. Black folks somehow landed in this and other plantation kitchens with no prior knowledge of food or cooking. Their most useful capabilities were in taking instructions, stirring the French pots, and serving the food when done.[7]

With regard to the Fossetts, just before Jefferson died he freed Joseph Fossett who moved immediately to Ohio, the state that saw its greatest years of African migration from the South between 1826 and 1829. In Cincinnati, where he landed, the African population rose from 4 to 10 percent during this period. In the midst of this community, Fossett opened his own blacksmith shop. Saving his money allowed him to eventually buy his wife and five of his children, all of whom came to Cincinnati in 1833. Mr. Fossett had arranged to secure liberty for his son Peter. However, when he tried to purchase Peter, the new owner refused to sell him. Peter later ran away but was captured and sold. It was his brother-in-law who bought him, however, and Peter was then sent to Cincinnati. After his arrival Peter made a connection with the catering establishment of Mrs. Kate Jonas who, in her day, was said to exhibit par excellence in this art. When she retired, Peter Fossett purchased her entire collection of chinaware, linen, and silver, the likes of which were not available anywhere in America. Peter became one of the leading caterers in Cincinnati and remained in the catering business until just a few years before his death. Cincinnati's most wealthy and aristocratic families were listed among his patrons.[8]

Joseph's son William, one of the first of five children to arrive in Cincinnati, went to work in his father's blacksmith shop. William later joined his brother Peter in his catering service, blending their talents to provide the most royal receptions and banquets in the city. The two men worked together until William was given charge of the service at a hotel at Niagara Falls, a position he held for a number of years. William returned to Cincinnati and opened his own successful catering business. He catered a number of important banquets, including the celebration of the opening of the Southern Railway, which took place at Music Hall. There were fifteen thousand guests in attendance. He also catered the Masonic banquet shortly after the burning of the Masonic Temple at Third and Walnut Streets. The Masonic banquet was held in the northern wing of the Music Hall, and there were so many guests that announcements made at one end of the hall had to be repeated for guests at the other end. One item discussed at the banquet was the purchase of the Scottish Rite Cathedral to replace the destroyed Masonic Temple. It was later purchased, and William B. Fossett was appointed the cathedral's caterer, a position he held until his retirement.

Like all "thinking" Africans, William, his father, and his brothers Peter and Jesse, along with Peter's wife, Sarah Walker Fossett, were actively involved in the Underground Railroad. Among the Whites in Cincinnati whose lives were rooted in slavery, both economically and politically, there developed abolitionists who worked with the Fossetts and other members of the African community, all of whom were blamed for the encouragement of Africans, both free Blacks and runaway slaves, migrating into the state. The antislavery influences of these "white fanatics" were seen as responsible for Africans "crowding out white labor," as well as for the rapid increase in "negro stealing." In this case, slaveholders complained that they "could not come to Cincinnati to trade, to spend the summer, or even to pass the night 'without having . . . negro servants decoyed or stolen away.'" Underground Railroad activity did increase significantly in Cincinnati in 1839 and 1840. Add to that, in June 1841, Ohio's Supreme Court held that every slave brought voluntarily by his master into Ohio was declared free. It was in a climate many Whites believed to be supportive of miscegenation and too friendly toward these Black "impudent wretches" that what was termed a riot broke out in September 1841; another broke out in 1843. Cincinnati had seen an anti-abolition "riot" in 1836, organized and carried out by mostly members of the status quo: lawyers, politicians, merchants, shopkeepers, and bankers. These same elites, who felt threatened by a change in the social order and who initiated and carried out assaults against Africans, were the same patrons and customers of Fossett and other African caterers in the city. However, Cincinnati Africans, it was said, "were well armed and more than willing to defend their homes with bullets." Consequently, there was less destruction of African property.[9]

Catering was how he made his living, but William B. Fossett was also the first president of the Society of Sons of Liberty, organized in 1853 to help his people before and after the war. After many years of service to the community, he died at his son-in-law's home on August 12, 1901. His brother Peter Farley Fossett had passed away several months earlier, on January 4, 1901, at the age of eighty-five, and his brother Jesse who had been a courthouse employee for many years died in the summer of 1900.[10]

The Fossetts' catering business continued after the older Fossetts died. Peter and Sarah's daughter, Edith, married John Miller, who had been in charge of a White caterer's business, Wilson and Reeder of Cincinnati. John Miller became virtually the head of the Fossett catering industry. When Miller died, Edith Fossett Miller, still very successfully carried on catering for many of the old families who were patrons of her father and husband.[11]

Despite the culinary expertise exhibited by Fossett and Hern and other Black chefs, the so-called French cuisine that Jefferson brought into the White House in 1801 has remained the food of choice for state dinners and other functions. However, if the truth be told, many presidents brought their own personal African American chefs to the White House, whose cooking they ate exclusively. Jefferson's successor, James Madison, had an all African staff, except for his French Steward, Jean-Pierre Sioussat. Numerous US presidents did bring in French cooks to prepare dishes and menus for state dinners at the White House, allowing the French cook to be designated as the official White House chef, which was also supposed to make a significant statement, in that the food presented represented the best and highest quality in preparation. But most of these presidents, in actual fact, could not stand French cooking.

President from 1845 to 1849, James K. Polk was the son of a slaveholder who held title to over eight thousand acres and fifty-three bondspeople. A slaveholder his entire life, Polk sold and bought more Africans when he became president. Auguste Julien, the son of Jefferson's French chef, Honoré Julien, was hired by Polk to prepare formal dinners during Polk's White House years. But Polk "resolutely avoided the French concoctions of Auguste Julien." His preference was for the dishes prepared by his slave cook on his Tennessee plantation, whom he had sent to him as his own personal chef at the White House.[12]

Polk's southern tour in March of 1849 stopped at New Orleans. A welcoming committee brought him ashore to a hotel where a breakfast had been prepared. The committee thought that they had prepared a sumptuous repast, but Polk, however, was not pleased. In fact, in his diary he comments: "All the dishes were prepared in the French style of cooking, and to one unaccustomed to it [it] was difficult to tell of what they were composed. Fish of every variety and prepared in various ways constituted a large part of the repast. . . . I could see nothing before me that I had been accustomed to, or that I should have deemed it safe to eat in my state of health and in a cholera atmosphere. I took a cup of coffee and something on my plate to save appearances, but was careful to eat none of it. As soon as an opportunity offered I asked a servant in a low tone if he could give me a piece of cornbread and broiled ham."[13]

———

Perhaps, along with that cornbread and ham, he would have favored some crusted potatoes and onions, with which I am sure his Tennessee cook was familiar. My father referred to the following concoction as "American style potatoes," which, when you get that crust just right, the word *satiated* comes to mind. You will dream about this dish after the first time you have had it. Serve alongside ham and eggs, and corn bread muffins, or as a side dish at dinner.

Crusted Potatoes and Onions

- About 4 large potatoes
- 2–3 large onions
- Approximately 3½ tablespoons EACH vegetable and olive oil
- Garlic salt with parsley, black pepper, dill weed, and crushed red pepper, all to taste

Peel potatoes and slice into 1/4 inch thick rounds. Peel and slice onions into 1/4 inch thick rounds.

Heat oil in a steel or aluminum skillet. DO NOT USE A NONSTICK UTENSIL because you want the potatoes to form a brown crust. Alternately add layers of potatoes, onions, and seasonings. Over medium heat, and with a spatula, cook and turn potatoes and onions every couple of minutes, as crusts form on the bottom. The more crusts that form on the potatoes and onions, the better, but cook and turn only until potatoes are tender. Makes a wonderful side dish for dinner as well.

African culinary artists were expert at preparing more than cornbread and broiled ham, and such expertise was not relegated to the White House or Washington, DC. Africans and Native Americans were continually used to help build towns and cities such as Boston, and to cook while doing so. For over a decade after its founding, Boston remained primarily a farming community, but eventually the area transformed into a heavily trafficked trading town. New Hampshire lumber and cattle and Grand Banks codfish found their way to Caribbean and European markets through the port of Boston. The same port received cattle from central and western Massachusetts, Rhode Island horses, sheep and dairy products, furs from New York, and grain from Connecticut.[14]

It was slave labor that produced the goods so vital to Boston's commercial success. And its success was also tied to African expertise brought from the African homeland in the area of combining spices and herbs not only for use in various culinary preparations but also for use in colonial medicine in New England and the Northeast during this century. Africans possessed knowledge of herbal curatives, and many produced their own compounds and used them as needed.

Knowledge of the use of various herbs and spices for medicinal purposes had been a common feature of African life for thousands of years. Traditional African methods of herbal cures were transplanted and continued to be used by herbal specialists in African communities here in the Americas. Caesar, a slave, discovered a cure for rattlesnake bites in 1780. The state legislature emancipated him. Black women such as Doctress Phillis of Barrington, Rhode Island, were recognized locally for their ability and expertise in African traditional medicine. Variolation was one traditional African medical procedure that was transferred to New England and used against the outbreak of smallpox in Boston in the 1700s. Various racist discourse on the subject gives the credit for the discovery and use of variolation to the so-called Turkish method of inoculation, and especially to a White man named Cotton Mather. The fact is, one of Cotton Mather's African bondsmen, Onesimus, taught Mather all about small pox variolation during this outbreak.[15]

The African method, by way of Onesimus, eventually saved many lives, as the outbreak in Boston threatened serious damage to life and commerce there and in surrounding areas and seaport towns such as Salem, Massachusetts. Salem was the sixth largest city in the United States in 1790, with close to eight thousand residents. Its commerce, by 1798, included Trinidad sugar, Port-au-Prince molasses, St. Vincent rum, Molasses Jamaican spirits, and Surinam cotton.[16]

One of Salem's future merchants, John Remond, made his way to Salem on board the *Six Brothers* on its journey home from Curacao, via St. Eustacia. Remond, a Black ten-year-old, managed to get on board this ship, alone, in Curacao without being noticed. In his possession was an "old fashioned round bottle of Schiedam gin" that his mother had given him, presumably to guard against illness. John wrapped a note around the bottle, on which was written, "Presented to me by my mother the day I sailed on the 25th of July 1798."[17]

Remond disembarked in Salem, and John Needham, the owner and master of the ship placed him under the care and supervision of his brother, Isaac Needham, who owned a bakery on High Street. Young Remond was given the job of delivering the bread to private homes, as well as to the ships that came and went in the port of Salem. It was a job such as those usually held by Blacks in Salem during this time, which included oystermen, fish vendors, hairdressers, barbers, mariners, clothes' cleaners, gardeners, chimney sweeps, laborers, and stablers. Other Blacks maintained boardinghouses or were servants for rich families in which some had been slaves until the Revolution.[18]

Sometime after his arrival in Salem, John Remond left for Boston to learn the barbering and hairdressing trade. During his stay he garnered a great deal of knowledge with regard to the catering business after he met Nancy Lenox, a free woman, born in Newton, Massachusetts, and known to possess considerable talents in the culinary arts. Remond returned to Salem in 1805, where he acquired living quarters in the newly completed Hamilton Hall, named in honor of Alexander Hamilton. At the age of nineteen, he opened barber, hairdresser, and catering businesses. Between 1805 and 1857 John Remond was the principal restaurateur in Salem.[19]

There were two stores on the ground floor of Hamilton Hall. The south side store was John Remond's, where he catered most of the affairs held in the hall. Soup was served at his store at 11:00 a.m. every morning. The first affair held in the hall was on the Thursday in Christmas week, 1805. It was reported that the kitchen had huge brick ovens and a fireplace, which John Remond made busy by preparing all sorts of fowls, pies, and cakes. To make the evening more memorable, music was provided by a band of African fiddlers, situated in a section of the hall's balcony.[20]

Remond married Nancy Lenox in Boston on October 29, 1807. She was a well-known fancy cake maker, and her skills would prove to be a crucial asset in helping to make her and her husband's catering business successful, as she was said to have done most of the cooking.[21]

All by itself, or accompanied by vanilla ice cream, this simple yet elegant and absolutely delicious gem is a tribute to cake baker Mrs. Nancy Remond. It is guaranteed to show off your baking skills.

Gingered Gingerbread Cake

- 2½ cups flour
- 1½ cups sugar
- 1½ teaspoons baking soda
- 2 teaspoons baking powder
- 1 teaspoon salt
- 2 teaspoons ground (powdered) ginger
- 1/2 teaspoon ground (powdered) cloves
- 1/2 teaspoon cinnamon
- 1/2 teaspoon nutmeg
- 1 cup shortening
- 1 gill (1/2 cup) dark rum
- 1 cup molasses
- 4 eggs
- 2 rounded tablespoons finely grated fresh ginger (outer skin removed)

In a large bowl combine dry ingredients and mix well. Add shortening and work into dry ingredients until mixture resembles coarse meal.

Make a well in the middle of mixture and into the well add rum, molasses, eggs, and fresh ginger. Mix these ingredients together in the well, and gradually stir rum mixture into dry ingredients until well blended.

Divide equal amounts of batter between two greased 8x8 inch square pans. Bake in a preheated 350 degree oven for about 30 minutes.

Nancy Remond's skills catered what was termed a spectacular event in 1809. Many painstaking preparations were made. "Vans" arrived from Boston, loaded with various fruits and game. Farmers were summoned for their fresh produce. As was the case with a number of African caterers throughout the nineteenth and early twentieth centuries, Remond was especially noted for his turtle soup. A two-hundred-pound live turtle was acquired for his delectable dish. Oysters were a new delicacy presented at formal affairs, and Remond's varied ways of preparing oysters established them as a mainstay for all important culinary events. In this case, the oysters were specially brought in for the governor of Massachusetts, Christopher Gore, escorted by the Company of Salem Light Infantry.[22]

I would like to digress for just a moment to mention that Christopher Gore was used to Africans taking care of his needs. Between 1825 and

1827, the last two years of his life, Gore's lavish home, known as Gore Place, located in Waltham, Massachusetts, was flawlessly run by Robert Roberts, an African. Roberts was born around 1780 in Charleston, South Carolina. He married Dorothy Hall in 1805; tuberculosis took Dorothy in 1813. They had no children. Late in 1813 he married Sarah Easton. They had twelve children. Before working for Christopher Gore, who had served as governor and senator from Massachusetts, Roberts had been a butler or manservant for Nathan Appleton.

Roberts wrote and published the famed *House Servants Directory*, considered the "final word on the correct and proper relations between servant and master and between master and servant." Published in Boston by Munroe and Francis in 1827, Roberts's book was believed to be one of the first commercially published books written by a Black person in the United States. Two later editions were published to accommodate its popularity, one in 1828 and another in 1843. Although it does contain recipes and instructions for how to market, how to carve, and how to preserve, as well as "receipts" for varnish, shampoo, and cleaners, *The House Servant's Directory* is very much a manual offering directives on the proper management of the household.[23]

Just as Robert Roberts became known as an outstanding community leader and was considered as occupying a special class of public and private servants, John Remond, the civic-minded businessman, belonged to a small and exclusive class of chefs, restaurateurs, and caterers. His manners and deportment lent an aristocratic air to special affairs held in Salem, such as those catered for the Salem Light Infantry Company between 1809 and 1863. The affairs were considered successful *only* because Remond was in charge of the service. During the thirty-seventh anniversary of the infantry, held on October 13, 1842, with many military guests in attendance, the proceedings temporarily halted in order for everyone to drink a toast to John Remond.[24]

A few menus have survived from John Remond's catering events. A "Publick Dinner," for example, was held at the Exchange Coffee House at Congress Square in Boston on Wednesday, July 30, 1823, in honor of Captain Isaac Hull. It was truly a feast. There were twenty-two items comprising the first course alone, including green turtle soup, green turtle steaks and fins, salmon, corned legs of pork, calves' head, ragout of veal, compote of pigeon, and fricassee of chicken. Some of the eleven items on the second course were ducks stewed with green peas, lobster fricassee, and roasted game birds. Rounding out the meal was, of course, an assortment of desserts.[25]

"Dinner on the Two Hundredth Anniversary of the First Settlement of Salem" was a particularly spectacular episode in Salem culinary history. It was held at Hamilton Hall on September 18, 1828. Preparations were made for 170 people. Forty-nine items are listed on the bill of fare. Remond's command of the turtle was presented in the first course. Green turtle pie was accompanied by green turtle soup, then came mutton, ham, beef à la doubé (beef daube), beef bouilli, sweetbreads, chicken pies, oyster pies, halibut à la mode, pigeons transmogrified, as well as other boiled meats. Roasted pork, chicken, beef, and an array of eight different game birds—including plovers, teals, quails, and doebirds (thought by some Boston epicures to be the best tasting game bird)—were breathtaking and luscious additions to the second course. Turk's Caps, and a myriad of fruits, pastries, jellies, and peach, apple, pear, and quince preserves rounded out the sweet presentations.[26]

Just imagine lamb chops sensationally flavored with whole cranberry sauce and simmered until fork tender with fresh green vegetables to produce a unique and tasty meal suitable for any anniversary or special occasion dinner.

Sweet Cranberry Lamb (or Pork) Chops Simmered with Collard Greens and Onions

- 4 shoulder blade lamb chops (or pork chops), a little over 3/4 up to 1 pound EACH
- Garlic salt, seasoned salt, black pepper, cilantro flakes, parsley flakes, paprika
- Flour
- A few tablespoons vegetable oil
- 2 large onions, sliced into rings

- 1 big handful of shredded collard greens
- 1 cup whole berry cranberry sauce
- 1½ cups chicken broth
- 2 to 4 teaspoons molasses, OR, sugar
- 1/2 rounded teaspoon garlic salt with parsley

Season chops with garlic salt, seasoned salt, black pepper, cilantro flakes, parsley flakes. Sprinkle generously with paprika. Coat with flour.

Heat oil in a large deep skillet or pot. Brown chops on both sides. Remove from heat and set aside covered.

In a small saucepan, combine cranberry sauce, broth, molasses, and garlic salt. Heat and stir just until cranberry sauce has completely melted.

Layer onion rings all over chops in skillet. Layer shredded collard greens over onions. Pour cranberry mixture over greens and chops. Bring to boil, lower heat, and simmer covered, on low heat, for 1 to 1½ hours, depending on thickness of chops, or until fork tender.

A similar menu was lavished on Supreme Court Justice Joseph Story, famed for rendering opinions *United States v. The Amistad* (1841) and *Prigg v. Pennsylvania* (1842). He was honored at a public dinner that was catered by Remond at Hamilton Hall on September 3, 1829. Forty-six items appear on the menu. Added to many of the same dishes, desserts, and fruits mentioned earlier were lobster ragout, baked codfish, roasted Bremen and Mongrel geese, ducks, plum tarts, tapioca, lemon pudding, water melon, green gages, and pineapple.

Catering dinners to honor people such as Justice Story was a common event for Mr. and Mrs. Remond. They would cater another dinner, served to Salem's Light Infantry and hosted by Boston's Light Infantry on Thursday, August 4, 1831, at Concert Hall. The bill of fare included soup, mutton, ham, tongue, turkey, fowl, oysters, beef à la Mode, roasted beef, pork, veal, chicken, pigeon, Mongrel geese, turkey, duck, partridge, and woodcock. On the list of desserts were puddings, pies, tarts, custards, ice creams, calves feet jelly, and Turkish caps.[27]

Throughout the Remonds' career, their catering services were much sought after in Salem and surrounding towns in Massachusetts. Some of the service contracts have survived, which shed light on the kinds of dinners they catered in the 1830s. One agreement was signed in 1830 for the Remonds to provide dinners for fifty-nine guests at a ball held at Hamilton Hall.[28]

Seventy-five persons would celebrate the installation of Rev. I. W. Thompson on March 7, 1832. It was agreed that the Remonds would furnish dinner for $1.50 per person. Pastry, cider, coffee, dessert, and "wine of a good quality" were some of the prerequisites. Remond was also to furnish coffee, tea, rolls, and cheese for the council on the morning of the event.[29]

Prerequisites would certainly have been in order for President Andrew Jackson's visit. He must have been celebrating as he planned his arrival at Salem in 1833. After all, he had signed the Indian Removal Act a few years earlier in 1830. Since Native Americans could not be allowed to stand in the way of White settler expansion, Jackson made certain that Native Americans in the southeastern United States suffered what became known as the Trail of Tears. In the case of Florida, the removal act also disrupted the safe haven some Native Americans provided escaped slaves. In fact, Jackson engaged in some expansion of his own when he increased his slave ownership from nine in 1804 to one hundred and fifty bondspeople by the time he left Tennessee in 1829 to occupy the White House. Unfortunately, the Remonds were not serving black-eyed peas and rice, which Jackson's slave cooks prepared for him at the Hermitage, his Tennessee plantation. It was agreed, however, that for Jackson's event the Remonds would provide dinner for between 150 and 200 or more persons, at from $3.00 to $3.25 per head. Since the contract specified serving mock turtle soup, "an abundance of cherries and strawberries," "the best Brown & Pale Sherry Wine[s] . . . to be supplied in such quantity as shall be required, with one course of Champaign," it can be ascertained that these were some of Jackson's preferences.[30]

Potatoes were very often a preference of dinner guests and were considered the "just right" accompaniment to any meat or fish dish. Treat yourself and family to this archival recipe or to my modern, good-for-every-occasion version that follows.

Potato Puffs

- Two cups cold mashed potato[es]
- 2 tablespoons butter
- 1 cup cream or milk
- Salt
- 2 eggs beaten light

Beat all until light and creamy; then pour into [a] deep dish and bake in quick oven until nicely browned.[31]

Potato Puffs with Cheese

- 1½ cups very hot mashed potatoes seasoned with 2 tablespoons butter
- A rounded 1/2 teaspoon garlic salt with parsley
- A little milk
- 1/2 cup shredded cheddar cheese
- 3 tablespoons butter
- 1/2 cup chopped onions
- Fine bread crumbs
- About 1 or 2 tablespoons butter for browning

Combine hot potatoes and cheese and stir until cheese has completely melted.

Melt 3 tablespoons butter in a large skillet. Add onions. Cook and stir until onions are golden brown. Stir onion mixture into potato mixture. Pour out a thick layer of bread crumbs on waxed paper. Place heaping tablespoonfuls of mixture on crumbs and generously coat on all sides.

Melt a little butter in the same large skillet. When hot, transfer coated puffs to the skillet. Flatten slightly. Allow puffs to brown until a crust develops, on both sides.

Cotillion parties, set up in the ladies drawing room, specified their preferences and were usually provided with items such as sponge cake, French rolls, wine, coffee, and lemonade. Musicians were hired, brought in from Boston. Ham, tongue, rolls, and coffee were served for a gentlemen's collation. Noticeably, for these and other events such as military balls, it was customary to have each male guest bring two ladies if they so desired.[32]

Along with cotillion parties, the Remonds catered military balls. For these occasions, cakes, cheesecakes, French rolls, sandwiches, and lemonade were considered customary refreshments. For the guests' additional culinary pleasure, Remond ordered bushels of oysters, which they prepared in a variety of dishes, at the price of $3.50 per bushel.[33]

Before, during, and after all of these functions, the responsibility of lighting and cleaning Hamilton Hall fell on Remond. When female guests arrived with their valuable camel's hair shawls, Remond provided ladies' maids who attended these wraps for the duration of the event. Remond set up a check system where each item was carefully numbered so that there would be no possibility of loss or confusion. This begs the question, did Remond invent the coat check system?[34]

The Phillips Library at the Peabody Essex Museum houses several invoices for services and goods that provide a glimpse into the Remonds' catering affairs. For example, the Remonds fed 123 people at a dinner hosted by the East India Marine Society on October 14, 1825. The bill came to $546.13. But this was nothing compared to the affair for the Marquis de Lafayette. A meeting of the committee for the reception of the Marquis de Lafayette's second visit to Salem in August 1824 and a massive formal dinner to climax that visit were both catered by the Remonds. York Morris, the famous waiter, was one of the hired servants for the dinner. Needless to say, the list of products brought in for Lafayette's dinner is extensive. Every detail appears to have been covered, including an order for two bottles of rosewater, which could have been used as a flavoring ingredient in Mrs. Remond's fancy desserts, or as a rinse for perfuming the table linens, or a rinse for the guests' hands and fingers.[35]

Whether it was supplying barrels of cranberries and onions to Black New York merchant Henry Scott, who specialized in pickled foods, or supplying flour, grain, and oats to David Pingree, or selling pickled lobster, John Remond operated a thriving business and was in constant demand for public and private affairs for over fifty years. The 1850 census has his assets listed at $3,600. He was listed as a "dealer in wines" in the 1870 census, his real estate holdings totaled $19,400, and his personal assets were assessed at $2,000. This is not surprising, because the events held in Hamilton Hall became "the pivotal occasion of a social life that now visibly aspired to those luxurious modes of social conduct consistent with affluence and national prestige." And, as a successful wine merchant, Remond began collecting fine rare wines in 1808, which he sold along with other goods in his ground-floor store. Thomas Downing, his friend and a famous fellow caterer and restaurateur of New York, sent six baskets of wine to Remond, shipped on the schooner *Anawan* in August 1831. Remond utilized numerous sources for obtaining wines.[36]

On Wednesday, November 7, 1866, an auction was held in Boston, showcasing John Remond's private liquor stock. An eight-page inventory of his valuable collection was printed, cataloguing his various brandies, cognacs, burgundies, port wines, brown and pale sherries, Madeira ports and wines, fish, palm tree and Cologne gins, Cordials, whiskies, and rums. Two interesting entries appear in the catalogue. One represents the bottle Remond carried with him when he disembarked *Six Brothers* at the age of ten. It still had the note attached to it. There was also a listing for a wine that carried the label "Judge Story." If this was not a bottle reserved for Judge Story, perhaps it was a bottle of wine Judge Story presented to Mr. Remond as a token of his appreciation for a fine meal served to him. Such courtesies were in vogue.[37]

Remond's economic success was heightened by his entry into the trading business. The Embargo Act, beginning on December 22, 1807, greatly limited trade and forbade ships to embark for foreign countries. By March 1809 the embargo had been lifted and with this came a rise in prosperity for the merchants of Salem. Merchants and masters of vessels were supplied with livestock purchased from Remond. Local newspaper advertisements in the mid-1820s list him as having for sale thousands of pounds of cheese, hams, and smoked beef, as well as curry powder, macaroni, East India soy, pickled walnuts, mushroom catsup, split peas, Newark cider, and oysters that he advertised as being able to cook "in various styles, and sent to any part of the town in a hot state," and "at the shortest notice." In addition to these items he sold ales and fine liquors, cider oil, corks, Virginia fig tobacco, and Spanish cigars.[38]

An 1844 advertisement in Marie E. Faben's *Hamilton Hall* is copied from an original and written by Remond. In it he advises the public regarding the renovation and refurbishing of Hamilton Hall and suggests its use for engagements, which would include "enchanting" and "entrancing" music played by the five-member Salem Quadrille Band. However, the most important advantage of visiting Hamilton Hall, he writes, is that for those who do not wish to cook, or those who would simply like to entertain friends, or for single gentlemen who cannot cook for themselves, the extensive cooking apparatus allows him to provide family style or other complete dinners. The Remonds' cooking and catering were so famed and highly valued that in 1859, after a "Lady's Ball" was held at Hamilton Hall, a poem was written by an "elderly lady," which described many of the functions held at the hall. The poem centered around a large glass bowl that the Remonds had used for this and numerous other functions, dating from the Hall's beginning.[39]

In 1848 just before he publicly announced his withdrawal from business because of ill health, the Remonds controlled a diversified entrepreneurial enterprise involving a wholesale monopoly on oysters and a substantial trade with merchant ships for many commodities and services. As an oyster dealer Remond often claimed, especially in print, that his competitors falsified the quality and quantity of their oysters. On December 9, 1848, Remond took out a front-page advertisement in the *Salem Observer*, offering at one dollar a gallon, or eighty cents a bushel, fifteen hundred bushels of New York oysters, which, the ad claimed, was more than anyone else had in the state of Massachusetts. In addition, he promised his readers that "there is not in the County of Essex, 150 bushels of New York oysters, except those on the North River flats." He ridiculed these merchants, adding that "every signboard erected would have on it 'New York Oysters' and some of these establishments had not had 50 bushels of New York oysters in three years."[40]

James L. Shearman, a close friend, business partner, and the husband of the Remonds' oldest daughter, Nancy, was an oyster dealer, as was his brother George. James continued the oyster business John Remond built at 14 Derby Square and at 5 Higginson Square following Remond's retirement. James also continued to run the Remonds' oyster bar, their ice-cream parlor, and their catering business for public dinners, suppers, and balls, often as far away as twenty miles outside of Salem.

John Remond's wife, Nancy, was his closest aide and always worked side by side with her husband to satisfy all customers. The Friday, October 19, 1849, edition of the *Salem Gazette* carried a first page advertisement that states, "Mrs. Remond would inform the citizens of Salem and vicinity, that she will continue to make CAKE, at NO. 5 HIGGINSON SQUARE, and respectfully solicits a share of public patronage. Cake of various kinds made to order at short notice—among which are Wedding, Plum, Pound, White, Bride, Currant, Taylor, Clay, Sponge, Composition, Election, &c. All orders punctually attended to." Marianne Cabot Devereaux Silsbee, writing her memories of Salem and the Remonds in 1887, stated that "Mrs. Remond . . . will be remembered for her charming manners and good cooking. Her mock-turtle soup, venison or alamode beef, and roast chickens, with perhaps ducks, and light, not flaky pastry, made an ample feast for a dozen gentlemen at the fashionable hour of two o'clock."[41]

Many years had passed since John and Nancy Remond first began selling soup "made from a superior fat turtle, weighing over 200 pounds, at 50 cents per quart." They had become the parents of eight children and were strict disciplinarians. Overseeing a large family, as well as multilayered businesses, John (called "Sir") and Nancy (affectionately referred to as "Marm") may not have physically gone out on the road campaigning in the antislavery movement as some Africans did, but they took as many opportunities as possible to demonstrate antislavery sentiments. John was said to be a life member of the Massachusetts Anti-Slavery Society. Nancy and daughters Caroline, Susan, and Sarah participated in the activities of the first women's antislavery society in the United States, the Female Anti-Slavery Society of Salem, organized in February 1832 by a group described as females of color. In addition, the Remonds were always a stop for antislavery lecturers, and their home received a number of fugitive slaves who were provided with nourishment, clothing, and shelter.[42]

John and Nancy created a family environment that nurtured success-ful attitudes, and they produced two children whose names were syn-onymous with abolition—Sarah Parker Remond, lecturing agent for the American Anti-Slavery Society, and Charles Lenox Remond, hailed as the first and most eloquent Black abolitionist lecturer before the appear-ance of Frederick Douglass. In addition to his work as an abolitionist orator, Charles Lenox Remond supplemented his income by opening a "Ladies and Gentlemen's Dining Room, especially for families, visitors to the city and private parties," on June 25, 1856, at 5 Higginson Square. The other children built extensive businesses, where they conspicuous-ly displayed antislavery literature and newspapers published by free Blacks.[43]

The Remonds' first-born daughter, Nancy, was born in 1809. She spent her early years working alongside her parents in the catering busi-ness. It was natural, then, that she would be an essential and integral partner when her husband, James Shearman, took control of aspects of the family business.[44]

Another daughter, Susan H. Remond, born in 1814, contributed her talents to the family catering business. Her mother passed on to her the culinary art of making breads, cakes, pastries, jellies, confections, and fancy, "more substantial desserts," which "were in constant demand and brought excellent prices." Susan operated a small and popular dining room, "where none were eligible to entrance save the most exclusive of the townsmen and their specially invited guests." Under her father's supervision, she served game and food of the finest quality, along with a great variety of wines, liquors, and cordials, no doubt from her fa-ther's collection. It was said that "from Susan's kitchen . . . she controlled the trade of Salem in culinary productions" and that, "Her kitchen was a Mecca where gathered radicals, free thinkers, abolitionists, female suffragists, fugitives of all sorts . . . there such found rest and refresh-ment for mind and body." Her culinary environment offered her patrons sympathetic surroundings, from which many drew renewed strength and hope. She was described as having a natural dignity that "courted friendliness but rebuffed familiarity." "Aunt Susan" welcomed children where she lived, allowing them to play, and she often treated them with goodies and dainties, which she distributed lavishly. She aided her ac-tivist siblings financially whenever she could.[45]

Daughters Cecelia, Maritcha Juan, and Caroline all learned skills in barbering and hairdressing, in all likelihood from their father, as well as from Miss Mary J. Marshall, a sales person for John Remond at his confectionery store in Newport, Rhode Island, during the summer. Cecelia Remond was the oldest wig manufacturer in Essex County at the time of her death in 1912. Partnered with Maritcha Juan, Cecelia had the "finest hairdressing saloon in Salem"—Salem was the shopping center of Essex County—for more than seventy-five years. In today's modern world of women who invest a great deal of money in hair weaving, it is interesting to note that Cecelia's husband, James Babcock, was an established hairdresser who published a book in 1872, titled *How Hair Is Wove*. All three daughters were accomplished business women, pioneers in female independence, who were trained in the art of manufactured ornamental hair wigs.[46]

The Remonds were free African caterers and restaurateurs who used the money they made from serving Whites to foster the growth and prosperity of their family as well as the antislavery cause. For many free Africans, participation in "the cause" would become as important a lifelong calling as preparing sumptuous meals for their livelihood. Whether taken on as part of their life's work or simply lending support only on occasion, there would be much work to be done.

Such was the case with one eastern seaboard colony, referred to as the most complicit in the US slave trade. With its currency garnered and wealth defined by the production of rum, this colony imported Africans to the Americas on a massive scale explicitly for that purpose, becoming the conduit for profits that built stunning mansions and some of the most prestigious libraries and schools in the country. The African presence would also build a culinary infrastructure that thoroughly enveloped the colony's mansions and homes, plantations, markets, steamboat travel, and hotels with a legacy of unparalleled cuisine.

4

TRIANGULAR TRADING AND THE "COLORED" COOKS OF RHODE ISLAND

Massachusetts was not alone in establishing the African culinary contribution. It was in 1696 that the *Sea Flower*, another east coast colony's first documented slave ship, arrived in Newport, Rhode Island. African labor was needed to build and develop a solid, lasting currency for Newport's economy and infrastructure. The best cooks were needed to play a major role at the helm of hotel and steamboat kitchens and in Newport's magnificent mansions built with the profits made by merchants, businessmen, and ships' captains engaged in the slave trade.

Africans in bondage produced taste tempting, healthy meals for colonists entrenched in the development and perpetuation of supplying commodities to the southern colonies and the Caribbean for the upkeep of slavery. As in every other eastern seaboard colony, slavery built commercial prosperity and infrastructure, including libraries, churches, and schools, which, in Rhode Island were considered among the finest in New England. Beginning in 1700, and for the next seventy years, Newport attained phenomenal maritime commercial success through the trade in commodities produced by Africans in slavery.[1]

The increase in slave population prompted a series of laws and regulations to control Africans as well as Native Americans. The myriad restrictions in place were cause for resistance and numerous cases of "fugitive" slaves. Slave owner Ambrose Knox wrote to David Barnes hoping to enlist his aid in retrieving Africans who had "stolen themselves." While testifying that racism, and thereby hatred toward Africans, was not relegated to the southern states, Knox nevertheless assessed that his "fugitive" bondspeople would prefer to work for him for free: "I am creditably informed that my poor Negroes are very anxious to get home by a person that has seen them, that they say they saw more liberty in their master[']s kitchen then they have had or ever expect to find in New England." The "freedom" about which Knox spoke was the freedom to create and prepare delicious, mouthwatering meals day in and day out. There were no restrictions on the creative process in the kitchen.[2]

Restrictive laws and regulations were in effect in every colony, and Rhode Island's codes and discriminatory laws severed any ties to economic stability for free Africans seeking to make a living at their skills as artisans or entrepreneurs. Cooking was one of the most important occupations in which an African could engage, whether as a personal domestic servant or as a self-employed shopkeeper. A French traveler, Brissot de Warville, observed that, "Those Negroes who keep shops live moderately, and never augment their business beyond a certain point. . . . [It] is obvious; the Whites . . . like not to give them credit to enable them to undertake any extensive commerce nor even to give them the means of a common education by receiving them into their counting houses."[3]

With its active involvement in the slave trade, eighteenth-century Newport evolved as one of the principal trading ports in the new colonies of North America. The item that became Newport's currency, however, the commodity that catapulted Newport, Rhode Island, to the height of its prosperity, to its "Golden Age," was rum. At the apex of the colony's activity in the slave trade, Newport merchants turned the entire economy and the livelihoods of its citizens on the production of rum. Rum had been manufactured in the Caribbean islands with the sugar and molasses grown and produced there. A cheaper way was found by bringing those items to New England for distilling. The foundation of the slave trade was now laid for Newport merchants.[4]

Distilled rum from Rhode Island was sold on the African coast in exchange for Africans, who were then transported to sugar plantations in the islands of the West Indies. Molasses from the sugar grown and harvested by Africans in the islands was transported to Rhode Island where it was manufactured into rum, and thus the infamous "Triangular Trade" was created. The rum industry produced such wealth that it provided employment for Newport's White residents just as General Motors would do for Detroit. Annual exports topped eight hundred thousand gallons before the legal tap was turned off in 1807.[5]

Rum production was only one of numerous areas in Newport in which Africans in bondage played an enormous part. Although the rum distillers owned a disproportionate number of slave laborers compared to silver and goldsmiths, furniture and cabinetmakers, Africans were also the purveyors of agricultural goods such as cherries, apples, pears, and other produce, from sloops near Newport docks. Selling various foods was nothing compared to the African involvement in food preparation.

Cooking and cuisine in the hands of the Black slave laborers took on tremendous importance. Purchased as slaves, Prince Updike and other Africans did all the work for the two most successful merchants in Newport's slave trade, Aaron Lopez and his father-in-law, Jacob Rivera. In addition to molasses, Lopez's ships imported cocoa and sugar. Updike turned the cocoa and sugar into chocolate, becoming famous as a master chocolate grinder.

George Gibbs Channing offers one firsthand account of food and cooking in early Newport. He speaks of his sickly condition as a child, but then his mother began to feed him entirely on milk and whitepot (pronounced "whitpot"), the "poor man's custard," which he claims is strictly a Rhode Island dish. Made of white cornmeal "ground in the southern part of Rhode Island," new milk, and molasses, he was unable to obtain it after leaving his native home. If only he could have taken a Newport cook to his new home, he laments, "all would have gone well," because, regarding Newport cooks, "such a treasure could nowhere else be found." Between whitepot and the treasured breakfast cake called "journey cake," or "Johnny cake," on which he was fed for three years, he relates, he began to grow and thrive and, according to him, became quite "an athlete of no mean pretensions."[6]

Perhaps the following taste-tempting recipe, with its nutritious preponderance of milk and eggs, would have helped Channing retain his health and stamina.

Chocolate Apple Bird's Nest Pudding

- 4 tablespoons butter
- 1/2 cup powdered cocoa
- 1 quart of milk
- 2 cups sugar
- 10 tablespoons flour
- 1/4 teaspoon salt
- 6 eggs, separated
- 3 teaspoons vanilla
- 1 large apple, peeled, cored, and thinly sliced

Place butter in a saucepan over low heat. When butter has melted, stir in cocoa and continue stirring until thoroughly blended. Remove from heat and gradually stir in milk.

In a bowl mix together sugar, flour, and salt. Gradually stir in chocolate-milk mixture. Beat in egg yolks, one at a time, then vanilla. Stir in apple slices.

Beat egg whites until they form stiff peaks. Fold into chocolate mixture.

Pour into a 2½ quart baking dish. Bake 1 hour in a preheated 350 degree oven.[7]

George Channing had other recollections of the cooks and shopkeepers during his youth. Boys who had a little money to spend would find their way to a small beer and cake shop on Mary Street, run by "an excellent colored woman named Mareer." According to Channing and another Newport native, Mrs. (May) John King Van Rensselaer, there was also Violet, who owned a goody shop, where she sold journey cake, whitepot, and candy:

Near a schoolroom "then lived a very worthy colored woman, named Violet, who kept exposed in a window-frame a few specimens of cake and candy, rendered very attractive by the neat and tasteful way in which they were arranged. A few of us urchins were furnished now and then with a few coppers; and hence followed early trading propensities with Violet. Other boys there were less favored with means for procuring similar gratifications, and they could only look wistfully at the sweets. The good-natured, kind-hearted woman was not slow in discovering the reason for this self-denial, and so on one day when the fortunate ones had retired and the unfortunates still lingered, she bid them go round the house, and then gave to each a copper, telling them they could now buy candy for themselves if they pleased. They soon found their way back, shouting to the old woman,—"A stick of candy, Violet!" and were supplied as promptly as would have been the best paying customers.[8]

African and Native American cooks in Newport were also known for their mastery in preparing soups and in making preserves from quinces, peaches, pears, and apples. Newport invested heavily in the turtle trade, and its ships steadily brought in fruits and turtle from Nassau and neighboring ports. These green turtles, Channing states, "required . . . a Rhode-Island colored cook to manufacture from it a soup that would satisfy the taste of the lovers of good living of that day. Before the wooden bridge was swept out to sea, which connected the island with Tiverton, nothing was more common after the arrival of live turtle, than for the 'lords of creation' at that day to arrange for a turtle-soup dinner at the bridge."[9]

One of those "colored" cooks was Cuffe (Cuffy) Cockroach. He was one of seven Africans owned by Benjamin and Jahleel Brenton in 1774. Cockroach lived with Jahleel Brenton, first at Cherry Neck. Following the death of Governor Brenton, he resided at "The Castle," one of the Brenton extensive agricultural homesteads at Hammersmith Farm. Cockroach was said to be "unrivalled when preparing a great dinner, but excelled particularly in making turtle soup." Gaining his freedom in the late eighteenth century, Cockroach was said to become Newport's first caterer. Although there were many fine caterers who followed his path, he was said to be "the founder of the craft in Newport." He organized, among other events, picnic parties held on Rose Island, Goat Island, and other islands in the harbor for early summer cottagers. After serving his legendary clam chowders or turtle soups, Cockroach would entertain all in attendance by dancing and playing his fiddle.[10]

Here is one dish that is guaranteed to inspire any artistic tendencies in all who sample it.

Fiddler's Clam Chowder

- 1/2 quart of clam meat, diced
- 1/3 cup lime juice
- 1/2 inch slice of salt port, cut into small chunks
- 2 large onions, chopped
- 2 tablespoons EACH flour and yellow cornmeal
- 3 cups water
- 2½ cups diced potatoes
- 1 large carrot, sliced into thin rounds
- 2 tomatoes
- 1 small green pepper, diced
- 2 tablespoons finely chopped dill
- 1 bay leaf
- 2 tablespoons EACH Worcestershire sauce and sugar
- 1 teaspoon EACH white pepper, black pepper, parsley flakes
- Salt to taste
- 4 cups milk

Combine clams and lime juice in a covered container and allow to sit for two hours.

Fry salt pork over medium to medium-low heat in a large pot. Remove fried salt pork and set aside. Add onions to rendered salt pork oil. Cook and stir over low heat about 5 minutes.

Combine flour and cornmeal with water. Stir flour mixture into onions in pot. Add clams, then remaining ingredients, except milk. Bring to boil, lower heat, and simmer, covered, until potatoes are tender. Add salt pork cracklings and milk and heat just to the boiling point, but do not boil. Taste for needed salt and pepper. Tastes better aged for 24 hours.

Another of the most celebrated Newport cooks during the colonial era was Charity "Dutchess" Quamino, who was born in the Motherland in 1739. The slave ship that carried her arrived in Newport in the 1750s during the height of Newport's Triangular Trade. Although a number of Africans brought into Newport were purchased for their skills in specific tasks, most of them were sold to the islands and the southern colonies. Ms. Quamino was purchased by William Channing to become nanny and cook for his family. While in the Channing household she began building a reputation for the sweet treats, cakes, and pastries she baked, and she became known as "the pastry queen of Rhode Island." During the occupation of Newport by foreign troops (about which she was said to have provided amusing accounts), even Jean-Baptiste-Donatien de Vimeur, comte de Rochambeau, praised her cuisine.[11]

In 1769 she married John Quamino (Quamine) who was born in Anomabu, on the Gold Coast, in the 1740s. He was sold into slavery as a child but later purchased his freedom in the mid-1770s. He and another free African, Bristol Yamma, were chosen by Reverend Samuel Hopkins, slave owner from Great Barrington, Massachusetts, and Reverend Ezra Stiles, slave trader and owner, to be tutored at New Jersey College (later renamed Princeton University) for missionary work in Africa. At the outbreak of the American Revolution, Quamino signed on with a privateer hoping to earn enough money to purchase his family's freedom. He was killed on board the privateer in a skirmish with the British in the fall of 1779. Still enslaved and now a widow, Dutchess Quamino continued to sell her pastries and baked goods throughout Newport. A year after her husband's death, she obtained her own freedom. As a free woman, she continued to produce her baked goods in the Channing house, the home of her former master, where she was allowed free use of the ovens to continue her culinary business.[12]

As Rhode Island households kept African men and women as servants, an African doing the cooking was normal procedure. "Aunt Hannah" and "Aunt Julia" provided the following recipes for sweet treats and baked goods in 1827 and 1837 Rhode Island.

Aunt Hannah's Cookies

- 5 cups flour
- 2 cups sugar
- 1 cup butter
- 1/2 cup milk
- Teaspoonful purlash[*]
- 1 egg
- Spice to taste

There are no directions other than, "roll very thin."

However, may I suggest:

Combine flour, sugar, purlash, and spices. Mix well. With butter softened to room temperature, work it into the flour mixture. In a bowl combine milk and egg and beat well. Stir milk mixture into flour mixture.

Turn dough out on to a floured surface and roll very thin. Cut circles in dough with a cookie cutter. Place circles on a cookie sheet and bake in a preheated 375 degree oven for approximately 8 minutes.

[*]Purlash, also spelled "pearlash," was a lye-based chemical used in baking from approximately 1789 to 1840. Cooks added purlash to dough so that when it started to cook it released carbon dioxide, which made bubbles in the dough. The dough would consequently rise, making the texture light. In the twentieth-century baking powder took the place of purlash.

Aunt Julia's Sponge Cake

- 1 cup flour
- 1 cup sugar
- 4 eggs
- 1/2 lemon

No directions here either, but here is one suggestion:

In a bowl combine flour and sugar and mix well. In a separate bowl combine eggs and juice from 1/2 of a lemon and beat well. Make a well in the center of the flour mixture and pour the egg mixture into the well. Gradually stir egg mixture into flour mixture. Stir just until well blended.

Transfer mixture into a greased and wax-paper-lined 8 or 9 inch cake pan. Bake in a preheated 350 degree oven about 15 to 20 minutes, depending on your oven.[13]

As "the most celebrated cake-maker in Rhode Island," Dutchess Quamino was able to accomplish a somewhat decent living. George Gibbs Channing, a relative of the slaveholding Channings, recalls the winter "subscription assemblies" for which Quamino spent a day and a half or more at the Channing residence, baking cakes and other treats for the party. Once a year, after moving to a small house on School Street, she invited the families of her former masters to a "tea drinking," complete with her famous pastries and cakes:

> In the course of each winter, there were held "sub-scription assemblies,"—the last one being Washington's birth-night ball, —when were provided sundry huge loaves of frosted plum-cake, manufactured by "the Duchess," the most celebrated cake-maker in Rhode Island. The work was done in our kitchen, having an ample oven, and required a day and night for its completion. This excellent woman was universally known in the town, and universally beloved. Late in life, she occupied a small house in School Street, still standing, and there annually entertained three families (whom she had faithfully served, until made free) with a most sumptuous "tea-drinking."[14]

Charity "Duchess" Quamino died on June 29, 1804, at the age of sixty-five. Many influential families in Newport assembled at her well-attended funeral. She was buried in the Common Burial Ground known as "God's Little Acre," located in a section bordering Farewell Street. God's Little Acre is considered one of the oldest and largest African and early African American burial grounds in the country. It is unique for its almost three hundred detailed grave markers, a very rare item afforded Africans during this era.[15]

Like Duchess Quamino, most African cooks in Newport during the slavery era worked for the most prosperous and influential Whites in the colony. But Rhode Island was a colony made rich by free African as well as African slave labor. Free African labor sometimes worked for the benefit of Africans themselves. There were some Africans residing in the colony who had either purchased their freedom or were born to Africans who had done so and who set up businesses for themselves in Newport. Many such businesses centered around food. One such Black entrepreneur was Isaac Rice. His home—built in 1815 by Rice's stepfather, Caesar Bonner—is still occupied by Rice's descendants today. Isaac Rice was born free in 1792 in the Narragansett area. In the early 1800s his family moved to Newport. Rice became a highly successful gardener in the early years of his life and was employed as landscaper for the wealthiest families, including for Governor Gibbs's estate on Mill Street, a portion of which became Touro Park. Rice also became one of Newport's early caterers, developing a well-known business on Cotton Court off Thames Street.[16]

Rice was involved in the Free African Union Society, the African Benevolent Society, and the Colored Union Church. Part of his education on slavery was provided by enslaved Africans; he listened to the horrendous stories of cooks and servants who were brought to Newport with their owners for the summer "resort" months. It was many of these accounts that inspired his work in the antislavery cause.

The Rice home, at the corner of William and Thomas Streets, was the Underground Railroad station in Newport, where many Africans on the run were fed and sheltered. Frederick Douglass formed an acquaintance with Isaac Rice after escaping to New Bedford, and from then on Rice and the abolitionist became good friends. Frederick Douglass, who was said to have stayed there in 1843 during his visit in Rhode Island to give a speech on abolition for the Massachusetts Anti-Slavery Society, along with Charles L. Remond, and Henry H. Garnett, made the Rice home their headquarters when they were on "freedom" tours in Rhode Island.[17]

In the later years of his life, Rice became sought after for the services of his large and fashionable catering establishment. He and another famous caterer, hotelier, and restaurateur, George T. Downing, were hired to prepare the foods for the reunion of all the returning sons and daughters of Newport in August 1859. The food was served on the lot south of the old Ocean House. Rice also provided help and assistance to George T. Downing and Colonel Thomas Wentworth Higginson in their efforts to desegregate Newport schools in the 1860s. For many years Rice served as clerk for the Union Congregational Church and was always a generous contributor. He died in 1866 and was buried in the Remington family plot in New Bedford.[18]

Before Newport satiated its appetite on Isaac Rice's scrumptious preparations, Newport's African population went into a spiraling decline during the start of the Revolutionary War. The decline continued through 1840. The war severely disrupted the local economy, and after the end of the war, migration to towns with a growing economic base, such as Providence, meant an overall population decline in Newport. A few Providence Blacks opened small cookshops (restaurants). But, as usual, Whites and Blacks competed fiercely for the same low end jobs, sparking racial tensions that peaked in a major race "riot" in the Snowtown section of Providence, on Gaspee Street, in 1831.

William Jordan, a thirty-year-old seaman, lived in the "upper storey" of a house that had a "cook shop" in the cellar, run by Richard Johnson. The cookshop was supposedly known for frequent fights and riots. Jordan testified that a crowd (mob) stoned the front of the house. There was gun play and the mob was supposedly fired upon. As Jordan "got most of his things out and away . . . the mob were engaged in front . . . and . . . cried out kill every negroe you can." Richard Johnson, who ran the cookshop in the cellar of the house on Olney Lane, lived there with his wife. According to his deposition, "the upper part of the house was occupied by black and white prostitutes and others used to frequent there and sailors used to resort there." The frequent fights that occurred there would usually end in the street, "where they would be dispersed by the watch." A week or ten days before the riot, Johnson was ordered out of his cookshop by the "City Counsel" due to "a disturbance and noise made by a woman in [his] cellar." Johnson closed his cookshop, but on the night of the "riot," the building was stoned, and later he could hear "the noise of the mob breaking and pulling down the house." Mobs continued "pulling down" African homes. When they finished, Olney Street was rendered uninhabitable. Johnson moved, first to Boston and then to New York.[19]

Whites in Providence had targeted Africans, their homes, and businesses for extinction much earlier. The diary of a White Pawtucket man records mob violence early in 1824, as well as in the fall of that year, during what became the Hardscrabble (Addison Hollow) "riots." On February 7, 1824, George F. Jencks wrote, "A gang of ruffi[a]ns to[re] down and destroyed the Negro house on the hill." There was more trouble in the fall of 1824. On October 19, Jencks recorded, "Last night the whites assembled on the bridge in Providence and went in a body to that part of the town oc[c]upied by the blacks and pulled down Ten of their houses and laid waste all the[i]re contents." The White mobs that drove Africans from their homes "carried off their furniture and sold it at auction in Pawtucket."[20]

When it comes to Africans with cookshops and in food service, Providence has a long history. In 1736, to be exact, Emanuel Manna Bernoon and his wife, Mary, opened what is believed to be the first oyster and ale house in Providence. Other caterers came into prominence and reigned in the late nineteenth century there. In Providence, Snow Street "had then a very extended reputation, as at the corner of Middle Street stood the residence of that Prince of Caterers, Scipio Brenton, and his somewhat numerous family of boys and girls." In addition, Joseph P. Hazard of South Kingstown left an 1891 memorandum in which he describes "Samuel Niles—a Mulatto—who was born without hair upon his head, and now lives at Narragansett Pier and keeps a Restaurant and is highly esteemed as an honest, useful, and respectable citizen. He was a servant of my late Father, Rowland Hazard . . . until my Father left Narragansett and became a citizen of Newport, R.I."[21]

Late nineteenth-century Providence, Rhode Island, was also home to "East Side Caterers" William H. Williams & Son, whose invoices read "SALADS A SPECIALTY." Williams & Son was the favorite catering service of the Providence Marine Society. Located at 21 Amy Street, Williams provided lunch and dinners for scheduled quarterly events for the Marine Society throughout, at least, 1895 and 1896. Williams also catered the society's Independence Day celebration dinners on July 4 and 5 in 1895, and July 4 and 6 in 1896. The fee for the daily luncheons was usually $7.00; the Independence Day dinners ran $220.00. Like most caterers, Williams also supplied miscellaneous items, such as chairs, for rent.[22]

Some Africans still residing in Newport continued to live with their former owners and worked as cooks and domestic servants, or they took jobs as domestic servants or as seamen on merchant and fishing vessels after settling into their own small neighborhoods. The post–Civil War period, from mid to late nineteenth and early twentieth centuries, saw African residents push for their own economic and personal financial achievement. Many became entrepreneurs and made their living as coopers, blacksmiths, house painters, laborers, gardeners, grocers, confectioners, restaurant owners, and caterers. Church-related programs, social clubs, and fraternal organizations were at the time the center of the recreation/entertainment activities of the African community—wherever it was located. Newport was no exception. However, growing entrepreneurial independence provided the African community in Newport certain essential services. Africans owned cafés and coffeehouses, such as the Cinderella Tea Room, the Richard B. King Coffee Shop, and Daniel A. Smith's Holly Tree Coffee House.

Daniel Arthur Smith was born in Washington, DC, and moved to Newport after the Civil War. In addition to his coffeehouse on Franklin Street, in operation in the early twentieth century and considered a cultural institution at that time, he opened a restaurant in the Bateman Building. His house on Mary Street would later become known for its dining rooms. Other restaurants, such as (George) Seaforth's Restaurant, the Laura Ricks Restaurant, the Red Deer Restaurant, Lizzie's Fish Shack (also called Fish Lizzie's, which became Daniel's Eatery), Williams' Restaurant, Smith's Lunch Room, Aura Spencer's Chicken Shack (early mid twentieth century), and Ton Ton's Eatery, and taverns would later be added to Newport's places-to-go roster, as well as venues where one could dine royally.[23]

There were other African-owned restaurant and catering establishments such as the Jacob Dorsey Confectionery Shop on Warner Street. Dorsey, who came to Newport from Maryland in 1851, at the age of thirty, is listed in late nineteenth-century city directories as a whitewasher. Dorsey's shop was a confectionery and bakery, which he operated with his wife between 1851 and 1900. Dorsey's baked goods shared the spotlight with those of the Allens. J. T. Allen settled in Newport in 1893, opened a restaurant with three private dining rooms at the Perry Mansion on Washington Square, and operated a catering business with his brother D. B. Allen, a "distinguished" baker. At the beginning of the twentieth century the Allen brothers owned the Hygeia Spa, a well--known café at Easton's Beach.[24]

Ernest Triplett also gained prosperity through his well-known catering services. However, Newport's most famous African caterer and businessman was George T. Downing. Mr. Downing's contributions to abolition and to the cause of civil rights, as well as his catering, restaurant, and hotel services span three states—New York, Rhode Island, and Washington, DC. Therefore, it will be necessary to discuss George T. Downing within the context of those states.

First, it is important to note that, beginning in the early to middle nineteenth century, from about 1830, and stretching to about 1910, Newport, Rhode Island, emerged as the queen of American summer resorts for the wealthy. The appeal of traveling to the area was facilitated by the luxurious conveyance of visitors from New York, Philadelphia, and the South via steamship, with the Fall River Line serving as the principal carrier. Once vacationers were in Newport, large resort hotels situated on Bellevue Avenue (where George T. Downing owned property) and in the Kay/Catherine/Old Beach section accommodated their land needs. Cooks, liverymen, domestic servants, teamsters, porters, stevedores, and waiters were needed for duties both on board ship and at the hotels. Africans were able to secure these personal service and oftentimes unpleasant jobs; they had, after all, secured them during slavery.[25]

The Fall River Line, which began operating in 1847, offered luxurious "palace" steamships, floating hotels that sailed Long Island Sound from New York City to Narragansett Bay and Boston by way of Fall River. The staterooms, halls, parlors, and salons were expensively furnished and carpeted, all lighted with elaborate chandeliers and sidelight fixtures. It was an overnight voyage to Newport, one relished by the rich passengers. The Fall River Line's sought-after ambience was provided by an all Black staff on all of its ships, excluding the ship's captain and officers. A White native Newport resident observed that, "The New York boats were frankly directed by black people. . . . The captains were always white people, but they'd [the blacks] would actually run the boat. They'd have three hundred or four hundred people on the boat and they had to feed them and wash them, as it were." It was customary for the porters, baggage handlers, and employees who assisted in all manner of general customer service to double as waiters.[26]

Dining on board one of the Line's floating palaces was its major attraction. The huge dining facilities, with its all Black culinary crew, offered numerous complex menus. Steamers such as the *Priscilla* carried between twelve hundred and fifteen hundred passengers each night during the summer season, and these passengers were amply fed. Provisions for the *Priscilla* for a single trip required a ton of roasts, steaks, and chops, 200 pounds of poultry, 240 dozen eggs, 500 loaves of bread, 100 gallons of milk, 300 pounds of butter, 300 pounds of fresh fish, and 100 pounds of coffee.[27]

In the middle to late nineteenth century, during the height of the Fall River Line's prosperity, George A. Rice became a legend as the line's African chief steward. As early as 1865 he worked on the *Metropolis* steamer. He was the principal organizer and manager of service, especially of the kitchens and the dining staffs on (among others) the *Puritan*, launched in 1889, the *Pilgrim*, and the *Priscilla*—all premier palace steamships. Rice was said to have commented to a passenger, regarding the large four-page menu on board the *Puritan*, that "there's more listin's in this menu . . . than [entries] in the [ship's] logbook." The *Priscilla* steamship, launched in 1894, garnered such a reputation that life on board the ship, including commendations for its chief steward, were depicted in a historical novel written in 1956. Rice's skills as overseer of the cuisine and as chief steward of the *Puritan* and the other ships were applauded time and time again in print.[28]

Apparently, Mr. Rice had planned to extend his services on land. The *Newport Mercury* for June 8, 1872, reported, "We understand that Mr. George Rice has purchased of Mr. Benjamin Bateman the property next north of the Mercury building and he will soon make much alterations in the premises as will enable him to open a first class restaurant. Mr. Rice, as steward of the sound boats, enjoyed the highest reputation, and we have no doubt he will be successful in his new undertaking." In the July 23, 1892, issue of the *Newport Mercury* an article appeared on page one, which stated, "Mr. Rice's forty years' stewardship on this line has made him too important a fixture to be allowed to leave it, . . . and shows the company's high appreciation of his valuable services." The *Newport Daily News* was just as keenly aware of the value of George A. Rice's services and supplied the following in its July 21, 1892, issue: "there is no question but that Mr. Rice has done very much to bring the reputation of the line in a culinary way up to its present high standard, and passengers of all classes unite in praising his uniform attention to every patron, whatever his social position."[29]

One of the specialties of the chef of the *Puritan* was orange fritters.

It was reported that "Rice's chef has made them a most popular dish." Incidentally, a five-page Fall River Line menu from 1925 has survived, which among numerous delicacies still lists orange fritters on the lineup. Banana and corn fritters were a hit as well. There were three in a serving; each serving cost thirty cents. Corn fritters were served "with a 2 oz. sealed jar of Pure Maple Syrup"—for an extra nickel.[30]

I do not know about you, but looking at a menu from the past that allows you to order a whole broiled lobster for $1.75, and a porterhouse steak for four people for $4.90 (and these are luxury cruise prices) *drives me crazy!*

Before we get to my mouth-watering breakfast cakes in orange, I would like to allow cookbook author, caterer, and Reconstruction Georgia state senator Tunis Campbell to offer his 1848 recipe for fritters, no doubt worthy of being served alongside George Rice's chef's orange fritters. Note that he adds wine or sherry to his concoction.

To Make Good Fritters

To make good Fritters—Mix half a pint of good cream very thick with flour, beat six eggs, leaving out four whites; add six spoonfuls of sack[*], and strain them into the cream; put in a little grated nutmeg, ginger, cinnamon, and salt; then put in another half pint of cream, and beat the batter near an hour; pare and slice your apples thin, dip every piece in the batter, and throw them into a pan with boiling lard."[31]

[*] *Sack* is an antiquated term referring to white fortified wine imported from mainland Spain or the Canary Islands. Sherris sack, from Jerez de la Frontera, later evolved into the word *sherry*, the English term for fortified wine from Jerez. Since sherry is practically the only one of the "sack" wines still widely exported and consumed, "sack" is commonly but not quite correctly quoted as an old synonym for sherry.

Now, for a sensual breakfast that puts the orange in the cakes.

Glazed Orange Breakfast Cakes

- 1½ cups flour
- 2/3 cup sugar
- 2½ teaspoons baking powder
- 1/2 teaspoon EACH salt and baking soda
- 3½ tablespoons butter, softened (room temperature)

- 2 tablespoons sherry or dark rum
- 1 teaspoon orange extract
- 1 cup orange marmalade
- 1/2 cup sour cream
- 2 rounded teaspoons finely grated fresh ginger

Combine dry ingredients in a bowl. Mix in softened butter until mixture resembles coarse meal. Make a well in the middle of the flour mixture. To the well add rum, orange extract, marmalade, sour cream, and ginger. Stir these ingredients together, in the middle of the bowl, in a tight circle. Gradually incorporate the marmalade mixture thoroughly into the flour mixture. Stir just until well blended.

Heat 2 tablespoons of oil in a skillet. Ladle spoonfuls in rounds in skillet. Brown on both sides. Heat additional oil in skillet as needed. Recipe can be cut in half, if desired.

For the glaze:

Combine 1½ cups confectioners sugar, 2 tablespoons orange juice, 1/4 plus 1/8 teaspoon orange extract. Mix until smooth. Drizzle glaze over cakes or muffins. Or top with regular syrup, if you prefer.

Orange fritters were just one delicious reason passengers flocked to the Fall River Line. From the 1840s to the 1930s, Africans employed by the Fall River Line made its prosperity. Fortunately, George A. Rice, a Maryland native, made an income that enabled him to educate three of his four children. The Depression, however, dealt a crushing blow to African employment. The Fall River Line had gone out of business by 1937, because of competition from automobiles, trains, strong unions, and new maritime regulations that forbade wooden ship construction for passenger transport.[32]

It was certain, though, that the vacationing Fall River Line passengers helped usher in hotel development. The first land accommodation built in Newport was on Catherine Street. The doors of The Brinley (later renamed Bellevue House) first opened in 1825. The Atlantic House, one of the grand mid-nineteenth-century hotels erected on Bellevue Avenue in the 1840s, became a major employer of African domestic service. Also constructed on Bellevue Avenue in the 1820s was the famous original Ocean House hotel. The largest and longest-lasting hotel was the second Ocean House, which replaced the original after a fire in 1845. The Fillmore House opened on Catherine Street between 1855 and 1857; sections of it still exist today.

Throughout the season the hotels provided the settings for dinners, concerts, balls, and galas of every sort, and the hotel owners did not want anything to upset the money being made. It was the hotel owners, other local merchants, and White Newport citizens who pushed and supported a petition, drawn up in 1835 and addressed to the Rhode Island state legislature, requesting the passage of a gag law curtailing the First Amendment rights of anyone speaking out against slavery. Abolitionist speakers and their activities were totally opposed, and for the activists this gag law was very dangerous. The fear Whites wanted to allay was that southern travelers would by-pass Newport as a resort destination if the local atmosphere was not friendly to visiting slaveholders. Like the rest of the North, Newport businesses were intertwined with those of the South, and Newport's dependence on a southern tourist clientele was part of its history.

One of the lasting effects of the construction of early hotels in Newport was the necessity of building new and functional thoroughfares, backstreets, and alleys that would provide ancillary services for visitors. One major street, Bath Road (renamed Memorial Boulevard), was created for the convenience of hotel patrons, as it made a path right through to Easton's Beach, one of the town's principal attractions, where the Allen brothers opened their café, Hygeia Spa.[33]

In the midst of the White-owned hotels was the Sea Girt House on Bellevue Avenue, built for the resort clientele in the fall of 1854 by Black restaurant owner and caterer George T. Downing. Born in New York City on December 30, 1819, he was the oldest son of the famous restaurateur Thomas and his wife, Rebecca West, Downing. As a second-generation member of the northern Black middle class, George T. was educated in the public schools of New York and was a graduate of Hamilton College in upstate New York.

Downing demonstrated unusual business acumen while still a young man. At the age of twenty-six, he extended the family business by opening a firm, George T. Downing Confectioner and Caterer, on Broadway in New York. The Astors, the Schermerhorns, and other New York social elites patronized his business.

Serena Leanora DeGrasse became his bride in 1841, uniting two of New York's leading African families. The couple and their children moved to Newport in 1844 or 1845. It was in Rhode Island that Downing enjoyed a long and successful career as a caterer and hotel owner.

At age twenty-seven, after receiving repeated suggestions to do so,

Downing first established a summer branch of his father's restaurant in Newport in 1846, leasing an estate at the corner of Catherine and Fir Streets. It was a catering and confectionery business specializing in fare for picnics and sailing parties, dinners and game suppers, and dishes for family suppers. Downing also advertised musicians for private parties. Each stage of his venture proved successful. In 1848 he leased another estate on what is now Liberty Street at the foot of Downing Street (a street named after him, adjacent to his property), and he purchased the property outright from William Smith in 1850. In 1849 he bought an estate from Charles Sherman, located at the corner of Downing Street and Bellevue Avenue. It was on this property that he built the luxurious Sea Girt House, which attracted wealthy White customers.

In 1850 he opened a catering house in Providence, Rhode Island, on Mathewson Street near Westminster, for which he advertised the sale of choice hot and cold dishes, game and New York oysters, and jellies, bisque de glace, Charlotte de Russe, ice cream and other confectioneries, and any other eatables for dinner, supper, or other entertainments. After two years the location was moved to a house on Benefit Street near College Street. Meanwhile, he continued conducting his business in Newport during the summer.[34]

The Sea Girt House offered an extensive menu. If an early morning breakfast was needed to get you through your day, you could satiate your appetite on lamb chops, ham and eggs, stewed kidneys or oysters, broiled or fried fish, various omelets, steaks, or chicken. Dinner delighted the palate with green turtle, oyster, Julian, or vermicelli soup; game dishes such as woodcock, quail, or partridge would warm the senses; broiled and fried oysters, crabs à la creole, and roasted goose, duck, veal, beef, lamb, and chicken were available to soothe and quell the hunger pangs. Southern-style fried chicken, chicken fricassee, pigeon compotes, chicken croquettes, beef with mushroom sauce, mashed potatoes, various cold dishes, desserts, and wines, all beckoned his patrons to assure they would dine well.

———————————————

To ensure that your dinner guests will consider yours an unforgettable meal, add this delicious offering to your menu as a lovely and memorable side dish with beef or chicken.

Mushrooms and Onions in Milk

- 4 or 5 tablespoons olive oil
- About 16 oz. sliced mushrooms
- 2 medium-large onions, sliced
- Approximately 1 teaspoon, or more to taste, garlic salt with parsley
- Black pepper, to taste
- 1/2 cup water
- 1/2 cup undiluted evaporated milk
- 1 teaspoon rice flour

Heat olive oil in a large skillet over medium-low heat.

Add mushrooms, onions, garlic salt, and black pepper. Cook and stir for about 7 minutes. Stir in water, and continue cooking and stirring over medium-low heat, stirring frequently, until onions are clear and very soft. Stir in evaporated milk. Immediately sprinkle rice flour over mixture and continue cooking and stirring to thoroughly blend ingredients.

When mixture begins to boil, allow to simmer about 1 to 2 minutes.

Serve as a lovely side dish with steaks, lamb or pork chops, and roast beef. It actually goes quite nicely with chicken as well.

———

Now you might impress your family and friends with this lunch or dinner treat. Downing himself would suggest that you take a bow.

Oyster Fritters

- 1/2 cup EACH flour and yellow cornmeal
- 2 teaspoons sugar
- 1½ teaspoons baking powder
- 1½ rounded teaspoons garlic salt with parsley
- 1/4 rounded teaspoon cayenne
- 1/2 teaspoon black pepper
- 4 tablespoons milk
- 1 teaspoon dark rum
- 1 egg
- About 8 to 9 ounces of oysters, drained
- Vegetable oil

In a bowl, combine dry ingredients and mix well.

Make a well in the middle of the flour mixture. Add milk, rum, then egg. Stir to mix well. Gradually stir milk mixture into flour mixture. Stir just until thoroughly blended.

Stir oysters into batter, making certain that oysters are well coated.

In a skillet or deep fryer, heat the oil. When hot, place spoonfuls of battered oysters in hot oil, and cook until lightly brown on both sides.

Buttermilk and Cream Sauce

- 1/2 cup buttermilk
- 1/2 cup UNDILUTED evaporated milk or cream
- 2 tablespoons, plus 1 teaspoon dark rum, divided
- 3 tablespoons molasses

- 2 teaspoons rice flour
- A rounded 1/8 teaspoon cayenne
- 1/2 teaspoon garlic salt with parsley
- 3/4 teaspoon finely crushed allspice

In a small saucepan, combine all ingredients. Stir until rice flour is thoroughly blended. Over medium-low heat, cook and stir just until mixture comes to a boil. Lower heat and simmer for about 20 seconds. Remove from heat. Cool slightly. Serve Buttermilk and Cream Sauce over fritters.

This sauce also serves as a delicious accompaniment to chicken or roasted duck.

After dinner one could stroll through the Sea Girt and admire its sumptuously furnished Brussels carpeting, brocade and rosewood chairs, and lace curtains. The lower story had a sitting-room for gentlemen, a ladies' "saloon" in the rear, and two spacious stores for the sale of "light and fanciful merchandise." There was also an ice-cream and refreshment "saloon." Downing's creams and ices were said to have won a worldwide reputation. It was his intention to keep on hand a varied and extensive selection of cakes and confectionery items in order to remain on a par with what could be found in New York and Boston.[35]

Downing's Sea Girt House was flanked by four stores on each side. It was situated on the Hill, opposite the Atlantic House, and offered panoramic views of the bay and adjacent islands and rivers. Sea Girt House was destroyed by arson on December 16, 1860, while the entire family was away in Boston. The loss was originally estimated at forty thousand dollars; a subsequent newspaper report lowered it to eighteen thousand dollars. Notified about the fire via Union Telegraph message, Downing was deeply hurt but not beaten. He immediately set in motion plans to rebuild. The land was turned into a large commercial block with numerous retail stores known as the Downing Block.[36]

Downing was energetic and ambitious and, with the help of his father, attained prosperity, influence, and a reputation, as his father had done in New York. In Whites' eyes this made Downing "arrogant," and "uppity." Never passive when it came to the struggles of his people, he was a conductor on the Underground Railroad, and active in the anti-slavery cause. The last two straws that could have possibly lit the match that burned down his hotel was his unyielding fight to desegregate Newport public schools. He also worked to overturn the law banning mixed marriages.[37]

In attempting to garner support for eradicating the separate school system—which for Black children hosted substandard curricula and facilities—Downing wrote a letter to Senator Charles Sumner dated May 28, 1855, in which he stated, "Yes there are established in this city 'schools e[x]clusively for colored children'—this I desire to destroy." Downing also asks Senator Sumner to use his influence with those in power in Rhode Island to desegregate its schools. Sumner replied, in a letter dated May 29, 1855, "You are right in your efforts to overthrow the wretched discrimination of color in your Public Schools; . . . In Massachusetts I have argued the whole matter before our Supreme Court at considerable length." Sumner then tells Downing: "You kindly allude to the influence which I may exert. Surely there you are mistaken. But I believe you are aware that whatever I can do will always be done for the cause of equal rights."[38]

Twenty years had passed since Downing first tried to enroll his children in a Newport school. Because of George T. Downing and other activists, in the fall of 1866 all Newport children were technically no longer restricted to certain districts, and they were now supposedly entitled to receive the same education regardless of race. Downing's twenty-year battle was said to have cost him a great deal of money, as well as many friends. The November 11, 1869, edition of *The Independent* published Downing's letter to the editor, in which Downing stated, "I believe that I would have been a millionaire to-day had I bowed to prejudice in this and like instances." In a letter written in 1877 to John Jay, a lawyer who represented and defended fugitive slaves (and grandson of the first Supreme Court Chief Justice, John Jay), Downing stated, "I have not enjoyed the patronage I would, had I been indifferent about my rights." He said that he knew the penalty of his being "a martyr to the cause" and "too independent in daring to cross and criticize prejudices" prevented him from enjoying "independent circumstances" (independent wealth, etc.) and was the cause of occasional reverses and hindrances in his business dealings and environment.[39]

By business standards Downing was indeed a success, as he was one of the most important of the entrepreneurs who developed the commercial section of Bellevue Avenue. Although some of his political activities were born as a result of focus on his own status concerns, he succeeded in another way. Downing was considered a symbol of success by the African community, as he was a fighting soldier in all of the issues affecting African people. Those issues, by 1860, would affect nearly 60 percent of African working men and 30 percent of African working women who earned their living as employees of Downing's Sea Girt House (before it was burned down), Atlantic House, Fillmore House, Bellevue Hotel, Pelham House, Park House, Bateman House, and the Aquidneck House.[40]

Downing, by all standards, was a remarkable caterer, restaurateur, not to mention political activist, in his day. Other Black caterers and restaurateurs during Downing's era may not have taken on the establishment as fiercely, choosing or forced instead to concentrate mostly on achieving economic success. Northern cities such as Philadelphia, the "City of Brotherly Love," would draw numerous Africans away from bondage in southern and Caribbean areas to plant new roots in northern soil. The interchange of wealth between northern cities and those territories built and maintained by slavery was not just in terms of material goods. The transplanting of African cooks to Philadelphia and other northern cities assured the upward prosperity of such cities, prosperity sustained by the culinary reputations born of the genius of its African cooks and chefs.

5

PHILADELPHIA

City of the Epicure's Epicures

W hether hawking foodstuffs at Congo Square (renamed Washington Square in 1825 to honor George Washington) or providing meals in private homes or commercial venues, Africans built Philadelphia's culinary reputation by dominating and commanding the catering and dining business in Philadelphia in the nineteenth century. African women in Philadelphia were not granted the luxury of being homemakers while their husbands single-handedly assumed the role of breadwinners. Even in upper-class African homes, African women did not possess the financial resources necessary for leisure comparable to White women of similar social status. Most African women usually worked as domestics in Whites' homes. Others took in laundry, which allowed them to work at home and still take care of their children. Still others found employment in the seamstress and milliner trades.

Many such as Flora Calvil and Polly Haine, well-known in their day, were street vendors, selling an enormous assortment of delicacies, from pepper pot to ginger cakes and candies. Food vending and street music were particularly in the hands of, and identified with, Africans. Philadelphia's Washington Square, located in the southeast section of the city, was known as Congo Square during the colonial period and was one of five original squares of the city. Enslaved Africans were brought to Congo Square and auctioned there before being transported to various locations in and around Pennsylvania. At a later time, and similar to the activities at Congo Square in New Orleans, Africans prepared traditional foods and engaged in dance and song, playing musical instruments similar to those used in West Africa and the Congo.

Another marketplace, located on Philadelphia's Callowhill Street between Front and Second Streets, was comprised of four buildings. However, Africans were not allowed to sell goods in any major shopping or marketing area where they competed directly with White merchants. As time passed, one popular open marketplace for free Africans was Head House Square. Melodious cries emanated from Head House Square, vendors hawking their fish, vegetables, fruits, and other foodstuffs, as well as prepared delicacies. Dressed in white, Africans selling pastries, herbs, jelly donuts, coconut cakes, "Baltimo' Crrraabs," and soups such as pepper pot, lined the square and the downtown landscape. One peanut vendor tried to outsell his competition by yodeling and playing the guitar while his dog did tricks on the back of a donkey.[1]

The marvelous flavors in the two soups that follow will overpower your competition on any day. For the first soup, in the African tradition, seafood and spices mix lovingly with coconut milk to create a palate-pleasing dish you will prepare again and again. Potatoes never tasted so good in the second soul-satisfying offering, guaranteed to make your dinner guests beg for more.

Shrimp, Sausage, and Crab Coconut Milk Soup

- 1½ pounds extra-large shrimp (21–25 per pound) in shells, and deveined
- 3½ cups water
- 5⅓ tablespoons butter
- 6 to 8 tablespoons flour
- 2 large onions, chopped
- 3½ cups chicken broth
- 1 15-ounce can creamed corn
- 1 medium-large tomato, chopped
- 6 ounces lump crabmeat (you can use canned, juice and all)
- 1/2 pound beef rope sausage, cut into very, very thin rounds
- 1/2 cup molasses
- 2 rounded teaspoons garlic salt with parsley
- 1/2 teaspoon EACH dill weed, cilantro flakes, and white pepper

- 1/4 teaspoon EACH cumin and parsley flakes
- 1/4 heaping teaspoon crushed red pepper
- Black pepper to taste
- A few shakes of cinnamon
- A few shakes of nutmeg
- 1 14-ounce can coconut milk
- Salt, if needed

Remove shells from shrimp and simmer shells in water, covered, for about 15 to 20 minutes.

In a large pot, melt butter. Gradually stir in flour, 2 tablespoons at a time. Continue cooking and constantly stirring until mixture turns medium-brown in color. Stir in onions and cook and stir for a minute or two. Strain shell water and add to onion mixture in large pot. Stir in broth and creamed corn, then tomatoes, crab, and sausage. Blend in molasses and all spices. Bring to a boil, lower heat, and simmer, covered, for 25 minutes. Stir in coconut milk, bring to boil again, and simmer, covered, 5 minutes. Add shrimp, bring to boil again, lower heat, and simmer, covered, for 4 to 5 minutes. Taste for needed salt, pepper.

Potato Soup

- 5 medium russet potatoes
- 3/4 of a medium-large sweet potato
- 1 pound "hot" roll sausage
- Approximately 1 tablespoon oil rendered from sausage
- 2 tablespoons sesame seed oil
- 2 big onions, chopped
- 8 cups chicken broth
- 1 cup water
- 1 15-ounce can cream-style corn
- 2 cups chopped collard greens
- 2 teaspoons garlic salt with parsley
- 1/2 rounded teaspoon white pepper
- 1/4 heaping teaspoon EACH dill weed, cilantro flakes, crushed red pepper
- 1/8 teaspoon basil
- 1/2 teaspoon or more, to taste, black pepper
- 2 tablespoons light molasses
- Salt, if needed, to taste

Cook potatoes in skins (microwave).

Flatten out sausage in a skillet and brown sausage on both sides. Remove sausage to a covered dish or wrap in aluminum foil. Reserve about 1 tablespoon of rendered oil in same skillet. Add sesame seed oil to skillet, heat, and add onions. Cook and stir for a few minutes. Remove from heat.

Blend together broth, water, and creamed corn in a large pot. Stir in onions. When cool enough to handle, remove skins from potatoes and add to pot, crushing and breaking up potatoes on the sides of the pot as you do so. Add collard greens, all spices (except salt), then molasses and blend well. Bring to a boil, lower heat, simmer, covered, for approximately 30–40 minutes. Taste for needed salt and pepper.

Trying to outsell the competition could not have been easy with the myriad African cultural and culinary influences migrating to Philadelphia from the southern states as well as from the islands of the West Indies. With that in mind, one or two points must be shared with the reader. Books such as *The Larder Invaded: Reflections on Three Centuries of Philadelphia Food and Drink,* published by the Library Company of Philadelphia and the Historical Society of Pennsylvania, offer a master narrative which states that the French arrived in large numbers in Philadelphia during the 1790s, initiated the catering industry, and then "trained blacks" in the art of cooking, thereby giving "rise to the great black catering families" who were successful in the nineteenth century.[2]

More than likely, if any French were arriving in Philadelphia during the 1790s it was because of the Haitian Revolution, and they were usually accompanied by their African cooks and servants. Therefore, any culinary techniques arriving with the French were, if not African in origin, at least Africanized by the time they got to Philadelphia. Contrary to the master narrative, constantly feeding us lies and misinformation, Africans brought their own culinary and business skills to Philadelphia from plantations and small businesses in other American states and from plantations in the Caribbean islands. Whether from Haiti, Jamaica, or Curacao, Maryland, Georgia, or Kentucky, Africans were in charge of the kitchens—and the culinary training practiced and exhibited by Africans anywhere in the Americas where Africans were found were culinary arts originating, honed, and passed down in the homeland, MOTHER AFRICA. Africans in the food industry in Philadelphia simply continued making a living in occupations they were well versed in and in which they had engaged elsewhere. *The Larder Invaded,* which bills itself as some sort of reference work, mentions merely five Black nineteenth-century Philadelphia caterers—and only two of those five, Bogle and Augustin (who received notice from White contemporaries), receive attention beyond a mere mention of their names.[3]

In their article "Fine Food for Philadelphia," G. James Fleming and Bernice Dutrieuille Shelton tell us that:

When the names of the Drexels, the Van Rensselaers, the Biddles, the Cuylers, the Lippincotts, and the Willings [and the DuPonts] are mentioned as successful nation-builders and hosts, no small amount of that success can very easily be placed on the laps of the Negro caterers of Philadelphia who "turned deals" and won issues through their medium as much as the city's "big wigs" did around conference tables, in legislative halls, and courts. . . . They were not just cooks or just caterers. They could cook, of course, but they were best of all organizers, food specialists, artists. They could decorate the greatest mansion for the most fastidious reception for royalty, and they could combine the best products of land and sea into the most intriguing dishes; they could manage affairs of state.

No social history of the City of Brotherly Love can be written without mention of these dark-skinned entrepreneurs who pioneered to make catering a lofty calling and who, through and by it, could build homes, educate their families, and pass on to succeeding generations foundations upon which they could build and carry on.[4]

One of the earliest culinary foundations in Philadelphia was laid by St. John Appo, born about 1755 on the island of Saint Domingue (Haiti). He left the island in 1791 or 1792, during the revolution there, and made his way to Philadelphia. He is recorded in the *Philadelphia Directory for 1804* as a waiter. In Philadelphia's *Census Directory for 1811, . . . Allotted to Persons of Colour*, he appears as a confectioner, firmly established at his location at 121 S. Sixth Street. Members of his family contributed to the musical renaissance of Philadelphia, becoming some of the city's most gifted musicians. His sons, William and Joseph, played in Francis (Frank) Johnson's band and orchestra, the best in the city, at the Walnut Street Theatre as early as 1824. William Appo later moved to New York State, where another branch of the family was established.[5]

A few Africans were able to break into the world of the small business owner as confectioners, cake bakers, and grocers, or they ran an oyster cellar or a small restaurant. During the late 1700s and on into the early nineteenth century, Africans continued to have a monopoly on the positions of common laborer and domestic servant. In Philadelphia, however, a number of Africans began to see their way clear to turn cooking and cleaning into a moneymaking proposition. The catering business raised these same Africans to positions of affluence and prominence, offering economic independence that, as W. E. B. Du Bois points out in *The Philadelphia Negro*, "transformed the Negro cook and waiter into the public caterer and restaurateur, and raised a crowd of under-paid menials to become a set of self-reliant, original business men, who amassed fortunes for themselves and won general respect for their people."[6]

When the capital of the United States moved from Philadelphia to Washington, DC, in the year 1800, Philadelphia remained a hub of business and finance. Throughout the nineteenth century, dining tables in Philadelphia made incomparable marks in the hands of African caterers and restaurateurs, making Philadelphia without a doubt the dining capital of America. There were French chefs employed in the city, but a veritable shortage of experienced people trained in the art of combined cooking and service opened the door for African economic advancement that was not available in most other areas of the country. "No other city in America," Dr. Henry Minton wrote in 1913, "has been so famed for its efficient and successful caterers as this, whose patronage was not confined by any municipal, state or even national borders." It became an agreed upon fact that "the best and most elegant service of food at balls and parties was provided by black business."[7]

This new economic development boasted many Black masters. The first, Robert Bogle, was born in slavery in Philadelphia in 1770, about eight years after the Queens Head was purchased by Samuel Fraunces in Lower Manhattan. Robert Bogle began his employment in Philadelphia as a waiter, but he soon conceived the idea that those who desired to entertain at home could avoid certain inconveniences by contracting him to purchase and prepare the foods needed for a formal dinner and to furnish the entire meal with his own staff. Advocating the organization of domestic service into a business, Mr. Bogle is credited with being the creator and founder of the business of catering in Philadelphia and in the United States. Although he opened an establishment on Eighth Street, near Sansom, in the first decade of the nineteenth century (making him one of the first prominent African caterers in America), there were other Black caterers before Bogle in cities such as New York, and a number of these were female.[8]

Owner and proprietor of then popular Blue Bell Tavern, he attracted much attention from Philadelphia's leading businessmen and politicians who often met at his establishment. His legendary catering skills soon made him the arbiter of palates in the city. Du Bois once wrote that Bogle's taste of hand and eye and palate set the fashion of the day. No event was considered appropriately tendered unless it was in Bogle's hands. Few could outdo his polish or his multifaceted services. Weddings, christenings, and funerals were always overseen by a hired director, who arranged all of the minute details. Bogle would perform all of the same duties normally carried by both butlers and directors, acting as a type of general butler for as many days, as needed, in the homes of the elite.

In addition to providing cuisine for important affairs, Bogle also demonstrated his business acumen as funeral director and undertaker. It was common for him to officiate at a funeral in the afternoon, evincing a most impressive solemn dignity and, on the same day, as a caterer displaying a manner both suave and pleasant while offering mouth-watering delicacies at a dinner party in the evening. Bogle was known to be witty, with a good sense of humor, but he also stressed a rigid adherence to details of form and method. His word was first, last, and only. For funerals he arranged family and mourners as he saw fit; his clients generally acquiesced without argument. The proper attire for morning funerals meant a high hat with a long silk band, a long staff, shad-bellied coat, ruffled shirt and sleeves, low shoes with black buckles, and black silk hose. Afternoon or evening affairs demanded white stockings and brilliant buckles.

Before his death in 1837, Bogle moved to Tenth and Pine. His private and public life was successful: his wealth allowed him to accumulate a considerable amount of real estate, and all three of his daughters profited from their father's earnings to become well-educated schoolteachers. Bogle was always active in the civic life of Philadelphia's Black community, and his descendants, including his daughter Amelia, who shared in the substantial real estate holdings left to his children, continued membership among Philadelphia's Black elite.

Included among Bogle's many White elite clients of Philadelphia was the president of the Bank of the United States, Nicholas Biddle. Along with other social gatherings, the Biddles gave at least one ball a year in their large town house. All of their events were largely under the professional care of Black men. Expressing what was termed his highest esteem for Bogle's showmanship, professionalism, and uncompromising attention to every detail in each facet of his business, Biddle composed a lengthy eight-verse, and now famous poem immortalizing him, titled "Ode to Bogle." Written in 1829 for his daughter Meta Biddle's "Ode to

Bogle" was more a mock tribute to Bogle. The "Ode" also mentions the bandleader Frank Johnson's smooth, quiet, and serene personality and demeanor. Biddle obviously enjoyed Johnson's African band; he hired Johnson to play at his parties. Various verses of the "Ode" mention "Roman punch," frosted cream, wedding cake, and "farewell poundcake," items undoubtedly on Bogle's menus. His menus also included meat pies and soups, which were said to be his specialties.[9]

Prepare the following irresistible dessert for the crowd that assembles for your next big gathering. It has been known to take many mourners' minds off their grief for the deceased.

Sorry to See You Go Cinnamon Swirl Sour Cream Poundcake

- 3 cups all-purpose flour*
- 3 teaspoons baking powder
- 1 teaspoon salt
- 1½ teaspoons baking soda
- 1/2 slightly rounded teaspoon cinnamon
- 1/3 cup, packed, light brown sugar
- 2½ sticks (1¼ cups) butter
- 3⅓ cups sugar
- 6 eggs
- 1 tablespoon plus 1¾ teaspoons pure vanilla extract
- 1¼ teaspoons pure almond extract
- 1¼ cups sour cream

Combine flour, baking powder, salt, and baking soda in a bowl and set aside. Combine cinnamon and brown sugar in a separate bowl and set aside.

Cream butter until light and fluffy. Gradually mix in sugar. Beat in eggs one at a time. Beginning and ending with dry ingredients, alternately add flour mixture and sour cream to butter mixture. Add both extracts with first addition of sour cream. There should be 4 flour additions, 3 sour cream additions.

Lightly grease a 9 inch tube pan (make sure to lightly grease tube as well) with vegetable shortening. Line tube pan, bottom and sides only, with wax paper. Pour 3/4 of batter into the tube cake pan. Sprinkle cinnamon–brown sugar mix over the batter, evenly. Pour remaining batter over cinnamon–brown sugar, spreading evenly. Bake in a preheated 350 degree oven 50 to 66 minutes, or until a knife gently inserted into cake comes out clean.

*Flour must be stirred many, many times before measuring, and then sprinkled into the measuring cups.

Coconut Sliced Almond Sour Cream Glaze

- 2 cups confectioners sugar
- A few tablespoons sour cream
- 3/4 teaspoon pure vanilla extract
- 1/4 teaspoon pure almond extract
- A touch of milk, if necessary, to make glaze stirable
- 1 cup sweetened flake coconut
- Almost 1/2 cup sliced almonds

In a bowl, combine sugar, sour cream, and both extracts. Stir in milk, if necessary. Mix until thoroughly blended and there are no sugar lumps. Stir in coconut, then almonds. Spread glaze on top and sides of thoroughly cooled cake. Allow cake to sit, tightly covered, for 24 hours before cutting.

While Bogle's elite clients showered him with praise and tributes, these customers were all tied to northern capital, which was joined inextricably to southern capital. Most, if not all, of Bogle's wealthy customers were connected to the support and maintenance of slavery and the slave trade. During this era Whites would not patronize African businesses unless they were totally racially restricted. However, since caterers tend to private functions, Bogle could have very well served both White and Black customers without complaint. To be sure, when Virginia-born Robert Bogle established himself by 1812 as the leading African caterer in the city, he introduced a system of catering contracts and trainee programs that ensured stable business practices for what had previously been marked by instability and erratic income earning.[10]

Bogle's place in the ranks of caterers after 1836 was taken by Peter Augustin, who migrated from the West Indies and opened a catering business between 1816 and 1818. Bogle was said to have helped the Augustins set up business. Augustin was in a distinct category of caterers who provided lavish entertainment for his wealthy White clientele.

Pierre (Peter) Augustin was a mulatto born about 1791 in Saint Domingue (Haiti). According to one source, Peter Augustin made a permanent move to the United States between 1810 and 1814 as chef to the Spanish ambassador. He was offered a lucrative position as chef for Barnum's Hotel in Baltimore. Mrs. Augustin, whom he married soon after his arrival, could not bear the thought of their children being born in a slave state, so the family moved to Philadelphia. The Augustins had three sons, Theodore, Jerome, and James.[11]

During the Augustins' early years in the city, up to 1818, their residence was located on Cedar Street, and Mr. Augustin was listed in the

Philadelphia directory as a barber and hairdresser. In 1818 he established himself as a confectioner and moved his residence to Walnut Street. Catering soon became his primary business, located at 139 Lombard Street, and from that point on the business took off. It has been written that for years his business vied with Thomas Dorsey's for first place in the catering arena. Others argued that, after Bogle's death in 1837, the Augustins had no true competitors.[12]

Considering that the leading caterers and purveyors of food in Philadelphia in the nineteenth century carried the names Dorsey, Stevens, Cromwell, Prosser, Minton, Price, Jones, Page, Trower, Shadd, Dutrieuille, and Bogle, this was high praise indeed for the Augustins—to be known as the establishment that made Philadelphia catering renowned both nationally and internationally.[13]

Reputation had it that no family exerted greater influence on the development of American gourmet cookery in the nineteenth century than the Augustins of Philadelphia. The family rose to great prominence, and Pierre (Peter) Augustin, according to records, "was not only an artist to his finger tips—literally and figuratively—but a canny business man as well." Augustin preparations were legendary, and in partnership with another African family of caterers, the Augustins wove a catering empire that helped to build the American catering industry as we know it today. The wealthiest families of the city and many foreign dignitaries were served by Augustin. His fame was worldwide, and his terrapin soups and stews often wound up in Paris.[14]

Nineteenth-century accounts of the Augustin catering affairs include those for which they flew solo as well as those that called for collaborative efforts. The banquet for General Lafayette, held in 1824, was overseen by the Augustins, but most of the food was prepared by Parkinson caterers, a White-owned business in Philadelphia. The famous military celebration for General George G. Meade in Washington, DC, in 1863 called for similar arrangements. In 1871 the Grand Duke Alexis of Russia was feted at a dinner dance for which the Augustins were hired; their services were also required for a huge banquet for General Ulysses S. Grant in 1879. Often, when the Augustins supplied only a portion of the menu, some of their most famous creations were in demand, such as oyster and chicken croquettes, terrapin, broiled oysters, and deviled crabs. Not only did they delight their clientele by catering parties and other functions in Boston, New York, Baltimore, and Washington, which they managed by owning a train car fitted with a kitchen so they could cook en route to their destination, they also served the public at their restaurant, which moved in 1863 to 1105 Walnut Street. Augustin's son Jerome joined the firm in 1863 and managed it until his death in 1892, and under him the restaurant enjoyed the reputation as the Delmonico's of Philadelphia.[15]

A private dinner was held at Augustin's restaurant on March 4, 1871, to honor the appointment of John W. Forney (the first Republican secretary of the Senate, serving from 1861 to 1868) to the position of collector for the Port of Philadelphia. A magnificently embossed and engraved menu was created for the occasion. A special wine was paired with each course. The bill of fare included oysters on the shell, served with hock (a type of wine); green turtle soup, served with sherry; salmon and lobster sauce, served with Madeira; filet de boeuf, champignons, roast capons, served with champagne; an assortment of vegetables; sweetbreads and croquettes, served with claret; roast saddle of mutton, served with burgundy; terrapins, served with champagne; an encore of oysters on the shell; dressed salad, fruits, brandy, and coffee. The work that entailed the tremendously ornate design of the printed menu for this occasion speaks to the trouble to which the Port of Philadelphia was willing to go in order to experience the exquisiteness of Augustin's lobster sauce and capons.[16]

While I would never try to compete with Augustin's lobster sauce, I suggest that you have a nice Chardonnay ready to serve with your preparation of this delicacy, lovingly ladled over your favorite baked seafood or vegetable dishes.

Crab Sauce

- 2 tablespoons butter
- 1 onion, chopped
- 1/2 cup water
- 1 chicken bouillon cube, OR, 1 teaspoon chicken bouillon granules
- 1/8 rounded teaspoon cayenne
- 1/8 teaspoon dill weed
- 1/2 rounded teaspoon garlic salt with parsley
- Several shakes of black pepper, or, to taste
- 6 ounce can lump crabmeat
- 12 ounce can evaporated milk, undiluted
- 2½ teaspoons rice flour

In a skillet, melt butter. Add chopped onion and cook and stir over medium to medium-low heat until onions start to brown. Stir in water. When mixture comes to a boil, add bouillon and mix well (if using bouillon cube, allow cube to soften in boiling mixture before crushing with a fork or spoon). Stir in cayenne, dill, garlic salt, and black pepper. Continue cooking and stirring for a couple of minutes. Add crabmeat, juice and all. Bring mixture to a boil, lower heat, and simmer, stirring frequently, until most of the liquid has been absorbed.

Stir in evaporated milk and mix well. Sprinkle rice flour over mixture. Stir until rice flour is well blended.

Bring mixture to a boil again. Lower heat and simmer, stirring continuously, until sauce has thickened. Taste for needed salt and pepper.

Private dinners continued to benefit from Augustin expertise. Following his father's death in 1847, James G. Augustin, Peter's son, took over the management of the business. Peter Augustin's widow, Mary F. Augustin, expanded the business under the title of Mary F. and Son. Both E. B. and Jas. K. Augustin came on board later. After the marriage of Theodore Augustin to the daughter of another famous catering family, the Baptistes, the Augustins merged with the Baptiste family to form the internationally known catering firm Augustin-Baptiste, located at 251–257 South Fifteenth Street.

Mr. Eugene and Mrs. Mathilde Baptiste started out in the French colony of Philadelphia, later called Society Hill, with limited means. Mr. Baptiste was a skilled cabinetmaker; Mrs. Baptiste was expert in the culinary arts. She gave birth to six children: Amelia, Clara, Eugene Jr., Jerome, Mathilde, and Adele. As the family was increasing, Mrs. Baptiste made the decision to try to make money selling some of her rare delicacies. She found that she had no trouble doing so. Her creations immediately attracted the attention of the fashionable set, the gourmets of Philadelphia. She and her husband began working together and expanding the business. They moved to Walnut Street but later settled at the Fifteenth Street address. The marriage of their daughter Clara to Theodore Augustin forged the merger of the two catering families.

"Aunt Clara," as she was known, was described as a diminutive, sharp-minded dynamo, and everyone stood in awe of her. She was a shrewd, hard-fisted bargainer who, as they say, ruled the roost. Together with her usual stern and aristocratic manner, she was a humorous, witty, and engaging conversationalist who would have her listeners in stitches. She also had a generous heart and was one to feel and show sorrow and sympathy over the sorrow and misfortune of others. Although childless, she had a strong motherly quality. Her brother Eugene Baptiste Jr. was the businessman who interviewed clientele and supervised the culinary staff, but he discussed all negotiations, suggestions, and arrangements with Mrs. Augustin. Following the death of their mother, it was Clara Augustin who actually ran the business, becoming its dominant figure. At the time of Clara Augustin's death, she was said to be the oldest woman in business in the state of Pennsylvania.

One aspect of their business was providing confectionery items. A confectionery department was set up in the establishment's basement; they hired a German pastry chef to oversee it. During the advent of World War I, the strained relationship between the United States and Germany caused the firm to "release" this chef, and they soon closed the confectionery. Augustin-Baptiste became a client of Sautters, an exclusive and expensive confectioner, located diagonally across from the Academy of Music on Locust Street. Sautters sold cookies, various tarts, and other sweets. Dexter's, which sold mincemeat and other pies, was another confectioner that received business from Augustin-Baptiste.

Augustin-Baptiste prepared dishes that became internationally renowned, as orders were shipped to London and Paris for Philadelphia elite who wanted to entertain "properly" while visiting Europe. Their delicious creations were packed in tins that were soldered shut for shipping, and many of these delicacies included chicken and oyster croquettes, for which both the Augustins and Baptistes were famous, lobster à la neuberg, stewed snapper (turtle), terrapin, oyster and lobster coquilles, and other items. One interesting and sad note concerning these overseas customers was that they never paid their bills until they returned to Philadelphia, and even then they had to be reminded. Looking for additional ways to expand internationally, Mrs. Augustin and her sister Mathilde Baptiste visited France and England together, just prior to or immediately following World War I.[17]

Property adjoining their house at 255 South Fifteenth Street was purchased and reconstructed to accommodate the demands of their phenomenally growing business. Mrs. Augustin designed the early colonial frontal structure, and she was quite involved in the supervision of the entire project. She was said to have watched every move the carpenters made. At one point she insisted that "the staircase from the first floor to the second [be] torn out and moved back a number of feet, because the builders had run it clear up through the banquet room to the front window." She told them sternly. "No, no! No indeed! That will not do! You will have the help standing up here staring out the window, instead of doing their work. So, move it!"[18]

The newly reconstructed establishment now had a banquet room and second-floor front, in which were held her own annual family reunions. Extending horizontally across the entire width of the building, just above the height of the front door, was placed a wide marble nameplate that read "Augustin and Baptiste." Mr. Peter Shelton, great grandson of Amelia Baptiste and her husband, Peter Albert Dutrieuille (another famous caterer who apprenticed with Augustin-Baptiste), still has the nameplate.[19]

The firm's culinary creations were enjoyed well into the twentieth century. For many years after the death of Thomas Dorsey, the Augustin's original firm was considered the leading catering establishment in Philadelphia. As late as 1910 the Augustins' place on South Fifteenth Street, which they owned with the Baptistes, was described as bigger and more valuable than it had ever been.[20]

For many patrons Augustin culinary creations evoked fond memories. Colonel John W. Forney, for whom the private dinner was given in 1871, once remarked about Peter Augustin's chicken croquettes: "The chicken croquette is the secret of Augustine—that of his sons, now that the original is dead—and it would be easier to obtain an advance copy of the President's Message than Augustine's croquette receipt. Delmonico, of New York, has sighed for it for years in vain." Apparently, Delmonico's, considered the first and last word in gourmet restaurants, gave exceptional praise to Augustin's creation. Augustin's reputation for croquettes had spread far and wide, and Delmonico's wanted to reproduce it but could not. Forney also stated that, in regard to terrapin and chicken croquettes, "the superiority of Philadelphia is universally granted." Well, after all, Philadelphia had all those African caterers, many of whom specialized in those two viands.[21]

The Library Company of Philadelphia states that "Lizzie Martin . . . an unknown entity among the multitudes of Philadelphia Lizzie Martins living in the 1890s" compiled a collection of recipes "record[ing] some of the rarest Philadelphia recipes and some of the best." The following recipe is from that collection and is claimed to be Augustin's own.

Augustin's Chicken Croquette Recipe (As claimed by the Library Company of Philadelphia and Lizzie Martin)

- 9–10 cups finely chopped chicken meat, or 6 cups chopped meat plus 2 cups bread crumbs
- 3 cups milk or cream
- 4 ounces butter
- 2 tablespoons flour

- 4 ounces onion, minced
- 1½ teaspoons salt
- 1/4 teaspoon cayenne pepper
- 1 teaspoon mace
- Bread crumbs
- Egg yolk

Put into a saucepan 1½ pints of milk or cream, when hot stir into it, 1/4 pound of butter and 2 tablespoons of flour, rubbed together and well mixed with some of the milk, 1/4 of an onion chopped fine, boil until it thickens, then stir in the chicken, which has been chopped very fine, and well seasoned with salt, cayenne, and mace—mix well—cool the mixture, form into shapes, roll in crumbs, and yolk of an egg, and fry. A chicken weighing 5½ lbs. will make 12 croquettes.[22]

Just thought I would compare what is considered to be Augustin's chicken croquettes with Augustine's chicken croquettes. Augustine was apparently the African cook for the Prescott family.

Augustine's Chicken Croquettes

Cut up your meat, chicken, add veal or sweetbread if you prefer. Take a quarter of a pound of butter to a chicken. Melt it thoroughly, add an onion chopped up fine and a tablespoonful of flour. Let all boil together. Add about a wine glass of cream, then mix in the meat, when mixed, put on a dish to cool. Make into shapes, dip in egg and cover with fine crumbs of bread, then fry in boiling lard laid on their sides. Don't put the mixture on the fire after adding the meat till going to fry, of course the white meat of cold chicken makes the nicest croquettes.[23]

In addition to their chicken croquettes and other culinary contributions, the Augustins were among the founding members of Philadelphia's St. Peter Claver's Roman Catholic Church. They were involved in and supported many African social organizations in Philadelphia and helped sponsor numerous charitable causes. It has been mentioned once or twice, however, that in many instances when Philadelphia Africans had to step up and be counted on issues that adversely affected their well-being, the Augustins were said to be "habitually absent on these occasions." Perhaps the Augustins and Baptistes and their relatives, the Dutrieuilles, and other African caterers and business people who served a White clientele were more reticent, or restrained, in their support of causes, and at least publicly, as some observed, suppressed their African backgrounds and connections as much as possible. They did not serve Blacks and could not serve Blacks at their establishments because Whites would not patronize them if they did.[24]

Signs of racism against free Africans were always evident in the North. Although the racism varied in intensity, it was universal. Different groups held meetings at St. Thomas African Episcopal Church to discuss this deplorable situation. One group included Absalom Jones, the famed sailmaker James Forten, and Cyrus Bustill, the prominent baker who had supplied bread to the Revolutionary Army.[25]

Bustill gave up his Burlington, New Jersey, business and moved to Philadelphia where he established a bakery at 56 Arch Street. His business there did not flourish as well as it had in Burlington. He never, however, expressed regret for moving. Even though he was not rich, whenever there was a call to help someone in need, he never failed to aid the cause of freedom and gave money and whatever means at his disposal to prove it. His table was always spread to alleviate, at no charge, both White and Black hunger. Bustill's youngest daughter, Grace, was about ten years old when the family moved to Philadelphia. She helped her father prepare his breads and biscuits. Bustill also taught her how to transmogrify, as he called it, his old pants into wearable trousers for his two young sons. Years later Grace lived next door, where she opened a Quaker millinery store.

In 1790, at the age of almost sixty, Bustill retired from the bakery business and threw himself completely into philanthropic work. He built a house on Third and Green Streets, where he opened a school and began teaching Philadelphia's African children. An assistant was hired to teach the upper grades, as Mr. Bustill's own education was limited. William Carl Bolivar, in his *Pencil Pusher Points* column published weekly in the Black newspaper the *Philadelphia Tribune*, wrote that Cyrus Bustill was one of the most important citizens of color, being noted as one of the first "colored" men to organize a school in the United States. Bustill also owned considerable property, some of which was passed down to his descendants, including a family burial plot on his Edgehill farm, in what was called Bustilltown. Mourned by everyone who knew him, Bustill passed away in 1806. His Quaker friends officiated at his burial ceremony.

Perhaps a strong sense of pride and deep consciousness runs in the family. Nathan Mossell married Gertrude E. H. Bustill, who was the granddaughter of David Bustill (Cyrus Bustill's son). Gertrude Bustill was the sister of Louise Bustill Robeson, mother of Paul Robeson, the renowned activist, actor, and singer.[26]

Despite the unwelcome environment and atmosphere of hatred, free and runaway Africans still headed straight to Philadelphia and entered into the lucrative field of the restaurant and catering business, as Robert Bogle did in the early part of the century. There was Richard Thompkins of Fourth Street near Walnut, for example. In addition, James Porter Sr. was hired as the first steward of the exclusive Philadelphia Club, initially located in the Napoleon residence on Ninth Street above Spruce. Mr. Porter later opened a restaurant at Eighth and Market Streets. His son George Porter was associated with his father's business. A contemporary catering family, the Prossers (father and son), were also prominent in perfecting restaurant catering and creating many famous dishes. It has been noted that caterers entering the business in Philadelphia in the second half of the nineteenth century learned technique, nuances, and recipes from the pioneer caterer James Prosser.[27]

James Prosser was born at Mount Holly, New Jersey, in 1782 and migrated to Philadelphia where he worked for a Hebrew family as a coachman. Not long after, he began his career as a caterer. His strength of character aided him in his tireless work ethics. His clients were always presented with the very best of everything available on the market, and he exacted from his employees the most scrupulous neatness in person and detailed attention to clients. As a result, his name and establishment became famous. Apparently, Bogle's touch was institutionalized in succeeding decades by James Prosser, about whom it was said that, "The name of James Prosser, among the merchants of Philadelphia, is inseparable with their daily hours of recreation, and pleasure."[28]

The senior Mr. Prosser, "a most gentlemanly man," was noted to have long been the popular proprietor of an oyster cellar, a fashionable restaurant, located at 806 Market Street. Terrapin (a North American freshwater turtle famous for its edible flesh) and clams were Prosser specialties. Prosser's clam soup and other dishes earned the title "legendary." One of the many White businesses and organizations that sought the cuisine and services of James Prosser was the Library Company of Philadelphia. In fact, it appears that the company hired Prosser exclusively, at least for a while. A few invoices and receipts have survived from as early as 1822 and as late as 1846, itemizing the various foods prepared by Mr. Prosser for dinners served at board meetings of the Library Company. Twelve dollars cash was paid to James Prosser on December 19, 1822, for twelve terrapins and six hundred oysters (I am assuming that this was the total bill). Lobster was prepared and paid for on April 27, 1846, according to a small account kept in April and May of 1846.[29]

This recipe is a combination of one that my grandmother created, and one from the recipe collection of the Hartwell-Clark Family Papers, representing the late nineteenth and early twentieth centuries. My grandmother added mace, celery, potatoes, and red pepper. She was also a little more liberal with the spices. The directions represent a much earlier time period.

Board Meeting Clam Soup

- 1 quart of clams, chopped up
- 1/2 cup finely chopped celery
- 2 potatoes, peeled and diced
- 3 to 4 cups seafood or chicken broth
- 1 quart plus 2 gills (1 cup) milk
- 2 onions, chopped
- 4 tablespoons butter
- 2 tablespoons flour
- 1/4 rounded teaspoon mace
- 1 teaspoon or more, to taste, black pepper
- 1/4 teaspoon or more, to taste, crushed red pepper
- 2 egg yolks, beaten

Combine the clams, celery, potatoes, broth, and a quart of the milk in a saucepan. Bring to a boil, lower heat, and simmer, covered, for 20 minutes. Melt butter in a separate saucepan or skillet. Add onions and cook until onions start to brown. Gradually stir in flour until well blended. Add onion mixture to clams. Blend in mace, black and red peppers. Bring to boil again, lower heat, and simmer, covered, for 10 to 15 minutes. Combine egg yolks and 1 cup of milk. Mix well. Blend egg mixture into soup. Bring to boil, lower heat, and simmer for 1 minute. Taste for needed salt, pepper.[30]

When Mr. Prosser, an elder in the Lombard Street Presbyterian Church, died on March 6, 1861, at the age of seventy-nine, his recipes and catering service had become an inspiration to others. During his years as a restaurateur, he employed John McKee, who was born of free mixed-blood parentage in Alexandria, Virginia, in 1820. While still very young McKee moved to Philadelphia. He began his livelihood as a restaurant waiter at Prosser's famous cellar restaurant on Market Street. Sometime later he married the boss's daughter and shortly thereafter opened his own place on Market Street known as The All Night Café. From a humble beginning he laid the foundation to become a wealthy Philadelphian and a noted philanthropist. Mr. McKee was elected colonel of the Thirteenth Regiment, Pennsylvania National Guard, and out of his own money paid for the equipment for the regiment, which amounted to seventeen hundred dollars. Like other caterers McKee invested heavily in real estate and engaged in land development, and by the time of his death in 1902 he was said to be a millionaire.[31]

McKee's line of work was clearly the way to go. Barbering, undertaking, upholstering, and cabinetmaking were important businesses for Africans to take up in Philadelphia, but no other occupations gained as solid a reputation in the city for Africans than confectioneries, restaurants, and catering. By 1838 there were on the books eight bakers and five confectioners.

Augustus Jackson was one of these confectioners, and it has been written that he introduced ice cream into the United States, by way of Philadelphia, in 1803. Now, Africans had long before introduced ice cream on southern plantations, including those owned by George Washington and Thomas Jefferson. It may be that Mr. Jackson introduced a version of it to Philadelphia, and beyond any doubt it was he and other African cooks who popularized its creation. For instance, Sally Shadd, relative of the wealthy African butcher and real estate investor Jeremiah Shadd, was claimed to have introduced ice cream to Delaware. In any case, Mr. Jackson, who operated an establishment on Goodwater Street, between Seventh and Eighth, where he monopolized the sale of the dessert for a dollar a quart, seems to have certainly created a more modern version of ice cream, comparable to how it is made today. The manufacture and sale of ice cream continued to be an important business well into the 1860s. There were two parlors on South Street among those supplied by Jackson's manufacturing plant, located on Walnut above Tenth Streets. His daughter continued his business for several years after his death. Another confectioner was Sarah Ann Gordon, who is also recorded as an ice-cream maker and seller.[32]

The following are a couple of recipes for summer's most delectable dessert. They are old ones, as you can tell from the directions provided.

Philadelphia Ice Cream

- 1 quart cream.
- 1 scant cup sugar.
- Flavor to taste.

Heat cream in double boiler until scalding hot, melt the sugar in it, flavor when cold.

Pineapple Ice Cream

Drain juice off 1/2 can pineapple, mix it with 1 teaspoon lemon juice. Mash pineapple through strainer, add sugar to taste, and mix with partly frozen Philadelphia or other ice cream—Pineapple preserve may be used or fresh fruit chopped fine and sprinkled with sugar—1/2 cup to 1 pint of fruit—[33]

Many more would follow in their culinary footsteps and find prosperity. James Le Count, who was related to William Carl Bolivar through Bolivar's mother, could easily have also made money in the undertaking business, as he was a carpenter before he became a caterer. Clayton Durham was a caterer who joined Richard Allen in the founding of the African Methodist Episcopal Church; his relatives migrated to Philadelphia from Virginia, where they reputedly figured prominently in Nat Turner's Rebellion. James Nixon, Cato Collins, Jeremiah Bowser (whose wife was related to Cyrus Bustill), the Bartholomew Brothers, Joseph Rogers, and John Price, then later John W. Page, Hans Shadd, Levi Cromwell, Andrew F. Stevens, Pierre Albert Dutrieuille, and his son Albert E. would all dazzle dinner tables everywhere while positioning their own culinary spotlights. Between 1845 and 1875, the triumvirate of Black caterers Henry Jones, Henry Minton, and Thomas J. Dorsey would "rule the [fashionable and] social world of Philadelphia through its stomach." It was during this era "when lobster salad, chicken croquettes, deviled crabs and terrapin composed the edible display at every big Philadelphia gathering, and none of those dishes were thought to be perfectly prepared unless they came from the hands of one of the three men named."[34]

Henry Jones was born of free parents in Virginia in about 1810. After migrating north, he arrived penniless in Philadelphia in the 1830s. Jones acquired some education and worked his way up from domestic service, refining his own skills while working in the service industry and in the homes of some of the wealthiest families in the city. In 1840 he began to supervise the entertainments of the wealthy merchants of Philadelphia. His catering enterprise started in 1843 and was built up by acquiring clients in the city and as far away as New York and New Jersey. Mr. Jones was known as a man of great care and faithfulness. Possessing a very pleasing disposition and great capacity for details, he immediately became a favored purveyor of foodstuffs and for thirty years operated a thriving business. He was noted for his mastery of the gastronomic art. While Mr. Jones did not always prepare every delicacy billed as the trademarks of the professional African chefs, he was said to know by tasting what was needed to complete a certain dish.[35]

Henry Minton, the youngest of the triumvirate, was born in 1809 or 1811 in Nansemond County, Virginia. He moved to Philadelphia in 1830, at the age of around nineteen. He was first apprenticed to a shoemaker, but not satisfied with this trade he got a job at a hotel as a waiter, an occupation in which he became very expert. Later, he opened dining rooms at Fourth and Chestnut where, between 1838 and 1845, through 1878, he achieved fame and became moderately wealthy as "the proprietor of a fashionable restaurant and resort for business men and gentlemen of the city." Mr. Minton's tables were said to be "continually laden with the most choice offerings to epicures, and the saloon during certain hours of the day, presents the appearance of a bee hive, such is the stir, din, and buz[z], among the throng of Chestnut Street gentlemen, who flock in there to pay tribute at the shrine of bountifulness." Minton's lobster salad, chicken croquettes, deviled crabs, and terrapin earned well-deserved accolades and notoriety throughout Philadelphia. It has been written that Mr. Minton amassed a respectable fortune on the sale of those four items alone. He died on March 20, 1883.[36]

Prepare this salad in large quantities for your family and friends, as it disappears rather quickly. Note that you will amass a fortune in accolades just as fast.

Lobster Salad

- 1 cup seashell pasta, uncooked
- 3/4 pound cooked lobster, shredded, or small, cooked shrimp
- 1/3 cup, plus 1 tablespoon matchstick carrots
- 4 tablespoons fried crisp, and crumbled, bacon
- 2 large whole green onions, chopped
- Almost 1/2 of a medium green bell pepper
- 1/2 teaspoon celery seed

The Honey Dressing

- 6 tablespoons olive oil
- 6 teaspoons red wine vinegar
- 6 teaspoons honey, filled to the brim
- 1½ slightly rounded teaspoons garlic salt with parsley
- 1/4 plus 1/8 slightly rounded teaspoon cayenne
- 18 dashes of black pepper

Cook pasta as directed on the package. Drain.

Transfer pasta to a large bowl or container. Allow to cool down for about 20 to 30 minutes. Add lobster, carrots, bacon, onions, bell pepper, and celery seed to pasta.

Combine dressing ingredients and stir for a couple of minutes to mix well.

Drizzle dressing over lobster mixture (make sure to stir dressing well just before adding to lobster mixture). Toss gently to mix and coat ingredients. Serve warm or chilled over Romaine or iceberg lettuce.

Choice offerings were ingrained in the reputations of other prominent Black Philadelphians. Some of them had previously been categorized as somebody's "property" in the slave states, but they rose to become famous caterers. These men were, in effect, it was argued, guilty of illegal seizure, because they had *stolen themselves*, just as Margaret Morgan had (Ms. Morgan moved to Pennsylvania from Maryland without being formally emancipated) in the infamous case *Prigg v. Pennsylvania*, 41 U.S. 539 (1842), and the Sierra Leone Africans in *United States v. The Amistad*, 40 U.S. (15 Pet.)518 (1841).[37]

Thomas Joshua Dorsey, the son of a female slave and her master from a Frederick County Maryland plantation, was said to have had the most unique character of the triumvirate of caterers in Philadelphia. As he and his three brothers were runaways and, thereby, "stole themselves," all four Dorseys could certainly attest to this nation's rules and laws regarding "property" and "piracy."[38]

Thomas J. Dorsey first appears as operating a boot- and shoemaking business in *A Register of Trades of the Colored People in the City of Philadelphia and Districts*, a pamphlet published in 1838 by the Pennsylvania Abolition Society. Dorsey's first appearance in *Philadelphia's City Directory*, in 1844, has him listed as a waiter. Between 1842 and 1860 various directories show that he found employment as a waiter at four different eateries. It is not until 1861 that the directory first lists him under the title of caterer. Africans in the business of catering were still referred to as "waiter" in the early nineteenth century, rather than by the professional title "caterer." This was illustrated clearly in "Ode to Bogle." It has been written that the Augustin family did not refer to their establishment as a catering house until 1865.[39]

Dorsey acquired almost no education, but he possessed a great intelligence and a naturally refined manner and taste, which he cultivated to the highest level. A *Philadelphia Times* newspaper article lauded his persona, his character, and his importance to the community. As a caterer he quickly achieved both fame and fortune. His own experience with the horrors of slavery had instilled in him deep compassion for his people and all those on the lowest rung of society along with a reverence for those who championed the causes of African people. He made certain to take a prominent part in every effort to change the misfortunes of his race, and in doing so he came into close contact with Frederick Douglass, Charles Sumner, William Lloyd Garrison, John W. Forney, William D. Kelley, and others, all of whom were guests at his table at his Locust Street residence. Dorsey's strong partisan prejudice on account of his relationship with certain statesmen was exemplified when a "copperhead" Democrat approached him to secure his services in preparation of a feast to which only Democrats were invited. Dorsey shook his head and said, "No, sir, I cannot serve a party which is disloyal to the government." Then, pointing to the picture of Lincoln, he continued, "And he is the government."[40]

Dorsey was always considered one of Philadelphia's high status caterers, who, because of his political awareness and unyielding demand for respect, became the most prominent in his field. His knowledge and understanding of his chosen occupation gave him total command of it. His reputation as a first-rate caterer was earned, as he embodied class, honesty, and style. Guests visiting his home or establishment could boldly state that he entertained lavishly. Dinner served at his establishment at 1231 Locust Street on December 27, 1860, for example, included oysters on the half shell, filet de boeuf-pique, canvasback duck, charlotte russe, ladyfingers, and champagne jelly. One or more of Dorsey's delicacies even graced the table at Charles Sumner's home. Sumner sent Dorsey a short note thanking him for "sending that product of your kitchen which was relished by myself & guests."[41]

Here are my own recipes for two jellies, which you will find deliciously accompany an assortment of crackers and hors d'oeuvres when completely chilled. Even better, they are must-have sauces with duck or poultry.

Champagne Jelly

- 1 cup of champagne or Chardonnay, divided
- 1 rounded teaspoon finely grated fresh ginger
- 1 envelope gelatin
- 4 tablespoons sugar

Pour 1/4 cup of champagne or Chardonnay into a bowl. Sprinkle gelatin over Chardonnay and let soften for a few minutes.

Pour 3/4 cup of champagne or Chardonnay and ginger into a saucepan. Bring to a boil. Pour boiling Chardonnay into gelatin mixture. Stir in sugar. Continue stirring until sugar has completely dissolved. Allow to cool down before transferring mixture to a covered container. Refrigerate until completely chilled. To use as a sauce for duck or poultry, refrigerate for about 10 minutes to thicken. Do not allow to completely chill.

Drunken Cranberry Jelly/Sauce

- 2/3 cup champagne or Chardonnay
- 1 tablespoon dark rum
- 1 cup whole berry cranberry sauce
- 1/2 cup plus 1 teaspoon sugar

Combine ingredients in a saucepan over medium heat. Continue stirring over medium heat until mixture comes to a full boil. Lower heat and simmer on low heat, uncovered, stirring frequently, for 10 minutes. Remove from heat and allow to cool down before transferring to a covered container. Refrigerate until well chilled. Serve with appetizers or as a sauce with roasted duck and other poultry.

And, from the 1827 and 1837 recipe collection of C. Dyer:

Wine Jelly

3 ounces of gelatin, soaked in 1 quart of cold water for 1/2 an hour, then pour it off and add 1 quart of boiling water. When cooled, add 1½ pounds sugar, whites of 3 eggs, beaten to a froth, juice of two lemons. Boil ten minutes without being stirred. Strain through [a] flannel bag, then add 1 pint of wine.[42]

Having firsthand knowledge of slavery was more than enough reason for Dorsey to entertain one visitor in particular at his residence. In June 1859, John Brown, who was preparing for his mission at Harper's Ferry, stayed at the Dorsey home during his visit to Philadelphia. No doubt, a delicious repast was prepared for the occasion. At the Dorseys' he met with caterers Henry Minton and Henry Jones, as well as Professor E. D. Bassett, John Saville (Dorsey's son-in-law), Alfred Morris Green, and Joshua B. Matthews. Brown received much moral support and material aid from these men, enabling him to carry out his plan. Brown also met with prominent Africans at the homes of Henry Minton and Reverend Stephen Smith. Harper's Ferry was the object of heated discussion and argument at both residences. Brown met Frederick Douglass in Rochester, New York, and very much wanted to enlist Douglass's moral, financial, and active support. While Douglass was said to believe in an uprising, he did not believe in Brown's Harper's Ferry mission. At a later meeting at Dorsey's home—no doubt accompanied by a delicious meal—Brown asked for endorsements from Professor Bassett, William D. Fortin, and John Saville. Saville did not oblige, but after Brown's capture, envelopes and other name- or address-filled memoranda found in Brown's pockets were the cause of a few Africans leaving the country temporarily.[43]

Thomas J. Dorsey and his wife, Louise, who performed much needed assistance in their social and economic lives, were culinary royalty and icons in Philadelphia. But, for all of their standing and influence in certain circles, for all of the accolades received from serving the wealthiest families in Philadelphia and various areas of Pennsylvania for their delicious dishes, they were still Blacks in America. Philadelphia served up a particularly hurtful insult to Mr. Dorsey during the visit to Philadelphia of the Russian Grand Duke Alexis in 1871. A grand reception and ball was given in the grand duke's honor at the Academy of Music. Dorsey attempted to purchase a ticket for admission to the gala, but the committee in charge of the affair (some of its members were no doubt clients of Dorsey) refused him. The next morning, on December 4, he wrote a letter to the grand duke, stating that he knew he had been refused admission because of the color of his skin. The letter attracted the attention of the *New York World* newspaper, and their leading editorial on December 11, 1871, covered this incident. This was a simple wake-up call, a reminder that Whites considered Black caterers, no matter how wonderful their sauces and stews, to be domestic servants and members of an inferior race, and the inferior race could never expect to be treated as their social equal.[44]

Before his death Mr. Dorsey built and enjoyed a national reputation. When he died, numerous obituaries and obituary editorials appeared in newspapers as far away as San Francisco. The *Pacific Appeal* wrote that Mr. Dorsey "was in many respects a remarkable man." The *Public Ledger* wrote, "Mr. Dorsey . . . was universally esteemed for his straight-forward honesty, common sense and business ability." Apparently, the Democrats never forgot Dorsey's refusal to serve them. The incident was mentioned in a very interesting piece that appeared in the Democratic weekly *Commonwealth*, a piece picked up by several other newspapers, such as *The Press*, which remarked, in part, "Dorsey, the negro feast furnisher, the great caterer, he who spread the tables for the marriage supper, or the ball, or the reception; he who gave character to any entertainment, and whose presence was more essential than the honored guests. . . . Philadelphia of modern times is in almost universal grief at the death of the negro Dorsey. He should have the satisfaction to know that his obsequies have unified the 'modern society' of the Union League–blessed City of Penn." I am certain that what Dorsey was indeed satisfied in knowing was that, when he died at the age of sixty-three on February 17, 1875, his wife, Louise, daughter, Marie, and son, William, were reported to be heirs to a quarter of a million dollars.[45]

Just as Bogle, McKee, Minton, and Dorsey were multiskilled, James Le Count was proficient in both carpentry and catering. Le Count and

James H. Teagle, barber, politician, and restaurateur, knew and practiced multiple trades, but food preparation was by far their favorite task. Choice meat dishes and unforgettable soups and desserts were their stock in trade. Richard Warrick, whose father, Richard, maintained the family tradition of involvement in the social and civic life of Philadelphia's African community, started out as a barber but later took up the occupation of caterer.

Caterer Warrick had been categorized in what was called a special class of blacks in Philadelphia. His wife was Emma Jones, a descendant of Absalom Jones, and the couple amassed a considerable fortune in catering and in real estate investments. Their son, Richard, a well-known dentist, along with Dr. Henry M. Minton (the grandson of caterers Henry Minton and John McKee and the great grandson of caterer James Prosser, as well as a founder of Douglass Hospital, Philadelphia's first African American hospital), and two other close friends, were the prominent figures who helped to found and establish Mercy Hospital, Philadelphia's second African American hospital. The Warrick family were members of the most exclusive social set in the city's African community throughout the late nineteenth and early twentieth centuries.[46]

Richard's caterer father was not alone. Levi Cromwell was born in August 1830 in Portsmouth, Virginia, the son of Willis H. and Elizabeth C. Cromwell. Against the laws of the state, Levi's father maneuvered to secure his son an education, which enabled him to do the clerical work in the extensive freight business that his father was involved in between the cities of Norfolk and Portsmouth. With the money his father made, Levi was able to buy his family's freedom, subsequently moving the family to Philadelphia in 1851.

Levi Cromwell gained employment in restaurants and then established himself in the oyster business. He finally opened his own restaurant at 227 Dock Street, opposite the Merchants' Exchange, and later moved to 117 South Second Street. Mr. Cromwell's fame as a caterer and restaurateur brought him enormous success, which allowed him to concentrate his efforts on supporting numerous African organizations and civil rights activities. He married twice. Levi Cromwell's "worth" was estimated at about fifty thousand dollars in 1879. He died on December 29, 1906.[47]

John S. Trower, a caterer known for his delicious ice creams, like Levi Cromwell and many other African business people, brought in money from White customers, which profited both Whites and the African economy and community. He was born in Northampton County, Virginia, in 1849, the son of Luke and Anna M. Trower, who were noted for their frugality and industry throughout the eastern shore of Maryland where they moved right after John's birth. They were mixed-heritage farmers of Indiantown who, although they had never been slaves or descendants thereof, were debtors on the land they worked. During his teen years John worked on the farm, saving every dime he earned. By the time young Trower was twenty-one, he had saved enough money to purchase the land and present the deed to his mother. With fifty-two dollars left over after paying for the farm, Trower moved to Baltimore, where he boarded with the family of Mr. and Mrs. Mack and found gainful employment opening oysters at a restaurant.[48]

In approximately 1870 he moved to Philadelphia and settled in Germantown, one of the more wealthy and prosperous communities. It was here that Trower opened a restaurant. The business took off immediately, and he soon added catering to his trade. A fellow caterer, John Holland, known for his napoleons, cream puffs, and other pastries, operated a prosperous business in Center City, Pennsylvania. Holland's services were called upon for one of the prenuptial affairs when a DuPont daughter married a Roosevelt son. Following Holland's death, William Newman purchased the business. Trower was later able to acquire this establishment, and the business was soon moved to Germantown, where the wealthy constantly sought out Trower's services. The accompanying profits and demand for a first-class caterer's establishment was more than reason enough for him to purchase and remodel the old and vacant Germantown Savings Fund building, which he purchased in 1876 for twenty-five thousand dollars.[49]

As a successful leading caterer, John Trower made a great deal of money from serving up rare dishes to the blue bloods of Germantown and surrounding vicinity. Most of his wealth, however, which reportedly amounted to $1,500,000, was made through wise real estate investments in Germantown and in Ocean City, New Jersey, where he and Mrs. Trower owned a summer residence. Caterer Colonel John McKee held, up to this time, the title of the richest "colored" man in the city. However, the money that John Trower accumulated forced McKee to surrender that title.[50]

In 1889 Trower won a contract to provide food services for Cramp's

Ship Building Company, on the Delaware. Cramp's was a huge corporation, one of the largest shipbuilders in the world. Not surprisingly, Cramp's maintained a "Whites only" employment policy; but, of course, cooking and cleaning up is personal, *domestic service*, and quite within the occupational bounds of an African's "place." Securing the catering contract was extremely profitable since Trower not only provided the elaborate banquets and luncheons that were part of the launching of a new ship but also provided the food on the trial trips, including the numerous war vessels built for the United States as well as those that were built for Russia and Japan. Among those vessels serviced by Trower were the *Yorktown*, the *Philadelphia*, the *Vesuvius*, the *New York*, the *Iowa*, the *Columbia*, the *Baltimore*, the *Minneapolis*, the *Newark*, the *Brooklyn*, the *Variag*, the *Retvian*, the *Mejedia*, the *Colorado*, and the *Pennsylvania*.[51]

John Wanamaker, the department store baron of Philadelphia, hosted many semi-official banquets during his appointment as postmaster general of the United States. Wanamaker hired John Trower to cater these affairs, including one elaborate reception in Washington. Garnering such lucrative business made it possible for him to hire other Africans and provide opportunities for these employees to gain business experience and training. He was very active in charity work and made aid and support to other Africans a primary goal. Being very much involved with church and religion, he founded an industrial school and a Baptist theological seminary in Downingtown, Pennsylvania. The farm he purchased for the seminary was held in trust until the Baptists of the state were able to assume the responsibility of purchasing the land.[52]

In 1909 John Trower's health began deteriorating. Two years later, on April 4, 1911, he died at the age of sixty-one at his home in Germantown. A second generation of the business was continued when John Trower Jr. merged with Thomas James in about 1936. Thomas James was inspired by John Trower to go into catering. This was before James married Susan Cowdery and became connected with the catering business begun by Martin Van Buren Cowdery.[53]

One of the desserts for which John Trower became famous was ice cream, and one directory in which he is listed as a confectioner is the 1907 *Philadelphia Colored Directory*. He formulated his own recipe and was known to carry his ice cream with him to his various catering jobs.

The following are two antique ice cream recipes from the late nineteenth and early twentieth centuries. I am certain that Mr. Trower would have appreciated these flavors from a fellow—lady or gentleman—ice cream maker.

Tutti Frutti Ice Cream

- 1 pint milk
- 1 quart cream
- Yolks of 5 eggs beaten light with sugar
- 3 cups sugar
- 1 lemon [its] juice and grated peel
- 1 glass pale sherry
- 1/2 pound crystalized fruits chopped

Heat milk almost to boiling, pour by degrees over eggs and sugar. Beat all together. Return to the fire and boil 10 minutes, or until set into a custard. When cool beat in the cream and half freeze before stirring in half pound fruit (crystalized) pears, apricot, cherries limes . . . chopped fine. Cover again and freeze hard. Beat the custard thoroughly.[54]

Coffee Ice Cream

Heat in double boiler 1 pint milk. When hot add 1/4 cup coarsely ground coffee. Steep closely covered 20 minutes; then add 1 scant cup sugar. Beat 1 egg [and] add [it to] 1/4 cup cold milk then gradually [add] the [mixture to] hot milk and coffee. Strain through cheese cloth. When somewhat cool add 1 pint cream. Freeze.[55]

When John Trower was not producing ice cream, he immersed himself in activities in his church. Many free African restaurateurs and caterers and other business and laypersons gave their time and attention to similar pursuits, as well as to clubs and associations. There were men's clubs such as the Delmonico Club, which was organized in about 1836 and was said to be named after the famous New York restaurant. By way of balls, picnics, and other fundraisers it acquired fame for its contributions to the antislavery cause, and for charitable funds geared to caring for the sick and arranging burials for its members and others in need. James Davis, an early member, continued operation of a restaurant located on Sixth Street, above Lombard, which was begun by a man with the last name of Cole.[56]

There were many other societies established for the intellectual stimulation of both Black males and females, such as the Female Literary Association of Philadelphia, founded in 1831, and the Female Minervian

Literary Society (or Association), established at the end of 1833. Indeed, Philadelphia has witnessed the opening and disbanding of numerous social and intellectual clubs, but there were at least two that were devoted to dining, whose "primal object" was "good food and fellowship." One of these was the Friday Night Dining Club, which was still in existence in the very early 1900s.[57]

The most noted, however, was the Ugly Club; its formal history was said to begin in Philadelphia in 1877. It was earlier, in the mid-1860s (about 1865), that a group of several Black New York caterers and other Black businessmen decided to enjoy their vacations and various recreations such as fishing and dining together in Newport, Rhode Island. After much discussion they formally organized what they called the New York and Newport Ugly Fishing Club. Members' names included James W. Mars, William H. Smith, Jeremiah Bowers, Robert Vosburgh (the poet laureate of the club), George Greene, Charles Hopewell, Richard Mays, James R. Braxton, and others. Their close association and social relationships with the Black Philadelphia caterers and businessmen led to the formation of the Philadelphia Annex, which came to be called the Ugly Club. The Philadelphia founder was the caterer Andrew F. Stevens, and the initial members were John W. Page, Charles H. Edwards, Levi Cromwell, Sylvester Coleman Sr., and William Warrick. Others such as George Bordley, Phillip A. Roberts, Martin V. Cowdery, John W. Holland, P. Albert Dutrieuille, Thomas De Witt, and John S. Trower joined later. The parent club officers all bore nautical titles, such as commodore, purser, and so forth.

The caterer members were already proven professional party givers, and they exhibited their talents as private hosts. History has it that in the era of "Commodore" Andrew Stevens, no social event in Philadelphia was reported more often in the Black press than the regular banquets of the Ugly (Fishing) Club. Dinners were held monthly, beginning in October and continuing through May of the following year. All of the members would invite guests (caterers and others) in from various cities. A partial list of guests from Baltimore included Howard Williams, Wyatt Archer, William E. Matthews, C. A. Fleetwood; from Washington, DC, Robert Graves. In fact, the Ugly Club had branches in Philadelphia, Baltimore, and Charleston.

By 1890 the Baltimore Annex of the New York and Newport Ugly Fishing Club was said to be the city's most elite African social organization. The Daniel Murray Papers provide a news clipping with the following description of the Philadelphia branch:

> Quite often there were interchanging courtesies between the parent club in New York and its offspring in Pennsylvania: and as the members of both organizations had "won their spurs" it is almost a yearly happening for trips either way, "to spread their legs under the mahogany," and not only to discuss the highest form of gastronomy, but to cement the good fellowship borne of a common purpose. In the matter of skilled cookery, decorations, appropriate bibibles and all the cognate things that appealed to the eye and palate, the Ugly Club dinners have never been approached. The mentor and mainspring was the late Andrew F. Stevens, and the long continued dinners were acknowledged by everyone as his due. Henry Ward Beecher once said that, gastronomy would, in time, become a science; so that one could order a steak, so as to add poetic taste, or a chop that would be cooked to foster oratory, . . . when in truth a chef could be able to advance men along any line in which he desired to shine. As a rule, these Ugly Club dinners arranged twelve courses, and the generous givers thought nothing of serving canvas back duck, terrapin or any of the most costly and toothsome viands. The bibibles run all the way from Hock to Crème de menthe but it was not altogether the appetite that was appealed to, because the members usually had a few choice guests at each dinner to make "the welkin ring" with story, speech, repartee, and all the other intellectual condiments, that are as much a part of a good feast as the eatables. . . . The men who held membership in the Ugly Club were public spirited as well, and many a movement for the general good grew out of its monthly gatherings.[58]

The *New York Freeman* reported that on May 10, 1885, the Philadelphia Annex gave its annual dinner at the home of Mr. Philip Roberts. It was described as a regal affair, quite in keeping with all of the standards of club affairs. The dining table was said to be "a marvel of decoration, the china being of the most approved pattern, the silver of unique design and the floral display in keeping with the rest." Dinner was served in twelve courses, with rich wines accompanying each course. In attendance were "Messrs. Page, Holland, Stevens, Warrick, De Witt, Bordley, Roberts and Coleman of Philadelphia; New York was represented by Messrs. Mars, E. and W. H. Green, Hopewell, Eato, Sturms, Mayes; also

Mr. Bass of Altoona, W.E. Matthews of Washington, D.C., and Messrs. William Brown and Benj. Sims of Baltimore." The following day the visitors who were still in town were provided lunch by Andrew Stevens.[59]

The *Philadelphia Tribune* carried news articles on banquets held by the Ugly Club Jr., one even mentioning caterer Preston Baker as having served "an excellent menu." The Ugly Club Jr. was said to exist in Philadelphia until sometime during World War I. *The Sentinel*, one of New York's newspapers, spoke of a dinner given in that city by the Ugly Club Jr. for a Professor Greener and his wife. The article presents a glimpse into the membership of the group, mentioning that members must have an income of at least one thousand dollars a year. It appears that the Ugly Club Jr.'s membership was composed of well-off younger men (probably sons of caterers and other business people) whom *The Sentinel* described as being "mere toadies to society," and "namby pampies."[60]

Other news articles written on the Ugly Club have suggested that by 1885, when it had been established as a prestigious African social organization, its members confined their activities to two exclusive social events, and that the club's reported main objective was to bring together at its annual dinners the best minds of the race in the country. These affairs, always held at the New York headquarters, regularly included a large number of guests from Philadelphia and carefully selected guests from other places. The first two decades after its founding saw its leadership chosen from the same group of individuals, such as James Mars and E. V. C. Eato, who were also members of the New York African Society for Mutual Relief.

Except for the publicity given its dinners, which were restricted to those men who had turned catering, food service, and hospitality into a science, the Ugly Club tended to avoid the spotlight. However, on Tuesday evening, May 12, 1886, in celebration of its twenty-first anniversary, the club sponsored a reception to which wives of members and guests were invited for the first time. On this night "the Club maintained its reputation for lavish but discriminating hospitality by an entertainment unsurpassed for elegance and brilliancy in the social annals of this city." Regarding the culinary portion of the evening, the supper was said to be "a matchless exhibit of caterer's art." Having so many first-class caterers taking part in the festivities, it was beyond speculation that, "in the way of exquisite dining, this club has never been paralleled."[61]

The founder of the Pennsylvania Annex of the Ugly Club, Andrew

F. Stevens, acquired fame as a leading caterer following the close of the Civil War. He was born on May 20, 1838, and "the cream of the business" became his clients. In 1884 (some literature has the date at 1887), Mr. Stevens founded the Citizens' Republican Club, one of numerous Republican political clubs that organized and flourished in the African wards before and after the murder on October 10, 1871, of Octavius Valentine Catto, a Black teacher, orator, baseball player, and activist who fought in the state capitol for equal rights. Catto's brother was a caterer from Bordentown.[62]

The Citizens' Republican Club quickly became one of the most prestigious Black men's clubs in the city. Over the next fifty years almost every Black man of any political stature was at some point in his career a member. Gambling and drinking were strictly forbidden in club quarters; however, its members embraced other activities. One of the entertainments sponsored by the Citizens' Republican Club was minstrel performances. Its company of performances was called the Soap Box Minstrel. Programs have survived showcasing twentieth-century performances. One performance was held in Musical Fund Hall on May 30, 1921. Another, possibly held on the same night, was "a one act farce," titled "Killing the Civil Rights Bill," the scene of which took place in the "Jarrisburg" Senate. On May 8, 1922, another Soap Box Minstrel performance, also held in Musical Fund Hall, was titled, "The Darktown Cabaret." Noteworthy is that many of their programs dealt with the politics of the day. The printed programs for the performances always included a large number of advertisements, publicizing various African businesses, such as Silver's Ice Cream Parlor and Confectionery, and the "home-cooking and hot rolls" at Robinson's Restaurant.[63]

After the show, one could visit the Venetian Tea Garden & Dining Rooms, located at 4051 Market Street. Open all night, it offered plenty of "good music, dancing, . . . private dining rooms and booths." There was also Attucks Cabaret, on Fifteenth and Catharine Streets, "With all the best to eat and drink." There were other night spots all along the black "Gold Coast," which stretched for two blocks along Seventeenth Street between Bainbridge and Lombard. Along these streets, luxury cars lined the front of restaurants and clubs packed with people until 9 or 10 a.m. Famous entertainers gathered and socialized with politicians, musicians, and sometimes less reputable folks at Green's Café, "the restaurant renowned from city to city," where steaks and chops were the specialty. In addition, you could choose from the Peacock, Woodson's Hotel, Dougherty's, and the Green Dragon Café, "the popular Café. The Right Place for an Evenings Pleasure," also open all night, where the owner was said to have had one of the best Chinese cooks in the city.[64]

A quieter evening might be had at a testimonial banquet given by the Citizens' Republican Club. A testimonial banquet program dated June 14, 1912, details "Toasts," or speeches given by club members during the banquet, which, on this night were made to "The Soap Box Minstrels: Origin, Achievements, Possibilities," "The Citizens' Republican Club: Its Relation and Duty to the Soap Box Social," "The Relation of the Club to the Enterprises of the Race," and "How Can the Club Improve Its Political Prestige."[65]

Well, a banquet is not a banquet without food. The menu included mock turtle soup, rock fish cutlets with cucumber sauce, fillet de boeuf with mushroom sauce, new potatoes, new peas, relishes, asparagus salad, cheese and crackers. Dessert and drinks completed the choice morsels; ice cream and cake, rasped rolls, beer, cognac, and coffee were served.[66]

———

This scrumptious asparagus salad may differ from the one served at the Citizens' Republican Club banquet, but it is guaranteed to win new friends, as well as to assure the return of dinner guests to your table.

Asparagus Salad
- 3/4 pound asparagus spears
- 1/2 cup matchstick carrots, cut down into small pieces
- 2 whole green onions, chopped
- 3/4 to 1 cup cooked green peas
- 1/4 teaspoon celery seed
- Fried crisp, crumbled bacon bits for garnish

The Dressing (for Asparagus Salad)
- Prepare "The Honey Dressing." See Recipe Index, using:
- 4 tablespoons olive oil
- 5½ to 6 teaspoons honey, filled to the brim
- 4½ teaspoons red wine vinegar
- 1⅛ rounded teaspoons garlic salt with parsley
- 1/4 slightly rounded teaspoon cayenne
- 16 dashes of black pepper

Cut "woody" area from the bottom of asparagus spears. Cut spears into cuts and tips. In a pot or skillet, cook asparagus in salted water for 5 to 6 minutes. Drain.

Allow asparagus to cool off for about 15 minutes. Transfer to a medium-sized bowl. Add remaining ingredients. Drizzle dressing over ingredients (make sure to stir dressing well just before adding to asparagus mixture). Toss gently to mix and coat well. Garnish each serving with bacon bits, if desired.

The Citizens' Republican Club's founder, Andrew Stevens, married Bella Cole of Philadelphia, who bore him two children. Highly respected and considered the doyen of caterers in the late nineteenth century, Andrew Stevens was the social leader of the African elite from the late 1870s. In 1894 he became the sixth African ever to win a seat on Philadelphia's Common Council, a seat he held until his death. After his death, on April 1, 1898, the family continued the catering business for a while. On May 24, 1920, the Citizens' Republican Club of Philadelphia marked the initial ceremony of Founder's Day, a ceremony to be observed each year on May 20 in commemoration of Andrew F. Stevens Sr.'s birthday, as its founder and first president.[67]

The Philadelphia Caterers' Association, over which Andrew Stevens often served as president, was not established until 1866. The association was considered a trades union, and its clubroom served as a clearinghouse for business and the employment of waiters. It was here that members convened and discussed their various business problems and issues, regulated prices, and exchanged constructive criticisms. Their Election Day banquets were considered important occasions for which each member contributed an exquisite dish prepared by them or their chefs. The association was said to have disbanded during World War I.

The Caterers' Manufacturing and Supply Company, a cooperative wholesale buying business, was not opened until 1894. Located on Thirteenth Street, it furnished the needs of caterers by housing supplies of tables, chairs, canopies, crystal ware, glasses, silver (including candelabra and candlesticks), rare china for special occasions, English, white ironstone chinaware for "stack feeds," linens, olives, pickles, and other foods and goods.[68]

Catering, along with cabinetmaking, barbering, and upholstering, had created an African middle and upper class, which had been, in Du Bois's words, purveyors to the rich. But the late nineteenth century was also the beginning of the end of what had been termed the "guild of the caterers." At the time Du Bois's *Philadelphia Negro* was published in

1899, he wrote that there were thirty-nine restaurants and eighty-three caterers doing business in the Seventh Ward, most of whom did part-time catering on a very small scale, or they were actually waiters, who worked under caterers. He reported that there were only about ten who did a large business bringing in, at least, between three and five thousand dollars a year. Andrew Stevens and Pierre Albert Dutrieuille were two who were still prominent. By this time, however, the profession, and its monopoly by Africans, was truly in decline.[69]

The decline was blamed on the much larger amount of capital being pumped into professionally run food service operated by White businessmen as well as on the new liquor licensing law, adopted in 1888, which dramatically raised license fees, which made it too expensive to operate certain types of establishments. A permit that cost fifty dollars and a letter from a politician now required a two-thousand-dollar bond and an annual fee of five hundred dollars (at a time when five hundred dollars was a good year's wages), which was then raised to nine hundred dollars. In addition, so-called fashionable society began to look to Europe to dictate what was "in." The large palatial hotel with its larger capital and accompanying restaurant boasting "French" flair and technique began to hold sway. But, as we shall see later, while it was the French and Europeans making all the money because of the changing fads in food and fashion, the real influence was still African.

Another consideration for the decline was worsening race relations and a rising tide of segregation, which spelled the collapse of the service-oriented economy that Africans had dominated for generations. As the service and artisan economies declined, the children of the "Old Philadelphia" African elite began to pursue educational opportunities outside of the family business. A number of the older African Philadelphians cite sons who abandoned the family business, because they saw it as "demeaning," as the reason for the collapse of the great African catering firms. After all, caterers formed the largest and were considered the most prestigious occupational group in African elite society during the nineteenth century. Catering was made up of individuals whose occupations were rooted in domestic service. To many, these individuals carried the stigma of "house nigger."[70]

One of the city's catering houses enjoyed tremendous accolades and lasted longer than any other. Interestingly, this catering house, with its skilled artisans of the culinary art, became the object of culinary affection for Philadelphia's men of the cloth. In fact, the Catholic Church in Philadelphia made eating well both a commandment and a natural law and thereby made its own laws regarding what heaven's earthly hosts would eat and drink, when and how often. It can be rightly stated that Philadelphia's Catholic clerics were determined not to do without the finest in culinary sustenance.

6

"THEM PIOUS EATS TREMENDOUS!"

Despite the rise in white supremacy and worsening race relations in the late nineteenth century, the names Augustin-Baptiste, Stevens, and Dutrieuille still maintained a firm hold on many a banquet, feast, and celebration. Peter (also known as Pierre) Albert Dutrieuille and his son Albert Eugene operated a catering firm that lasted from 1873 to 1967. Whether it was cream of celery soup, filet of beef, macaroni, and potatoes and peas for eighty for the E. I. DuPont de Nemours Company; or rock fish cutlets with sauce, filet of beef, and candied sweet potatoes for the Philadelphia Skating Club; celery soup and broiled chicken for the Triangle Rod and Gun Club; or deviled crabs, chicken salad, chicken croquettes, and lobster cutlets with sauce for "Miss Knowles," Dutrieuille catering served many elite households and various businesses all over the state and was considered by wealthy Pennsylvanians to be the best.[1]

The elder Dutrieuille, Peter Albert, was born in Philadelphia, and just like Andrew Stevens, in the year 1838. After attending public school he was taught shoemaking and followed that trade for several years.

Noticeably, African catering and other business families very often intermarried and gave their offspring the same or similar names as the parents. This was so often the case that it sometimes becomes a bit confusing (to this writer) to determine the relationships and, sometimes, who was who.

Mr. Dutrieuille married Amelia Baptiste, daughter of the legendary caterers, in November 1864. He obviously saw the financial success that catering afforded, so he joined his in-laws' firm as an apprentice. After absorbing a good foundation in both the culinary and business aspects of the industry, Dutrieuille made the decision to open his own business in 1873. His home served as his establishment, located at 108 South Eighteenth Street, just below Chestnut Street. Four years later, on July 26, 1877, their son, Albert Eugene, was born.

When Peter Albert opened his business, he was staunchly frugal, retaining records, in minute detail, of every penny he and his family spent. The Dutrieuilles' skill, business acumen, and dedication made their fame and fortune, and as their business took off they purchased a new four-story building located at 40 South Nineteenth Street, just above Chestnut, where he and Mrs. Dutrieuille conducted their business and lived for the rest of their lives. Peter Dutrieuille was characterized as impeccably neat, austere, and autocratic. Mrs. Dutrieuille, very much a part of the operation, served the firm by maintaining a close watch, in her genteel manner, over the mechanics of the culinary department and the staff, and by working at all times as hard and as many hours as the employees.[2]

Their success attracted much attention from many Philadelphia financial tycoons. Among his fashionable clientele were the Drexels, the Biddles, the Thompsons of Rosemont, Pennsylvania, and Thomas De-Witt Cuyler, a name that carried tremendous influence. It was Cuyler who offered to finance Peter Dutrieuille in opening a branch of his catering services in New York City. Of course, all such matters are family decisions; Mrs. Dutrieuille reportedly firmly rejected the proposal. Even though the decision was made to center and maintain the business in Philadelphia, many Dutrieuille creations gained international fame by way of overseas clientele, although not on as extensive a level as the Augustin-Baptiste firm.[3]

Mrs. Dutrieuille was famous in her own right. Her credo was "Waste not, want not!" She always observed the custom of serving tea in the late afternoon. But her "tea time" was often turned into mealtime. If there was any oatmeal left from breakfast, she would turn it into a delicious custard-type pudding or dessert. When friends dropped by for a brief visit, they would be urged to stay and eat. "Oh, you must have some tea," she would quietly insist, "before you leave."[4]

Coffee and tea lovers will find this creamy and delicious oatmeal dessert a must-have with their favorite hot beverage.

Oatmeal Coconut Custard Squares

- 1 9-inch unbaked pie crust
- 2 cups hot, cooked oatmeal
- 2 tablespoons butter
- 2/3 cup, plus 1 tablespoon sugar
- 1/4 teaspoon salt
- 1½ cups undiluted evaporated milk
- 2 well-beaten eggs
- 1½ teaspoons vanilla extract
- 1/2 teaspoon coconut extract
- 1 cup sweetened, angel flake coconut
- 1 tablespoon rice flour

Line a 9x9 inch square baking pan with the unbaked pie crust.

Combine hot oatmeal and butter and stir until butter melts. Blend in sugar, salt, and milk. Stir in beaten eggs, vanilla, and coconut extracts and blend well. Add coconut, then rice flour, and continue stirring until there are no lumps of flour left.

Pour mixture into baking pan with the unbaked pie crust. Bake in a preheated 425 degree oven for 35 minutes.

Amelia Baptiste and her husband believed in civic duty. Between 1870 and 1872 Peter A. Dutrieuille was, respectively, second lieutenant and first lieutenant in Company F, Thirteenth Regiment Infantry, National Guard, Pennsylvania Brigade, First Division, Uniformed Militia, of the City of Philadelphia. In about 1885 he was a member of the Social Club and of the New York and Newport Ugly Fishing Club. He was both a member of the charter group as well as a board member of the Frederick Douglass Memorial Hospital.

Peter Albert Dutrieuille was one of the organizers of the Caterers' Manufacturing and Supply Company. He served several terms as president—and as president and vice president during his connection with the Philadelphia Caterers' Association. He promoted the Pioneer Building and Loan Association, referred to as "one of the best of its kind in Philadelphia." Mr. Dutrieuille was the loan association's sole treasurer for over twenty-four years. Other affiliations included working as president of the Negro Historical Society, as treasurer of St. Mary's Catholic Beneficial Society, and as a member of St. Peter Claver's Holy Name Society, for which he was chosen to serve the Holy Communion Breakfast in the church's school auditorium for the First Holy Communion of three of his grandchildren's Sunday school class. He and W. E. B. Du Bois shared membership of a literary club, which held many of its meetings at the Dutrieuilles' home. Six years before his death, an article published in the *Commercial Journal* on December 31, 1910, summed up Peter Albert Dutrieuille's culinary success:

> We have in this city a number of the best caterers in the East . . . men, who from broad experience, have truly made catering a fine art. Prominent among the foremost of these is Mr. P. Albert Dutrieuille, who for many years, has had charge of the gastronomic features and feasts of a very generous proportion of the most elite and exclusive social functions that have been given in this city. It is with especial pleasure, therefore, that "Commercial Journal" is privileged to note that . . . Mr. Dutrieuille has entered the social season better prepared than ever to meet the demands of the most exacting, aristocratic patronage one could readily conceive, and Philadelphians who know him of old, may be assured that his talent and skills for rendering the very best service will continue unchanged.[5]

The gold standard of catering would continue in the hands of Peter Albert Dutrieuille's son, Albert Eugene (Al, and Allie to his close friends). Albert Eugene was educated in Philadelphia schools. At an early age he began assisting his father, thereby becoming acclimated to the business located in the fashionable Rittenhouse Square area. In a ceremony at St. Patrick's Catholic Church on December 25, 1900, he married Florence May Waters. As the years passed, business continued to grow and flourish, requiring his attention for much longer working hours, very often twenty-four hours a day. During World War I he headed the concession at several army camps, one of which was Indiantown Gap. Little by little, Peter Albert relinquished more and more authority and responsibilities to Albert Eugene, while maintaining his own strict reign and control. When Peter Albert died in 1916, Albert Eugene was promoted to head of the family business. Samples of receipts from the

1920s through the 1950s, carrying the company's letterhead, indicate that Albert Eugene was now in charge, but his father's name remained on the stationery, serving to assure patrons that the business was maintaining its reputation and was still in competent hands. Fortunately, inheriting the business meant inheriting the help as well.[6]

His parents' employees had obviously been an integral part of their success; they stayed with Albert Eugene until they died or were too old to work. Of the new employees hired by Albert Eugene and his wife, most remained in their employ for the rest of their working lives, although a few did leave to pursue other options. John Cleaver and Claude Giles were two chefs who worked for Albert Eugene. Cleaver eventually formed his own catering firm; Giles went to work for Philadelphia National Bank, which had its own kitchen for wining and dining the board members. Albert Eugene did make some changes of his own. One was in the area of transporting foods. His father had always hired vans to make deliveries. Albert Eugene purchased his own. In his new role he dealt with a multitude of struggles that accompanied the business, but he never failed to win friends and increase the business's clientele among the fashionable set, and especially with the Catholic Church.[7]

It would be easy to increase the clientele and win friends if you served the Virginia ham. It was a favorite menu item at numerous affairs. The Mutual Assurance Company was a business client that chose Dutrieuille quite often, engaging him to prepare lavish meals for their dining pleasure. Albert E. Dutrieuille catering records for the 1920s through the 1930s show that, in addition to Virginia ham, many of the company's repasts included caviar, oysters on the half shell, deviled crab, sweetbread paté, Guinea squab, lobster à la Newburg, consommé with okra, okra soup, black bean soup, Philadelphia and Baltimore terrapin, oxtail soup, corn fritters, salmon steaks, chicken croquettes, planked shad roe, fried smelts with tartar sauce, and turkey stuffed with truffles and chestnuts (and it was not even Thanksgiving!).[8]

One of A. E. Dutrieuille's many customers was Jos. Doran, whose office was in the Commercial Trust Building in Philadelphia. He ordered at least two Virginia hams between February 23 and March 26, 1915. Doran wanted one ham express shipped to his son John H. Doran in Kingston, Luzerne County, Pennsylvania, but at the same time he insisted that Dutrieuille "Take all the time necessary to prepare [and] cook it as it should be." Dutrieuille fulfilled many orders for Virginia hams for

Easter celebrations. Doran's ham order on March 26 was for just such an occasion.[9]

Thanksgiving had come and gone when Albert E. Dutrieuille served the Library Company of Philadelphia a fourteen-pound turkey and cranberries on December 2, 1920. Clearly, the Library Company had kept up its preference for African caterers. One hundred years after James Prosser's creations were regular fixtures at Library Company dinners, its dependence on Dutrieuille's catering services was constant throughout the 1920s and 1930s. Juniata terrapin, creamed spinach, oxtail soup, oysters on the half shell, roast saddle of mutton with currant jelly, filet of sole, salmon steaks, Long Island duck, potato croquettes, wild rice, Guinea squab, and Brussel sprouts were delicacies prepared for the board members' indulgence at lunch and dinner at the Library Company.[10]

Another must-have was stewed snapper turtle and especially terrapin, which were considered two of the most sought-after delicacies. They were consistently ordered for luncheons, dinner parties, and banquets. Both were specialties of a number of caterers in Philadelphia and Baltimore. Both were, quite literally, mainstays, and practically no catering event was complete without an order for one or the other. Colonel John W. Forney, who was feted with Peter Augustin's terrapin at Augustin's restaurant in 1871, wrote in 1879, "Terrapin is essentially a Philadelphia dish. Baltimore delights in it, Washington eats it, New York knows it; but in Philadelphia it approaches a crime not to be passionately fond of it."[11]

Albert Eugene Dutrieuille's grandson Mr. Peter Shelton shared with me in a telephone interview some of his recollections of growing up in the midst of his grandparents' catering environment. Mr. Shelton stated that as a child he never went into the basement of the establishment because there were always turtles crawling around everywhere. He said that the cooks would grab them by their tails and drop them in boiling water. The pots were huge and heavy copper and steel cauldrons; "you could barely lift them when they were *empty*." Mr. Shelton mentioned that two of his grandfather's expert turtle chefs, John Cleaver and Claude Giles (mentioned earlier) both prepared the firm's world-famous terrapin, chicken croquettes, and lobster Newburg.[12]

The Catholic Church in Philadelphia and in numerous surrounding Pennsylvania towns would have never argued with the accolades bestowed upon the Dutrieuilles and surely would have given several "high fives" to express agreement on the issue of the quality of Dutrieuille catering, since it was the Dutrieuilles whom it constantly engaged. However, the Catholic Church in nineteenth-century Philadelphia had no use for African parishioners. Although they accounted for about 3 percent of Catholic church-attending Africans in 1838, the number of African Catholics in Philadelphia increased over time because of immigration and migration. In 1886 a group of African Catholics, tired of the discrimination forced upon them in three local churches, organized as the Peter Claver Union. Finally recognized by the Archdiocese of Philadelphia in 1889, they found a home for their parish in 1892, the St. Peter Claver Roman Catholic Church, at formerly Fourth Presbyterian Church. For many years St. Peter Claver was the only church in Philadelphia's archdiocese where African parishioners were welcome. The members of St. Peter Claver's parish clung to strong traditions; however, the Catholic Church was increasingly identified as the religious bastion of Irish immigrants. In Philadelphia, between 1850 and 1870, Catholic parishes tripled in number, increasing from twelve to thirty-six; there were already nineteen parish schools before 1860. The Irish were in fact attracted to areas where manufacturing was established, and wherever an Irish neighborhood developed a church was built. Irish wages were contributed—and it has been written that the Irish were the primary agents and chief contributors—to the network of parish churches that were built throughout the city.[13]

I must confess that any discussion of the Catholic Church in Philadelphia brings to mind the Dutrieuille catering firm under Albert Eugene Dutrieuille, as well as a certain newspaper story. I am not in any way comparing Mr. Dutrieuille to the person quoted below, and I certainly intend no disrespect to Mr. Dutrieuille. The story is filled with so-called Negro dialect, but the point remains quite clear. The story goes like this:

> A friend of mine who was giving a large dinner once called on old T., the negro caterer to arrange the dinner and take the trouble off her hands.
>
> "Yes, ma'am," said old T., "I'll look out for it all; but fust I want to know who de company is. Is there any clergymen and them kind a-comin'?"
>
> "Certainly," said my friend; "but why do you ask such a question?"
>
> "Oh," says old T., "if they's clergymen and that sort comin', you must get more to eat and drink. Them pious eats tremendous!"[14]

Significantly, Albert Eugene was "exceedingly active" in all aspects of the Catholic Church. Up to shortly before his death he had been very active in the Society of St. Vincent DePaul, on whose behalf he took time to visit hospitals. He brought magazines, cigarettes, and occasionally his delicacies, which he personally distributed to the patients. He attended the society's luncheons and dinners, whenever time allowed, and sometimes contributed financially to their rallies. This and other benevolences led him to become particularly favored by the hierarchy, the head of which was the archbishop of Philadelphia, Cardinal Dennis Dougherty, and the visiting archbishop, Gerald P. O'Hara, who became apostolic delegate, in London, to the pope.

Albert Eugene's daughter Mrs. Bernice Dutrieuille Shelton reported that Archbishop O'Hara once spoke long distance to her father to "wish him well." Mrs. Shelton writes, "It came to the point in our father's business career that he steadily gained almost a complete monopoly of the Catholic clergy's business: ordination breakfasts, forty-hour luncheons, visiting celebrities (reverent potentates from other parishes, here, or from overseas) banquets—most of which were, of course, presided over by Dennis Cardinal Dougherty; Jubilees, silver and golden, and on and on." She further states that the clergy clients were from "almost every church (Catholic) throughout the city and environs, sometimes as far away in Pennsylvania as Phoenixville, Scranton, etc."[15]

And indeed they were. The firm had numerous clients, but the Catholic Church outdid them all in frequency of requested services and in money spent. Please note that the following few catered events mentioned here do not even begin to sample the long list of clergy and their sponsored events that were catered and recorded by Albert E. Dutrieuille throughout the 1920s and 1930s. Some of Mr. Dutrieuille's catering records, from 1920 to 1939, have survived, but they in no way indicate the amount of business he garnered from the clergy before or after those dates. Menus and invoices for dinner service for convents such as the Convent of Our Lady of Angels in Glen Riddle, Pennsylvania, and other church celebrations that appear after the 1930s, have also survived.[16]

Reverend D. C. Meuemyou, of Chester Heights, Pennsylvania, ordered dinner for May 31, 1920, at a cost of $118.00. Besides fruit cup and chicken soup, the twenty-five dinner guests enjoyed brook trout with sliced cucumbers, fried sweetbreads with spinach, roasted lamb with mint sauce, new peas, potatoes, and asparagus. And of course, the usual accompaniments to just about every catered lunch and dinner were rolls and butter, cakes, olives, nuts, mints, and coffee.[17]

The average amount spent by the clergy was in the neighborhood of $120.00—a fortune in the 1920s. Reverend McMahon of Bustleton, Pennsylvania, spent a little more ($166.50) for his luncheon party for thirty on October 3, 1920. He insisted that his oysters on the half shell be served "well iced" with horseradish chili sauce and lemon. Together with mushroom bisque and different vegetables, the diners were showered with whole, braised sweetbreads, roast turkey stuffed with chestnuts, assorted ice creams, fancy cakes, and Roman punch.[18]

Whether or not you decide to include a priest or two at your next luncheon party, excite everyone's appetite with this hearty mushroom soup. Make plenty just in case "them pious" come calling.

Mushroom Bliss

- 2 tablespoons sesame seed oil
- 3 tablespoons vegetable oil
- 12 ounces sliced mushrooms
- 2 large onions, chopped
- 1/8 teaspoon whole allspice berries, finely ground
- 4 cups chicken broth
- 2 cups beef broth
- Black pepper to taste
- 3 teaspoons garlic salt with parsley
- 1/3 cup dark rum or sherry
- 1 cup cream

Add sesame seed and vegetable oils to a medium-large pot. Add mushrooms, onions, and ground allspice. Cook and stir over medium-low heat for a few minutes. Stir in chicken and beef broths, then black pepper and garlic salt. Simmer, covered, over low heat, for approximately 40 minutes. Add sherry and bring to boil. Lower heat and simmer, covered, 5 minutes. Stir in cream and bring just to a boil, but do not boil.

Then there was the Silver Jubilee for Father Buckley, which was celebrated at three different venues on June 8, 1920. It seems that Father Buckley and the Catholic Church believed their celebration was more important than the law. After all, Prohibition went into effect on January 16, 1920. At the convent and rectory at Forty-Eighth and Lancaster, and at another location on Elsworth, 165 people were wined and dined. Along with other classics, they enjoyed clam broth with whipped cream, roasted ham and greens, roasted duck, and two quarts each of sherry and whiskey to accompany their mint juleps, all to the tune of $771.50. No doubt, the frequency of this lawbreaking behavior of drinking and carrying on was often.[19]

Similar events, such as the Investiture dinner for Right Reverend Monsignor Jas. Nash on May 3, 1921, provided fruit cup, Bellevue broth, lobster Newburg, baby lamb, broiled spring chicken, asparagus and various vegetables, vol au vent (pastry shells filled with seafood or chicken in cream sauce), paté de foie gras, tomato aspic, salad, ice cream and strawberries, ginger ale, and to round out this auspicious occasion, Monsignor Punch. (You want to bet on what kind of "punch" was in the punch?) The grand total came to $762.00.[20]

Now, the cardinal actually had his own punch. "Cardinal Punch" was prepared for Reverend Jas. Duffy and his sixty guests at a $210.00 broiled sirloin steak fete on May 8, 1921. Well, I guess we should not fret over it; maybe Duffy was *studying* to become cardinal. At any rate, on April 9, 1928, the real cardinal, "His Eminence D'Cardinal Dougherty," ordered dinner for twelve. Perhaps they needed to save room for a few gin and tonics, because it was not a particularly spectacular affair; it included only honey dew melons, oysters, soup, chicken patties, lamb chops, asparagus, potatoes, peas, salad, with strawberry shortcake, apple pie, and ice cream for dessert. Roman Punch was the drink of choice for the cardinal's dinner with the apostolic delegate on March 7, 1923. If memory serves me, the Roman Punch that I know is flavored with champagne, rum, curacao, and/or brandy. It probably went quite well with oysters on the half shell, clam bouillon with whipped cream, baked shad, spinach omelets, and other goodies that were in attendance along with the cardinal's twenty-six guests. Reverend P. F. O'Neill's dinner for sixty, and supper for twenty, on February 4, 1924, included Roman Punch to wash down three hundred oysters on the half shell and Virginia ham and greens. His bill totaled $299.97.[21]

———————

I know that the following concoction is known as Roman Punch in some circles, but let's be real. I simply call it as I know it to be. And it tastes good, too.

Pulpit Pimp Punch

- 1 cup Syrah
- 1/3 cup blackberry brandy
- Grenadine (to dress the drink as the cardinal would dress, and to lightly sweeten)

Combine all ingredients except grenadine and mix well. Pour into glasses over ice. Add a little grenadine to each serving.

———

If this one does not make you tell everything you know, then maybe it has already knocked you out. Apparently, the higher your rank, the stronger the punch. Who can say how many thirsts this will quench if you do not hold on to it for yourself. If you do, maybe only one.

Confession

- 2 tablespoons orange juice
- 2 tablespoons lemon juice
- 1/3 cup champagne
- 3 tablespoons dark rum
- 2 tablespoons blackberry brandy
- 1 tablespoon curacao
- About 4 teaspoons sugar, or more, to taste
- 1 tablespoon egg white, that has been beaten into stiff peaks

Combine all ingredients except egg whites. Mix well and thoroughly chill. When ready to serve, ladle punch into cups. Stir egg white into each serving.

While the priests were slinging cocktails and oysters, the Great Depression hit in 1929, which meant a slowdown, and most often, a stop in wages, and therefore a vast change, to put it mildly, in eating habits. During the years of the Great Depression, the average family income, if there was one, was $1,500 a year. In 1930 the Committee on Unemployment Relief was organized, and it raised $3,840,000 to aid Philadelphia's poor families. It was replaced in 1931 by the Bureau of Unemployment Relief. When relief money was exhausted, poor families depended on friends, relatives, community breadlines, and soup kitchens. To make matters worse, in 1932 the mayor fired thirty-five hundred city employees in order to save Philadelphia twelve million dollars in salaries. But 1933 was said to be the worst year for Philadelphia: 11.5 percent of Whites, 16.2 percent of Blacks, and 19.1 percent of foreign-born Whites were jobless. Well, maybe the average person did not have enough to eat; "Them Pious," my dears, were another story.

Banquets will always stand out in the midst of starvation, especially since the Depression years did not force a slump or slowdown in catered events for the Catholic Church. Apparently, during some of those years, money was no object. In 1934 there were at least seventy-one catered affairs for individual priests, five for convents, five for Catholic churches, one for a Catholic school, and two for a Catholic club. I guess that the priests were particularly depressed during the Depression the following year and needed many culinary pick-me-ups, because in 1935 there were at least ninety-nine catered affairs for priests, seven for convents, seven for Catholic churches, one for a Catholic school, and one for a monastery. In 1936 there were again at least ninety-nine events for priests, and eight for convents. Seeing as there are fifty-two weeks in a year, the average was about two dinner parties each week for those years. And remember, we are talking only about the Dutrieuille catering records.

Various catering events recorded in Mr. Dutrieuille's records show the difference between what priests and nuns were served for the exact same affair. Right Reverend Monsignor Jas. A. Mullin and his golden jubilee on January 13, 1935, for example, served the king of soup, terrapin, along with ham and greens, roast turkey and cranberries, potato balls, string beans, and fancy cakes to seventy-five priests at the rectory. The forty convent sisters taking part in the celebration were served cream of celery soup, roast turkey, beef, candied sweet potatoes, peas, and regular cake. The entire bill was $277.50.[22]

Well, it is a good thing Prohibition was repealed in 1933, although it was still the height of the Great Depression. The Catholic Church was known for its strict attitude toward sex (hmmm), and the total abstinence movement against alcohol (Oh, I see!). These aspects of Catholicism were encouraged by the "strong and concerted leadership of the clergy." All of this is interesting for a number of reasons, because on October 28, 1935, in addition to oysters on the half shell, Virginia ham and greens with white potatoes, roast turkey with chestnut filling and cranberries, filet of beef with creamed mushrooms and baked stuffed potatoes, Nesselrode pudding with rum sauce and pumpkin pie, Reverend John J. McMenamin made certain he and his forty dinner guests had their share of Manhattans and Side Car Cocktails, which required both whiskey and rum. Reverend P. J. McGarrity's bill, in the amount of $147.35, for services on November 4, 1935, included the price for his rum and whiskey mint juleps.[23]

Speaking of Nesselrode pudding and other desserts, when A. E.

Dutrieuille catered for an Italian priest, rum cake and zuppa inglese (a custard and cake confection) were purchased from an Italian bakery in South Philadelphia. For other "feeds" (as Dutrieuille called them), he purchased many of African caterer John Holland's famous pastries. Holland's and African caterer John Trower's ice creams were favored by the Dutrieuille firm as well. Much of the ice cream and items such as Nesselrode pudding were purchased from Abbott's Alderney Dairies, located at 212–240 Lombard Street.[24]

During the years leading up to A. E. Dutrieuille taking over the business, there was a steady rise in racism, in discrimination, and in segregationist mentality, which engulfed Philadelphia along with the rest of the nation. As African businessmen were losing their predominance in certain occupations and African caterers were abandoned by their White clients, Italians, Irish, and other European immigrants replaced Africans as waiters in restaurants and as bellhops in hotels. Undoubtedly, this was a direct result of a resolution passed by the Hotel Men's Association in New York in August 1912, which stipulated that no hotel employing Africans should be rated as "first class." Consequently, four major Philadelphia hotels replaced their all-African staffs with Whites.

This had been an ongoing pattern and practice throughout the nineteenth century as well. White workers in San Francisco in 1889, for instance, replaced all of the African employees at the Palace Hotel, following protests of the White cooks' and waiters' union. In Philadelphia, Abbott also owned Abbott's Dairy Restaurant on Chestnut Street, which was known to employ African waitresses exclusively. In 1910, when Whites objected to their presence, Abbott's moved the African staff to the basement counter. For White customers, however, the basement was not far enough away. In September 1913, every African employee was dismissed. At the same time that Abbott's was making changes in its employee roster, about a mile away the fiftieth anniversary of the Emancipation Proclamation was being honored with the Emancipation Proclamation Exhibit, a fair celebrating fifty years of African progress in business and industry.[25]

One area in which there was eventual progress was the inclusion of service by African caterers to African clients and customers. Mrs. Shelton, A. E. Dutrieuille's daughter, wrote that in later years he did accept the patronage of some of his own, which sometimes included his children's classmates' functions, weddings, commencement celebrations, and so forth. For example, the African American newspaper the *Philadelphia Tribune* was a customer on December 29, 1923. Dr. Henry M. Minton, at Mercy Hospital, ordered chicken croquettes and potato salad on June 18, 1935, and deviled crabs, chicken salad, and potato chips on June 21, 1935. A. E. Dutrieuille catered a dinner for fifty people for Dr. E. T. Hinson at Mercy Hospital on April 16, 1935. Stewed snapper turtle and sweet potato surprise were two of the items on that menu. On January 21, 1936, Dr. Minton ordered one dozen oyster croquettes, a popular item also favored and ordered for twenty persons by the Ugly Club on October 16, 1936.[26]

Looking at one more order for the church, since oysters were so popular and such a regular feature at catered affairs, it would come as no surprise that for Holy Thursday, on April 18, 1935, Reverend H. T. Mc-Fall would have Mr. Dutrieuille include them, on the half shell, for his fifty-four guests (five will get you a hundred that none of the guests was a parishioner). Together with roasted jumbo squabs with creamed celery sauce, a whole roasted baby lamb, filet of beef, Bellevue broth, sweet potatoes, asparagus, salad, ice cream, strawberries, apple pie, and fancy cakes, and the usual coffee, olives, celery, radishes, salted nuts, mints, rasped rolls and butter, and of course, the charges for the chinaware, linen, silver, glasses, waiters, cook, dishwasher, and transport costs, the cost for this feast totaled $250.68.[27]

Now I ask you, shouldn't the Irish have given more thought and attention to where the Catholic Church was spending parishioner dollars (on booze and oysters) than they did to constantly warring against Africans over jobs? But maybe you think I am being too hard on the priests. Perhaps you are right, and it is just like the Academy Award–winning song tells us: "It's HARD out here for a pimp." Nevertheless, when it came to being fed, most people did not come close to the bill of fare enjoyed by the Catholic clergy during the Depression era. This era, from 1929 through the 1930s, was a time of charity ventures for Florence May Waters Dutrieuille and her husband, Albert Eugene. During the Depression years, the Dutrieuilles were noted for their daily feeding of the hungry. At least one hundred unemployed men of all ages gathered at their back door each week. The Dutrieuilles provided a full meal, free of charge, to each person. No one was ever denied a meal. One of Mrs. Dutrieuille's children commented to her that some of them should not have been fed. She responded, "I'd rather give to someone who didn't need it, than learn later that I had let your father turn away someone in real need."[28]

Culinary pursuits had always been a part of life for Florence May Waters Dutrieuille. Roscoe's, in Los Angeles, is not the first chicken and waffles establishment in the United States. When Florence and Albert Eugene were first married, she opened "Maryland Fried Chicken and Waffles restaurant in North Philadelphia. She probably got her recipes from family members living in Princess Ann County in Maryland. North Philadelphia was all White and Jewish back then. Apparently, she did not keep it going for very long, opting instead to work with her husband's catering firm.[29]

Nine in the morning, or twelve o'clock at night. You cannot go wrong with this one. All hours are the right hours to keep this one going.

Chicken and Corn Pancakes (by the way, I'm a pancake girl)

The Chicken

The flavor is in the seasoning and coating. Season chicken with garlic salt, seasoned salt, black pepper, cilantro, parsley flakes (or your favorites), and *a little cayenne*. The chicken should be *spicy*.

Coat with paprika and flour. Fry in bacon grease, or a combination of oils: sesame seed,* vegetable, and/or bacon

The Pancakes:

- 1/2 cup EACH yellow cornmeal and all-purpose flour
- 1½ teaspoons baking powder
- 1/2 teaspoon baking soda
- 1/2 teaspoon salt
- 2/3 cups sugar
- 1 egg
- 3 tablespoons vegetable oil
- 1/2 cup creamed corn
- 1 or 2 tablespoons milk, if needed

Combine dry ingredients in a medium-sized bowl and mix well.

Make a well in the middle of the dry ingredients. Into the well add the egg, oil, and creamed corn. Gently mix these ingredients together, gradually stirring egg mixture into dry ingredients. If mixture becomes too thick to stir, add a little milk, one tablespoon at a time, and mix just until well blended.

Use as waffle or pancake batter.

*Sesame seed oil is not a southern staple, but I sometimes use it in combination with peanut or vegetable oil because it gives the dish a delicious different flavor. It is available at larger supermarkets and at Asian and Indian groceries.

This is another old recipe for waffles from Harriet, a cook known to the Prescott family.

Waffles, Harriet's Recipe

"A note beside recipe 'This is excellent.'"

- 1 quart of milk
- 8 eggs
- 1/4 pound of butter
- A gill (1/2 cup) of yeast
- A little salt
- Flour, "enough to make a batter the thickness of griddle cakes"[30]

And work together they did. Mr. and Mrs. Dutrieuille were part of the "Old Philadelphia" Black elite when Albert Eugene Dutrieuille retired in 1967 at the age of eighty-nine. A founding charter member of the socially prominent Olde Philadelphia Club, which came into existence in about 1929, he was the last surviving founder when he died at age ninety-six on April 25, 1974. When A. E. Dutrieuille passed away, his was the last of the old-line prominent Philadelphia catering dynasties, signaling the end of an era of unsurpassed culinary creativity in Philadelphia, creativity that garnered the highest marks for "American" culinary achievements.[31]

The African American culinary service sector would continue to maintain a foothold. In some cases the wives would carry on the business after the death of their spouse. That foothold had become entrenched in other parts of Pennsylvania, such as Harrisburg. Slave and free Africans resided in Harrisburg and Dauphin County as early as 1790. In later decades the county's free Africans boasted a well-organized society, which formed protection committees and took on slave hunters. Pennsylvania became the key state, the center, or "middle passage" of the system of the Underground Railroad, and several Africans in Harrisburg, such as William Pap Jones (one of the founders of the Wesley AME Church in Harrisburg), Joseph C. Bustill (schoolteacher and grandson of Revolutionary War bread baker Cyrus Bustill), and the George Chester family, to name just a few, were some of its most prominent operators.[32]

Dauphin County was a central vein in the Underground Railroad— and the hub of the "central route" in Pennsylvania was the city of Harrisburg. The center of social and political activity and a noted Underground Railroad station in Harrisburg was the restaurant that George and Jane

Marie Chester owned and operated, located near the courthouse on Market Street. From 1831 through 1834 Mr. Chester was the capital's only agent for *The Liberator*, William Lloyd Garrison's newspaper, which he sold at his restaurant. Together with the delicious food served (Mr. Chester was an oysterman, and contributed to the delicacies served at the restaurant) and a congenial atmosphere and hospitality, the restaurant soon became what was considered a hub of local abolitionist activity for both Blacks and Whites. It was at the Chesters' restaurant that Africans congregated, organized anticolonization meetings, and planned protection from recapture for fugitive slaves as well.

Many of the city capital's most important events demanded catering by George and Jane Marie Chester, "and on major public holidays it became something of a tradition to dine at their restaurant." When George died on October 15, 1859, the family resided at 305 Chestnut Street. Author R. J. M. Blackett reports that Jane Marie moved the family residence and the restaurant. To be certain, Mrs. Chester remained in Harrisburg and continued the business as Harrisburg's "principal caterer," renowned for her homemade taffy. But taffy was only one specialty served up by Mrs. Chester and advertised in Harrisburg's local newspaper. Soft shell and deviled crab, turtle and chicken soup, "terrapins, oysters in every style," chicken salad, ice cream, "and all the other delicacies of the season" were among her claims to culinary fame. Mrs. Chester was still known for her culinary hospitality in 1885, as Harrisburg's African-owned newspaper, the *State Journal*, mentions on the first page of its January 24, 1885, issue that Mrs. Chester gave an impromptu reception for visiting gentlemen from Hollidaysburg and Altoona.[33]

"The Housekeeper's Department," "Hints for the Housekeeper," and "Hints for the Housewife," columns in the *State Journal*, offered household cleaning tips and remedies as well as recipes.

Excellent Breakfast Cakes

Three eggs, one tablespoonful of sugar, one coffee cup of sweet milk, one cup of warm water, three tablespoonfuls of yeast, flour enough to make a stiff batter. Leave the whites of the eggs until the latter has risen, then add them; a pinch of salt is needed. If started the night before, these cakes are delicious. They will be as light as puffs.

Oyster Cakes

Chop and pound some veal in a mortar, with an equal quantity of oysters, mix well and add some bread crumbs and a little beef suet finely shred; moisten with some of the liquor of the oysters, season with pepper, salt, and a little mace, bind together with a well-beaten egg, form into rather long shaped flat cakes, and fry a light brown in well-clarified dripping; serve as fish cakes.[34]

Rubber Cookies

Two cups of molasses, one-half cup sugar, three cups flour, one table-spoonful soda, one large tablespoonful vinegar and one egg. Mix soft and bake quickly.[35]

Cough Syrup

One gill [1/2 cup] of Jamaica spirits, one of molasses, one teaspoonful of powdered alum, one of paregoric [an opiate used to treat diarrhea], one of licorice. Steep all in the spirits, and heat to the boiling point. When cold, give a teaspoonful when the cough is troublesome.[36]

At about the same time that Jane Chester was hosting receptions, Mr. Wm. Adore was the proprietor of the United States Hotel Restaurant in Harrisburg. Meals were served at all hours, including "oysters in every style." In later decades, Pennsylvania's capital boasted Mr. G. W. Scott who, "during his life time was the leading caterer of [Harrisburg]." When he died Mrs. G. W. Scott, a well-trained businesswoman, was, in 1903, still carrying on the business in Steelton.[37]

We cannot leave Pennsylvania without mentioning Philadelphia's William A. Potter. Born in 1829, Potter was a native of the city and another of its most noted caterers. As a young adult he worked for the old music firm of Lee & Walker. He eventually left to set up his own catering business. Mr. Potter was in charge of preparing the food for the collation served on July 4, 1856, in honor of the establishment of the *Public Ledger*. The White House was served by Mr. Potter on three occasions. In addition, he provided the dinner given for General Grant in Philadelphia at the end of the Civil War. Potter remained in the catering business until illness prevented his continued activity. He died at the age of eighty-three on May 13, 1912, after an illness of several years.[38]

Philadelphia was legendary as a center of gastronomic pleasures during and beyond the era of slavery. Other east coast enclaves, however, were not without their African culinary legends. Some became culinary pioneers in the process. In New York state, one such pioneer created a snack that initiated a multibillion-dollar industry in the United States. Another ran a pickling establishment—housing pickles, preserves, and jellies—that was "the only one of its kind run by a Negro businessman in the city." Through various club-related and charitable activities, many members of the food service community in New York made important social and political impacts on the daily lives of Black folk, in the tradition of Samuel Fraunces's Tavern, as well as lasting impacts on the taste buds and eating habits of New Yorkers in general.[39]

7

"OUTCASTS AND INDIGENT SONS OF AFRICA"

New York's Nineteenth-Century Chefs, Caterers, and Restaurateurs

*I*f you could afford to have your meals professionally prepared, New York was the place to eat. African caterers were numerous in New York, and their services have a long history. According to Booker T. Washington, whose mother was the cook for the plantation where his family was enslaved, catering in New York City began with African females. Between 1780 and 1820 Cornelia Gomez, great grandmother of Dr. P. W. Ray of New York, was among the most recognized of Black female caterers. She was said to cater for the most prominent families in the city, such as the Rhinelanders, Goelets, Robinsons, and Gerrys. She was succeeded by "Aunt" Katie Ferguson, who stayed in business until about 1820. Washington states that catering had been almost totally in African hands, and that African men "[took] it up where the women left it."[1]

Resort towns such as Saratoga Springs, New York, were home to African residents who were largely hotel service people in the early to mid-1800s, working as chefs, cooks, waiters, and maids. African musicians were employed at the hotels as well. While serenaded by Frank Johnson's very own music compositions at Congress Hall Hotel and United States Hotel in Saratoga Springs, you could experience wonderful dining treasures supplied by Mrs. Anne Northup. She and her husband, Solomon Northup (another popular musician), were year-round residents, and both worked at the United States Hotel, which opened in 1824.[2]

The Northup family moved to Saratoga Springs from Kingsbury, New York, in 1834. Mr. Northup worked as a violinist during the winter season. He also worked as a laborer on the Troy and Saratoga Railroad while it was under construction. Mrs. Northup held a reputation as an outstanding cook and was regularly relied upon at the hotel, as well as at other dining rooms in Saratoga Springs and other towns. It would be remiss of me not to mention that Anne Northup had been hired to take charge of the "culinary department" at Sherrill's Coffee House in Sandy Hill, twenty miles away. In the latter part of March 1841, on one of her days there, her husband, Solomon, was approached on the street by two slave dealers pretending to be interested in hiring him as a violinist to play for a circus. Solomon Northup, a free African, was drugged, kidnapped, and sold into slavery—a common occurrence in America. His riveting narrative, *Twelve Years a Slave* was published in 1853. It chronicles his life and some of the lives of Africans with whom he suffered on plantations in Louisiana. After Mr. Northup's rescue, he returned to his family at Glen Falls, in Warren County, where his wife was in charge of the kitchen at the Carpenter's Hotel.[3]

In 1860s Saratoga Springs, many African women like Anne Northup were cooks, washerwomen, or servants. About 96 percent of African women who worked were employed in these positions. The remaining 4 percent were listed as seamstresses or as working in tailoring. African women and men were the domestic service people for a number of old and new enterprises in Saratoga Springs.

For the wealthy, attending the horse races was still a popular pastime. Rich men such as the first Cornelius Vanderbilt came each summer to display their "trotters" and to play bid whist all night. However, New York's legislation called An Act More Effectually to Protect the Free Citizens of This State from Being Kidnapped, or Reduced to Slavery, which passed on May 14, 1840, made it difficult for southerners to visit northern terrain accompanied by their army of African servants. Many simply stopped coming, which was a loss of about one and a half million dollars per season for Saratoga Springs. After the Civil War, the southern contingent of tourists reappeared in droves. The John Morrissey Club House, a gaming house built in 1869, sparked the creation of twelve gambling houses in Saratoga Springs by 1873. African cooks and chefs were prime additions to these houses.

Two large hotels, the Grand Union and the United States Hotel—which burned down in 1865 or (some date it at) 1867 but was rebuilt and opened in June 1874—were the playpens of many of these tourists. They were major employers of Africans. Dolly Carey, employed prior to Anne Northup, was said to be the first pastry cook at the United States Hotel.

On many occasions Africans trained as teachers and college students took jobs at the hotels as cooks, kitchen help, waiters, ushers, porters, and bellmen because teaching positions and industrial or other skilled jobs were not open to them. One Saratoga resident stated that, "In the Grand Union Hotel, the head bellman and the headwaiters were all black men, and they had the whole charge of the hotels."[4]

Saratoga had its legendary waiters such as John Lucas, who held the title of headwaiter at the United States Hotel before he died in 1888, but it also had its legendary chefs. Presidents Grover Cleveland and Chester A. Arthur; Senators Thomas F. Bayard, Arthur P. Gorman, Edward Murphy, Thomas G. Nast, and Thomas A. Hendricks; Governors Horatio Seymour, Alonzo B. Cornell, David B. Hill, and Roswell P. Flower; wealthy financiers William H. Vanderbilt, Pierre Lorillard, Berry Wall, E. T. Stokes, Wm. M. Tweed, Thomas B. Laflin, John Chamberlain, and William R. Travers, and a host of other rich and well-known customers, all made the trek to the restaurant of one legendary African–Native American chef in Saratoga to indulge in his culinary creations. Jays, Frito-Lays, and others are in debt to this chef whose decision one day to respond sarcastically to a customer complaint (or so the story goes) launched the creation of a multibillion-dollar snack business in the United States.

The setting was Saratoga Lake. Accommodations at Saratoga Lake served as the watering holes for many visitors during the summer months. There was Meyers's lake house on the eastern shore. Patrons could not wait to get a table to partake of its special creamed potatoes, broiled black bass, and game dinners. Avery's lake house was on the east side of the lake at Fish Creek. Avery's was also the place for game as well as fish dishes, and the eatery overflowed with customers.

Then there was Cary Moon's lake house. Moon's was particularly celebrated for its fish dinners. The chef at Moon's was George Crum who later opened his own roadhouse restaurant. It has been written that citizens "remember Crum's even if they never dined or visited George Crum's place at the south end of Saratoga Lake." In addition, "few prominent men in the world of finance, politics, art, the drama or sport failed to eat one of Crum's famous dinners." Crum's woodcock, which he considered to be the "king bird" and "the only bird fit for a gentleman's table," and partridge, lake bass and brook trout, potatoes and corn fritters were legendary in New York, Chicago, and Boston, as well as in Paris, London and Rome. Well, perhaps there is some truth here because story has it that an invalid traveled nine hundred miles to sample one of his woodcocks. Generous monetary offers were made to lure George Crum to take charge of other kitchens. He could not be persuaded; "even Delmonico's was forced to give up the attempt to get him in the kitchen at Twenty-sixth-st. and Broadway."[5]

William H. Vanderbilt, noted businessman and one of the nation's wealthiest men, was a regular visitor to Saratoga Lake and was said to be extremely fond of canvasback ducks. He did not like the way they were cooked in town (Saratoga) so he sent a few to George Crum to get him to offer his rendition. Crum supposedly had never cooked a canvasback, but because he knew he could cook anything, he gave them a try. Crum later stated that the ducks were kept on the coals for nineteen minutes. They must have turned out well because Vanderbilt was reported to have said that "he had never eaten anything like them in his life." Consequently, Vanderbilt sent Crum many customers.[6]

The steady flow of customers proved lucrative, as Crum did not hesitate to charge "Delmonico" prices. Quality was of the utmost importance, and he kept his tables supplied with the best ingredients. There were specific breeding ponds for his trout, and many of the foods served— such as the butter, milk, and chickens, and ingredients for breads, pickles, corn dodgers, muffins, and flapjacks—were raised or prepared on his own small farm, which he was said to tend himself when possible. His business became so popular he had to turn people away. One day Judge Henry Hilton and his party were directed by Crum to a rival house for dinner on the other side of the lake. The judge left but returned an hour later, however, adamant about eating at Crum's. Hilton reportedly told Crum, "George, . . . you must wait on us if we have to remain in the front yard for two hours." Crum replied, "I can cook for as many as can eat here, . . . but I can't get waiters enough to look after the tables properly."

Everyone was made to wait their turn, regardless of their "status" or "position." The food and the service were said to be worth the wait, so no one objected. Once he kept both Jay Gould and William Vanderbilt waiting for an hour and a half. When Crum came into the dining room to apologize to Jay Gould, "the 'wizard' said that he understood the rules of the establishment and would willingly wait another hour."[7]

Crum reportedly never had an assistant in the kitchen, although I must say I find this hard to believe. He was said to make his own fires and no other hand touched the broiler. The cooking was done over open fires of charcoal. His lake bass was cooked slowly, twelve inches above the burning embers. Turned at least twelve times, the fish was basted with Crum's own famous sauce on each turn. Those who had the pleasure stated that no further seasoning was required because any condiment would spoil the delicious flavor. Stewed potatoes were served with each bass, trout, and game course. It was a recipe known only to his Native American wife. Many guests came there just for the potatoes. She prepared the side dish in a house twenty yards from the dining rooms, and when Crum needed a dish of potatoes he tugged twice on a wire attached to a bell to let her know to send more to the kitchen.

Here is a delectable side dish destined to call for encores. Sh-h-h! Let's keep the ingredients a secret between you and me.

Potatoes and Spinach in Buttermilk

- 4 medium potatoes, peeled and sliced into rounds
- 2 strips thick-sliced bacon, OR, 3 strips regular sliced bacon
- 1 large onion, chopped
- 1/8 to 1/4 teaspoon crushed red pepper
- 1/8 teaspoon dill weed
- About 2/3 cup cooked salad spinach
- 1 cup EACH chicken broth and buttermilk
- Black pepper, to taste
- 1 heaping teaspoon garlic salt with parsley
- 1 heaping tablespoon, plus 1½ heaping teaspoons sugar
- 2 rounded teaspoons rice flour

Boil potatoes in water until done, approximately 30 to 40 minutes. Drain completely. Cover tightly if not using right away.

While potatoes are cooking, in a large skillet fry bacon until brown and crisp on both sides. Remove from skillet, reserving bacon drippings. When cool enough to handle, crumble bacon.

In the same skillet, add onions, red pepper, and dill to bacon drippings. Cook and stir until onions start to brown. Add crumbled bacon and spinach. Stir in chicken broth and buttermilk, then remaining ingredients. Bring to a boil over medium-low heat. Simmer for a minute or so to allow sauce to thicken.

Fold in potatoes. Allow to heat thoroughly, and serve.

Having succeeded in building an important name for himself in the culinary world, George Crum's next venture was to establish his own restaurant. He was born in Malta in 1828 to a Native American mother and a mulatto father named Abe Speck (Speck was Crum's real name). Abe Speck was a horse jockey who moved to Saratoga from Kentucky. Abe's son George was raised learning how to hunt deer and fish, the main sports attracting visitors to the lakes and streams of the Adirondacks. As he grew older George became famous as a guide, hunter, fisherman, and cook, and his services were in great demand. At nineteen he became the sole hunter for a wealthy family who dismissed their five live-in hunters after giving Crum a trial run. Paid $150 a month, Crum kept their pantry full with the best fish, game, and game birds. As an Adirondack mountain guide he prepared his own meals, which were described by hunting parties who were allowed to share his fare as absolute genius. George left the Adirondacks, returned to Saratoga Springs, and was employed as a cook at Moon's lake house.

There are a number of stories as to how Crum's most famous creation came into being, but the one most continuously told is that one day in 1853, while Crum was busy in the kitchen, one of Moon's diners complained to a waiter that his fried potatoes were cut too thick and asked to have some new ones prepared (one source claims that the customer sent the potatoes back two or three times). Crum sarcastically responded by shaving some potatoes paper thin and dropping them in hot oil. Salting them first, he sent them out to the customer never expecting to receive approval. But the customer did approve. The customer loved them. Crum prepared more and passed them around to the kitchen staff, as well as to Mrs. Moon, the owner. Crum's "Saratoga chips"— that is, potato chips—received rave reviews. They were soon on menus throughout the country and, as everyone knows, are now an American institution. The man who invented the potato chip died on July 22, 1914, and was said to have left behind a small fortune. And "small," unfortunately, is the correct term, because the fortune did not include rights to what would become massive profits for Jays and Frito-Lay's and all of the other potato chip companies. As a kid myself, and as many kids and adults could testify, it was hard to put down a bag of potato chips once you started munching. Jays brand had as it motto, "Can't stop eating 'em." And they were right.[8]

With culinary skills like those of George Crum, Saratoga Springs was certainly not adverse to having Africans cooking for both its locals and its visitors. Some hotels such as the Worden Hotel advertised in the local newspaper, *The Saratogian*, specifically for colored chef cooks. However, unless you were self-employed and ran a small business such as Laura Branch's lunchroom or John Stewart's restaurant, working in Saratoga Springs was your *summer* gig. Therefore, Africans had to find employment to carry them through the winter months. When the season ended and Saratoga's hotels closed, dining-room chefs had to take their culinary talents to hotels in other towns and cities. A few, such as Robert Jackson, were known to run their own catering establishments in New York City and elsewhere during the winter months.[9]

During the winter months, soups and stews are mainstay meals. Armed with a captivating aroma, the term "delicious" describes the following concoction, and it is guaranteed to keep you going through any season.

Cream of Potato and Mushroom Soup

- 3 medium or medium-large russet potatoes
- 5⅓ tablespoons butter
- 5⅓ tablespoons flour
- 2 big onions, chopped
- 6 cups chicken broth
- Chopped collard greens, about 2 cups
- 8 ounces sliced white mushrooms
- 1/4 heaping teaspoon dill weed
- About 1 teaspoon parsley flakes
- About 1/2 teaspoon cilantro
- Black pepper to taste
- 1 12-ounce can evaporated milk

Microwave potatoes in skins. Allow to cool before handling.

In a medium-large pot melt butter. Stir in flour, blending until smooth. Cook and stir butter-flour mixture until medium-brown in color. Add onions and cook and stir for a couple of minutes. Add broth, then collards and mushrooms. Peel potatoes. Add potatoes to pot, breaking potatoes up with a fork on the sides of the pot as you do so. Stir in dill, parsley, and cilantro. Simmer 40 to 45 minutes. Add milk and bring just to a boil.

Whether in the winter months, spring, summer, or fall, cooking and catering was, after all, in the correct or acceptable realm of employment for Africans. New York began incrementally ending slavery between 1799 and 1827 (reportedly it was not until the 1840 census that there were no slaves listed in New York), beckoning a steady migration of Africans to New York after that year. The establishment of African American businesses, therefore, was a response to the exclusion of Africans in the labor force, not to mention a response to creative achievement and meritorious invention. Some Africans in Brooklyn, in the early to mid-nineteenth century, responded similarly to their exclusion from the labor force and, as "outcasts and indigent sons of Africa sold oysters and crabs about town on Sunday." Late nineteenth- and early twentieth-century Brooklyn had its small group of African businessmen, whose clients were mainly from the African community. Among those whose businesses included food service were William Pope, owner of the Square Café, and John Connor, who operated the elite Royal Café, about which it was said, "only a few white café's can surpass it in beauty or in up-to-date service." In addition, Professor B. H. Hawkins owned the New National Hotel and Restaurant.[10]

Just as Samuel Fraunces's Inn and Tavern was famous for its food during New York's colonial period, in early nineteenth-century New York (the 1830s specifically), the best drinks, "segars," and breakfasts were found at Cato's Tavern (or Roadhouse), an early version of a "sports bar." Cato Alexander's clientele included numerous horse-race fans. It was situated midway along the Harlem speedway ("the famous five or six miles that paralleled the Hudson River, through what is today Manhattan's upper west side, near Morningside Heights and Columbia University, to 'the pretty village of Harlem'") on the Post Road at what is now Fifty-Ninth Street and Second Avenue. Witty and popular, this African barkeeper served "unadulterated brandy" and sold cigars made to his specifications that were shipped to him directly from Havana, Cuba. If ordered in advance, Cato would provide breakfast. Early nineteenth-century touring Irish actor and comedian, Tyrone Power (great grandfather of the famed actor Tyrone Edmund Power Jr., who died in 1958), stated that at Cato's, "A woodcock and toast as served up by him on these occasions is a thing not to be forgotten." However, according to Power, the drinks, as concocted by "this distinguished spiritous professor," were even more unforgettable because, "Cato is a great man, foremost amongst cullers of mint, whether for *julep* or *hail-storm*, second to no man as a compounder of *cock-tail*, and such a hand at a *gin-sling!*" Another of Cato's unforgettable cocktails was Rum Punch, which may have been slightly responsible for the merry manners of the elites such as the Stuyvesants, the Van Courtlandts, Lydigs, and Beekmans of that day.[11]

I cannot say definitively that my composition is exactly like Cato's. However, rest assured that my version will be responsible for *your* merry manners.

Rum Punch

- 1 cup 151 proof white rum
- 1 cup dark rum
- 1 cup coconut rum
- 2 cups orange juice
- 1 cup pineapple juice, or if you prefer, lime juice
- 2 cups sprite or 7-Up
- Fresh, finely grated nutmeg

Combine all ingredients, except nutmeg, and blend well. Pour into old-fashioned glasses over ice and, if desired, garnish with finely grated nutmeg.

Whether in the occupation of bartender or cook, caterer or domestic servant, barber or coachman, laborer or stevedore, seamstress or hairdresser, bootblack or chimney sweep, sailor or hotel waiter, Africans in New York dominated most of these positions for generations and were uncontested in the quality of their service. One fact was undisputed: "At one time the best food that could be procured in New York City was that furnished by coloured caterers." Thomas Jackson helped to prove the point. During the decades preceding the Civil War, Jackson serviced "the most exclusive parties and most fashionable weddings." Thomas Jackson was considered the arbiter of all things gustatory in New York in his day.[12]

One of the most remarkable businessmen was Henry Scott. By his own perseverance and determination Scott launched one of the most successful pickling establishments in New York prior to the Civil War. By 1839 Henry Scott and Company was open for business at 217 Water Street, where he warehoused a large stock of, among other items, pickles, preserves, and jellies that were in constant demand. His business lasted for many years as "the only one of its kind run by a Negro businessman in the city."[13]

By the 1850s Scott was known to principally supply ships and other oceangoing vessels, although he also did business with African caterers and restaurateurs such as Thomas Downing, who operated the famed oyster house on Wall and Broad Streets, as well as the Remond catering family of Salem, Massachusetts. And, like Thomas Downing and the Remonds, and "every thinking [African] man and woman," Henry Scott was involved in activities and organizations established to try to eradicate the wonton racial discrimination that saturated African existence. He was on the board of trustees, for example, of the New York Society for the Promotion of Education Among Colored Children, founded in July 1846. *The Manual of the Board of Education of the City and County of New York* for 1848 and 1849 lists Scott as the society's president. He was a contributor to the *Colored American* and other newspapers, espousing the hypocrisy of racism in public accommodations. Martin R. Delany included mention of Henry Scott in his 1852 treatise, *The Condition, Elevation, Emigration, and Destiny of the Colored People of the United States*, in which he stated, "There have doubtless been many a purser, who cashed and filed in his office the bill of Henry Scott, without ever dreaming of his being a colored man." In providing an assessment of Henry Scott's character, Mr. Delany stated that "Mr. Scott is extensively known in the great City, and respected as an upright, prompt, energetic business man, and highly esteemed by all who know him."[14]

Henry Scott was in the company of fellow African businessmen during the early and middle decades of the nineteenth century, as several refectories and eating houses were opened over time. From about 1836 until January 1839, Thomas Van Rensselaer's (or Rensellaer) Temperance House was a popular one, located at the corner of William and Ann Streets. Van Rensselaer, too, was a "thinking" man, prominent in abolitionist and equal rights activity in New York.

In 1839 Van Rensselaer's Temperance House moved to the corner of Wall and Water Streets, occupying the Phoenix building. During the celebration of West Indian emancipation, Thomas Van Rensselaer and his wife advertised the opening of their second establishment under the Broadway Tabernacle. His advertisements and editorial notice in *The Emancipator*, published under the auspices of the American Anti-Slavery

Society, called specific attention to his room under the Tabernacle, and to his "excellent eating house," which society members and friends were urged to patronize. Judging from the location of the establishments, his patrons were White.[15]

In 1820 James W. Mars was born in New York City, and he would become an eminent churchman and caterer. In 1841 Mars became confirmed as a member of St. Phillip's Episcopal Church, the church of choice of a number of free Africans. The White pastor of St. Phillip's would become a focal point after the passage of the Fugitive Slave Law of 1850, mainly because he swore to uphold and abide by that law. At any rate, Mars became senior warden in 1850, a position he held until his death on November 16, 1906. Early on he learned the catering business and in 1856 was placed in charge of catering and food service for the Hanover National Bank of New York. He remained with Hanover until "disabled by age." In 1877 he helped to organize the Newport Ugly Fishing Club, the membership of which was primarily caterers and others "devoted to good living." Like many forward-thinking free Africans who wanted to serve their community in that era, Mr. Mars sought participation in politics. In 1880 he was a candidate for assemblyman on the Republican ticket in Brooklyn; he lost by seven votes. He died at his residence in Brooklyn, survived by his wife, three sons, and two daughters.[16]

While Cato established himself as the famous purveyor of cocktails, and the sale of oysters and crabs became the livelihood of Brooklyn's "outcasts and indigent sons of Africa," over six million dollars' worth of oysters were sold in New York each year by 1850. *The 1866 Guide to New York City* reports, "The consumption of oysters in New York is immense; it having been computed that the daily consumption is valued at $15,000, and that some 1500 boats are constantly engaged to obtain the supply for this city alone." The Earl of Carlisle, in his *Travels in America*, remarked that he had made the acquaintance of the Jays, the Hamiltons, and the Livingstons, and that he had lodged at the "splendid" Astor House, and that he could "not refrain from one, . . . rather sensual allusion to the oyster cellars of New York. . . . every one seems to eat oysters all day long." Eastern seaboard varieties of oysters included Blue Points, Mattitucks, Cape Cods, Lynn Havens, Chesapeakes, Peconics, as well as Little Neck and Cherrystone clams. With such an unrivaled demand, most of the local beds were said to be exhausted by 1880.[17]

However, a settlement of free Africans living in the area of Staten

Island known as Sandy Ground, also referred to as "Little Africa," has been called this country's oldest existing community of free blacks from the nineteenth century. Sandy Ground emerged in 1850 in the rural township of Westfield, in Richmond County, Staten Island, New York. Most of the residents of Sandy Ground were in the oyster business and first occupied the area in the 1830s and 1840s. A number of African families owned land in nearby areas earlier than that, but a larger group of free people of color migrated from Worcester County, in and around the town of Snow Hill, Maryland, and formed, with the previous settlers, a vibrant, thriving community.[18]

In nineteenth-century Maryland the oyster trade supported the largest processing and packing industry of its kind in the world. The market for oysters seemed insatiable; the supply seemed inexhaustible. Africans working in the oyster industry in 1852 in Worcester County, Maryland, were particularly restricted because Black competition was considered an injury to the oyster business. The state spent a great deal of time on legislative and judicial activities attempting to force all free Africans to leave the state. However, by this time most of the oystermen had already left Maryland, settling their families, boats, and oysters in the same business on Staten Island. It was also during the 1850s and 1860s that Africans began to move to Staten Island from New York City, settling in rural Westfield in part to avoid the crowded city ghettos being rapidly occupied by Irish and German immigrants. Beginning with its earliest settlement, Staten Island was known for its high quality of oysters, especially those obtained from Prince's Bay, approximately four miles from what would become Sandy Ground. It is a historic community of African oystermen who, from the second half of the nineteenth through the early twentieth century, "delighted the palate of prosperous New Yorkers and residents of other American cities" by way of the products of their skill and labor. Seeding, dredging, hauling, sorting, and shucking oysters was physically demanding labor that brought worthwhile profits. But oysters were not Westfield's only economic base. Farming was also a major part of life, accomplished from what was once characterized as useless soil. The *Staten Island World* on September 3, 1910, referred to Sandy Ground as "the most fertile garden spot of Greater New York. The Agricultural Society invited people from down there who grow things to exhibit them at the county Fair."[19]

It was during Reconstruction that Sandy Ground Africans made the most headway and economic success in the oyster trade. The 1880s and 1890s saw the peak of prosperity; those years were Sandy Ground's "Golden Age." When oyster beds seeded in Lower New York Bay failed, Sandy Ground moved its commerce to Kill Van Kull, but after 1900 capitalism and racism took over the oyster business. New York City oyster merchants applied political influence, established racist hiring practices, mobilized racist stereotypes, and invested capital to solidify the industry as their domain. Through their control, "the New York State legislature imposed a licensing procedure for oystermen, requiring registration of beds, license costs, and taxation of bed by area. New laws covered bed tenure and transfer, and allowed the oyster merchants to accumulate thousands of acres throughout New York harbor. The merchants soon became oyster-capitalists, as they called themselves, owning vertically integrated corporations with hundreds of steam and diesel-powered boats, thousands of acres, and control over marketing and shipment of oysters."[20]

When the oyster capitalists began buying up shoreline property in Prince's Bay, the primary location for oyster planting, Sandy Ground and other local oystermen resisted by combining a "property-based approach with the traditional relations of the industry." Without shoreline access to the beds, loading and docking would be difficult. The Prince's Bay Oyster Company was formed in response to this dilemma. It bought several hundred feet of shoreline for "free use of those occupied in the oyster industry, whether owners of stock in the company or not." Unfortunately, this did not solve the problem. In response, the oyster capitalists denied the validity of "customary practices" and attacked the local oystermen, defining them, in print, as "self-interested, backwards, and ultimately, criminal." The oyster capitalists refused to allow natural growthers (oystermen who cultivate and gather oysters from natural beds) to work the planted beds after the end of the season, an act that pushed the common oysterman practically out of the business. In addition, the oyster capitalists refused to buy seed oysters from the natural growthers; they developed methods of oyster cultivation not dependent on natural beds.[21]

The finishing touch to the attack on Sandy Ground's oyster culture was the mobilization of a system of racism against the African oystermen. The oyster capitalists imposed racist labor practices, pigeonholing the hiring of Africans in positions as deckhands and shore hands. Most of the big companies would not hire African men at all. Needless to say, merchants would not buy seed or mature stock from Africans. Also, in 1910 the natural growthers were defined as bandits and renegades, and oyster capitalists knew they could make that tag stick because the physical and visual image of the "outlaw/criminal" natural growther was presented by the oyster capitalists as the African male. No more than one-third of the growthers were African; however, the oyster capitalists' trade journal, *The Oysterman*, carried racist cartoons implying that all growthers were both African and criminal.[22]

Oystering as a trade was all but finished in Sandy Ground by 1916 because of industrial pollution from New Jersey and the town's inability to compete with corporate-run agriculture and aquaculture. Ultimately, "competition with the whites caused many problems." Residents sought other occupations, such as wrought-iron mastery, midwifery, and well-digging. Some grew crops for self-consumption and sale, such as strawberries, sweet potatoes, melons, and tomatoes.[23]

The nineteenth-century demand for oysters had been a tremendous one and made a fortune for some in the business. In the early 1800s, Boston Crummell, father of future African American intellectual leader Alexander Crummell, was one of many who met the demand, as he was a New York caterer and oysterman who harvested and sold the bivalves. Like a famous fellow New York oysterman, Thomas Downing, Crummell was able to provide financial stability for his family in New York, at least through 1835. Between 1824 and 1834 Crummell is listed in *Longworth's Annual New York Directory* as an "oysterman," with his address at 6 Broad Street. In the 1834–1835 edition he is listed at 3 Amity Lane. *Longworth's American Almanac, New-York Register, and City Directory* for 1835–1836 lists Boston Crummell, again as an oysterman, located at 548 Broadway.[24]

But in the 1830s and 1840s, before oyster restaurants "fell into the realm of nostalgic recollection," the greatest concentration of these oyster cellars, as they were called, was located on Canal Street. For the tradesmen and businessmen of the district, oyster cellars provided breakfast, lunch, and dinner. A "Canal Street Plan" was offered, which was an all-you-can-eat setup for six cents. It was said that, if the establishment thought you were pigging out and getting too much for the money, then "a bad oyster would turn up to curb a glutton's appetite." For the proprietor, the bigger the oyster the more servings it would provide. Some oysters could be cut into three or four pieces, depending on size. A plain array of condiments accompanied raw oysters: lemon juice, vinegar, oil, salt, pepper, and mustard. Another fifteen cents added to your bill would purchase a bowl of stew, normally served for dinner, containing at least three dozen oysters, together with a "generous slab of bread and butter, salad, and a relish or two."[25]

Now, the menus at most cellars were limited to raw, fried, or stewed oysters. Well, there were cellars, and then there were *cellars*. Thomas Downing's oyster cellar on Broad Street was said to be "the very model of comfort and prosperity with its mirrored arcades, damask curtains, fine carpet, and chandelier." Oysters were considered an epicurean delight, and Downing made them his specialty. His menu established and sealed his reputation by offering "unusually elaborate dishes," such as scalloped oysters, oyster pie, fish with oyster sauce, and an especially delectable poached turkey stuffed with oysters. His award-winning pickled oysters, together with his boned and jellied turkeys, were particularly popular during the holidays.[26]

I have chosen here a few samples of coveted "receipts" from the nineteenth century for some of the same savory menu items that Downing prepared.

Nat's Receipt for Stuffing Boned Turkey

One pound of fresh pork minced, a loaf of bread, crust cut off, & soaked in water, 3/4 pound butter, nutmeg, onions, pepper & salt.

Receipt for Pickling Oysters

Take the Oysters from the shell as free from liquor as possible; put a layer of them into a jar—sprinkle them over with pepper corn and mace—then a layer of Oysters, then pepper [corn] and mace, until the jar is full; pour as much Vinegar into it as it will hold—then put the jar in a pot of cold water over a slow fire—when the water boils the Oysters are done. They will keep for any length of time."

Roast Turkey with Oyster Dressing

Make a stuffing of fine bread crumbs, minced parsley, pepper and salt to taste, and a large spoonful of melted butter. Chop 30 oysters fine and mix thoroughly into the bread crumbs. If the mixture [is] . . .

dry, moisten with a little of the oyster liquor. Fill the [cavity] . . . and body of the bird with this stuffing and sew up carefully, bend the legs and wings close to the body, place in a baking pan, and pour a large cup full of boiling water over the fowl. Roast 15 to the pound, basting often.

Scalloped Oysters

Take a quart or more of oysters from the liquor. Strain the liquor. Put a layer of oysters in a dish and cover with cornmeal and butter— Then a layer of oyster and so on until the dish is full[.] there should be some pepper on each layer. Po[u]re the liquor on and let it soak in[.] Put butter on top then bake until sufficiently brown.

Oyster Sauce

Put 1 pint of oysters in [a] saucepan and let them just come to boiling point. Strain and remove the beards; add to the oyster liquor [liquid] an equal quantity of milk & a liberal quantity of butter. When hot and smooth add the oysters. Heat again without boiling, season & serve. Thicken with flour smoothed in the milk if desirable.[27]

Thomas Downing's restaurant, which occupied the basements of two small buildings, was in the financial and shipping section of the city. There were also three other African-owned eating houses in this same district: Henry Johnson, located at 13 Fulton Market; Lawrence Chloe, whose place was at 5 Front Street; and Stephen Simmons, whose eating house employed White domestics. They were all frequented by White bankers, brokers, merchants, and other elite clientele, many who also resided in this district in stately homes, but it was Thomas Downing, George T. Downing's father, who became and remained the most famous African caterer and restaurateur in New York between 1830 and 1860.[28]

Thomas Downing's Oyster Bar was located at 3, 5, and 7 Broad Street at the corner of Wall Street. It became famous as one of the best eating establishments in New York. Not only was Downing's "the only house to attract the aristocracy as well as ladies in the company of their husbands or chaperones," it was also the favorite haunt of a regular crowd of distinguished businessmen from the Merchants' Exchange, nearby banks and customhouses, as well as leading politicians of the day and others "who believed in the marked superiority of colored cooks."[29]

Samuel J. Tilden was among those who enjoyed repasts at Downing's. An opponent of what would be referred to as Radical Reconstruction, Tilden won the popular vote in 1876 over his Republican opponent, Rutherford B. Hayes, in the most disputed and controversial presidential election of the nineteenth century. At a dinner for Senator Eugene Casserly, Tilden stated: "It is but yesterday that he [Casserly] and I were sitting over a chop at Downing's in Broad street, long before Broad street was the scene of the transactions which Mr. Schell knows are going on there now. There were no crowds, and but a few solitary persons around each of the tables of our respected and respectable colored friend who then was the Delmonico of New York."[30]

Countless others made Downing's their headquarters. Some of the most recognizable names of the day included William M. Price, district attorney; Samuel Swartwout, collector of the Port; Abraham R. Lawrence, president of the Harlem Railroad; and Jonathan I. Coddington, postmaster. There was also the Quaker banker and broker Jacob Barker; auctioneers Wilmerding and Jones; James B. Glentworth, "the pioneer of political pipe layers" and inspector of tobacco; Bobby White, president of the Manhattan Company; Fitz-Greene Halleck, bookkeeper for the author of *Marco Bozzaris* and *Fanny*, John Jacob Astor; and many more who saw Downing's as the place to "network," leave a message, or just to have a great meal. Reminiscences of life in the financial district of New York always included Downing's: "To rise early in the morning, to get breakfast, to go down town to the counting-house of the firm, to open and read letters,—to go out and do some business, either at the Custom house, bank or elsewhere, until twelve, then to take a lunch and a glass of wine at Delmonico's; or a few raw oysters at Downing's."[31]

Thomas Downing was born in January 1791, in Chincoteague, Accomac County, Virginia. His parents were freed by a Captain John Downing, who was a Methodist. Captain Downing supposedly adhered to the doctrine of limiting Methodist membership to nonslaveholders. Along with the usual chores engaged in as a boy, Thomas Downing went fishing, raked for oysters, dug clams, and caught terrapin. Henry A. Wise, who would later become governor of Virginia, was one of his boyhood playmates.

As the troops marched north in the war of 1812, so did Thomas Downing. Stopping in Philadelphia, he went to live at the famous Joe Head House, where the proprietor, Joseph Head, kept a private Gentleman's Restaurant and Club House. It was while living there that he learned how to prepare terrapin, creating a recipe that thereafter remained the family's secret. Many years later, New York's Astor House was the scene of a meeting of connoisseurs who did their part as tasters in a competition of stewed terrapin preparations. Vying for the number one spot were cooks from Philadelphia, Washington, Baltimore, and New York. When the final judgment was made, "the award of superiority was given to Downing's preparation."[32]

Thomas Downing arrived in New York City in 1819, bringing with him his knowledge of oysters and terrapin and a desire to go into the business of preparing and serving food. He presented a letter of introduction to Mr. Wm. Hudson, who turned him over to his nephew Philip A. Bell, who became the editor of *The Elevator*, a paper published in San Francisco, and co-owner of the *Colored American* newspaper. Mr. Bell helped Downing gain employment with William Bunker, keeper of Bunker House, on Broadway. Shortly thereafter Downing opened his own business at 5 Broad Street.

Downing studied the nature and habits of oysters. He soon knew and understood every minute detail of every aspect of their formation, growth, and age. His expertise enhanced his business, so much so that it was soon enlarged to include 3, 5, and 7 Broad Street. In describing Thomas Downing's routine, his son George has stated: "For a long time he used to leave his bed at two o'clock in the morning, take a skiff, row himself across the North River to the Jersey Flats, which in those days were loaded with superior native oysters. There he would tong as many as time admitted, and row himself back across the river and offer his delicious fresh bivalves to a continually increasing number of customers. His fame spread in all directions."[33]

The demand for oysters meant that competition for the best ones was tremendously high. Downing was known to pay the highest price for the best. However, he had to employ different "devices" to get what he needed. Sometimes he would be waiting at a dock at midnight to bargain for the best oysters, while other proprietors would be at home asleep. On other occasions he would take a boat out to an incoming vessel, bargain, and transfer the choicest goods to his boat before it reached the docks. He would then park his load at a point on the wharf, go back to the oyster vessel, which was now docked, and bargain for a portion of the oysters that the vessel had left. Thus, he assisted the captain in selling more easily the less desirable oysters. Often he would bargain for an entire cargo, forcing his competitors to plead and negotiate with *him*.

Downing was said to be a favorite with the oyster boat captains because Downing paid them well and "treated them in a generous manner when they came to his house."[34]

Downing's was the place to be, and it was the fashion for the elites to bring their guests to lunch at 5 Broad Street. Downing's reputation spread across the Atlantic. Lord Morpeth, Charles Dickens, and many more well-known foreigners visited his establishment and ate his fried oysters. Downing shipped fried and pickled oysters to the West Indies, as well as large numbers of raw, pickled, and fried oysters to Europe. Europeans knew only too well who the reigning kings of food preparation were. Colonel Harmon Thorne was said to have created a sensation in Paris during his residence in Europe when he spared no expense in having his receptions stand out in regal splendor beyond anyone else's. In order to outrival all competitors, he made sure his guests feasted on fried oysters prepared by Thomas Downing at 3 Broad Street in New York, which were said to taste as though they had been prepared right there on the spot. In 1847 Downing prepared and shipped a barrel of very lovely pickled oysters to Queen Victoria. The Queen responded to his gift by asking Com. Joseph Comstock to deliver to Mr. Downing a letter accompanied by a gold chronometer watch engraved with her initials.[35]

By way of his food, Downing was connected to the initial opening of a number of businesses. His culinary preparations were enjoyed during numerous events such as the launching of ships and steamboats, including the introduction of steam in transatlantic navigation, the early establishment of the express business, the extension of the Erie Railroad to Dunkirk (when more than a hundred guests were invited to take a ride to Lake Erie), and with mining and coal operations, and canal navigations. His services were also sought after for receptions, luncheons, and dinners for annual elections at banks and insurance companies, and on government and other official occasions.[36]

Holidays were other occasions when Downing's catering services were a must. His notices to his customers in the *New York Herald* advertised his preparations of pickled oysters, boned turkeys, and alamode beef, jellied or without, "for the adornment of the New Year's Day Table," which could be "sent to any part of the City, Brooklyn, or Jersey City, or elsewhere." It was, therefore, not always necessary for Downing to be physically on the premises. Sometimes it was just his oysters that took a bow.[37]

While he rendered services at various venues, he was never one to take credit where it did not belong. In a notice posted in the November 9, 1844, issue of the *New York Herald*, Downing issued a correction concerning the late dinner served on board the steamship *Great Western*:

> Sir—I do most respectfully beg leave to correct a mistake in your paper—that is to say, that the entertainment on board of the Great Western, for the reception of the invited guests, on Wednesday last, which was supposed to have been got up by me. Although I was not there; and as usual furnished the oysters; yet I had no hand in getting up the dinner, and did not arrange the table; and if I had, I could not have done it with more taste and elegance than it was arranged by my friend, the steward of the ship, Mr. Crofford.[38]

Thomas Downing's invoice letterhead from the 1850s reads:

> New York Bought of T. DOWNING. OYSTER AND DINING SALOON, Established, 1820 3 and 5 BROAD STREET, N.Y.

and to the left of "Bought of T. Downing," printed in a box, it reads:

> Pickled and Fried Oysters for Shipping and Family use; prepared to keep in any climate. Parties supplied with all the necessary articles, and superintended when required Oysters delivered to any part of this or adjacent cities. Confectionery, &c.

Thomas Downing's business card reads:

> DOWNING'S OYSTER & DINING SALOON ESTABLISHED, 1820. 3 & 5 BROAD STREET, N.Y. Pickled and Fried Oysters for Shipping and Family use; prepared to keep in any climate. Parties supplied with all the necessary articles, and superintended when required. Oysters delivered to any part of this or adjacent cities. CONFECTIONERY, &C.[39]

Since Downing was no stranger to handling public functions, and because Charles Dickens was no stranger to Downing's morsels, it should come as no surprise that Thomas Downing was asked to cater the Boz Ball. The Boz Ball was held on February 14, 1842, to honor thirty-year-old Charles Dickens, who had arrived in Boston with his wife the day before.

The Boz Ball, held at the Park Theater in New York, was termed "the greatest affair in modern times." The decorations and ornaments for the occasion were described as elaborate, with great splendor and taste. As many as two thousand persons showed up with tickets, as well as another five hundred who were guests of the members of the reception and planning committees. One-term ex-mayor Philip Hone, a wealthy Whig merchant and friend of John Jacob Astor and Presidents John Quincy Adams and Martin Van Buren, was a member of the reception committee and instrumental in planning the ball. One of the planning committee's decisions was to have refreshments set up on several floors and also in what was called the Green Room, which was set aside for members of the committees and their families. Hone was one of Downing's regular clientele. The preparation of food and libations was placed in the hands of Thomas Downing, "the great man of oysters," who, Hone recorded in his diary, received twenty-two hundred dollars for the evening.[40]

"The great man of oysters" attracted many virulent racists to his restaurant. These patrons loved the food prepared by African people but hated the African people who prepared it. George Templeton Strong, one of New York's leading attorneys, placed himself firmly in this category. His diary makes several references to eating at Downing's oyster house. On December 30, 1859, Strong "dined on roast oysters at Downing's, and spent the afternoon on duty at Bank for Savings." On April 13, 1860, he wrote, "John Van Buren at the counter [at Downing's Oyster Cellar] devouring his shilling's worth of bivalves."[41]

At least two additional diary entries mention him having lunch at Downing's. One entry indicates that on one "hot and busy day," Strong took his "usual lunch of roast clams at Downings's." We can see that churchgoer Strong was all in favor of dining at Downing's, but he was in firm opposition to clergy or laypersons representing Downing's church, St. Philip's African Episcopal Church, at the Episcopal conventions. With the help of attorney John Jay, grandson of Supreme Court Chief Justice John Jay, Thomas Downing and fellow African vestrymen of St. Philip's won representation for St. Philip's, after waging an eight-year battle. Strong, a vestryman at Trinity Church, expressed his personal views on the battle won by the Africans of St. Philip's: "Another Revolution. John Jay's annual motion carried at last, and the nigger delegation admitted into the Dioc.[esan] Convention. J. J. [John Jay] must be unhappy— aching void, as when one's stomach liver & other innards have been dexterously taken out." Three years later it was still a pill Strong could not swallow. On Sunday, October 12, 1856, he recorded, "Niggerism has got into the [Episcopal] General Convention at Philadelphia. . . . It was that Proteus of Abolitionism in a new disguise."[42]

Strong, like many others in the city, considered lunch at Downing's and oyster eating a mainstay of culinary life. No wonder oysters wound up as the center of blame for an outbreak of cholera, as well as a few deaths within those segments of society. In his diary Strong mentions specific individuals known to have enjoyed the bivalves who were among the victims, thereby causing an "oyster panic" in New York. On October 31, 1854, Strong wrote that even though the oyster panic was subsiding, the numbers normally found at Downing's and George W. Brown's (apparently another oyster restaurateur) were still down because of the scare. Downing may have lost an enormous amount of business, but according to Strong, he managed not to lose his sense of humor. Strong writes, "The former venerable Ethiop [Downing] says: 'If any gentleman can prove he died of the oysters I works in, I'll pay his expenses to Greenwood [Cemetery].'"[43]

Thomas Downing's establishment was always categorized as of a "leading and profitable character." Highly respected throughout New York City, Downing himself was characterized as "benevolent, kind, and liberal minded, his head was always willing, his heart ready, and his hands open to 'give'" as well as "one of the most respectable . . . aged colored men in this city. His private character is without reproach."[44]

No doubt one of the reasons Downing earned such accolades was because of the actions he took when the great fire broke out in December 1835. When the water supply was exhausted, he had the firemen roll out barrels of cider and vinegar from his storage loft to quench the flames. Downing was one of about six persons, "who by indefatigable and somewhat hazardous exertions, saved the buildings in the rear of the South Dutch church from burning, although we had neither engine nor water, but . . . VINEGAR, several pipes of which happened to be in the adjoining yard. Nothing but these exertions of Downing and a few others prevented the conflagration from extending through to Broad street. A million dollars at least was thus saved from destruction."[45]

If that was not enough, one of New York's leading newspapers was greatly indebted to Thomas Downing for its continued existence. Downing loaned the owner of the *New York Herald* ten thousand dollars to carry on the paper through the bank panic. "Had not Downing come to the pecuniary assistance of the elder Bennett [the owner]," states New

York's *Town Topics*, "the *Herald* would not have lived a year. To the day of his death Bennett was grateful for this service and often acknowledged it by editorial notices of Downing's business that could not have been bought for any money." It is interesting to note that many years later, when the *Herald* was under different ownership and was supporting the views and policies of President Andrew Johnson, the paper was said to have commented, "Downing [son, George T.] had better stick to his oysters and let politics alone." This was an interesting statement when you consider that it was oysters and Downing family politics that allowed the *Herald* to exist as long as it did.[46]

Now that the accolades from some of his patrons have been noted, it is time for us to remember that Thomas Downing was a man of African descent living in nineteenth-century America. No one would deny that his culinary talents were considerable. However, this simply was not enough to shield him or any other person of African descent from an environmental vise designed to crush and degrade.

Everyone loves a talented chef, someone who can prepare a meal for you that stays in your memory, your psyche, long after the tantalizing morsels have been washed down with a good Chardonnay or Syrah, iced tea, or Kool-Aid, and long after the heavenly aromas have dissipated. This was how people felt about Downing's preparations. However, everyday existence for Downing and all other free Africans in New York was saturated with discrimination, in employment, public places and transportation, education, and professional organizations, "firmly established not by law but by custom." In fact, these customs were firmly established by *law*. As historian Edgar J. McManus notes, "Their [free Blacks] isolation was complete. The Negroes were in a very real sense a population in quarantine, trapped in a system of racial bondage in many ways as cruel and intolerable as slavery."[47]

As noted, many of Thomas Downing's clientele were businesspeople in the transportation sector. However, when it came to public transportation in New York, even if you were a highly successful and tremendously popular restaurateur, it did not matter how delicious your meat dishes or how succulent your sauces, or how highly esteemed your cuisine, or the difficulty your clientele had doing without it. Up to the passage of Charles Sumner's Civil Rights Act of 1875, Africans in New York lived firmly under "Jim Crow." Thomas Downing—one of the wealthiest African businessmen in New York City, whose oyster house was patronized by the wealthiest of Whites, including the president of the Harlem Railroad—was beaten by agents of the Harlem Railroad when he attempted to ride on that line.[48] The *Colored American* noted that:

> The abuse of Downing by the Harlem Rail Road agents, is an act which we hope will be dealt with according to its merits. Downing is an intelligent, respectable citizen, possessing considerable property, and universally esteemed by those who have been accustomed to visit his refectory. . . . But Downing is a *colored man*, and therefore may be kicked out of a Rail Road car and wantonly beaten at pleasure. It is not the first time that this shameful abuse of colored people has been perpetrated by the agents of the Harlem Road. A very respectable, well dressed colored man (an Elder in a Presbyterian church) and his wife were turned out of one of the cars in a manner equally unceremonious, a month or two ago. In that case, however, we believe no blows were inflicted. It is time those outrages were put a stop to.[49]

Downing took the railroad to court. As expected, "the jury returned a verdict against the plantiff." This would not be the last time Downing's presence on public transportation would wind up recounted in the news.[50]

Downing was, of course, not the only African to experience discrimination and violent reaction to attempts to use public facilities. Henry Scott, New York's famous African pickle merchant, was prompted by his own experiences and those of friends to write an editorial titled, "To the Public," concerning racial discrimination in public accommodations. The fact is, in the 1830s, a driver of a public conveyance, for example, "could use a whip to force a Negro to stay off an omnibus, and a threat to invoke the law would meet with laughter." A pamphlet issued in 1837 by the New York Zoological Institute, located at 37 Bowery, clearly stated, "People of color are not permitted to enter, except when in attendance upon [white] children and families." Restaurant owner Thomas Van Rensselaer decided to challenge the Zoological Institute by showing up with his family. He and his family were stopped at the door and not allowed entry. He was forcibly removed by two officers but not before he was punched in the chest.[51]

Augustus Washington, "a man of color" and an acclaimed Black daguerreotypist, stated in 1851 in an issue of the *African Repository*, an organ of the American Colonization Society:

[Africans] are shut out from all the offices of profit and honor, and from the most honorable and lucrative pursuits of industry, and confined as a class to the most menial and servile positions in society. . . . They are excluded in most of the States from all participation in the government; taxed without their consent, and compelled to submit to unrighteous laws, strong as the nation that enacts them, and cruel as the grave. They are also excluded from every branch of mechanical industry; the workshop, the factory, the counting-room, and every avenue to wealth and respectability, is closed against them.

In other words, whatever his or her wealth or education or talents, the African is excluded from social and economic equality and freedom. African status in America was clear: "whether slave or free, . . . the colored is by nature a subordinate race; and that [under] no circumstances, can [the Negro] be considered equal to the white."[52]

New York Whites were determined to do their part in maintaining White supremacy. With economic, judicial, educational, social, and political discrimination in place, the only thing left was mob terrorism against Africans. In New York in 1834 there were a number of terrorist attacks targeting both Africans and abolitionists, organized and engineered by mobs of working-class Whites as well as merchants, bankers, clergymen, lawyers, and others of property and standing. The continuous violence resulted in a full-scale massacre beginning on July 7 of that year. Over a three-to-four-day period anti-abolitionist terrorists murdered Africans, inflicted injuries on many more, and severely damaged or demolished at least sixty dwellings, six churches including the St. Philips African Episcopal Church, and other homes and meeting places that were owned and frequented mostly by Africans.[53]

Philip Hone, a lover of Thomas Downing's viands and certainly one of Downing's biggest culinary fans, attended a meeting held on August 27, 1835, by (in his words) "those opposed to the incendiary proceedings of the abolitionists." Hone concluded that he needed to attend this meeting in order that "persons of character should be present" to convince southerners "that the incendiaries constitute an inconsiderable proportion of our citizens, and to prevent any violence which might possibly be attempted by turbulent persons." Hone's personal diary reveals, as diaries usually do, a person's true thoughts. Hone's March 25, 1842, diary entry is titled "Abolition and Fanaticism." He records that a member

of the House of Representatives resigned his seat under pressure because of his introducing a set of resolutions justifying the slave revolt on
board the *Creole,* as well as his "asserting other ultra-Abolition doctrines,
which he afterwards withdrew, but he had gone too far."[54]

For free Africans fervently serving the cause, their mission was something more than philosophical or moral posturing. It was personal. Free
Africans understood that they carried an inextricable bond with their
sisters and brothers in slavery; that they were joined together at the
head and chest, body and soul. New York Africans who worked as chefs,
cooks and caterers, and restaurateurs in their own places of business as
well as in first-class hotel dining rooms or private homes not only shared
with their enslaved brethren the culinary customs of Mother Africa, such
as roasted duck and other poultry, oyster stews, green turtle soup and
terrapin, seafood and vegetable stews, fried sweet potatoes, roast partridge and other game meats, they also shared common life-and-death
struggles with those who made the plantation and major city lifestyle,
culinary and otherwise, possible. It is for this reason that, as Maritcha
Remond Lyons points out in her autobiographical narrative, "Memories
of Yesterdays, All of Which I Saw and Part of Which I Was," "Every
thinking man and woman was a volunteer in the famous 'underground
railroad.'" Lyons's parents' connection with the "railroad," a part of their
business that they referred to as "keeping a cake and apple stand," had
helped a thousand people reach freedom through their "station" in New
York.[55]

It is not surprising then that Thomas Downing's establishment, his
oyster house, was said to be the New York City headquarters of the Underground Railroad. Hundreds of fugitive slaves were fed and clothed in
his spacious cellar before being guided on their way to Canada. Thomas
and Rebecca Downing's children would naturally be brought into the
family business, in more ways than one. Beginning in the late 1830s,
the eldest son, George T., worked diligently together with his father in
political, antislavery, and educational organizations in New York City.

George T. Downing was born on December 30, 1819, in New York
City. He began his business career in 1842 as a caterer at 564 Broadway,
at Fourth Street, in New York. He was just a youth when he became an
agent in the "railroad." George would prove, by way of his activities
in Rhode Island, New York, and Washington, DC, to be just as fierce a
fighter for equal rights as his dad was, if not more so.[56]

The times never allowed Downing to be soft. The second Fugitive Slave Act was signed into law by President Millard Fillmore and passed by Congress on September 18, 1850. Since the law threatened the liberty of *all* Africans, emigration to Africa, Canada, and elsewhere became a major topic of discussion. Having established successful culinary businesses here, George T. Downing felt the solution was to stay and fight. He and other New York African leaders formed a watchdog organization in response to the new law—the Committee of Thirteen (not to be confused with the US Senate's Committee of Thirteen)—which sought to resist execution of the Fugitive Slave Act as well as of colonization and racial discrimination against Africans in New York City and Brooklyn. George T. Downing's Committee of Thirteen was composed of his father, Thomas Downing, with Dr. James McCune Smith, Philip A. Bell, William J. Wilson, T. Joiner White, Robert Hamilton, Ezekiel Dias, Jeremiah Powers, Junius C. Morrell, John T. Raymond, William Burnett, and John J. Zuille, who served as chair of the committee in the 1850s.[57]

In such a fiercely segregated mid-nineteenth-century New York, African organizations made unified attempts to educate their children with private subscriptions and limited New York State money. *All* New Yorkers with an income were taxed, and those taxes paid for *all* schools. Due to racism and segregation, African children could attend only two schools; both were designated for "colored" children. Concerned about the lack and poor quality of educational opportunities available to African children, and obviously in a position to make contributions, it was restaurateurs George T. Downing and Thomas Van Rensselaer, sailor's home keepers William P. Powell and Albro Lyons, Alexander Crummell, Dr. James McCune Smith, Philip A. Bell, Charles B. Ray, and other African caterers, restaurateurs, educators and businessmen who incorporated and created the New York Society for the Promotion of Education Among Colored Children, founded in July, 1846. The Society's two schools were "subject to the general supervision and direction of the Board of Education for the city and county of New York, *but [were] under the immediate government and management of the said corporation* . . . ." (italics added). Pickle merchant Henry Scott was its president in 1848 and 1849. Those same years lists Dr. James McCune Smith as the Society's treasurer. John J. Zuille, a contributor to and sometimes manager of the *Colored American* newspaper, was a teacher at Colored Public School No. 2 in the 1840s.[58]

Even though attempts were made by the Black "Who's Who" of New York to fight and resist racial discrimination and to educate Black children beyond the confines of food service, cooking and cuisine were still major occupations for Black people in the nineteenth century. Unfortunately, becoming a member of the food service community, and thereby maintaining your "place" in society, did not remove the precept of African inferiority or lessen the incidence of violence and brutality against Blacks in America. With this in mind, stepping forward in time just a bit, I want to mention Fanny Belkizer, a well-known African cook for well-to-do families in New York, and wife of the well-known and highly respected African caterer William Belkizer. Mrs. Belkizer recounted in writing what happened to her in December 1886. She wanted to speak and tell the story herself, but it was her husband who read her statement to a *New York Times* reporter. Mrs. Belkizer had attended a society meeting one Monday evening, and on her way home passed the corner of Thirty-Third Street and Eighth Avenue. Officer McGinley of Captain Washburn's district was standing on this corner, and when Mrs. Belkizer passed he made insulting remarks to her. When she let McGinley know that she resented his remarks he kicked her in her side. He then struck her in the face with his club, breaking her jaw bone in two places and dislocating it on one side. He then arrested her and locked her in a cell overnight, where she received no medical attention. When she appeared in court before the judge the next morning in blood-stained clothing and unable to speak—her jaw hanging limp and bloody—McGinley told the court Mrs. Belziker had been drunk and disorderly the night before. It was during this hearing she was fined ten dollars plus costs, based on the sole testimony of Policeman McGinley.[59]

Since every African woman, whether cook, nurse, or teacher, is considered a person of *ill repute, a slut and a whore by nature*, did McGinley utter insulting comments to Mrs. Belziker along those lines? As Dr. Evelyn Higginbotham states, "Violence figured preeminently in racialized constructions of [gender]. From the days of slavery, the social construction and representation of black [gender] reinforced violence, rhetorical and real, against black women and men." Continued belief in the precept or ideology of African inferiority found its base in the 1829 Supreme Court opinion in *State v. Mann*, authored by Judge Thomas Ruffin, who ruled that slaveholders, whether permanent or temporary, had absolute authority over their slaves and could not be found guilty of committing violence against them, because "the power of the master must be absolute, to render the submission of the slave perfect."[60]

Fanny Belkizer's assault was a continued example of the mentality that decided one of the most devastating legal cases for African women in the history of this country: *State of Missouri vs. Celia, a Slave*. A child of fourteen when purchased, Celia performed the duties of a cook. Her primary function, however, was to provide sex for the sixty-year-old, "active churchman," Robert Newsom. Despite at least two Missouri statutes that were explicit in assuring women the protections of the law against such abuse, Celia was hung after she killed Newsom when he tried to force himself on her while she was ill and pregnant with Newsom's second or third child.[61]

Judge A. Leon Higginbotham's and Anne F. Jacobs's invaluable article "The 'Law Only as an Enemy': The Legitimization of Racial Powerlessness through the Colonial and Antebellum Criminal Laws of Virginia" explains "the duality of the slave" and outlines the "ten precepts of American slavery" (a duality and precepts just as applicable to the free African in America in the nineteenth century, and also to African Americans in the twenty-first). As in Celia's case, the African is "always property, sometimes a person, and never a citizen." Higginbotham quotes the abolitionist William Goodell who states that "the slave 'can know *law only as an enemy, and not as a friend*'" because the slave is always "chattel," but "becomes '*a person*' [only] whenever he [or she] is to be *punished*! . . . He [or she] is under the *control* of law, though *unprotected by* law [original italics]." The guiding principle is that Africans must be made to realize and accept their place and limitations—that is, their "wretched status." This "wretched status," predicated on the precept of inferiority, is the base on which present-day culinary apartheid and the culinary master narrative both still stand.[62]

Any disrespect or assault experienced was sanctioned *by law*. Frederick Douglass understood this when he wrote a letter to restaurant proprietor Thomas Van Rensselaer in 1847, congratulating Van Rensselaer on starting the *Ram's Horn*, a Black newspaper that began publication in New York on January 1, 1847. Douglass's letter also mentions the editor of the *New York Sun*, who attacked Douglass in the May 13 issue, criticizing a speech Douglass gave before the American Anti-Slavery Society during which Douglass criticized the treatment of Africans in America. The editor stated, "*Freedom of speech should receive, in this country, the greatest* latitude . . . . *There is, however, a limit to this very freedom of speech. We cannot be permitted to go into a gentleman's house, accept his hospitality, yet* abuse *his fare, and we have no right to abuse a country under whose government we are safely residing and securely protected* [original italics]." Douglass analyzed the editorial, and in sharing his thoughts with Van Rensselaer he stated that "a gentleman's house and the government of this country are wholly dissimilar." He then makes a clever comparison between a cookshop (restaurant) and the government of the United States, and he tells Van Rensselaer that when he makes this comparison no disrespect is geared toward him. Douglass writes:

> Let cook shop represent Country—"Bill of Fare"—"Bill of Rights"; and the "Chief Cook"—Commander-in-chief. . . . Enters editor of the *Sun* with a keen appetite. He reads the bill of fare. It contains the names of many palatable dishes. He asks the cook for soup, he gets "dish water." For salmon, he gets a serpent; for beef, he gets bullfrogs; for ducks, he gets dogs; for salt, he gets sand; for pepper, he gets powder; and for vinegar, he gets gall; in fact, he gets for you the very opposite of everything for which you ask, and which from the bill of fare, and loudmouthed professions, you had a right to expect. This is just the treatment which the colored people receive in this country at the hand of this government. Its Bill of Rights is to practice towards us a bill of wrongs. Its self-evident truths are self-evident lies. Its majestic liberty, malignant tyranny. The foundation of this government—the great Constitution itself—is nothing more than a compromise with man-stealers."[63]

One of Downing's Oyster Dining Saloon's most frequent patrons, George Templeton Strong, was in total sync with America's ideology, his words reflecting today's sociopolitical thought as it refers to culinary apartheid, when he stated, "Our slavery system says . . . You and your descendants are and shall be forever deprived of every privilege, right, and attribute of humanity which can be directly or indirectly reached by our legislation or our social system. Being slaves, you are, of course, not entitled to the fruit or benefits of your own labor."[64]

Well, woven into law was racist ideology, passed down, just like recipes, by courts and legislation. The following year after Strong wrote those words, the Supreme Court decided Missouri's most famous slave law case, *Dred Scott v. Sandford*, which was "by far the most articulate and authoritative defense of the precept of black inferiority ever mount-ed by the American legal process." This decision clarified for all time that *the founding of the United States never took into consideration the inclusion of Africans as citizens or members of the society.* Therefore, Africans, slave or free, *could never count on protection from the courts,* much less protection from marginalization and being made invisible in America's social and culinary history.[65]

Thomas Downing—the African restaurateur and caterer, prominent in the African community life of New York City, and about whom it was said he had made "three fortunes"—was fully aware of this when he was summoned (one source states that it was actually his son, George T.) to the state supreme court in 1860, for refusing to state the value of his holdings. When Downing went to court he let the judge know that he would refuse to take the oath, refuse to be sworn in, because, "by the Dred Scott decision, he was deprived of all the rights of a citizen, and was held to be a mere chattel." In other words, since "property could not own property," why should he be subjected "to be[ing] examined as a judgement debtor"? Now, this stumped the judge temporarily, and "an application was made to Judge Sutherland, to settle the qu[e]stion." Sutherland stopped to take careful aim at this one because he could in effect break the law. Sutherland "decided that for the present purpose, he [Downing] might be considered a human being, and a citizen." Sutherland's decision, then, did take the position that the *Dred Scott* decision was illegal—or could simply be set aside, for the moment. And, at this moment, we must note Judge Higginbotham's treatise on the duality of the slave (or any person of African descent). Downing, and all free Africans, according to the *Dred Scott* decision, were merely "slaves without masters," and thereby just as powerless as the slave. Slave or free, as with Celia, the African could become a "person" for the purpose of enforcing criminal law against him or her, making him and her "under the *control* of law, though *unprotected by* law."[66]

Being hauled into court in the attempt to hold his finances up to scrutiny did not stop Downing from continuing to use the money he made from his restaurant and catering to contribute to the cause of his people. The Downings gave to and were involved in many venues created to help their African brethren get a financial foothold. In July 1850, a couple of months before the Fugitive Slave Act was passed, George T. Downing became a member of the executive committee, with Frederick Douglass as a vice president, of the American League of Colored Laborers, which was formed for the purpose of uniting African men in the trades, to foster training and administer advice in the agricultural, commercial, and mechanical arts, in order that members could move toward and gain the position of the self-employed artisan. The league assisted in setting up a fund to help Africans start up independent businesses, such as restaurants, barbershops, funeral homes, and so on, because there was a sharp difference in annual earnings between White and African in the same occupation, resulting from the dependency of Africans on White business owners for employment.

Since the African's job ceiling had been limited to occupations defined as dirty, brawn only, or labor intensive, African cooks and caterers, waiters, domestics, and longshoremen were especially vulnerable to discrimination. For example, the proportion of Africans in positions such as waiters was high; however, African waiters actually did not compete with Whites for better-paying jobs in that category, because Africans were restricted to the hotel or restaurant that offered the lowest income in the business. In addition to working these lowest-rung employees for much longer hours, these houses offered low or no gratuities, a key element of income, which thereby affected total annual earnings. The same was true for many in the catering industry (which also included the wait staff). Most were sent to second-class "houses" or functions rather than to first-class dining halls.[67]

Still of concern to Thomas Downing and members of the United Anti-Slavery Society of the City of New York were their brethren who were still forced to work for free. Formed on December 5, 1855, the organization held its first meeting at the hall of the Phoenix Society. Pro-slavery sentiment was just as strong with New York merchants as it was with White immigrants. Fear of the consequences of abolitionist activities— African economic competition—controlled the mindset of European immigrants in New York. Racist ranting from politicians and newspapers succeeded in inflaming and inciting economically insecure White workers. The displacement of African workers that took place, however, was the exact reverse of what was being preached.[68]

Antiwar and anti–draft law editorials flooded the media, and not much else was needed to start one of the bloodiest race massacres in US history. The signing of the Emancipation Proclamation on January 1, 1863, spelled for Whites an unleashing of an even greater pool of labor competitors. Then, in March 1863, the Conscription Act was enacted, because of the Civil War's manpower shortage. All male citizens between twenty and thirty-five and all unmarried men between thirty-five and forty-five years of age were subject to military duty. Eligible men were entered into a lottery; however, those who could hire a substitute or pay the government three hundred dollars could avoid service.[69]

On the first day of the so-called Draft Riots, violence was confined to military and government buildings. By afternoon, however, mob violence had escalated, turning into wholesale terrorism against all Africans and anything that symbolized African economic, social, or political independence. Whites attacked an African fruit vendor and a nine-year-old boy on the corner of Broadway and Chambers Streets. A mob visited Downing's Oyster House on the first evening of the riots, where it was said the police put down a "demonstration" before moving on to try to quell other terrorist activities. During the five days of mob terrorism, in which longshoremen took a very active part, Africans were murdered, and their property and that of any one who supported them was destroyed. Since the real reason for the violence was labor competition, terrorism was also centered on cooks and waiters and other Africans tied to menial employment at hotels and restaurants.[70]

Maritcha Lyons lived with her family in New York at the time of the Draft Riots. Her mother, Mary Joseph Marshall, had worked for the Remond catering family of Salem, Massachusetts. Maritcha's grandparents Joseph and Elizabeth Hewlett Marshall had previously settled in New York, purchasing four lots in what is now the Central Park area. Her grandmother later opened a bakery in the basement of their main house after her husband died. Maritcha's mother married Albro Lyons, who went into a business partnership with William P. Powell. It has been mentioned that Lyons and Powell were both trustees, along with George T. Downing, of the New York Society for the Promotion of Education Among Colored Children. One could always find William P. Powell and Albro Lyons on the front lines fighting for equal rights and abolition just like the Downings. Powell also ran the Colored Seaman's Boarding Home, which had been instrumental in securing jobs for African seamen, such as cooks and stewards, on board ships "at the highest wages."[71]

Since all Blacks were targets, especially those with means, it is little wonder that the mob made three attempts to break into Maritcha's family home. The third attempt was successful and resulted in its destruction. Fortunately, the family managed to take refuge with a neighbor, and they were later taken by the police to the Roosevelt Street ferry. The family reached the Williamsburg section of Brooklyn before continuing on to Massachusetts, where they stayed with the Remonds for a while. The Lyons were welcomed at the Remonds', because of Mrs. Lyons's former association with the family, and because Remond's daughter Maritcha (whose first name had been given to Maritcha Lyons), had been Maritcha Lyons's mother's bridesmaid. Providence, Rhode Island, was the final destination as a place of residence for Maritcha Lyons's family. Albro Lyons traveled back and forth to New York until he was certain he would not be able to revive his business. He finally decided that Rhode Island would have to be home to the trade he had learned in his youth— the manufacture of ice cream.[72]

The battle was certainly not over. Africans in America cooked and provided culinary sustenance for Black, and especially White, fighting forces. They also carried arms and fought valiantly in the Civil War, believing that freedom and justice would be rewards within their reach. In a few years the Civil War was over, but the emancipation battle continued. Blacks would still command America's kitchens, but some would also take on the fight, by way of elected office, to help attain those dreams of freedom and justice so justly earned.

8

RUNNING THE KITCHEN
AND RUNNING FOR OFFICE

*T*he Civil War's manpower shortage that led to the 1863 Conscription Act and the Draft Riots soon found a remedy in the recruitment of Africans, who had been imported in large numbers into tidewater Georgia and South Carolina to expand the state economy and build the wealthy rice aristocracies. Africans served as fighting soldiers and in every other capacity. Now, when it came to feeding those troops there were a few African culinary royals who were known for their ability to entice volunteers. Their support of the effort to end slavery by feeding the troops was just as important as those who carried guns into battle. These culinary royals emerged from the occupation of caterer or restaurateur, or even barber, to become leading African political figures during Reconstruction.

Massachusetts Senator Charles Sumner communicated with his African confidant, the caterer and future Massachusetts legislator Joshua B. Smith on December 25, 1862, stating he was happy to assure him that the president was now in favor of employing African troops at posts on the Mississippi River, in South Carolina, and in other southern areas. George

T. Downing wrote to Charles Sumner a couple of months later, declaring, "I speak with a knowledge of the feelings of your fellow citizens of African descent when I urge upon you the importance of some assurance being given the above class of citizens, by the government, that they shall have all the protection . . . for the defence of their country . . . this is most important to secure colored volunteers in the north; a proclamation from the President to this effect would have a tremendous influence in obtaining volunteers."[1]

Although President Lincoln now wanted former slaves to sign up, he had a real problem with the idea of Africans as recruiters. All of that changed, however.[2]

George T. Downing came very highly recommended for the post of quartermaster in a letter dated July 13, 1863, from Frederick Douglass to Secretary of War Edwin McMasters Stanton. After praising Downing as an experienced businessman, one with character and ability, Douglass stated that "the appointment of Mr. Downing would have an excellent effect upon the colored citizens all over the north and tend to facilitate colored enlistments . . . in Pennsylvania and elsewhere." Subsequently, Downing wrote to Charles Sumner, stating, "I am the more assured of my ability to discharge the duties of a Quartermaster with credit to myself and in the interest of the government." Downing also asked Sumner if he might be able to secure Downing's name. Sumner apparently took it a step further and wrote a letter of recommendation for George T. Downing "for the post of Quartermaster, in our colored forces, as a *commissary* [original underscore]."[3]

Secretary of War Stanton must have believed in the soundness of the argument. He was, after all, used to depending on John Sidney Butter, another African who had been in Stanton's service prior to 1861. Butter became one of the top-rung, first-class caterers in Washington, DC, and because of his reputation in September 1871 he was given a "confidential messenger" position in the US State Department under Secretary Hamilton Fish. Stanton made George T. Downing a brigadier quartermaster for "colored" troops. Downing was instrumental in organizing several African regiments in Rhode Island and Massachusetts, "but not until he obtained from Governor [John A.] Andrews . . . of Massachusetts written assurances that he would exert the whole power of the State to secure for every soldier equal and exact justice, to prevent any discrimination on account of color." The Commonwealth of Massachusetts Head-Quarters, by Special Order, No. 281, dated March 7, 1864, gave George T. Downing and his brother Peter authorization to recruit for the Fifth Regiment of Calvary, Colored Massachusetts Volunteers, under General Order No. 32 of 1863.[4]

The majority of Africans who served as soldiers in "White" regiments were enlisted in the occupations of undercooks, wagoners, and teamsters. In August 1862 General Sherman, commanding the Fifth Division Tennessee Army, ordered that his regiment commanders could employ a limit of sixty-five Africans per regiment as company cooks and teamsters, and although included on the muster rolls, they would not be armed or uniformed. General Rosecrans, commander of the Department of the Cumberland, issued a statement five months later that two Africans per company would be employed as company cooks, as well as laborers and nurses.

A section of an act passed by Congress provided that for every thirty men in a company, one cook was to be provided; two cooks for each company of over thirty men. The president was also authorized "to cause to be enlisted . . . two under-cooks of African descent, who shall receive for their full compensation ten dollars per month, and one ration per day—three dollars of said monthly pay may be in clothing." There were cases where Africans were hired on as cooks or undercooks but actually performed as soldiers and were treated as such and were thereby enlisted in what were supposed to be White regiments. However, on the muster-out forms much evidence is shown that there was irregularity in payments to African cooks and soldiers, and in the "last paid" columns of the forms the remark "never paid" appears. Such inequality was of no concern to Frederick Douglass. He opined in the same letter to Secretary of War Edwin M. Stanton in which he recommended Downing for brigade quartermaster, "I am one of those colored men who say office or no office, equal or unequal pay, bounty or no bounty, the place for colored men is in the army of the United States." Douglass might have been equally unmoved by the fact that African servants of commanding officers would sometimes participate in major battles and end up severely wounded. Since they were not enlisted men, they were not entitled to veterans' assistance from the government. Thus, the "place" of Blacks as soldiers in the War Between the States was sometimes relegated to invisibility.[5]

Blacks' invisibility permeated more than one battlefield. If ever there was a statesman who understood the "place" of Africans in America and who worked on behalf of Black people, both before and after the Civil War, to change the idea of what their "place" should be, there are few to rival Tunis G. Campbell. He was a creative chef and a culinary artist who performed what was termed America's "menial" labor. But Campbell was also a labor organizer, and his 1848 *Hotel Keepers, Head Waiters, and Housekeepers' Guide* was a cookbook with numerous recipes, as well as a home and hotel dining room management manual. His thesis maintains that one of the most important tenets of an employer/employee relationship is decent and fair treatment of labor. His interest in labor relations ran very deep. Laborers in food service such as waiters consisted of large numbers of African males, and waiters' wages and working conditions were miserable.

African waiters did try to better the lot of themselves and fellow workers. In March 1853, they placed themselves at the center of a movement for better wages by forming a coalition called the Waiters' Protective Union Society. They sought wages of eighteen dollars a month. By the first week in April, a number of hotels agreed to their demands. Their group soon received an invitation from a White waiters' organization to participate in a meeting of White waiters—that is, *attend* the meeting, *not join* the White organization—in order to advise them [White waiters] how they might do the same. Five hundred White and African waiters employed at hotels, saloons, restaurants, and in private homes met in the Grand Street Hall. White waiters at the Astor Place and other hotels, however, tried to break up the possible interracial alliance by pitching fears of African competition. While all of this was taking place, Tunis Campbell was instrumental in forming another Black waiters' union, the First United Association of Colored Waiters. The association's intentions were "to improve the status of black waiters for the good of the black community." Campbell and his group were denounced as traitors by Waiters' Protective when Campbell's group vowed not to strike with the White union, should the White union fail to achieve its goals.[6]

Tunis Campbell was born on April 1, 1812, in Middlebrook, Somerset County, New Jersey, the seventh of nine children of the blacksmith John Campbell. He was the only African child in attendance at a school in Babylon, Long Island. In 1832 after he and his parents had been living in New Brunswick for two years, he established an anticolonization society and vowed "never to leave this country until every slave was free on American soil." Campbell joined the Methodist Church after leaving school, which prompted him to start lecturing and preaching. Moral reform and temperance were his platforms, and this made Campbell possibly "the first moral reformer and temperance lecturer that entered the Five Points, in the city of New York."[7]

Between 1832 and 1842 Campbell worked as a hotel steward in New York City. From 1842 to 1845 he was the headwaiter at New York's Howard Hotel. The Adams House in Boston employed him from 1848 until 1853. It was here, in 1848, that Campbell's first book, *Hotel Keepers, Head Waiters, and Housekeepers' Guide,* was published. It was a cookbook and one of the earliest manuals written on the supervision and management of first-class restaurants and hotel dining rooms. More than a cookbook, Campbell's *Guide* is a strict, systematically detailed, technical procedure on every facet of cooking and serving for hotel dining. Campbell's book presents his own innovations for waiters on how to organize the dining room and takes waiting tables to new heights of efficiency. In addition, his *Guide* not only outlines waiters' responsibilities, he also discusses proper labor/management relations, telling employers they are equally responsible to treat employees with dignity and respect, which offers an interesting analysis of labor and race relations in the North during the period.[8]

Tunis Campbell was lauded for his service and his recipes prepared at the Howard Hotel in New York and the Adams House in Boston. The following succulent treats are Campbell's own, samples from his cookbook/management guide.

To Roast a Shoulder or Leg of Mutton Stuffed

Stuff a leg of mutton with mutton-suet[*], salt, pepper, nutmeg, grated bread [bread crumbs], and yolks of eggs; then stick it all over with cloves, and roast it; when it is about half done cut off some of the under side of the fleshy end in little bits; put those into a pipkin[**] with a pint of oysters, liquor and all, a little salt and mace, and half a pint of hot water; stew them till half the liquor is wasted, then put in a piece of butter rolled in flour, shake all together, and when the mutton is done enough take it up; pour the sauce over it, and send it to table.[9]

[*]Suet is the hard fat around the kidneys and loins of beef and mutton. It is used in cooking and for making tallow, which was used in the production of

soap, candles, and the lubrication of locomotive and steamship engines until the 1950s.

[**]A pipkin is an earthenware cooking pot used for cooking over direct heat from coals or a wood fire. It has a handle and three legs. Late medieval and postmedieval pipkins had a hollow handle into which a stick could be inserted for manipulation.

To Roast Mutton, Venison Fashion

Take a hind quarter of fat mutton, and cut the leg like a haunch; lay it in a pan with the back side of it down, pour a bottle of red wine over it, and let it lie twenty-four hours; then spit it [put it on a roasting iron], and baste it with the same liquor and butter all the time it is roasting, at a good quick fire, and two hours and a half will do it. Have a little good gravy in a boat, and currant jelly in another.[10]

To Make Brown Celery Sauce

Stew the celery in little thin bits, then add mace, nutmeg, pepper, salt, a piece of butter rolled in flour, with a glass of red wine, a spoonful of catchup, and half a pint of good gravy; boil all these together, and pour into the dish. Garnish with lemon.[11]

To Make Maccaroons

Take a pound of almonds, let them be scalded, blanched, and thrown into cold water, then dry them in a cloth, and pound them in a mortar; moisten them with orange-flower water, or the white of an egg, lest they turn to an oil; after this take an equal quantity of fine powdered sugar, with three or four whites of eggs; beat all well together, and shape them on wafer paper with a spoon. Bake them on tin plates in a gentle oven.[12]

To Make Lemon Puffs

Take a pound and a quarter of double refined sugar beaten and sifted, and grate the rinds of two lemons, and mix well with the sugar; then beat the whites of two new-laid eggs very well, and mix them well with the sugar and lemon peel; beat them together an hour and a quarter, then make them up in what form you please; be quick to set them in a moderate oven; do not take off the papers[*] till cold.[13]

[*] "The papers" could refer to using what today we call cupcake cups or liners.

Perhaps Campbell's outline of proper labor/management relations was precisely what was needed. George Seely, the owner of New York's

National Hotel, where Tunis Campbell was headwaiter in 1853, agreed to the waiters' demand of eighteen dollars a month just about a week before Campbell formed the First United Association of Colored Waiters. Headwaiters "were in supervisory positions and had a better chance of becoming owners and reaping the rewards of the new capitalism." It was exactly those types of job-related footholds as well as the antislavery activity that fueled resentment and hatred among European immigrants against Africans.[14]

Some years later, in 1861, Tunis Campbell was a partner and general agent of the unfermented bread manufacturers Davies & Co., located on the corner of Third Avenue and Fourteenth Street in New York City. He was now married with three children, one an adopted son. His firm garnered a contract to supply bread to the Sickles Brigade at their camp on Staten Island. As he was a good businessman and a stickler for detail, Campbell insisted that they weigh his bread when he delivered it to the commissary. They did not want to weigh it, but Campbell refused to unload and leave it until they either signed his receipts or weighed the bread and gave him vouchers for the weight. A month or so later a committee was appointed in Washington to inspect the commissary department and the sanitary condition of the troops on Staten Island, and Campbell was ordered by the chief quartermaster of the US army, General Eaton, to be one of the inspectors.[15]

Your dinner guests will not have to worry about the weight of these biscuits. Light and fluffy, they almost melt in your mouth. These will not only hit the spot, you might want to eat *them* instead of the rest of your dinner.

Sweet Potato Biscuits

- 3 cups flour
- 2/3 cup sugar
- 5 teaspoons baking powder
- 1 teaspoon EACH salt and baking soda
- 7 tablespoons vegetable shortening

- 2 cups cooked sweet potatoes, slightly packed (break potatoes up with a fork; DO NOT mash out all of the lumps)
- 1 cup sour cream

Combine all dry ingredients in a large bowl. Work shortening into dry ingredients until mixture resembles coarse meal.

In a separate bowl, combine sweet potatoes and sour cream.

    Gradually stir sweet potato mixture into flour mixture until a dough is formed.

    Turn dough out onto a floured surface. With very lightly floured hands, knead dough for a few minutes. Flatten dough out to 1/2 inch or desired thickness. Cut circles with a floured glass or cookie cutter. Place circles 1 to 2 inches apart on an ungreased cookie sheet (preferably nonstick), and bake in a preheated 375 degree oven for 15 to 20 minutes. Makes 12 to 16 large biscuits.

Inspecting the sanitary condition of the troops was as close as Campbell would get to serving in the Civil War, as his request to serve in some capacity in the war was denied. However, when the fighting ended, General Rufus Saxton, assistant commissioner for the Freedmen's Bureau for South Carolina and Georgia, named Campbell superintendent of islands for Georgia.

It was Campbell's extraordinary ability to master order and organization and his attention to detail as headwaiter in the dining room that enabled him to lead freed African communities in Georgia from the state of exploited chattel to a revolutionary program for equality. Campbell had previously requested to be sent to the Sea Islands in Georgia, where he was placed in charge of Burnside, Ausaba, Saint Catherines, Sapelo, and Colonel's Islands, "with orders to organize and establish governments on the Islands; protect freedmen and refugees for thirty miles back from the seashore." Campbell governed these islands for two years, during which time he brought in three teachers and paid them at his own expense.[16]

By June 16, 1865, Campbell had settled 214 adults and 98 children on Sapelo Island and 200 adults and 117 children on Saint Catherines. On Saint Catherines Campbell wrote an elaborate constitution, organized a senate and a house of representatives, a judicial system with a supreme court, as well as a 275-man militia.[17]

By December 15, 1865, Campbell managed to settle 369 people on St. Catherines. Since the government rations were inadequate to support and maintain food necessities for that many people, it was fortuitous that the soil on St. Catherines and the other Sea Islands was able to provide well in terms of diversified crops. The islands averaged fifteen feet above sea level and crops flourished in those sandy soils. A great variety of vegetables were grown, including sweet and white potatoes, fruits and melons, sugarcane and corn. In addition, there was an abundance of game birds, raccoons, rabbits, deer, and wild boar; saltwater streams provided oysters, clams, mullet, turtle, crab, prawns, shrimp, and trout. Abandoned plantations provided cattle, which now roamed the islands; these were slaughtered for food or sold with surplus produce at Savannah's markets.[18]

Campbell provided the newly arriving Africans "with up to forty acres of land on which they could establish homesteads. By February 1866, he had parceled out land in varying acreages to approximately 425 freedmen and their families." Individual parcels of land were established all over the island, allowing the freedmen and -women to increase their hold over the entire island, and the militia units in place increased the freedmen's sense of autonomy and allowed them to practice self-reliance by establishing and maintaining independent families and farms.[19]

The philosophy of "separatism for strength" was adopted, and it worked. The freed Africans controlled their own labor, made their own decisions on numerous farm problems, and lived in "collective autonomy." As far as the government was concerned, this was not the intention. President Andrew Johnson placed the Georgia islands under Davis Tillson's direction, who fired Tunis Campbell, invalidated most of the land grants, forced Africans into labor contracts with former masters, and made certain that the freedmen and -women were once again badly exploited.

Wanting to continue work on behalf of his people, Campbell purchased (with his own money as a down payment) 1,250 acres of land in McIntosh County, on mainland Georgia, where the freedmen would pay a yearly rent toward outright ownership. The move proved fruitful. Campbell organized the BelleVille Farmers Association, which functioned like a city government. The freedmen raised chickens and trapped wild hogs to supplement their diet of turtles, oysters, and other seafood.[20]

By 1867, with the so-called Radicals in control of Congress, the first Reconstruction Act was enacted on March 2, over President Johnson's veto. On March 23 and July 19, 1867, Congress passed two supplementary acts, again over the president's veto. Under federal guidelines, all qualified voters were to be registered, elect delegates to rewrite state constitutions, and set up state governments. Tunis Campbell held a prominent position in fulfilling these goals. He still struggled to help uplift his people, and with Congress cracking open the door for greater reform, he decided to seek political office to hopefully open the door all the way and thereby help legislate away discrimination and further his people's gains. He campaigned for the state senate seat, as well as a seat for his son Tunis Campbell Jr. for the state house of representatives.

Having established positive public images, Tunis Campbell was one of three Africans elected to the state senate. His son was elected as the representative for McIntosh County. Campbell, along with Foster Blodgett, was appointed by the Georgia state central committee to go to Washington to work on behalf of reconstruction in Georgia.[21]

Caterer, cookbook author, and now senator, Tunis Campbell represented McIntosh, Liberty, and Tatnall Counties. He had been fighting for land rights for Black people since St. Catherines. The necessity of Blacks owning land and having the accompanying property rights was not lost on Tunis Campbell, and he understood the imperative at least as well as, or even better than, Thaddeus Stevens and Charles Sumner, both of whom spoke on behalf of Black landownership. Campbell encouraged the efforts of self-employed farmers and laborers in the rice or timber industry to acquire land and supplement their earnings by growing crops of their own to sell, such as corn, sweet potatoes, rice, oats, and small amounts of cotton.

The idea was for Africans to become totally self-sufficient agriculturally—and as close as possible to it, economically. He was also aware that African laborers were now supposed to be paid laborers, and many planters were often at odds with the workers in terms of wages and length of the workday. Campbell often counseled McIntosh County Africans on labor contracts, insisting that they not sign lengthy term agreements, because if workers later found that the contract was not in their best interest and then failed to complete the terms of the contract, the employer could have them sent to prison. Campbell was also an activist in changing the labor system from one of coercion, racism, discrimination, and intimidation to competition in an open market. In a land where the planter class was used to making its wealth from exploitation of African labor, this move made Campbell extremely unattractive and a disruptive element to the purposes of McIntosh County planters.[22]

Some Whites testified that "Campbell exercises great influence over the Negroes of this County." They did not believe that Campbell could be put in jail without bloodshed, because "if they [authorities] had put him in jail the niggers would have put the jail in the River." Campbell was willing to ask for protection from President Grant to oppose any law Blacks considered unjust or oppressive. If that protection failed to materialize, Campbell was reported to have said, "we will have to act," because "colored people had one resource left, which was dear to every freeman's heart, and that was the musket and Bayonet." Campbell asked his citizens to adhere to law-abiding behaviors; however, the social climate also dictated that they bear arms. Africans began to carry rifles in the streets, refused to yield sidewalks to Whites, and refused to address Whites by titles. Ironically, a White newspaper responded to the prevailing atmosphere by stating, "Wherever they are in the majority . . . a white man has no rights which the African is bound to respect."[23]

The consequences of Campbell's untiring efforts on behalf of Blacks in McIntosh County gave Campbell much in common with Huey P. Newton and the Black Panther Party for Self-Defense in the 1960s and 1970s. Campbell, like Minister of Defense Newton and the Black Panthers, understood the right of and the need for Africans to bear arms—and to use them when necessary in self-defense. Africans defending themselves with guns against armed attacks was something White America refused to accept. What followed was constant, concerted, omnipresent efforts to bring Campbell down by keeping him so wrapped up in arrests and legal battles (one of his arrests was for violation of [are you ready?] the Ku Klux Klan Act of 1871, also called the Civil Rights Act, or the Force Act of 1871, enacted to protect African Americans from violence perpetrated by the Ku Klux Klan) he would not have the time or the energy to fight for anything else. The idea was to break and destroy Campbell, just as the US government did its very best, using some of the same tactics, to break and destroy Huey P. Newton and the Black Panther Party.[24]

Racism and money guided the efforts to keep Campbell and Black McIntosh County subordinate. Tidewater Georgia and South Carolina had been the home of a rice aristocracy that prospered from enormous amounts of slave labor. During the antebellum period the crescent of the south Atlantic seaboard from Georgetown District, South Carolina, southward to Glynn County, Georgia, was known as the Rice Kingdom of the world. By 1720, for example, rice was grown "upon every 'seated' river" in South Carolina, from where over seventeen thousand barrels were exported in 1724, and over one hundred thousand barrels by 1761. Just as in Louisiana, South Carolina planters particularly sought, and placed a higher value on, Africans from the Upper Guinea and Senegambia regions because of their advanced knowledge and expertise in grain and rice cultivation, and in agriculture in general. The increasing numbers of Africans imported into South Carolina during the eighteenth century corresponded with the expansion of the state's economy based on cultivation of indigo and rice in the Sea Islands and in the hinterlands. Thus, locked into a system of rice production transplanted from the Motherland, the African "Old World" heritage in rice agriculture was reinforced.[25]

Margaret Creel in her treatise *"A Peculiar People"* argues that there was an early cultural dominance in the Carolina Lowcountry of BaKongo peoples of Kongo-Angolan origin, followed by Senegambians and those from the Windward Coasts, and that "it was the BaKongo influence that served as incubator for many Gullah cultural patterns." Most assuredly, African culture survived the Middle Passage, as evidenced in traditional retentions of the Sea Islands Gullahs, not only in rice cultivation but also in cuisine, language, arts and crafts, and religion.[26]

It has been written that the Gullahs' lifestyle characterized farm-to-table cuisine. Their culinary practices were African cooking traditions adapted to American soil—soil tied to seasonal availability, dependence on the environment, and based on necessity. Gullah traditional dishes such as red rice, okra soup (there are as many varieties as there are Louisiana gumbos), which is almost always prepared with a tomato base, perloo (pilau), Hoppin' John (or Carolina peas and rice), one pot meals, and numerous shrimp and seafood entrees are always accompanied by or mixed with rice. These are southern staples, and they are African in origin.

Here is one of many examples of rice bread recipes prepared and showcased on South Carolina's tables in years long gone. Notice, Mrs. Kirkland claims both Jane and Jane's recipe.

"From Mrs. Kirkland's Jane," Rice Bread

One Quart of Rice Flour—A little more than One half Pint of good yeast—Pint of lukewarm water—About a teaspoonful of salt, or more if necessary—One Egg—One Tablespoonful of Butter—First Put the Rice Flour and yeast and salt in a Large Pitcher, then pour in the water gradually and stir until the ingredients are well mixed together— Set the Pitcher by the fire until the mixture rises well—it will take about two hours to rise—Now break the egg and throw it in, melt the butter and mix with it a little *warm milk if you have it*, if not a warm water will do, and mix all well together in the Pitcher, and then empty the whole into a pan, and set the pan into a *warm not hot* oven and let the bread remain there about a half hour to rise, before you apply a sufficient quantity of fire to the oven to bake it thoroughly— it does not take a very long time to bake——From Mrs. Kirkland's Jane.[27]

The culinary and material civilization imported from Africa to the Americas has been noted by one French historian. Although referring to Africans in Brazil, the same holds true for Africans brought to the Americas in general: "the slave did not arrive in America [culturally] naked. He brought with him a sense of sedentary life and of agriculture, while his wife brought a concept of domesticity. . . . He brought as well culinary recipes, a sense of dietary balance . . . medical formulas and plants unknown in America."[28]

African culinary concepts were practiced by the enslaved as well as by free Africans. Free Africans, regarded as a bottomless fund for state taxation, were listed as engaging in thirty occupations in nineteenth-century South Carolina. A number of these occupations employed free Blacks who were famous for their culinary skills. One free Black was Abigail Jones, wife of Jehu Jones Sr., Charleston's most popular hotelier. Jones also owned many valuable pieces of property on Broad Street, Charleston's most important business area. Born in Charleston in 1769, he began his career as an expert tailor and opened his own business. Unfortunately, his White patrons did not always own up to paying for services rendered. Jones frequently had trouble collecting the money owed him. One such incident prompted Jones to sue Thomas Wilson in the court of common pleas for an unpaid bill.

Jones owned a small house on Coming Street left to him by his mother, who was said to be "a woman of some means." In the early 1800s Jones acquired land in Wraggsboro, and on Logan and Beaufain Streets, which proved lucrative investments. In 1802 he began to invest in real estate in Charleston and on Sullivan Island. In 1809 he purchased property, a house and lot, behind St. Michaels Church on Broad Street. Six years later he bid thirteen thousand dollars at a public auction for the adjacent house at 33 Broad Street, located on Charleston's main commercial thoroughfare. This property was referred to as Jones' Lot. Jones expanded the property into Jones' Long Room; the latter house was turned into the famed Jones' Inn, or Jones' Hotel, and was considered the beginning of the tradition of fine hotels in Charleston.[29]

Travelers all over South Carolina and beyond, extending their stay in Charleston, were well acquainted with the Jones' Hotel, with its "antique and mixed" architecture and large convex windows. So advanced were the décor and the culinary fare of Jones' Hotel over any other encountered between New Orleans and Charleston that it caused one commentator to remark, Jones has "all the luxuries of the table;" and "iced claret to convert Diogenes into a *gourmet* [original italics]." The luxury of Jones' iced claret might have converted Diogenes into a gourmet." Patronized by White elites (including the governors of the state and prominent military officials) and European travelers (including the British actor Tyrone Power), the Jones' Hotel was highly praised for its comfort and its fine food.

> His house was unquestionably the best in the city and had a widespread reputation. Few persons of note ever visited Charleston without putting up at Jones', where they found not only the comforts of a private house, but a table spread with every luxury that the country afforded. The Governor always put up at Jones', and when you were travelling abroad, strangers would speak of the sumptuous fare at Jones' in Charleston and the elegance and correctness of his house. Jones continued in the popularity of his house for many years, reared a beautiful, intelligent, and interesting family; at the same time accumulated about forty thousand dollars.

The English traveler Thomas Hamilton was so taken by Mr. and Mrs. Jones's methods of catering that he wrote: "Every Englishman who visits Charleston, will, if he be wise, direct his baggage to be conveyed to Jones' hotel."[30]

One of the most important components of the Jones' Hotel was Abigail (Abby) Jones's cooking. Jehu Jones's wife was an excellent and, by all accounts, famed pastry cook. Mrs. Jones may indeed have run one of the earliest African cooking schools in America. The hotel not only boarded the White elite but also apparently "served as a center for the training of house servants and slaves in the art of cooking." An advertisement for a runaway slave provides insight: "100 Dollars Reward, will be paid to any one who will apprehend and lodge in any goal of this State or Georgia, my Negro woman Charlotte, who ran away in July 1821. . . . She is a good plain and pastry cook having been taught both at Jones' in Charleston; and it is not improbable that she is engaged in some such establishment in Georgetown or Charleston unless harbored by some of her relations or friends." Another advertisement stated, "At private sale a first rate man cook, taught at the hotel of Jehu Jones, and has cooked for years for one of the first families of this State."[31]

Versions of the following were representative of Abigail Jones's offerings.

Rice Bread

Half a pint of Rice boiled soft, when cold stir in one pint of ground rice [rice flour], 2 large spoonsful of leaven or yeast and a teaspoonful of salt, and 1/2 a teaspoonful of soda . . . Place it to rise for some 3 or 4 hours, then bake. When cold, cut it in thin slices and toast it, to be buttered.[32]

White Sauce for Boiled Chickens

Knead, with a spoon, a large spoonful of Butter, with 1/2 a pint of Wheat Flour, mix, gradually in 1/2 a pint of milk & the beaten yolks of 3 eggs, with a gill of cream & a little Mace. Let it boil, stirring, all the while, to prevent curdling & to keep it smooth. A little chopped Parsley may be added, or oysters.[33]

Abigail Jones's cooking was Jehu Jones's main asset. However, Jones was not without material assets. As well as holding shares in the Planters' and Mechanic's Bank in Charleston, he also owned a hotel on Sullivan's Island, considered a fashionable resort for Charleston's so-called crème de la crème. His hotel in Charleston maintained its prestige for many years until Jones left the state. The steady increase in the African population, as well as the Denmark Vesey revolt, prompted the implementation of additional harsh, restrictive laws and legislation. Despite the Jones family's "superior" status in the community, one of those laws heavily impacted on Jones, his daughter, and his grandson. If free Africans left South Carolina, for any reason, they were not permitted to return.

Jehu Jones, like other Africans in America, understood that being categorized as a "free" African in America did not mean one was free from oppression. Some free Africans looked to Liberia, to Africa, for the promise of opportunity and respect denied them in America. Jones, already having built lucrative businesses, left South Carolina at the invitation of the American Colonization Society in New York to assume the role of editor for a newspaper that the Colonization Society proposed to publish in Liberia. Unfortunately, Jones never went farther than New York, where the Colonization Society abandoned him. He was prohibited from returning to South Carolina, and most of his property was sold. Jones did repeatedly petition the legislature for permission to return. He apparently succeeded, as his burial is recorded in the register of St. Philip's Church in Charleston. The size and depth of Jones's wealth must have been considerable. Despite his losses, when he died his estate was said to be valued at over forty thousand dollars.[34]

When Jehu Jones died in 1833, his stepdaughter, Ann Deas, took over management of the hotel. Financial difficulties in the mid-1840s forced Deas to relinquish control of the hotel. Free Africans John and Eliza Seymour Lee, who owned the Mansion House (reputed for "good management and excellent cooking [that] went unchallenged" and said to have been owned by Jehu Jones at one time), took over operation of the hotel in 1847. Eliza Seymour Lee, daughter of the famous cook Sally Seymour, had previously operated Lee's Boarding House, renowned for the finest meals in Charleston. Her reputation for good cooking went far beyond the usual accolades. The food prepared by Mrs. Lee was so heralded that visitors to the boardinghouse often requested her to teach their slaves in her style of cooking, and these requests she sometimes accommodated.[35]

Sally Seymour (Martin), a slave, was freed by slaveholder Thomas Martin in 1795. She worked as a pastry cook and trained her daughter Eliza, who took over the business and won additional fame for her preserves, cakes, pies, jellies, as well as entrees in general. Seymour's two sons, fathered by Thomas Martin, moved north to make a better life for themselves. Faced with hardship, they resorted to making a living by pickling and preserving, the way their mother taught them. A man named Heinz heard about their methods of pickling and preserving and expressed deep interest. Heinz bought their recipes and rights, and the J. H. Heinz & Company was soon on its way to packaging the "57 Varieties" (Heinz was said to pick the number "57" because he liked how it sounded). Every time you pour ketchup on your hamburger and fries or use Heinz's India relish, mustard dressing, or any number of other Heinz products, you can thank an African woman in Charleston, South Carolina, for her creations.

⎯⎯⎯⎯⎯⎯⎯⎯

Sally Seymour was one in a long line of Black cooks who made every dinner, every event they oversaw, more memorable because of their culinary presentations. Various pies and preserves, such as these two below, always adorned the tables of the elites who could not do without the Black cook's expertise.

Corn Pie

Grate green or mutton corn[*], or corn that is harder than mutton corn, on a potato grater. When grated, add milk, . . . and black pepper, so as to make the mixture soft, then place on a dish, a layer of the above mixture and a layer of shrimp, chicken or other meat, alternately, and bake in an oven. If you have no shrimps, chicken or meat, then place the above mixture in a dish alone and bake in the same manner. The mixture should be seasoned with salt. When made without meat of any kind, it is a good substitute for bread.[36]

[*]Mutton corn: Sweet corn that is just ripe enough to be eaten; roasting ears.

To Make Tomato Preserves

Take them while quite small and green; put them in cold clarified syrup, with an orange cut in slices to every pound of tomatoes. Simmer them over a slow fire for 2 or 3 hours. There should be equal weights of sugar and tomatoes. If very superior preserves are wanted, add two fresh lemons to three pounds of tomatoes, pare thin the rinds of the lemons, so as to get none of the white part; squeeze out the juice, mix the parings, juice and cold water sufficient to cover the tomatoes, and put in a few peach leaves and powdered ginger, tied up in bags. Boil the whole gently for three quarters of an hour; take up the tomatoes, strain the liquor and put with it a pound and a half of white sugar for each pound of tomatoes. Put in the tomatoes and boil them gently till the syrup appears to have entered them. In the course of a week, turn the syrup from them, heat it scalding hot, and strain it . . . to the tomatoes. Prepared in this way, [they] resemble West India sweetmeats.[37]

Charleston, South Carolina, produced other culinary artists who, like Abigail Jones and Eliza Lee and her mother, Sally Seymour, were unequalled in the repasts set before their customers. African caterer Thomas R. Tully's restaurant on King Street, where he partnered with a mulatto pastry cook, Martha Vanderhorst, attracted extensive White patronage as well as the Black upper class. Tully was considered by Whites "an oracle in matters culinary." His specialties were cake baking and other confectionery items, items that helped them garner much success through catering.[38]

Tully was trained by Nathaniel Fuller, for whom Tully worked. In the 1840s Fuller sold game and other meats such as turkeys, quail, bear, and venison at Charleston's market at 68 King Street. Fuller was also a popular caterer, overseeing the meals at meetings and banquets given by the Charleston Light Dragoons, the St. Andrew's Society, the chamber of commerce, and the Phoenix Fire Company. Two of Charleston's most important social events, the St. Cecilia Ball and the Carolina Jockey Club Ball, were catered by Fuller. Eliza Seymour Lee also catered the Jockey Club Ball on another occasion.

Considered Charleston's prince of caterers by 1860, Fuller opened Bachelor's Retreat Restaurant at 77 Church Street, offering breakfast, lunch, dinner, and supper, with meat preparation his specialty. The premises were leased with the assistance of the slaveholder William C. Gatewood. When Gatewood died the following year, Fuller was bequeathed either additional financial assistance or title to the building, a bequest that Gatewood's wife, Madeleine, refused to honor. Fuller continued operating his restaurant and catering society events until an illness forced him to close his doors for about two months. Now behind on his rent and with the building subsequently put on the market for sale, Fuller relocated his prize recipes to a not-so-luxurious venue on Washington Street.[39]

Georgia's nineteenth-century rice cultivation was no less impressive. From around 1820 until the Civil War, the Altamaha River valley, considered the very lifeblood of the town of Darien in McIntosh County, was conducive to heavy agricultural activity in the production of rice. The US agricultural census of 1860 reported that there were 5,800 acres of rice under cultivation in McIntosh County, yielding 195,000 bushels. During the 1840s and 1850s Georgia was second only to South Carolina on the world market in the production of rice. Production of rice in the districts of Savannah, Ogeechee, and Altamaha Rivers reached their peak in 1861. The 1860 agricultural census reported that 1859 Georgia rice planters cultivated 52.5 million pounds of rice, compared to 119 million pounds in South Carolina. In Georgia the Altamaha River delta, which includes McIntosh and Glynn Counties, produced 11.2 million pounds alone. There were ninety-six rice planters on the Georgia tidewater in 1860, twelve in McIntosh County, and six in neighboring Glynn. This rice-growing area—with its handful of planters "representing the greatest concentration of wealth the antebellum South had ever seen"—was eventually obliterated as the result of the Civil War and the liberation of African bondspeople.[40]

By the 1870s Darien was a booming timber town. Rice was still grown in McIntosh County. Cultivation was comparable to the most productive areas on the coast, but it was nowhere in the same league as during the antebellum period.[41]

For many, rice was still king, and queen. Numerous rice dishes, by way of Black cooks, came out of this region. Tunis Campbell produced a number of recipes of his own.

To Make a Rice Soup

To two quarts of water put three quarters of a pound of rice, clean picked and washed, with a stick of cinnamon; let it be covered very close, and simmer till your rice is tender; take out the cinnamon, and grate half a nutmeg; beat up the yolks of four eggs, and strain them to half a pint of white wine, and as much pounded sugar as will make it palatable; put this to your soup, and stir it very well together: set it over the fire, stirring it till it boils, and is of a good thickness; then send it to table.[42]

To Make a Rice Pudding

Beat half a pound of rice to powder. Set it with three pints of new milk upon the fire, let it boil well, and when it grows almost cold, put to it eight eggs well beaten, and half a pound of suet or butter, half a pound of sugar, and a sufficient quantity of cinnamon, nutmeg, and mace. Half an hour will bake it.

You may add a few currants, candied lemon, citron-peel, or other sweetmeats; and lay a puff-paste [crust] first all over the sides and rim of the dish.[43]

In 1876, while rice and timber remained lucrative endeavors for the counties' residents, sixty-three-year-old Tunis Campbell was put on a chain gang. Convicted on a trumped-up charge of malpractice in office and for inciting an insurrectionary spirit among the people of his district, Campbell was leased out for a year clearing land with 119 other convicts on a plantation owned by T. J. Smith under Georgia's horrendous convict leasing system.[44]

Perhaps the highlight of his incarceration, if there was any, was the "box of nourishments and medicines—clothing, soda-crackers, sugar-cakes, pound-cake, strawberry and other preserves, pickled eggs, etc.," that Mrs. Campbell sent him every month. During his imprisonment, Mrs. Campbell and their daughter, Catharine Amelia (Cassey), lived in Atlanta. Every dollar Mrs. Campbell collected from the sale of medicines she made during the winter, as "her knowledge of the medicinal quali-ties of roots and herbs was very extensive," and from the sale of black-berries she picked in the woods and strawberries from the fields around Atlanta, she used to try to free her husband.[45]

At any rate, after eleven years Tunis G. Campbell had been perse-cuted out of Georgia. McIntosh County, where he had led the center of radical politics in Georgia, was returned to the control of planters; the rest of the state followed suit. Campbell's memory, however, lingered at least through the first decade of the twentieth century. His example and legacy would be a rallying point of thought and solidarity for McIntosh County residents, and a rallying point of theory, and massacre, perpe-trated by Whites, in 1906 Atlanta.[46]

Just as cookbook author, caterer, and hotel dining room manager Tunis Campbell had become a leading political figure during Recon-struction, other African political leaders of this same era emerged from the occupation of caterer or barber. Born free in Richmond, Virginia, in about 1820, John J. Smith moved to Boston in 1848. He originally lived on Anderson Street and then on Pinckney Street; he later moved to Ja-maica Plain and Dorchester. He was a diligent abolitionist who learned the barber trade and opened a shop in Boston near the corner of Howard and Bulfinch Streets. Located in the West End section of the city, Smith's barbershop became a favorite gathering place, a rendezvous, where "se-cret councils" of abolitionists congregated. Smith was intimately ac-quainted with Charles Sumner, the noted senator and abolitionist, as well as with Wendell Phillips. Sumner was said to have "become so fond of Smith and the gossip [prevalent] . . . there" that whenever "he could not be found at his home or office, he could usually be located at Smith's shop."[47]

After the Civil War, John J. Smith went into politics and served three terms—1868, 1869, 1872—in the Massachusetts House of Representatives. He was reportedly the only African to be elected three times to this position. He represented the Sixth Suffolk District in Boston and shared representation with F. W. Lincoln and a gentleman named Codman. Like many Africans in the late nineteenth century, he did not look closely at individual candidates, and refused to see any negatives in the Republican Party, and thereby "declared himself to be a Grant man first." In 1881 Smith represented Ward Nine of Boston in the Common Council. But if that was not enough, he was also placed in charge of the Massachusetts State House restaurant, a position he kept until 1888. He returned to the hair trade, and for the remainder of his life he operated a hairdressing emporium at No. 4 Exchange Place. He had married a Black woman from Nova Scotia, with whom he had six children. When he died at home on November 4, 1906, in Dorchester, Massachusetts, he was survived by his Boston schoolteacher daughter, Harriet, and a son, Hamilton.[48]

Boston was also the home of Massachusetts's "prince of caterers," Joshua Bowen Smith (no relation to John J. Smith). "He resembled," it has been said, "in character and standing," Prince Hall, an earlier Boston abolitionist, civic leader, leather dresser, sometimes caterer (according to Proceedings of the One Hundredth Anniversary of the Granting of Warrant 459 to African Lodge, at Boston Mass.), and founder of what would become the African Prince Hall Grand Lodge (#459) of Massachusetts. One version of Joshua B. Smith's early life indicates that he was born to slave parents in 1815 and eventually fled to Boston as a fugitive slave from North Carolina in 1847. Another states that he was born in 1813 in Coatesville, Pennsylvania, and that a wealthy Quaker was responsible for him attending public school. The latter version has Joshua B. arriving in Boston in 1836, where he obtained a job as headwaiter at the Mt. Washington House. It was while working at Mt. Washington that Smith met both Robert Gould Shaw, who would later become colonel of the famous all African Massachusetts Fifty-Fourth Regiment, and the Massachusetts senator and abolitionist Charles Sumner.[49]

Joshua B. Smith found employment for a number of years in the home of Robert Gould Shaw's parents. He also worked for Thacker, the leading African Boston caterer. Smith subsequently established his own very successful catering business, which opened in 1849. Just as Scipio Brenton held the title "prince of caterers" in Rhode Island, Joshua B. Smith held that same title in Massachusetts. For more than twenty-five years his establishment thrived, and his patrons represented abolitionist organizations, private individuals, as well as Civil War troops, many of which he recruited.[50]

When it was Smith's turn to step up to fight slavery, he did not stumble. During the 1840s Africans in Boston stood up and acted in defense of fugitive slaves. A Committee of Vigilance was established with both Africans and Whites among its members and leaders. Joshua B. Smith was a member of the executive committee. As with other African businessmen of his day, much of the money he made from cooking and cuisine was spent on activities that benefited his people. He was considered a radical abolitionist who took a leading role along with Lewis Hayden in an organized resistance to the 1850 Fugitive Slave Act. He was involved in the armed rescue of the apprehended fugitive slave Shadrach Minkins. His activities naturally drew him to Senator Charles Sumner whose own work and pronouncements on behalf of abolition was "a bitter pill" for Whites north and south but endeared him to the hearts of Africans in America. Smith wrote to Sumner in 1860 regarding Sumner's speech titled "The Barbarism of Slavery." He thanked Sumner for what he felt was a "very masterly speech . . . before the Senate in exposition of the monstrous iniquity of American slavery." Smith goes on to confess to Sumner that his experience and observation with the developments of slavery have left him with "no confidence in the abolition of slavery by any existing political party." He had therefore decided to engage in a movement that he and others came up with to undermine the cotton kingdom in America, "to attack slavery in its financial importance, by establishing a company of cotton growers, in Central Africa, where cotton is indigenous and peren[n]ial growing in wild profusion all over the country." Smith even enclosed with the letter an accompanying circular that explained the plan. Unfortunately, I was unable to locate this circular in the Charles Sumner Correspondence Collection.[51]

Smith catered many important events such as the annual Independence Day dinner on the Fourth of July for the City Council of Boston.

Smith always furnished a magnificent bill of fare. For the 1846 dinner there was salmon with Harvey Sauce, mutton with caper sauce, turkey with oyster sauce, chicken with celery sauce, ham, tongue, and beef. But we are not finished with the meats: turkeys, ducks, chickens, geese, pigs, veal, beef, and lamb with mint sauce rounded out the roasted items. The "entrees" included Fricandeau veal, mutton cutlets, curried chickens, brown fricassee chickens, white fricassee chickens, potted pigeons, ala-mode beef, scalloped oysters, stewed oysters, oyster pie, lobster salad, lobster "plain," chicken salad, and bird pies. If that was not enough, game meats, woodcock, and squabs made their appearance as well. Pastries included five flavors of puddings, as well as apple, gooseberry, mince, and custard pies, and "Turks caps," charlotte russe, cream cakes, meringues, jellies, "blown jumbles," and other items. "Dessert" took the form of six different fruits, nuts, together with strawberries and cream, ice cream, orange sherbet, Roman Punch, and cake! To quench any additional thirst, lemonade was served.[52]

Here is one more stellar performance from your kitchen that will ensure your place of importance for your most memorable events. Because of the rum—and for flavor you and your guests will never forget—age this cake for twenty-four hours before serving.

Independence Day's Summer Fruitcake

- 1½ cups all-purpose flour*
- 1/2 teaspoon salt
- 1½ teaspoons baking powder
- 1/2 teaspoon baking soda
- 1/4 teaspoon EACH cinnamon, nutmeg, and cloves
- 3/4 cup butter
- 1½ cups light brown sugar
- 3 tablespoons white sugar
- 3 eggs
- 1/2 cup EACH mango puree, and mashed bananas
- 1/3 cup dark rum
- 2 teaspoons vanilla extract
- 1½ teaspoons coconut extract
- 1/2 cup sweetened angel flake coconut, slightly packed

Combine flour, salt, baking powder, baking soda, cinnamon, nutmeg, and cloves in a small bowl.

In a large mixing bowl, cream butter until light and fluffy. Add sugar 1/2 cup to 1 cup at a time and blend well. Add eggs, one at a time, beating well after each addition.

Beginning with dry ingredients (flour mixture), add flour mixture to butter mixture alternately with fruit, rum, and extracts. Begin with dry ingredients, end with dry ingredients. There should be 4 additions of dry ingredients, 3 additions of liquid ingredients. Mix well, but do not beat or stir too much.

Stir in coconut by hand and mix well.

Lightly grease a tube pan. Line with waxed paper. Pour batter into pan. Bake in a preheated 350 degree oven for about 42 minutes. Cool thoroughly before removing from pan.

*Flour must be stirred many, many times before measuring, and then sprinkled into the measuring cups.

Glaze for Summer Fruitcake (optional)

- 1/2 cup confectioner's sugar
- 2 teaspoons mango puree, or coconut milk
- 1/2 teaspoon vanilla extract

Combine glaze ingredients and mix well. Spread glaze over top of completely cooled cake, allowing it to drizzle down the sides.

The dinner in 1848 was billed with the same delights, except that Smith served the salmon with chautney and anchovy sauce, and he added lobster mayonnaise on the list of entrees, and the pastries included Washington Pie and cake of various kinds. Meats such as Saltpetred beef, and the addition of Biscuit Glasca and Charladonies on the pastry list, as well as the serving of coffee, were seen at the dinner provided in 1849. For the seventy-seventh anniversary of American Independence (July 4, 1853), as was his custom, Smith went over the top. There were so many meats and entrees, desserts, and fruits, my stomach felt filled just reading through these printed menus. A pamphlet published by "A partnership between the Federal Reserve Bank of Boston and the Museum of African American History, Boston and Nantucket" contains a brief biography of Smith, in which is mentioned another Fourth of July dinner Smith catered in 1865, at which "more than 1,000 people" attended.[53]

Since Washington Pie was a favorite pastry prepared by Joshua Smith and very popular during the nineteenth century, I present the following "receipt" from a nineteenth-century collection.

Harriett's Washington Pie

One heaping coffee cup of flour, one even coffee cup of sugar, 4
eggs beaten separately, a piece of butter the size of an egg. Not quite
1/2 a teaspoonful of cream of tartar, not quite 1/4 spoonful of soda.
Mix the butter and sugar together, then add the eggs. Then the soda
dissolved in a little water. Put the cream of tartar in the flour and add
it to the other ingredients the last thing. This makes 2 pies, 4 pans to
be baked pretty low oven, 7 minutes, watch all the time. When cold,
spread nice apple sauce (with grated lemon peel) between (or other
preserve, if it pleases).[54]

Smith oversaw numerous other main events. On one occasion Sumner
told Smith he enjoyed the account of the supper at the opening of the
Boston branch of the Smithsonian. And since Sumner enjoyed a comfortable, friendly relationship with Smith, his words then took a more
serious turn. Sumner added, "I am disgusted with the colored people in
Washington. I wished them to nominate one or two of their own number
as an example to the freedmen at the South. . . . They allowed themselves
to be frightened by politicians who said that 'it would not do'—'that it
would have a bad effect on the elections at the north.' . . . Though in one
of the wards they had a majority, they have not nominated one of their
own color." To Sumner this was a serious mistake. He continued, telling
Smith, "Wormley told me a day or two ago that they meant to give me
a serenade before I left. I told him . . . that I would not take it, and that I
did not want anything of the kind from people who abandoned in this
way their own cause."[55]

The issue of African representation was crucial to Sumner, as Africans elected to office could help push through needed legislation.
Sumner wrote to Smith, inviting him "to come to Washington and inspect [Sumner's] new quarters." With this invitation he included a letter
from "a colored delegate to the Constitutional Convention in Louisiana." Sumner responded to the delegate's letter, stating, "the presence
of colored men in the Senate and House of Representatives is needed to
complete the triumph of our cause."[56]

Smith and Sumner's relationship lasted until Sumner's death. Smith
arranged lodging at the Coolidge House at Bowdoin Square for Sumner
when he traveled back to Boston. Sumner visited Smith's place on Bulfinch Street where he was among Smith's guests at a dinner for M. P.
Bradlaugh. Also in attendance were H. L. Pierce, Mr. Hooper (Sumner's

wife's ex-father-in-law), the former governor Emory Washburn, William Lloyd Garrison, and Thomas Russell. Their relationship seemed to include, however, Smith—as well as his caterer, hotelkeeper friend James Wormley—attending to some of Sumner's needs, such as purchases of supplies, the hiring of servants, and other arrangements for Sumner's Washington and Boston homes. Payments for services were involved, as Sumner did ask Smith to forward his bills. Perhaps, since Smith and Wormley were in the "service" business, they were the best persons to approach; they both would certainly know the best people to hire. A broken chandelier was shipped to Sumner, and it was Smith, whose whole nervous system was reportedly "shattered" at this time, who dealt with the problem.[57]

Smith apparently received a number of invitations from Sumner to visit him in Washington, which included offers for Smith to stay at Sumner's home. Responding to Smith's scheduled visit to DC, Sumner states, "The Collector writes that you are about to visit Washington. Come direct to my house. The room is ready. I hope that I shall be more at leisure than I was when you were here before." After stopping at Wormley's Hotel on March 4, Smith stayed with Sumner, just before Sumner died, for three days—March 6, 7, and 8, 1874. During this stay Sumner introduced Smith on the floor of the Senate.[58]

Following one visit to Washington, Smith showed his gratitude to Sumner by sending him various foods, because, as he stated, it had been "the only visit of my life where I felt at home." There were a number of occasions when Smith purchased fresh salmon from the Kennebec River, which he sent by express to Sumner. He also sent pheasants and Winter Nellis pears, English cheese, a Massachusetts turkey, brook trout and other seafood from Plymouth Rock, as well as grapes, peaches and strawberries from Mansfield, Massachusetts.[59]

Smith sent Sumner foods; Sumner sent Smith books. Smith also sent victuals, such as beef, to hotelkeeper and fellow caterer James Wormley. While Joshua Bowen Smith lived deep in the realm of cooking and cuisine, he did not relegate himself to it. In 1873 Smith was elected to the Massachusetts legislature, representing Cambridge from 1873 to 1874. He shared representation of the eighth Middlesex District with John W. Hammond and Asa P. Morse. During Smith's tenure, he served on the Federal Regulations Committee. According to Smith's obituary in the

July 7, 1879, issue of the *Boston Evening Transcript*, he also held the office of inspector of the marine hospital at Chelsea.[60]

Joshua Smith did not hesitate, while working in the Massachusetts legislature, to become very active in the attempt to rescind the resolution of censure against Charles Sumner. Sumner had introduced in the Senate, in 1872, a resolution to remove the names of battles and victories from the regimental colors of the United States with the hope that "good-will among fellow-citizens can be assured . . . through oblivion of past differences"—that is, in the hopes that differences between the North and South remaining from the Civil War might be healed. The Massachusetts legislature denounced this battle flag resolution as "an insult to the loyal soldiery of the nation" and as "meeting the unqualified condemnation of the people of the Commonwealth." When the censure was finally rescinded in February 1874, Massachusetts Governor W. B. Washburn appointed Joshua Smith to personally deliver the official copies of the document to Washington. Sumner entertained Smith as his guest, giving a grand dinner one evening, "to which many prominent men in Washington, D. C. were invited."[61]

Grand dinners were Joshua B. Smith's stock in trade, and he made a considerable fortune catering important functions in Boston. One such occasion was the banquet at Harvard on October 19, 1860, given for the prince of Wales during his visit to the city. The Harvard librarian John Langdon Sibley kept a diary in which he recorded details of local events and affairs, including those at Harvard. At nearly three o'clock, as the dining commenced, Sibley writes, "J.B. Smith, the colored caterer, had, through a misunderstanding, neglected to provide hot coffee or any hot drink, & as Englishmen never drink cold water, & there was no other drink, the President apologized to the Prince, who excused it in a courteous manner, saying a glass of wine would do just as well. Thereupon the President was obliged to say there was no wine & that it was contrary to the laws of the college to have any on public occasions. Before long, however, coffee was brought. After partaking of cold chicken, salads, etc. ab[o]ut twenty minutes the party went off amid cheers."[62]

Smith catered numerous entertainments for Harvard College (now Harvard University), and other organizations, which enabled him to provide lavish events for national antislavery bazaars as well as for the twentieth anniversary (January 24, 1851) of William Lloyd Garrison's *The Liberator*, for the Massachusetts Female Anti-Slavery Society, and for the celebration of the issuance of the Emancipation Proclamation. During this celebration, Wendell Phillips unveiled a bust of John Brown, created by William H. Brackett. Although Smith did not ask for payment for these festivities, he was presented with a check for one hundred dollars, a mere fraction of what he spent for the size of the reception.

Smith's catering service also allowed him to employ Africans who had "stolen themselves"—fugitive slaves—whom Smith shielded from slave hunters "who searched for their prey in Boston restaurants." Smith in *The Liberator* "advised every fugitive to arm himself with a revolver," for defense against recapture. Two of the most famous fugitives were Ellen and William Craft. Notable abolitionists such as Theodore Parker, Robert Gould Shaw, George Luther Stearns, William Lloyd Garrison, and of course, Charles Sumner were won over by Smith's culinary skills and became friends of the "prince of caterers."[63]

It would have been good if serving as a member of the state legislature meant that Smith could come to his own aid as well as he aided Sumner. As mentioned earlier, Smith's catering service extended to meal preparation for army soldiers. It was during the Civil War that he spent and lost a great deal of his money as the caterer for the first volunteer regiment raised in Massachusetts, the Webster Regiment, named after Daniel Webster's son Fletcher Webster.

The Webster, or the Twelfth Massachusetts Regiment of Volunteers, was organized by Fletcher Webster in April 1861; he was made colonel of the regiment in May. In describing the regiment's pastime in June, Lieutenant Colonel Benjamin F. Cook writes, "Drills and dress parades marked the time till the close of the month," in addition to "Choice music in abundance, both instrumental and vocal; frolic and games of all kinds, in the quarters and on the parade-ground . . . receiving and entertaining friends and distinguished visitors; frequent visits to the city; plenty of food, of good quality, furnished by Caterer J. B. Smith,—all served to make the time pass very pleasantly." By June 26, 1861, 850 additional men had joined the Webster Regiment, mustered into service, and the regiment "was afterwards filled to the full number required."[64]

Since Fletcher's father had a punch named after him, I have no doubt that the boys, during their frolic and games, imbibed many a thirst-quenching libation such as the following.

Daniel Webster Punch

- 2 dozens lemons
- 2 pounds sugar
- 1/2 pint green tea
- 1 pint Benedictine
- 2 quarts brandy
- 3 quarts claret
- 2 quarts Jamaica rum

> Mix well. Strain. Bottle overnight. Pour into punch bowl in the morning with ice and fruit.[65]

Joshua Smith had fulfilled his role for the regiment. In his petition for reimbursement submitted to the Commonwealth of Massachusetts, Smith states "he was employed by the committee for recruiting the 12th Mass. Regiment (Col. Webster) to provide rations for said regiment from April 22 to July 23 1861, and, also, to furnish three days' rations on their departure for the rest of [the] war, . . . that he did furnish such rations to the entire satisfaction of the Quarter Master and of all parties concerned, and that *the agreed price was fifty cents for each ration to the privates, and seventy five cents to the officers* [italics added]." As the regiment "frolicked," "entertained," and made trips back and forth to Boston, the time must have passed very pleasantly because the bill came to $40,378. Smith also bore expenses for additional costly services, for which he never asked to be repaid. He was of the mindset, like most Africans of the era, that he wanted to do his part, and more, to render service and support to the effort to end slavery. Smith's act of feeding the troops was just as important as those who carried guns and fought in the war.[66]

Smith's petition states that "he [Smith] inquired of His Excellency, the governor, whether he, said Smith, would be paid by the state, and was answered that he would be so paid." Now, Massachusetts Governor John Andrew took a particular interest in Smith "because he was the only caterer in Boston who had the means, pluck, and patriotism to undertake the job," and because *Smith and the governor agreed to an amount that was less than what other caterers charged*. Smith's prices were said to be "just, fair and reasonable according to the market value of the subsistence furnished."[67]

Smith was needed because what better way to lure young men into voluntary duty during war than to assure them that they will be provided with a Black chef's cooking, and of such quality that they would never miss home? On Smith's presenting the bill to the Executive of the State on or about July 26, 1861, Andrew refused to pay it, stating, "no funds had been appropriated by the legislature with which he could legally pay." However, catering and subsistence bills accrued by all other regiments throughout the state were paid for by the state and Congress reimbursed them "without regard to the amount allowed, or to be allowed by the Government of the United States." Smith, "in order to obtain payment was obliged to send to Washington where only thirty cents could be received for each ration, to his great loss." A payment of $23,760.80 was finally received, which fell short by $16,617.20.[68]

Smith's original request for reimbursement and claim for the difference between the agreed price and the sum received, dated January 18,1879, was under consideration by both the Massachusetts House of Representatives and the state senate. In one senate statement, dated March 7, 1879, it was "Resolved, That the Governor and Council . . . are hereby authorized to pay to Joshua B. Smith . . . his just and equitable due, *not exceeding the price paid by the Commonwealth for subsistence for other organizations at the same time* [italics added]." On March 11, 1879, the claim was "read and referred to [the Senate] Committee on Finance." A House statement, dated April 17, 1879, gives the exact same authorization as the senate's March 7, 1879, "resolve" but adds, *"provided, that if the Governor and Council shall judge it . . . to adjust the alle[d]ged claim by arbitration, they are hereby authorized to do so, in such manner as they may think best* [italics added]." Then, sometime in April 1879, the Massachusetts House and Senate enacted, "An Act Relative to the Claim of Joshua B. Smith against the Commonwealth [of Massachusetts]." Section 3 of this printed document states, "The case shall be tried in open court by three of the justices of said superior court without a jury," with the following added, just for Smith, in handwritten script, *"who shall have authority to decide, whether anything, and if is, what amount is legally or equitably due from the Commonwealth to the petitioner* [italics added]." Section 4 states, "And if the final decision is in favor of the Commonwealth, . . . the claim shall be forever barred." It was clear that they were setting up their own arbitrary "legal" barriers to keep from paying him, and it should come as no surprise that they never did pay all that was owed. During the month of April the petition was sent back and forth for "consideration." Apparently, on April 18, 1879, it was read and rejected; a motion was made on April 21 to reconsider. On April 22 the motion was lost. Unwilling to submit to defeat, Mrs. Smith states that on May 14, 1879, her husband filed a petition in the office of the Clerk of the Superior Court for Suffolk County for reimbursement of their $16,617.20, plus "interest thereon."[69]

Even after Smith was cheated out of his fees, he spent additional money related to the war. Another campaign in which Smith was thoroughly involved was a movement to erect a monument to the soldiers of the Fifty-Fourth Massachusetts Regiment and their colonel, Robert Gould Shaw, who had become a martyr in the cause of abolition. It has been written that it was Joshua Smith who conceived the idea, initiating the project beginning in the fall of 1865. He pledged five hundred dollars of his own money and raised funds in the local African community, in addition to enlisting the help of his friend Charles Sumner. In 1897, twenty-three thousand dollars had been raised and the monument erected on Boston Commons.[70]

Joshua B. Smith died on July 5, 1879. His was said to be an impressive funeral, attended by many well-known people of the day, and was held at his home at 37 Norfolk Street in Cambridgeport. He is buried at Mount Auburn Cemetery (plot #1562, Cypress Avenue), the same cemetery where Senator Charles Sumner, Supreme Court Justice Joseph Story, and other famous people are interred. According to the Mount Auburn Cemetery archivist Brian Sullivan, Mount Auburn was never segregated. Interesting information, but none of this helped Smith or his widow. Smith's estate wound up in probate court, as debts had accrued from expenditures for the Twelfth Regiment, contributions to the abolitionist cause, and the law suit, totaling $22,596.99. His chinaware, glass, crockery, cooking utensils, table service, and other articles related to his catering business were given an estimated value of $1,350; the oil painting, "The Miracle of the Slave," left to him by Sumner, was valued at one hundred dollars.[71]

With his personal estate valued at $2,150, and his real estate holdings valued at $4,016.62, his estate certainly could not clear up such outstanding debts. In August 1880, Moody Merrill, administrator of Smith's estate, petitioned to sell Smith's real estate "for the payment of his debts, and charges of administration." Smith's widow, Emeline Smith, had also petitioned probate court to "allow her some parts of the personal estate of said deceased, as necessaries for herself."[72]

In the fall of 1879, the court granted her a total of $750. This small pittance from her husband's estate forced her, at age fifty-five, to go to work as a nurse and housekeeper. Although her husband's petition for the balance of the money owed was still pending in Superior Court, and there was every indication that the case would be dismissed, Mrs. Smith refused to abandon the fight. She filed "Petition of Emeline I. Smith, Widow of Joshua B. Smith, for an Allowance in Consideration of Services Rendered to the Commonwealth by Her Husband," and such was presented before the state Senate on February 3, 1880.

With regard to her petition, in which she asked for "a suitable allowance," according to Massachusetts Supreme Judicial Court Archives and Records Preservation, on April 24, 1880, the Commonwealth of Massachusetts approved a payment to Mrs. Emeline Smith "as a gratuity, in consideration of services rendered the Commonwealth by her late husband . . . in furnishing subsistence to the twelfth regiment of Massachusetts volunteers." The payment was for five thousand dollars, all of which she owed to debtors. Since there was no way to force compensation for the African's work at its true worth and value, the commonwealth felt it did more than enough in offering far less than what the state owed the Smiths, and far, far less than what her husband's work had earned and accomplished for the country.[73]

Two other points come to mind. The hiring of Joshua Smith would not be the first or last time that African cooks and their cuisine were used and actually advertised as a draw to sell potential recruits on joining the ranks during the Civil War. And on this occasion it was not just any cook—it was Massachusetts's Prince of Caterers. Smith was not called the "Prince" of caterers merely because of his culinary skills. Joshua Bowen Smith served the United States, in every way a person could.

It is also crucial to mention that Emeline and Joshua Smith had a daughter who died before both of her parents. Had she been living at the time of their deaths, impoverishment is what would have been handed down to her. Refusing to pay the Smiths the money owed them bore the same results as if he and his wife had been victims of one of the numerous massacres (termed "riots" by historians) that left Africans in America in ruins, forcing them to *pass down poverty, for generations to come.*[74]

The best politicians and political activists, so they say, use every form of diplomacy they know of to try to sway someone to their way of thinking. Therefore, diplomacy takes many forms in politics. One or two African caterers and restaurateurs in Washington used their expertise in the kitchen to try to limit and hopefully reverse "passing down poverty." Culinarily, they imposed their ideas and fought for change in their lives and the lives of their Black brothers and sisters. In providing Washington's politicians culinary sustenance as well as lodging and a place to "hang out," they found themselves indirectly creating, supporting, and maintaining the political theater under construction in the nation's capital throughout at least twelve of the post–Civil War years. This political theater on the one hand sought to exclude Africans, unless they knew how to cook, and on the other would find Africans involved, however briefly, in the fight to secure rights and protection for African people.

9

HOTELIERS, DINING ROOMS, AND CULINARY DIPLOMACY IN THE NATION'S CAPITAL

During the Reconstruction era, from 1865 to 1877, African culinary experts in Washington, DC, used their political and racial consciousness, by way of their expertise in the kitchen and service industry, to bring attention to and effect positive change for African economic, social, and political conditions. A few of these experts were among the eleven thousand free Africans who lived in Washington, DC, in 1860. Generally speaking, the economic position of the majority of those Africans was, as to be expected, limited in terms of the kinds of occupations available. As was the custom, the African's subservient role in society was relegated to cooks and laborers, domestics, and other jobs in the "service" capacity. The rich and influential, both nationally and internationally, were drawn to the capital's style and elegance provided in every venue by these "servants."

The 1850 census listed, for the first time, every individual's occupation, and of the 1,658 Africans categorized, 905 listed their job as "laborer"; 158 as "domestic" or "servant." A heavy demand for service-related occupations ensued in the 1850s, and by 1860 there were close to 3,000 free African cooks, servants, nurses, and washerwomen. Other Africans earned their living by producing and selling oysters, crabs, poultry, and vegetables, fruit produce such as strawberries, and nets, baskets, and firewood. Their merchandise was marketed at one of the District's public markets or was peddled in carts along the streets. Only small amounts of money could be made this way; however, one woman was able to save four hundred dollars, which she used to purchase her husband's freedom.[1]

Municipal regulation of vendor and hawker sales took the form of licensing requirements. Initially, such licensing garnered revenue to finance the Chesapeake and Ohio Canal as well as to build, support, and maintain White-only public schools. An October 28, 1802, ordinance required hackney coaches, stages, and carriages to obtain an annual license from the mayor for a fee of ten dollars. The following spring another ordinance was passed requiring peddlers, wine and liquor sellers, venues with billiard tables, and others to obtain licenses. Grocers, firewood sellers, and others found themselves on an expanded list over the years.[2]

African-operated eating places and hotels were becoming a feature in Washington, and the Snow Riot in 1835, involving the African owner of a restaurant, was an excuse for the passage of even more licensing ordinances. At the corner of Sixth and Pennsylvania, Snow's Epicurean Eating House, a popular restaurant owned and operated by Mr. Beverly Snow, became the target of rioting in 1835. A number of issues were said to instigate the occurrence such as the growing number of Africans in the nation's capital and an alleged assault by a slave on the widow of the famous architect of the US Capitol Building and Octagon House, Mrs. William Thornton. At any rate, rumors spread that Mr. Snow made unkind remarks about the wives of White mechanics who worked at the Navy Yard. Snow denied he had said anything of the kind. His denial was not accepted, and the growing intensity for Snow's blood to flow in the streets instead of through his veins forced him to leave town and move permanently to Canada.

When the looting and vandalism began it was concentrated on Snow's restaurant. However, hell bent on terrorizing the African community and using as their excuse the claim of seeking abolitionist literature, the rioters moved on to attack African homes, businesses, churches, and schools. They wreaked particular violence and vandalism on African schoolhouses, such as those operated by Mary Wormley and John F. Cooke.

As a result of the riot, new licensing laws were enacted purposely aimed at deterring Africans from moving into Washington and in the hopes of discouraging current residents from remaining. An 1836 ordinance prohibited the mayor from granting any license to a free African for the purpose of trade other than driving carts or carriages, and even this permit was restricted to Africans residing in Washington before the ordinance was passed. Specifically, Africans, or anyone acting on their behalf, could not be granted a license to sell alcohol, operate a tavern, restaurant, or any type of eating establishment in Washington. Due to lax enforcement of the licensing regulations, Snow's restaurant reopened within a year, owned and operated by another African, Absalom Shadd, who also reportedly ran a hotel. Shadd sold the restaurant twenty years later for twenty-five thousand dollars.[3]

Lax enforcement of the licensing laws also allowed several African-owned restaurants and hotels to prosper prior to the Civil War. A Mr. Selden kept a hotel on the avenue, between Fourteenth and Fifteenth Streets. African management was also in place under Alfred Cook at The Hope Club Hotel on F Street, between Fourteenth and Fifteenth, as early as 1845. John Kugjohn ran an oyster house on the northeast corner of Pennsylvania Avenue at Fifteenth Street. Lettie Thompson, known as "Aunt" Lettie, was the proprietor of a famous eatery on F Street near the Ebbitt House hotel between Fourteenth and Fifteenth Streets. James Johnson ran a very prosperous confectionery and catering business on Fifteenth Street where the Corcoran building was later built. In 1834, on Pennsylvania Avenue between Fourteenth and Fifteenth, stood a fruit store operated by a Black man named John Brown, who by the 1840s became a confectioner and caterer. In a later era, Blacks such as Lucinda Seaton Chase, mother of W. Calvin Chase Sr., publisher and editor of the *Washington Bee*, opened the Ice Cream Saloon and Confectionery Resort in her home to help make ends meet after her husband, William H. Chase, was accidentally killed. Alexander Peterson was the keeper of The Buckingham, on Fifteenth Street near K. Peterson catered to a coterie of army and navy officers. The city's John Andrew Gray was yet another hotelier.

Gray was born in Washington, DC, to free African parents on June 15, 1829, and received a "colored" private school education. At one time he was a waiter at the Washington Club on Lafayette Square. Gray's hard work garnered property sometime before the Civil War, and he became the owner of the house on Fifteenth Street rented by Philip Barton Key, US district attorney. Key rented the property for the purpose of carrying on a tryst in 1859 with the wife of Daniel E. Sickles, a congressman from New York. The ill-fated adulterers were discovered, and on February 17, 1859, Sickles shot and killed Key on the northeast corner of Pennsylvania Avenue and Lafayette Square.

John A. Gray might have had tenants with questionable morals, but he was still considered one of the leading caterers in Washington for many years. He later became proprietor of the Hamilton House hotel, owning the corner on which the Union Trust Building was subsequently built. He also owned the corner of I and Fifteenth Streets, where the Normandie Hotel was located.

In March 1869 Gray was contracted to cater the Inaugural Ball for General Ulysses S. Grant, which was held on March 4 in the new cash room of the US Treasury. I guess that news of Gray catering the event spread far and wide because the entire town showed up. These were the days when even the uninvited would show up in droves and eat you out of house and home. The committee in charge botched and bungled the evening by not coordinating the guest list with who they allowed inside, and then there was a problem with the amount of food ordered. The evening was described this way: "The attendance was so great that all semblance of order was destroyed and in their eagerness to be served, a panic ensued and the guest[s] seized whatever was available. In the scramble many elegant gowns were utterly ruined. The same disorder existed in the coat rooms and many wraps were torn asunder by frantic guest[s], and hundreds after waiting until daylight were at last compelled to accept ill assorted head gear and many to wind their way home and without any." To make matters worse, they tried to blame their own disorganization on the Black man. The inaugural committee initially kept refusing to pay Mr. Gray the full amount. Gray held his ground, however, and a deal was struck with him donating $250 of his $9,750 fee to the Lincoln Monument Fund.[4]

Gray was a school trustee in 1867 and a city councilman in 1871 for the District of Columbia. In 1871, Georgetown, Washington City, and Washington County were combined under one territorial form of government, overseen by an eleven-member council and a governor. Gray, Frederick Douglass, and Adolphus Hall, a local miller, were appointed members of the governor's council. On May 5, 1907, Gray and his wife celebrated their golden wedding anniversary. He was still in active business in 1910 at the age of eighty-one. He died very suddenly on April 12, 1911.[5]

Other well-known Washington, DC Black caterers included Isaac N. Cary, John Smallwood, Gurden Snowden, Samuel Middleton, James Penny, Thomas Martin, James L. Thomas, Charles Watts, John J. Johnson, as well as Richard Francis and William Andrew Slade. A few of these men became well-known culinary artists by way of DC's White-owned establishments. Many famous restaurants, inns, and taverns owned and run by White men had garnered outstanding reputations because of their African cooks. Richard (Dick) Francis, "a pleasant-faced mulatto, fifty-eight years old," was considered "a splendid appointment" as the new Senate caterer, according to a western congressman who had just heard the news. The congressman was quick to remark, "I have known Dick in his business for over twenty years and have a profound respect for him. His mint-juleps and cocktails made for him a great reputation here a number of years ago which has clung to him ever since, and as for *recherché* dinners and terrapin suppers, I don't believe he has his equal anywhere." One of the most famous White-owned restaurants in DC was John Hancock's, located on the south side of Pennsylvania Avenue near Thirteenth Street, which had been the place of employment of Richard Francis since 1848 when he first came to the city. In the business for over thirty-five years, Francis was hired by Andrew Hancock to manage Hancock's as a caterer. From that moment on he was on the premises six days a week, "opening the house at 7 o'clock in the morning and closing at midnight."[6]

During an interview at Hancock's Francis told the newspaper reporter that, "In old times this house was the rendezvous of prominent gentlemen, and during the sessions of Congress it was a common thing for Senators and Representatives to come up here from the Capitol when they wanted a good drink. Senator Benton was a regular visitor, and . . . he never drank unless I waited upon him. . . . Henry Clay was another regular visitor. His steady drink was old Bourbon straight." Francis also told the reporter, "Yes, I am to cater for the next Senate, and hope to have the Senate restaurant open between the 1st and the 15th of next month. I am familiar with the business, and hope to be as successful in meeting the Senatorial taste as I have been with the gentlemen I have waited upon here." Born at Surrey Courthouse in Surrey County, Virginia, Richard Francis had a son, Dr. J. R. Francis, who practiced medicine in DC.[7]

Senator Tom Benton also made numerous personal appearances at the Senate's "Hole in the Wall" for the purpose of imbibing. He liked mixed drinks, and Francis kept a bottle of the finest brandy set aside for him. "This he took," said Francis, "with a little soda, when in a hurry."[8]

Even though I think that Senator Benton would prefer his spirits a tad more "neat" than the following, I nevertheless present to you a couple of mixed drinks. The first is made with Benton's favorite—brandy—together with Apollinaris water and white wine, a combination that continued to be popular in some circles well into the late nineteenth and early twentieth centuries.

White Wine Punch

- 8 oranges, juice extracted
- 4 lemons, juice extracted
- 1 cup white rum
- 2 cups brandy
- 1 cup granulated sugar
- 2 or 3 slices of pineapple, cut up
- 3 quarts white wine
- 1 cup curaçao
- 1 quart Apollinaris water*

Combine orange and lemon juices, rum, brandy and sugar. Stir until sugar dissolves. Add pineapple. Pour mixture into a stone jar and let stand overnight. Strain into a punch bowl. Add white wine, curaçao, and Apollinaris.[9]

*Apollinaris water, the "Queen of Table Waters," is a sparkling, very rich mineral water with 100 percent source carbonic acid and no artificial carbon dioxide added. Described as "highly effervescent," Apollinaris was considered to have an agreeable flavor alone or mixed with wines or spirits. It was also said to provide a great relief for seasickness. Considered an elegant and sophisticated addition to various elaborate rituals surrounding multi-course meals, it is often served to cleanse the palate between courses or to "mediate" the effects of large amounts of wine. It was very popular in the nineteenth century.

Martini Cocktail
For one cocktail

- 1/2 teaspoon orange bitters
- 1 teaspoon curaçao

- 1/2 glass dry gin
- 1/2 glass dry vermouth

Serve very cold with . . . ice . . . The rim of [the] glass may be moistened with [the] juice of lemon and . . . dipped in sugar.[10]

William Andrew Slade began his career in Washington in the livery business. He was born in Alexandria, Virginia, in 1815. His move to Cleveland, Ohio, when he was still a child allowed him to receive a decent education. Later, after relocating to Washington, DC, Slade became involved in the livery business. The livery business and the driving of hackney coaches was a particularly popular licensed occupation. Africans who were able to purchase a carriage and pay the license fee could actually do well financially, as many travelers reported that their transportation bills while staying in Washington amounted to thirty dollars a week, and in one case, twenty-five dollars a night. Livery vehicles were in continuous demand from the dinner hour until five o'clock in the morning.[11]

In addition to the livery business Slade had also garnered knowledge of catering, and since he saw a potential in Washington for making a living at it, he became a caterer. His reputation spread far and wide, and he became a leader in the field. Described as so fair in color that he could pass for White, Slade was also said to be an intelligent, educated person who started with a clerical position—one of the earliest African clerks appointed—and was later made steward of the White House by President Abraham Lincoln. He continued his stewardship under President Andrew Johnson. Slade oversaw other staff members, such as the doormen, the coachman, and the White House cook, Lizzie Mitchell, who lived in with her two children. When William A. Slade died of heart disease and dropsy (edema) at his home on March 13, 1868, he was survived by four children, Louisa, Libbey, Jesse, and Andrew. President Andrew Johnson attended his funeral, a fact followed by "much and much gossip."[12]

You would think that a president who thought so much of his African steward that he would attend his funeral would be on board, or would certainly not object, when Congress passed the suffrage bill in December 1866, extending voting rights to African American males in the District of Columbia for local elections. Many were rightfully worried that the bill would fail to pass. George T. Downing expressed his concern in a letter to Charles Sumner in which he stated he was "repeatedly questioned by friends, mostly by colored persons, as to whether the bill granting the elective franchise to the col[ore]d people of the District of Columbia will probably pass the Senate by a two thirds vote over the probable veto of the President." Johnson did veto the bill. Johnson's position was that you cannot have African men trying to take part in civic affairs by voting, and pouring drinks for you at the same time. Congress, however, moved swiftly to override the veto. When the bill passed, many African males became very active in politics, organizing a number of Republican clubs around the city.[13]

And, since Andrew Johnson loved having drinks poured for him, he brought additional gossip upon himself when he stopped for a drink at a place run by another noted African Washington caterer, Samuel Proctor. Born on March 2, 1828, in Baltimore, Maryland, Proctor served early in his career as assistant steward to Commodore Barney, with whom he sailed on a number of cruises. In 1849, after returning to DC, he was employed by the Smithsonian Institute and also began a catering business. By 1860, numerous customers and their guests were singing his praises as a caterer.

In February 1861 Proctor was hired by the Washington local committee to provide pre-inauguration services for President-Elect Abraham Lincoln in a house on Franklin Row on K Street between Twelfth and Thirteenth. Having learned of a plot "to offer him indignities and possibly assassinate him," President-Elect Lincoln arrived in Washington several days ahead of schedule and without the knowledge of the local committee. Since the Franklin house was not quite ready, Lincoln stayed at Willard's Hotel, which employed an African headwaiter, George Washington, described as "gorgeous." Proctor, however, had gone to considerable expense and expected recompense. To compensate Proctor, a decision was made "to give him a place in the Capitol, where he could cater to the taste of the Senators and Members, as he . . . [would] . . . do at their homes." A room formerly used as the Senate post office and a little tower room were redone for him. This famous tower room on the Senate side of the US Capitol was called the "Hole in the Wall." From 1861 to 1863 it was run by Samuel Proctor and James Penny; Proctor later ran it alone. The story goes that the Hole in the Wall became even more famous on March 4, 1865, when Vice President–elect Andrew Johnson visited and "imbibed too freely of its liquid refreshments, and was visibly affected thereby and only by heroic action was saved disgrace."[14]

Since I prefer to say what I mean, the story was that Johnson got stinking drunk. The night before, Johnson partied, fortifying himself with whiskey at the home of his friend and secretary of the Senate, John W. Forney. The next morning—that is, inauguration day—he drank three more "tumblers" of whiskey.

Since whiskey was Johnson's drink, perhaps he would have enjoyed a tumbler or two of Wild Cherry Bounce, the history of which is known as a libation prepared back in the day by enslaved cooks for George Washington and his guests.

Wild Cherry Bounce

Place cherries in glass jars, or anything which can be closed tight. Allow one tablespoonful of granulated sugar to each quart of cherries—more or less—and cover with . . . whiskey (the better the whiskey, the better the bounce). Let stand six weeks, then strain the juice through cheesecloth, adding a rich syrup of boiled sugar and water, and more whiskey to taste. It is my impression that if at this stage it could be placed in a small whiskey cask, the flavor would be greatly improved by standing for some months.

"A friend in Kentucky"[15]

Andrew Johnson is mentioned in the memoirs of Isaac Bassett, a sixty-four-year employee of the Senate. Isaac wrote that on the day of the inauguration, Johnson returned some bottles to the Hole in the Wall. Mr. Robert Carter, the caterer who Isaac reports was in charge of the Hole in the Wall at the time, remarked, "Why, he has not dr[u]nk any. The bottles are both full." Hearing this remark, Isaac decided he must have been wrong to conclude that Johnson was drunk: "Anything unusual in his appearance or manner was the result not of drinking, but of his exhausted physical condition from travel." Isaac soon after wrote, "As an act of justice to the memory of A.J. I feel it my duty to correct the report so unduly circulated at the time that Andrew Johnson, at the second inauguration of Mr. Lincoln, and his own as Vice Pres't, was under the influence of liquor. . . . Mr. Johnson . . . was perfectly sober, but fatigued and weak. He had travelled all the preceeding night." (Yeah, right.) How sweet of Isaac to try to clean up A.J.'s reputation. Now, I do not know *how* Johnson was prevented from disgracing himself because whether Johnson's visit to the Hole in the Wall was before or after the inauguration, or perhaps both before *and* after the inauguration, history has it that he was drunk when he gave his inauguration speech on March 4, 1865.[16]

The Daniel Murray Papers report that in 1865 the Hole in the Wall was incorporated into the extension of the Library of Congress, at which time Proctor was given the restaurant quarters later used for senators, called the Senate Saloon, which he held until late 1871. Proctor's November 1869 advertisement in *The Critic* states, "Visitors to the Capitol will find the finest quality of Refreshments, Game, Fruits and Ice Cream And all the Luxuries of the Season, In the Elegant Saloon immediately under the Senate Chamber." Samuel Proctor died at Hillsdale on September 22, 1887. In 1898 the quarters were converted into a toilet room to serve the Senate committees located in the "Old Library Space." The dining room for senators became in 1899 the committee room of the Senate Committee on Pensions.[17]

Politicians, just like Andrew Johnson, have been known to partake of numerous "remedies" in order to brace themselves against the chilblains, whether it is chilly or not.

Tom and Jerry "For a Winter Night"

Mix egg and sugar together till of a consistency of hard cold sauce. Put in bottom of mug about an inch of old Medford or Jamaica rum then scald some milk (not boil). When rum is in the mug add two tablespoons of sugar and egg mixture then pour on scalded milk.[18]

During the Hole in the Wall's most popular period, "lunch consisted principally of ham [and] bread [and] other simple eatibles, but the supply of liquors was quite liberal. The ham [and] bread was paid for out of the contingent fund of the Senate [and] was entered in the accounts as horse hire, until it became too expensive, and it had to be given up, as it was patronized too liberally by members of the House of Representatives. After the Sergeant-at-Arms closed it up it was turned over to a man by the name of Robert Carter, an excellent caterer."[19]

One should also note that in Robert L. Harris Jr.'s article, "Daniel

Murray and the Encyclopedia of the Colored Race," Daniel Alexander Payne Murray, the nineteen-year-old who was selected by Ainsworth R. Spofford to be his personal assistant at the Library of Congress in 1871, is mentioned as having a caterer brother who managed the US Senate restaurant called The Hole in the Wall. David Rapp, in his article, "The Man in the Library," states that Proctor was Daniel Murray's half brother. Daniel had moved to Washington from Baltimore at the age of nine to work for his brother. The Hole in the Wall was celebrated as having attained a worldwide reputation, and distinguished visitors to the Capitol from every section of this country and from abroad never left the city until they had been given a glimpse of the notables and sampled the menu of what was considered to be an epicurean retreat.[20]

Just as senators enjoyed world-renowned food at the Hole in the Wall, members of the House of Representatives dined daily and nightly at their restaurant operated by George T. Downing, who took over its management in 1865. Under Downing, the restaurant in the House of Representatives acquired the reputation of drawing *the* rich and influential from all over the country. This establishment occupied two very stylishly furnished rooms, and its proprietor was described by one of his patrons, Dr. John B. Ellis, as having "decidedly the most elegant manners to be seen in the Capitol." Dr. Ellis goes on to say that Mr. Downing is from New York, "where he is well known to all lovers of good living, and has opened in the Capitol one of the best restaurants in the Union. His bill of fare contains every delicacy of the season, and his dishes are served in a style which would not shame Delmonico himself."[21]

The House restaurant traditionally serviced members who worked late into the evening. As far back as 1834, the "refectory," as it was then called, was run by local vendors and provided beefsteak, partridge, and veal cutlet at twenty-five cents each; mutton chop, a cold lunch, or a bowl of soup for twelve and a half cents; one pint of stewed oysters for a quarter; one half pint of stewed oysters, or one dozen raw oysters, for twelve and a half cents (six and one-fourth cents for one half dozen raw oysters); and one dozen roasted oysters for eighteen and three-fourths cents. As far as beverages, a cup of coffee or a small glass of punch cost twelve and a half cents; a glass of spirits, including gin, brandy, whiskey, and so on cost six and one-fourth cents each; a bottle of port or cider, twelve and a half cents; and a pint of draught beer was six and one-fourth cents.[22]

When the Capitol expanded in the 1850s, the House restaurant (Members' Dining Room) moved to the South Wing. By 1865 the quality of its offerings expanded as well. In a telephone conversation with the curatorial assistant of the Office of History and Preservation of the US House of Representatives, I asked if Downing's was the House's first restaurant. The assistant responded, "No," but "under Downing the level of the restaurant was raised to a much more luxurious level." Downing did indeed raise the standard of the Capitol dining experience, and he used his position to continuously push for racial equality while doing it.[23]

As George T. Downing prepared sumptuous meals for members of the House and their guests, a hotel located on the corner of Fifteenth and H Streets was becoming the most fashionable and widely known African-run hotel and dining room of the nineteenth century. James Wormley, proprietor of the famous Wormley Hotel, set the standard for hotelkeepers both throughout the nation and worldwide. With the succulent fare offered in its dining room and attention to every detail throughout the hotel, politicians were making Wormley's the most popular political rendezvous in the nation's capital.

James's father, Lynch Wormley, was able to give James his start in business. Both Lynch and his wife, Mary, were always said to have never been slaves, having "lived as free people with a wealthy Virginia family." After their move to Washington, Lynch Wormley made the decision to go into the livery business. He purchased a hackney carriage and harness from William Galloway on December 21, 1818. With license in hand, Lynch Wormley came into prominence in the city as a successful proprietor of a livery stable located on Pennsylvania Avenue between Fourteenth and Fifteenth Streets, NW, near Willard's Hotel. Possessing unlimited entrepreneurial spirit, he also ran the Liberia Hotel on E Street between Fourteenth and Fifteenth Streets.[24]

As hard as they worked, Mr. and Mrs. Lynch Wormley found time to produce eight children. The Wormleys owned a small brick building on E. Street, near Fourteenth, NW. It was in this little house with two rooms, plus attic, that James was born on January 16, 1819. An old Irishman turned the house into a saloon during the Civil War; its cellar was used for storing barrels of ale and whisky. The building has since been torn down.[25]

From his early youth James was noted for his diligence, pursuit of labor, and perseverance. Like his father, he acquired the rudiments of education and added to it by numerous endeavors. James began as a hackney driver for his father's stable and later purchased a vehicle of his own, which he used to carry visitors to Washington's leading hotels such as the Indian Queen, the National, and the Willard. While engaged in this service he came into contact with and made quite an impression on numerous leading public figures, some of whom would later become members of his clientele as well as supporters of his other business ventures.[26]

James was twenty-two when, in 1841, he married Anna E. Thompson, of Norfolk, Virginia, and although he had built a highly successful hackney service, he left the business and became a steward on board a US ship commanded by Allen McLane. Several years later he was hired to steward several of the splendid Mississippi River steamboats. California's gold rush lured James to the goldfields there, but he failed to strike it rich (one or two biographies state that he never even made it to California) and returned to Washington. Upon his return to DC he was hired again as steward of the original and popular Metropolitan Club, located at Fifteenth and H Streets (which later relocated across the street), the site that later became his world-famous Wormley's Hotel.[27]

Although a few sources state that the business started shortly before the Civil War, the Wormley Family Papers include a page that mentions that James Wormley began the catering business in the early 1850s on I Street, near Fifteenth, right next door to a successful candy/confectionery store run by none other than his wife, Anna. One of his many catering gigs was aboard a cruise on the steamboat *City of Baltimore*, for Civil War Major General George Brinton McClellan, who invited Secretaries Seward, Welles, and Bates, Commander Dahlgren, along with Mrs. Frederick Seward, the wife and daughter of Admiral Goldsborough, and other ladies. Wormley extended his catering business to include a restaurant, and they both proved extremely successful, quickly garnering popularity with the city's political elite and patrons from various parts of the country. Major General McClellan ate often and luxuriously at Wormley's restaurant, where, almost every afternoon, he also hosted elaborate dinners, with a variety of wines, for at least twenty guests.[28]

George Templeton Strong was another patron. Strong was in Washington in July 1861 and apparently had a hard time finding a comfortable place to sleep. He notes in his diary that he visited every hotel in the city without finding shelter. He says he "got in at the National, and was assigned a cot in a large omnibus garret room—one of eight or ten," which was "worse than [his] room at Willard's." He goes on to say that he "shifted again that night to *Wormley's*, a quiet little place in 'I' Street, where Van Buren, Agnew, Bellows, Gibbs, and I messed together and fared well." So, after he complained about everything he encountered in Washington, including the mosquitoes, the best time he had was when he sat down to eat at the Wormley House. Too bad for Strong that Wormley's Hotel did not open until 1871, because I am sure it would have been his *first* stop.[29]

Wormley's first inn and restaurant on I Street, Wormley House, provided healthy and satiating sustenance for weary travelers, such as the following.

To Make Asparagus Soup

Take five or six pounds of lean beef cut in lumps, rolled in flour; put it in your stew-pan, with two or three slices of fat bacon at the bottom; then put it over a slow fire, and cover it close, stirring it now and then till the gravy is drawn; then put in two quarts of water, and half a pint of ale. Cover it close, and let it stew gently for an hour, with some whole pepper, and salt to your mind: then strain off the liquor, and take off the fat; put in the leaves of white beets, some spinach, some cabbage lettuce, a little mint, some sorrel, and a little sweet marjoram powdered; let these boil up in your liquor, then put in the green tops of asparagus cut small, and let them boil till all is tender.[30]

To Make a Baked Bread Pudding

Take a pint of cream, and a quarter of a pound of butter, set it on the fire, and keep it stirring; when the butter is melted, put in as much grated stale bread as will make it pretty light, a nutmeg, a sufficient quantity of sugar, three or four eggs, and a little salt. Mix all together, butter a dish, put it in, and bake it half an hour.[31]

Wormley's restaurant was said to be an especially attractive watering hole for many of Washington's Radical Republicans. Not only was the food superb, but Wormley kept the choicest varieties of wines and sherries, some of which had been purchased from the sickly Lord Lyons at auction when Lyons sailed back to England. Wormley's was where

Charles Sumner and Vice President Henry Wilson both met and forged a warm and lasting relationship with James Wormley. However, you did not have to be a "Radical Republican" to be drawn to Wormley's culinary masterpieces. The fame of the restaurant and Wormley's dishes became a focal point of the five senses of attorney and politician Reverdy Johnson.

One of Reverdy Johnson's claims to fame was his role in the Dred Scott Decision. "Probably the most respected constitutional lawyer in the country," Johnson was one of the four counsels representing the slave-owning defendant in the 1857 decision. Now, just because Reverdy was a personal friend and staunch supporter and defender of Chief Justice Roger Taney, whose majority opinion made it clear that Africans had no rights that Whites were bound to respect, and just because he later argued in the Senate against the Civil Rights Act and the Fourteenth Amendment (both of which passed in Congress in 1866 and the latter was ratified in 1868) on the grounds that inclusion of Africans as citizens was contrary to the Dred Scott decision, what does *that* have to do with his fetish for a Black man's turtle soup?[32]

Reverdy Johnson and Wormley got together on a professional basis in 1868 when President Andrew Johnson appointed Reverdy Johnson as minister (ambassador) to the court of St. James. Reverdy Johnson, like all other rich businessmen and politicians who came in contact with his cuisine, loved Wormley's culinary preparations, especially his terrapin and roasted duck. He saw the English as "stiff and cold and in need of warming up." He wanted Wormley's dishes to accomplish the task. Knowing that the English would not know how to prepare these dishes, Reverdy persuaded Wormley to temporarily leave his wife and four children and accompany him to England as the embassy's steward, with the primary function of supervising the preparation of his favorite dishes, which included diamondback terrapin from the Chesapeake Bay and the Potomac River. Wormley transported Chesapeake Bay and Potomac River terrapin across the Atlantic, keeping them fresh until it was time to cook them. Johnson's guests were enthralled. James Wormley brought fine dining to England, and every meal thereafter "cemented Wormley's reputation as a connoisseur of fine foods, and greatly increased the demand for his services in Washington." Wormley, as "Diplomatist on Dishes," "used terrapin and canvas-back to the same end that the Ambassador used notes and protocols." Wormley's "culinary diplomacy" delighted the ambassador's dinner guests and won him many English friends, "largely contribut[ing] to Mr. Johnson's diplomatic success."[33]

Well, following Reverdy's two-year appointment, he returned to his law practice in Annapolis, Maryland. He was called moderate in his politics regarding post–Civil War reconstruction of the South. Reconstruction acts that would guarantee the rights of and provide suffrage to former bondspeople were passed by "radicals" such as Thaddeus Stevens and Benjamin Butler. These laws would also prevent former Southern rebels from regaining control of the state governments and mistreating Black southerners. However, all of this was viewed as wrong and unconstitutional by President Andrew Johnson, and he repeatedly blocked their enforcement, while publicly expressing his defiance of the "Radical Republicans." Secretary of War Edwin M. Stanton was the only member of Andrew Johnson's cabinet who supported the Radical Republicans' program for reconstruction. When President Johnson dismissed Stanton and appointed General Ulysses S. Grant in his place, thereby defying the Tenure of Office Act, which made it impossible for the president to dismiss important government officials without the permission of the Senate, the House of Representatives, by a vote of 126–47, formally moved to impeach Johnson on February 24, 1868. On May 16, 1868 the Senate failed by one vote to convict Andrew Johnson on articles of impeachment. Did I mention that another one of Reverdy Johnson's claims to fame, besides his wine collection, was that the senator from Maryland was instrumental in securing the president's acquittal?[34]

During Johnson's impeachment procedure, there was no moratorium on eating; everyone had to eat, including Charles W. Woolley, who was "under arrest for refusing to testify before the board of managers of impeachment." It seems that following the vote to impeach Johnson, the Select Committee of the Managers of Impeachment was formed to prosecute the case before the Senate. However, after the May 16 vote against conviction, the committee decided to address the alleged corruption permeating the impeachment trial. Charles W. Woolley, a lawyer who oversaw "Whiskey Ring" cases brought before the Bureau of Internal Revenue ("the manager or one of the managers of the concerns of that body of men who are defrauding the government" with regard to the whiskey trade), was subpoenaed for questioning by the committee regarding his alleged participation in a scheme to buy the votes of several senators. Well, Woolley tried to arbitrate the outcome of his situation by having a Dr. Bliss send the committee a "certificate" stating that Woolley was "unable to leave his apartments, and confined to his bed by reason of irritative fever—sequella of gastric derangement," on one of the days he was ordered to appear. On another day that he was ordered to testify, he arrived two and a half hours late. When he did testify, he lied, and when he was not lying, he absolutely refused to answer questions. In short, he showed general noncooperation and contempt for the House of Representatives "and hindered the investigations ordered by the House, by contumacy in refusing to answer questions, by evasion, and by avoidance." As a result, on May 25, 1868, a report was presented before the House by Benjamin F. Butler, one of the seven representatives on the committee, and a resolution was offered and passed that same day directing Woolley to be arrested by the Sergeant-at-Arms. Now, you would think that *total* punishment would have followed; that they would have found the least accomplished cooks, serving the worst meals available. From May 25 through June 11, however, at a total cost of $37.70, Woolley's meals were provided by George T. Downing. It truly sounds as though Woolley must have had more friends than enemies in the House. Under these circumstances, he probably did not mind being under arrest. He might have been incarcerated, but he ate well.[35]

Meanwhile, having established an even greater reputation through his "culinary diplomacy" abroad, Wormley returned to Washington to find one positive change was being made in the area of racial discrimination. Congress had exclusive legislation over the District of Columbia, and in 1866 Charles Sumner took particular interest in requesting a place on the Senate District Committee. Sumner had introduced a bill in Congress permitting Africans to be summoned for jury duty and as officers in the government of the District. The bill finally passed. For James Wormley, it was even more positive. Wormley wrote to Sumner in June 1869 enclosing not only the several bills that Sumner asked to be forwarded to him (a service that shall be discussed shortly) but also a certain certificate. Wormley let Sumner know that Wormley had been drawn as one of the "Grand Jurors" for the city of Washington and the enclosed certificate was to that effect. Wormley states, "This is but another step upward, and still greater evidence that your arduous labors [o]n our behalf have not been in vain. . . . If there is anything you wish me to attend to in Washington please let me know."[36]

Washington's National Archives provides the following document:

"In pursuance and by authority of the act of Congress, approved April 20, 1871, entitled 'An act to amend the act approved June 18, 1862,['] entitled 'An act providing for the selection of Jurors to serve in the several courts of the District of Columbia': It is ordered that Sayles J. Bowen, George W. Phillips and James Wormley, citizens of the District of Columbia, be, and they are hereby designated as officers to make the lists of Jurors for service in the Supreme Court of the District of Columbia, instead of the officers designated by the said amended act."[37]

Unfortunately, racial discrimination did not disappear from the capital just because Wormley was selected for jury duty. On Saturday, October 2, 1869, Africans were thrown out of the National Theatre in Washington for "Obtrud[ing] themselves into the dress circle." It was one of James Wormley's sons, James T., and two other Africans, who were ejected and arrested. The *New York Herald* reported that "Mr. Wormley contends that he has as much right to go in the best parts of the theatre as any other person, provided he is willing to pay the price demanded by the managers." The National took their money as payment for the best seats but tried to force them to sit in the "Negro" section. The theatre's managers were said to be "determined to exclude negroes from all parts of their theatre, except that which is specially set apart for them until the highest court decides otherwise, when they say, they will be compelled to close their theatre."[38]

While the newspapers were giving space to segregation and discrimination confronting Africans at White-owned establishments, the news media was also publishing accusations of discrimination *perpetrated by* George T. Downing at the House Restaurant. Apparently, a Washington correspondent of *The Independent* wrote that he had been told "even Downing, the well-known colored caterer and keeper of the House Restaurant, does not venture to entertain his colored brethren, his white customers laying down the law of exclusion to him." Downing fired back with an editorial in *The Independent* clearly defining his position. He spoke of the "obstacle" to success because of a "cramping, depressing prejudice" and stated that having employed "the most accomplished waiters" and applying "the energy [he has] given to business," and "the mastery of it" put into every dinner and party, he might have become a much richer man, a "'railroad king,' a Vanderbilt, a Stewart," he continues, "had it not been for the prejudice against my color, or had I catered thereto." Downing states that he should demand his every right as a man, which included determining who eats at his restaurants. He continues, "To exclude a customer because of his color has never been laid down for me, either in the Capitol or any place over which I have ever had control. No person has been proscribed on account of color in the House Restaurant in the Capitol since I have had charge thereof. Consistency forbids that I should be a party to any such proscription. . . . I deny that any person had ever been, since I have been in business, refused accommodation in any house of mine on account of their color . . . I have accommodated both white and colored in my places of business, at all times . . . at times when it cost me something to do so."[39]

If the Washington correspondent for *The Independent* had bothered to check before making assertions "to the detriment of a person," as Downing himself put it in the same editorial, he would have discovered that Downing was always on the front lines actively working to break and destroy the color line, and that "everywhere his plume was seen in the thickest of the fight for unconditional civil rights and universal suffrage, with Douglass, Sumner, Phillips, Garnet, Garrison and Ward." On occasion Downing had to deal with the mentality of his African brethren who had inculcated the habits taught by the racist and discriminatory Washington environment. An African headwaiter, who had served under the previous proprietor at the House Restaurant, frantically sought out Downing, informing him that "some colored people had called for dinner." Mr. Downing responded, "Serve them and send to me any one who may complain." Downing was also instrumental in having the galleries of the Senate opened to people of color on the same terms as for Whites, as well as helping to overturn the nine o'clock curfew for Africans.[40]

Downing's presence in the city goes back as least as far as the Civil War. While on a trip to Washington in connection with the enlistment of troops, he came in contact with Rhode Island House Representative Nathan Fellows Dixon II, who was elected as a Republican to the Thirty-Eighth and three succeeding Congresses (from March 4, 1863, to March 3, 1871). Dixon suggested to Downing that he take charge of the restaurant in the House of Representatives in Washington. After careful consideration, Downing accepted the challenge and in 1865 took over the restaurant's management, which he held for twelve years. His success after five years could certainly be measured by looking at the census. The 1870 census for Washington, DC, lists Downing's real estate as valued at seventeen thousand dollars and his personal estate at twelve thousand dollars.[41]

At the outset of his management of the House Restaurant, Downing made his reputation known in numerous circles in Washington. He dug right in, seeking to combat racism through his personal contacts with Charles Sumner and other legislators and gaining respect and confidence as he did so. Downing spoke out against and lobbied on issues such as the horrendous treatment of Africans traveling on the Baltimore and Ohio Railroad between Washington and Baltimore. He shared his concern with Sumner who raised the issue on the Senate floor concurrent with pending legislation affecting the railroad.[42]

As head of the House Refectory, Downing interacted daily with politicians and leading statesmen of both parties. He was often asked his opinions concerning matters of legislation and in certain areas of diplomacy. According to some sources it was George T. Downing who was instrumental in having the first Negro appointed to the diplomatic corps of the United States. Ebenezer Don Carlos Bassett, appointed in 1869 by President Ulysses S. Grant as minister-resident and consul general to Hayti (Haiti), was said to be America's first Black diplomat. He was also reportedly the first Black student to integrate Connecticut Normal School in 1853, which gives him a one-hundred-year jump on *Brown vs. Board of Education*. Bassett was later appointed principal of a public grammar school in New Haven, Connecticut, and while there took classics, math, mathematical science, and literature classes at Yale.[43]

Judging from the tone in correspondence Bassett forwarded to Downing, they seem to have been on very friendly terms, as his letters express warmest regards. In one letter, Bassett mentions having lunched at Wormley's restaurant with the first African member of the US Senate, Hiram Rhoades Revels, who filled the position vacated by Jefferson Davis about ten years earlier, and J. P. Root, minister to Chile. This would also clearly indicate that, like Downing, Wormley had no intention of towing the color line by restricting his restaurant to White patrons.[44]

Ebenezer Bassett also became a friend of Frederick Douglass, who was one of President Grant's appointees to a commission sent to Santo Domingo (Dominican Republic) in 1871. Grant was quite anxious to annex Santo Domingo. This poorly disguised thrust into imperialism on the part of America forced Massachusetts Senator Charles Sumner, chair of the Foreign Relations Committee, to vigorously oppose the idea before Congress.[45]

Even though Sumner persuaded the Senate to reject the proposed treaty, Grant still hoped to gain support for and find a back door to annexation. He created a commission, consisting of Andrew D. White, president of Cornell University; Dr. Samuel Gridley Howe, the noted Boston reformer; former Senator Benjamin F. Wade; and as assistant secretary to the commission, Frederick Douglass.[46]

Douglass was, for the most part, treated equally during the expedition to Santo Domingo. However, on the commission's return, "On the voyage from Charleston to Washington, Douglass was denied admission to the dining room by the captain of the Potomac mail packet" *Georgiana*. Commission members White and Howe argued with the officials of the steamer, but they refused to reconsider. White and Howe were said to become so furious that they left the dining room. The captain offered to set up a table for the White commissioners and Douglass in a separate room, but they all declined. Note that, "the President, on whose invitation [Douglass] had joined the Commission, never uttered a word in rebuke of this exclusion."[47]

Douglass returned to Washington wholly supporting US expansion and the annexation of Santo Domingo, mainly because, apparently, he supported the Republican Party to the exclusion and subordination of everything else—including accepting racism against himself. Douglass was hit with a second slap in the face, once again proving that it was alright for Black hands to serve the White man's table but they were never welcome to dine there. All four commissioners returned to Washington on March 27. Three days later, the three White commissioners were invited to dine at the White House. Everyone knew Douglass was in town. The day before the dinner, on March 29, Douglass presided as chairman at the Republican Convention to nominate a delegate to Congress from the District of Columbia; on taking the chair he made a speech. Douglass, however, was not invited to the March 30 dinner at the White House.[48]

Douglass was hurt, deeply; but he refused to admit it publicly. Douglass made all kinds of excuses for Grant's racism. The *New York Times*, in several articles, took the position that if Douglass said it was not important, why was everyone, especially Charles Sumner, making such a big deal over it. Douglass stated, "I should be ashamed to charge the omission to invite me as an offense against me or my race. The President was under no obligation to invite me to dine with him. . . . It is enough that I am with all my heart laboring to elect U. S. Grant President of the United States for a second term. I certainly should not so labor if I thought him capable of offering me an insult because of the color of my skin."[49]

However, in a private conversation between James Wormley and Douglass, "shortly after [Douglass's] return from St. Domingo," Wormley asked him if he dined with the President and the Commissioners. Douglass responded, "no, and for a good reason[:] I was not invited." Douglass is further quoted as stating, "it is no use to deny it, but I feel it sorely." In a later conversation with Wormley on the same subject, at Douglass's son's house, Douglass is said to have remarked, "I felt it keenly." Wormley told all of this to Charles Sumner, who then quoted Douglass's true feelings of having been slighted in a letter to Commissioner White, which all wound up discussed in the *New York Times*. In his letter to White, Sumner added that Douglass stated, directly to Sumner, that "the President's neglect in not inviting him to dine, . . . was more noticeable," and that "an invitation from the President would have been a proper rebuke to those who had insulted him."[50]

Frederick Douglass accepted the appointment of assistant secretary against the absolute condemnation of James Wormley. One evening Drs. Francis J. Grimke and Edward Wilmot Blyden were driven out in one of Wormley's vehicles to Wormley's farm, just outside of the city, where the three men dined and engaged in chat, particularly on racial issues. The subject of Douglass's appointment came up about which Wormley voiced tremendous displeasure, telling his guests that in accepting this position, Douglass "compromised his dignity." Wormley saw the offer as "an insult." Grimke quotes Wormley as stating that if he (Wormley) had been given the offer, he would have "spit in General Grant's face." Wormley apparently saw that this commission was not formed in the best interests of Africans anywhere, and Douglass, as assistant secretary, would not be expected to act or influence policy. Douglass's name, and the color of his skin, would be used to open certain doors wide enough to accomplish Grant's purpose.[51]

Intent on "resettling" the newly freed bondspeople, as well as making money from the island's rich resources and opening the door to lucrative real estate investments, Grant surely felt he could use a black face to appease Africans here in America as well as abroad. However, in rushing headlong into campaigning for and blindly giving support to

Grant (the same Ulysses S. Grant chosen by racist Andrew Johnson to replace Edwin M. Stanton, supporter of Radical Republican programs) and the Republican Party, Douglass actually invited Grant's mistreatment. After all, when the commission returned from Santo Domingo, annexation was still a dead issue. Therefore, as Sidney M. Willhelm asks, *"who needs the Negro?"*[52]

Grimke and Blyden's visit was topped off with dinner. Grimke reports that "the evening ended with a delicious oyster supper, which we all thoroughly enjoyed."[53]

Scalloped Oysters (Entrée)

For 1 quart solid oysters use 1 pint pounded cracker crumbs, 3 ounces of butter, 1 gill cream, 1/2 gill oyster liquor, pepper and salt to taste. Butter baking dish and cover bottom thickly with cracker crumbs, wet with oyster liquor and a little cream, then add a single layer of oysters, salt and pepper and a bit of butter on each oyster, then more crumbs, oysters and so on, until the dish is full, top layer being crumbs dotted over with bits of butter. Set in oven with cover and bake until juice bubbles up to the top, then remove cover and brown. A glass of sherry or Made[ir]a may be poured over before browning.[54]

An evening at James Wormley's dinner table had, by this time, become an even more memorable event. Wormley's plans to become a much more successful businessman took a turn in 1871 when he acquired a building on the southwest corner of H and Fifteenth Streets (1500 H Street, NW), and with his older property on I Street serving as an annex, he opened Wormley's Hotel. Now, supposedly Wormley ran into some monetary difficulty after taking on the hotel. There were said to be mortgage payment issues, leading to an arrangement with Congressman Samuel Hooper of Massachusetts (Charles Sumner's wife's ex-father-in-law), to purchase the building, who then rented it to Wormley. It has also been written that it was with Congressman Hooper's initial aid that Wormley purchased the building. The hotel was said to have opened on December 1, 1871. In a letter to Wormley dated September 28, 1871, Sumner comments, "I am here for 3 days with Mr. Hooper who read me a letter from Washington saying that you will make out of the Hotel

$25,000 the first year. Good! Three cheers!" Congressman Hooper, it would seem, had been made privy to certain intimate details of the venture. Please note, however, that when the hotel was sold in 1893, it was purchased from James Wormley's son James T. Wormley. The Wormleys, therefore, did own the hotel.[55]

Open only a few months, the word was out: the Wormley Hotel was a hit. Senator Charles Sumner wrote to his Black caterer friend Joshua B. Smith, "Wormley is very successful. He is sure that his is the best house in the country. He expects to pay for his furniture out of this year's profits." Conveniently located near the White House, the Treasury and Navy Departments, and Lafayette Square, the hotel was the ideal accommodation for business travelers and dignitaries. Dining and lodgings at Wormley's soon became among the most sought-after in Washington. Contemporaries of the era describe the hotel's gracious rooms and amenities as "superb, the cuisine elaborate and refined, and the service perfect." An 1884 account states:

> [Wormley's] ranks at the head of Washington's best establishments of that kind. Elegant in all its appointments and most efficiently managed, it has gradually won the reputation it enjoys at present. For years it has been patronized by our most eminent men, and is the general rendezvous for the foreign aristocracy visiting our country. All the late presidents, . . . enjoyed the hospitality of its well-known proprietor. The hotel . . . was enlarged in 1881. A large number of sleeping apartments and dining rooms for private dinner parties have been located in this addition. . . . The house is arranged for the accommodation of 150 guests, and is provided with all the newest improvements as to elevators, telephone, and heating apparatus; electric bells are introduced throughout the premises; . . . its general management is such that nowhere, neither in the United States nor abroad, can a better appointed hotel be found.[56]

Yes, it is true. Wormley's was one in only a handful of establishments housing a telephone. The Executive Mansion's telephone number was 1; Wormley Hotel's telephone number was 13.[57]

The hotel stood five stories high. Its offices and dining rooms were located on the first floor; parlors and guest rooms were on the upper four floors. Furnishings in the guest rooms and throughout the hotel were said to be luxurious. The rooms at Wormley's Hotel in 1876 rented for the daily rate of five dollars and were "the largest and airiest of any in town." The halls and corridors were wide and spacious. The parlors accommodated both ladies and gentlemen. A first-class barbershop and a bar, renowned for Wormley's choice wines and spirits, were in the basement. And since "dining in Washington is a great element in politics," the most important aspects were the firsthand reports indicating:

> [Wormley's] hotel is the only stopping place for epicures, for its table is
> world renowned. . . . nowhere is such comfort attainable as under Mr.
> Wormley's organization. The house has always maintained the lead for
> its culinary facilities and admirable table. Its bills of fare are remarkable
> for many reasons. The catering for this house is done upon a methodical
> scale, and every section is laid under contribution to secure the choicest
> luxuries—game, fowl, meats, fish, fruits, etc., for the larder, and which
> are prepared under the supervision of a skilled *chef.* The dining-room
> service is admittedly the best in Washington, while the tariff is very
> moderate.[58]

One of the reasons the culinary department at Wormley's received such a high rating was because the season's freshest and tastiest viands were provided by Wormley's very own farm. He and his son William owned property and at least two country houses during the 1870s and 1880s on what was then called Pierce Mill Road, near Fort Reno (Reno and Van Ness) in upper northwest Washington. Most of the foods prepared at the hotel had as their ingredients products grown on his property. In addition, this author can personally attest to the beauty and exquisiteness of the table settings. Mrs. Freida Wormley, mother of James Wormley's great grandson Stanton L. Wormley Jr., graciously invited me to visit her home in Washington, DC, where she allowed me to peruse the magnificent crystal and gold-trimmed wine and water goblets, the gleaming silver eating utensils, and some of the choice chinaware used at the Wormley Hotel.[59]

Since Wormley guided his hotel with what was considered a soundness of judgment and a degree of ability not found elsewhere, and he put Washington on the map as having an establishment considered the epitome of perfection in hotel keeping, his roster of guests would surprise no one. Senators, members of Congress, cabinet officers, and other dignitaries made Wormley's their home. The hotel was the Washington home of Vice President Schuyler Colfax. John Hay resided there in 1879 while he was assistant secretary of state; he sent personal correspondence to Wormley. New York Senator Roscoe Conkling was a resident during 1879 and 1880. Among the coterie of New England statesmen and politicians who also made Wormley's their Washington home were Senators Anthony of Rhode Island, Merrill of Vermont, Dawes and Hoar of Massachusetts, and several Massachusetts members of the House. Included in this group was Massachusetts congressman William W. Crappo, who was on the committee on banking and currency in the Forty-Sixth Congress; he chaired the committee in the Forty-Seventh Congress. He was also the author of, and skillfully carried through to become law, the bill for extending the charters of national banks. His numerous interests and activities included a onetime presidency of the Flint and Pere Marquette Railroad as well as having shipping and New England cotton industry concerns and reached far in "placing the United States in the forefront of commercial nations."[60]

General Winfield Scott—"Old Fuss and Feathers," who loved "tarrapin," canvasback duck, and the hams of his native Virginia—was said to have stayed at the "Wormley Hotel." However, the hotel opened in 1871; Old F and F died in 1866. Actually, he occupied rented rooms at the Wormley House on I Street, the business James Wormley had established prior to the Wormley Hotel. Also, Theodore Roosevelt, on his return to Washington from a ranching and hunting expedition in the Northwest in 1889, opened personal headquarters in a back room of the Wormley Hotel, which he used to round up votes from the new congressmen from Washington, Montana, and North and South Dakota for electing Thomas Brackett Reed of Maine as Speaker of the House, for the Fifty-First Congress (1889–1891).[61]

While Thomas Downing's Oyster and Dining Saloon was the "political rendezvous" in New York, Wormley's was most assuredly the "political rendezvous" in DC. Wormley's hosted the diplomatic set, including Congressman Caleb Cushing, also from Massachusetts, who served as minister to Spain from 1874 to 1877. The Marquis and Madame de Noailles and Señor and Madame Flores lived and entertained at Wormley's. Lodging at Wormley's had been contracted by the government for the majority of the delegates to the International Marine Congress, and from October 1889 to April 1890 for the Pan American Congress. The Pan American Congress was said to be the First International American Conference. Wormley's special appeal to foreign visitors and dignitaries, "who generally thought American hotel accommodations horrible," attracted the English Joint High Commission on the Geneva Award. The hotel was very popular with titled Englishmen who visited Washington. The German legation was housed at Wormley's during the years following the unification of the German states. The 1880s also saw members of the diplomatic corps from Chile and France listed as residents at Wormley's. Shortly before James Wormley died, Lord Coleridge, Chief Justice of England, reserved nine rooms at the hotel.[62]

One of Wormley's specialties was private dinner parties, "and the most elaborate and successful of the season [were] always given here." Washington lobbyist Sam Ward entertained profusely and rotated his larger lobbying dinners among Wormley's Hotel, the Metropolitan Club, and sometimes John Chamberlain's club. Wormley's maintained the same focus for the rich and famous as a central resort as did the Hoffman and the Fifth Avenue in New York at that time. And sometimes this center of social activity drew patrons who did not pay their bills in a timely fashion; some not at all. John W. Forney, the same collector for the Port of Philadelphia who praised Augustin's chicken croquettes in *The Epicure* and was feted in 1871 with a dinner at Augustin's restaurant in Philadelphia, wrote to Wormley, stating, "Mr. Stevens has just called to tell me that he has paid his bill which he owed to your Hotel, and I am very glad to know it particularly as he used my name with you. Nothing gives me more pain than that you should lose anything by any person claiming to be a friend of mine." Forney definitely knew where to find the very best in African purveyors of cuisine.[63]

"Mr. Stevens," according to Forney, did finally pay. The same cannot be said of Emory Storrs. Clearly, love or loyalty for any political party can be bad for the Black businessman's wallet, and dangerous for Black folks in general, in the long run. In the early 1870s, as the anecdote goes, Emory Storrs was touted as Chicago's great advocate and orator. He was sent to Washington as an attorney in connection with the charges against Anton Hasig, editor of the *Staats Zeitung*, who was connected to the operations of the Whiskey Ring. Now, Storrs, together with his wife and son, landed at Wormley's, where he extended royal hospitality during his residence in Washington. When Storrs checked out of Wormley's, he left the hotel proprietor a check for services, which amounted to a little over fifteen hundred dollars. Unfortunately, Storrs's check was returned to Wormley stamped "NO FUNDS." Time passed and there was a September campaign in the works in Maine. The Republicans hired Storrs "to stump the State, which he did with telling brilliancy." The Democratic congressional committee found itself in a desperate situation, and having heard about Storrs's bad check, sent an inquiry to Wormley asking if it were true. When Wormley confirmed that he still held Storrs's bounced check, the representative of the committee told Wormley that they would pay the entire amount owed him. Wormley was willing to accept, except he first wanted to know why they would pay it. The explanation given was that "Storrs was hurting the Democratic party in Maine and they proposed to use the check and drive him out of the state." Wormley was said to have replied, "The check is not for sale, gentlemen. . . . I am a Republican and my race owes its freedom and its opportunities to the Republican party. I will not do what you ask to injure my friend." Storrs's bad paper was still in Wormley's safe when Wormley died.[64]

It was not so much the Republican Party that was owed such trust and allegiance by Africans in America but, rather, only a few individuals who happened to have been Republicans. These included Charles Sumner, who had been a longtime firebrand in Washington. There was never surprise in Sumner constantly upsetting southern slaveholders and their supporters.[65]

Sumner spent time at both Wormley's and Downing's establishments. Downing also catered to Sumner's culinary needs outside of the House Restaurant. Downing was away in Virginia when he received a letter from one of his employees at his restaurant in Washington. The letter prompted him to write to Sumner explaining that he regretted his absence from Washington, as it deprived him of the pleasure of complying with one of Sumner's requests. Since Downing's chefs did not know how to prepare oysters the way Sumner liked them, he offered to prepare them himself and send them to Sumner. The son of the Great Man of Oysters of New York continues, "I shall be in Washington a day on my way north when I will, with pleasure, prepare you some. . . . [P]repared as you like them, they are not so delicate when prepared to keep."[66]

Wormley also pampered and catered to his many wealthy patrons in numerous ways. He operated a roadhouse, or clubhouse, for owners of racehorses, and a racetrack was on the property, which the owners used to try out their horses. The roadhouse was said to be "a famous breakfast or dinner rendezvous for Washington celebrities during several decades following the Civil War." The resort was located on Rockville Road near Wisconsin Avenue. Catering to the wealthy and influential, it was also known as the summer extension of the Wormley Hotel. Wormley, therefore, was the perfect person to get Sumner's horses in shape for selling.[67]

In a discussion of Wormley's Hotel and its summer extension, it is important to mention that, just as Wormley served members of his own race at his restaurant he also served them at his hotel. Francis Grimke tells us that statesman and pan-Africanist Dr. Edward Wilmot Blyden was a guest at the Wormley Hotel. Dr. Grimke states, "Dr. Blyden, at this time on his visit to this country and city, was stopping at the Wormley Hotel." However, the conversation that took place regarding Frederick Douglass's appointment to Santo Domingo and the wording of Grimke's statement places Blyden there before the hotel was actually opened, unless he was commenting on Blyden having stayed there at a later date. James Wormley established Wormley House on land that his father owned on I Street, and this was the precursor to Wormley's Hotel. As mentioned, the Wormley House on I Street offered many of the same services. There would not have been many Africans who could have afforded to stay at either establishment anyway, but those who did come were accommodated. Again, this is indicative that Wormley did not adhere to the prevailing discrimination.[68]

You could count on pressure, courtesy of Charles Sumner, against the prevailing discrimination. On May 12, 1870, Sumner introduced his Civil Rights Supplement, which he felt would make any other legislation on this issue unnecessary. Downing wrote to Sumner twice in reference to the supplement, the second time letting Sumner know that he (Downing) had written to Senators Trumbull, Edmonds, Stewart, Anthony, Conklin, Wilson, and Nye, urging them to pass Sumner's Civil Rights Supplement. Downing continues in his letter:

> If left friendless, unprotected and dependent, they may hope for a
> certain amount of consideration and protection, when the conciliatory
> move would be to vote the Democrat into place. If your bill supplemen-
> tary to the civil rights act shall not pass, . . . would it be strange if he
> should not vote the Republican ticket? It would . . . [take] consideration
> on my part before I should feel at liberty to condemn him, unmeasur-
> ably, for not doing so. I would like that each Republican Senator should
> know that this is my feeling in the matter, and that it is the feeling of
> intelligent colored men.[69]

Clearly, restaurateur Downing's words and convictions carried weight with Sumner, who gave a speech on January 31, 1872 at the Forty-Second Congress, second session, in which he pressured for passage of his supplement to the Civil Rights Bill. In his argument with Senator Morrill of Maine, Sumner allowed "colored fellow citizens" to "speak"—that is, he read letters and testimony from Africans attesting to the necessity of passage of this bill. He read a statement from R. G. L. Paige, member of the House of Delegates of Virginia; E. A. Fulton, a resident of Arkansas; and one from Edwin Belcher, president of the Georgia Civil Rights Association. But it was the words of George T. Downing who Sumner "put face to face" with Senator Morrill, an opponent of Sumner's bill. Downing's name, along with his views and writings, was constantly used during Sumner's argument to counter and "answer" Morrill's opposition. Morrill summed up Sumner's presentation by stating sarcastically and with contempt that Sumner "brings in Mr. Downing . . . and with an air of triumph calls upon me to answer, and calls upon the country to see how I am overthrown by Mr. Downing, 'a colored fellow-citizen!'" Sumner had sent Downing a copy of his speech some days earlier. In response, Downing wrote, thanking him for the copy of the speech, as he was "proud to be remembered by so good a man." And "I borrow my daughter[']s words," Downing wrote, "God bless Charles Sumner."[70]

Momentarily leaving the hotel and club kitchen and all other labor behind, on December 9, 1873, approximately 330 delegates came together for the National Convention of Colored Persons, which assembled in the hall of the House of Delegates. The gathering was comprised of leading African men from all over the country. Organizing this event was the Pennsylvania Equal Rights' League. Chartered in 1864, the league called on Congress to pass the Civil Rights Bill. It sought to "compel the tyrant to loose his hold on the poor, and still forever the assumptions based alone on color." A few days later Sumner presented to the Senate an intelligently written, five-page petition asking for the passage of the Supplementary Civil Rights Bill. It eloquently outlined once again the necessity of calling attention to and eradicating the intolerable treatment of African citizens who are "shamefully outraged." The petition was called "Memorial of the National Convention of Colored Persons, Praying to be Protected in Their Civil Rights," and it was written by restaurateur George T. Downing.[71]

Downing and Wormley were present at Sumner's very last plea to pass the Civil Rights Bill. They were both at Sumner's side during his last hours after he suffered a massive heart attack. Downing was holding Sumner's hand when he passed away at ten minutes to three on the afternoon of March 11, 1874. Among the few allowed in the room at Sumner's home where he lay dying was Judge E. Rockwood Hoar, to whom Sumner spoke several times stating, "Judge, the Civil Rights Bill; don't let it be lost." At 2:50 p.m. Dr. Lincoln had his hand on the senator's pulse while George T. Downing held his other hand. "Suddenly there was a convulsive movement of the muscular system, the Senator grasping the hand of Downing so powerfully that he almost crushed it. Then, with a sudden throwing up of his hands, the Senator expired."[72]

Downing and Wormley, as well as Hoar and three other of Sumner's closest associates, have since been depicted in a painting representing the last moments of Sumner's life. Sumner's caterer friend Joshua Smith was bequeathed a valuable Tintoretto painting (some have written it was merely a copy), *The Miracle of the Slave*, which Sumner was said to have purchased in Venice. Smith became a member of the planning committee, or "Committee of Arrangements," for the commemoration services for Charles Sumner, held in the Music Hall at the State House before the executive and legislative branches of the Commonwealth of Massachusetts on June 9, 1874.[73]

Downing shared his deepest regards for Sumner with his sister Julia Sumner Hastings, then a resident of San Francisco, who responded to a letter from Downing the following year. She tells him in part, "I shall always remember with tender gratitude your kind care of my dear Brother in his last sufferings,—and shall cherish gratefully the memory of all who were with him, in his last hours . . . yourself and Mr. Wormley." She continues, "Please express my heartfelt gratitude to Mr. Wormley—and accept it for yourself."[74]

Washington's two most famous purveyors of fine cuisine were not the only Blacks who provided Sumner with memorable meals. A few days before leaving to return to his home in Washington for the last time, Sumner dined with George S. Hillard, the friend of his youth, already smitten with paralysis. An eyewitness recounted the scene:

> The two friends talked till nearly twelve o'clock, recalling old and intimate days. . . . When they parted, it was almost in silence, with a long clasp of hands, as if each felt it was for the last time. It so happened that

we had colored servants. The old cook had been a slave in Georgia, and was greatly excited over the preparations of a dinner for the man who was to her the deliverer of her race. Mr. Hillard told Mr. Sumner what a solemn occasion it was to her. Mr. Sumner said it was the custom in some places to send a glass of wine to the cook when the dinner was un-usually good, and begged permission to do so, which he did, rendering the old woman almost beside herself with pride. The servants had told me of their earnest desire to see the great man, and I asked Mr. Sumner if he could gratify them. He assented, simply and readily. I shall never forget how he looked as he stood in the doorway of the dining-room, al-most filling it in height and breadth, while those two poor, homely black women, one of them scarred by injuries received in slavery, reverently kissed his hand. It was a scene full of significance. . . . I also remember that the kitchen department was demoralized for some days following.[75]

Forget the glass. This delightful concoction will certainly have guests raising a toast to you and sending you whole bottles of wine.

Corn Chowder with Prawns

- 3 slices bacon
- 10 prawns in shells, remove shells (but do not discard) and de-vein
- Seasoning for prawns, all to taste: garlic salt, black pepper, asafetida* (or an aromatic spice of your choice), ground cumin
- Rice flour
- 1 egg, beaten
- 1 tablespoon butter
- 2 to 3 teaspoons sesame seed oil
- Shells from 10 prawns
- 2 cups water
- 6 cups chicken broth
- 2 15-ounce cans creamed corn
- 1/4 teaspoon EACH ground cumin and dill weed
- 1/2 teaspoon EACH cilantro and crushed red pepper
- 3/4 teaspoon parsley flakes
- 3 teaspoons garlic salt with parsley
- Black pepper, to taste
- 2 onions, chopped
- 1 medium roasted red pepper, chopped
- 2 tablespoons sugar
- 1 tablespoon dark rum
- 1/2 pint whipping cream
- Crisp, cooked bacon, crumbled, one slice per serving

In a skillet cook bacon until crisp. Remove from skillet and set aside. Reserve oil from bacon.

Place prawns in a bowl. Season prawns with spices. Stir and toss until well coated. Roll prawns first in rice flour, coating well, then in egg. Heat butter and sesame seed oil in skillet. Brown prawns on both sides. Set aside, covered.

Simmer shells in water, covered, for about 15 to 20 minutes. *Strain* and discard shells.

In a large pot add shell water, broth, and creamed corn. Stir in next seven spices. Crumble crisp bacon and stir into pot.

In reserved bacon oil in skillet add onions. Cook and stir until onions brown. Transfer onions and oil to pot. Stir in roasted red pepper and sugar. Simmer, covered, about 15 minutes. Add rum and browned prawns. Simmer, covered, about 5 minutes longer. Stir in cream. Heat just to boiling, but DO NOT BOIL. Taste for needed black pepper or other seasonings. Garnish servings with additional crumbled bacon.

*Asafetida has an onion-like smell when exposed to heat. It is the dried gum resin from several species of the *Ferula* plant. Available in lump or powdered form (you would need the powdered) at Indian groceries.

Sumner's dying wish came to pass (parts of it anyway), and twenty months after the Civil Rights Act of 1875 was signed into law the country was in the midst of a presidential election. The contenders were the Democratic candidate, Samuel J. Tilden, the same Tilden who liked doing lunch with his politician friends at Downing's Oyster House, and the Republican, Rutherford B. Hayes, both opponents of "Radical" Reconstruction. On the same day that Hayes accepted the nomination, the town of Hamburg, South Carolina, was embroiled in a so-called race riot. Another six-day "race riot" took place at nearby Ellenton, South Carolina, on September 15 through September 20. It was clear that "many Southerners and some Northerners justified the resort to force as the only means by which the whites could obtain redress for the wrongs which, they alleged, had been inflicted upon them by a Negro majority." Ulysses Grant's Attorney General Taft wrote to Hayes, letting him know that "it is a fixed and desperate purpose of the Democratic party in the South that the negroes shall not vote, and murder is a common means of intimidation to prevent them."[76]

At any rate, Tilden won the popular vote over the Republican Hayes in the 1876 election. However, Florida, South Carolina, and Louisiana all sent two sets of electoral votes to Congress. Congress attempted to thwart a crisis by creating a fifteen-member commission that would decide which set of votes was valid in each case. The commission voted eight to seven to award twenty disputed votes to Hayes. For these votes, promises from Hayes were made to the southern states, negotiations were held, a bargain was struck, and Hayes was declared the victor. The reassurances given to southerners' demands through Hayes's representatives, all of which outlined and mapped out each step in the betrayal of African "Americans," had already been ongoing but were finalized at secret conferences held on February 26 and 27, 1877, in rooms, with accompanying succulent mealtime sustenance, at (are you ready?) the Wormley Hotel.[77]

Hayes kept his promise. "The Compromise of 1877," the "Wormley Conference," the "Wormley Agreement," or the "Wormley Bargain," all terms used interchangeably in history books, had, in absolute terms, killed Reconstruction and reinvigorated the precepts of African inferiority and powerlessness, allowing Rutherford B. Hayes to become "the principal presidential architect of the consolidation of white supremacy in the South, during the post-Reconstruction period."[78]

I assume Wormley did not know. Politicians were always showing up on his doorstep as guests, and these did what politician guests always do: hold conferences, talk politics, sleep, drink, and eat. After all, they were not going to ASK Wormley if they could come to his hotel and fashion plans to betray his people. But just imagine! The plot to betray Africans is consolidated at a hotel owned by one! And worse: the deed carries the Black man's name—into posterity.

Now, like all good "architects of white supremacy" Rutherford B. Hayes had to have his African cooks and servants. He took office in 1877 as the wealthiest president of the nineteenth century. Life for Hayes's family, which included five children, was made easy by more than a dozen servants, some of whom had been employed at the White House under Ulysses S. Grant, and some of whom accompanied the family from their home in Ohio. Africans Winnie Monroe and her daughter Mary had been with the Hayes family for years; Winnie performed double duty as the children's nurse and the family cook, while Mary was Mrs. Hayes's maid. It was said that Mrs. Monroe "annoyed the other White House servants by referring to herself as the 'first colored lady of the land.'" She was apparently known for "tantrums and moodiness," so they say.[79]

John Alex Simms joined the White House domestic staff as steward during the Hayes administration. He remained only two years—from 1877 to 1879. Simms was born in Upper Marlboro, Prince George County,

Maryland, on November 9, 1830. He landed in Washington, DC, while still a child in about 1837. He received a "fair education" at Reverend John F. Cook's school, located at the corner of H and Fourteenth Streets. Simms was elected five times by the Baltimore Conference as a lay delegate to the General Conference of the AME Church, and he represented the John F. Cook Lodge, No. 1185 (which he founded) four times. Simms was also active in the establishment, in 1841, of Union Bethel (Metropolitan AME) Church. He initially entered government service as a messenger in the Ordinance Bureau in 1849, but he left the following year to follow the gold rush in California. He came back to DC, however, and was transferred to the Board of Construction of the Navy Department in 1853. In 1877 he was appointed White House steward by President Hayes. Hayes made a few changes in 1879, and Simms was given another position. John Simms was said to hold "many positions of honor under the municipality of Washington, D.C." He was twice married, first on May 8, 1849, to Martha A. Shorter, who died in Washington, DC. His second wife was Lorena M. Butter, whom he wed in 1900. In 1912, at the age of eighty-two, Simms held a position in the Ordinance Bureau of the US War Department. "One of the oldest colored residents of the City of Washington," and "exceptionally conspicuous and prominent in social and civic work during the whole of his career for the uplift of his race and the community in general," he died at his residence, 1181 New Hampshire Avenue, on March 31, 1918.[80]

James Wormley, too, was well-known not only for his dining room but also for his superb service. Where Wormley's patrons were concerned, he often went over the top in providing those services. Wormley frequently gave attention to his clients' personal needs. On occasion their needs required him to pay patrons' expenses out of his own pocket and then wait to be reimbursed. Henry Adams, for example, placed the transportation of his horse and other articles to his home in Wormley's hands. A. Gregory felt close enough to Wormley (and it also attests to the amount of money that Wormley earned) to ask him for a loan of one thousand dollars, which, Gregory says, "will probably be given back in the beginning of October when I expect money from Russia." Charles Sumner was a client, and he had relied on Wormley to purchase much of the furnishings in Sumner's home, as well as seeing to it that his home and furnishings were properly tended. After Sumner's death, Wormley purchased some of these items at auction and brought them to the hotel where he set up what he called the Sumner Parlor, exhibiting his tremendous esteem for the human rights advocate. Artist Henry Ulke was commissioned to paint three portraits of Sumner, one of which was hung in the parlor as well. Another full-length portrait was ordered by the Haitian government in recognition of Sumner's opposition to the San Domingo annexation; it was hung in the Senate chamber in Haiti's capitol.[81]

The year before his own death, Wormley presented Sumner's portrait, from his Sumner Parlor, to the state of Massachusetts. It was Henry L. Pierce, former Massachusetts state representative, who wrote to Wormley, thanking him for the portrait. Pierce noted, "Your intimate relations with Sumner during the latter years of his life, and his high regard for you, are well known to many here and give special interest and value to your gift. I and my associates feel honored by being selected to represent you in this matter of the presentation to the state, and we will take the necessary steps to that end as soon as the General Court convenes in January." Pierce himself had formed "intimate relations" with Wormley's Hotel and dining room. He had been a guest at the hotel, and in early February of 1874 Pierce gave a dinner at Wormley's for the Massachusetts delegation, which Sumner attended. Wormley's gift to Sumner's home state, originally hung in the Massachusetts State Library, is now a part of the Massachusetts State House Art Collection and hangs on the second floor of the Massachusetts State House of Representatives, outside of Doric Hall.[82]

Wormley had been ill for some time when he was hospitalized at Massachusetts General Hospital in Boston in 1884. He underwent what was considered a successful surgery on Wednesday, October 15, but by Thursday evening his condition had deteriorated. James Wormley died at 1 p.m. on Saturday, October 18, 1884, from "Vesical Calculus (bladder or gall stones)," and "Peritonitis." He was sixty-six years and nine months old. His remains were returned to DC where his body was laid in state in the Sumner Parlor at his hotel. The officiating clergymen were Reverend Byron Sunderland (who later married President Cleveland and his bride, Frances Folsom) and Reverends William Waring and Francis J. Grimke. Among his pallbearers were the former African senator from Mississippi, Blanche K. Bruce, ex-mayor James G. Berret, John F. Cook, John T. Given, Isaac Landis, M. W. Galt, Henry Birch, and R. H. Gleaves. Honorary pallbearers included White owners of Washing-

ton's other leading hotels—the Ebbitt House, the Arlington Hotel, and
the Riggs House—as well as William Henry Smith. Out of respect for
Wormley, the flags of Washington's principal hotels flew at half-mast on
the day of his funeral.[83]

Wormley left an estate estimated at over one hundred thousand dollars, which his sons were said to have invested and doubled by the end
of the century. He is known to have said, with regard to his success, that
he owed his success to the prompt and timely payments to his employees and of his bills. A charter member of the Washington Chamber of
Commerce, Wormley was said to have little interest in politics and therefore was not a radical or an activist. He was not, however, interested
only in business with no thought or interest in his people. James Wormley's place at 314 I Street was the dropping off place for food, money, and
clothing collected for the newly freed bondspeople in Washington and
for those who were migrating from other parts of the South into Washington in 1863, at the time when slavery had just been abolished.

Of course, his relationship with Charles Sumner certainly suggested
that the two men shared common convictions. On February 8, 1871,
Sumner argued in the Senate against efforts to continue segregated
schools in DC. In attempting to gain support for his argument he read
a statement that had been prepared by James Wormley and William
Syphax (known for his efforts to secure quality education for Washington's African children), regarding their demands for integrated schools.

There is an indication, too, that Frances and William Seward, the abolition activists, worked with James Wormley in Underground Railroad
activity. Francis B. Carpenter, a visitor to the Sewards on one occasion,
noted that, "Among the visitors in the evening was Mr. Wormley, the
well known colored landlord of Washington." Carpenter writes that after "greeting him [Wormley] cordially and introducing him to his other
guests," Seward stated, "Wormley and I went into the emancipation
business a year and a half before Mr. Lincoln did, down on the James
River. How was it Wormley—how many slaves did we take off on our
steamer? 'Eighteen,' replied Mr. Wormley."[84] The *Christian Recorder*, in
their praise of Wormley, offered:

> To speak of Wormley as a gentleman most exactly describes him. . . .
> He was a "colored man," but this color never stood in his way. . . . He
> was a caterer, a hotel keeper . . . yet he attracted around him the most

distinguished me[n] of his time. . . . You would see him one moment respectful[ly] receiving an order for a dinner and the next in close and confidential conversation with Charles Sumner. . . . [H]e never sou[ght] the friendship of men merely because they were prominent. . . . The prominent men sought out Wormley, and were proud to know him."[85]

Francis J. Grimke had long before described Wormley by stating, "He was a manly man, a man who respected himself and who demanded respect from others. A man was a man with him. There was nothing cringing or obsequious about him in his contact with white people, as so many colored people are. He was a race man, in the sense that he was thoroughly interested in the welfare of the race."[86]

The operation of the hotel continued under the direction of Wormley's two sons, William H. A. Wormley and James T. Wormley. In 1870 James T. Wormley was said to be the first graduate of the Medical Department, in the pharmacy program, from Howard University. After receiving his degree, James T. set up an apothecary business at the corner of L Street and Connecticut Avenue, North, to which he planned on adding a soda fountain. Only one of the brothers was said to be in charge of the hotel when the economic downturn in the 1890s forced the sale of the hotel in December 1893 to Charles E. Gibbs, former manager of the famous Ebbitt House in Washington. Gibbs continued to operate the hotel under its original name until 1897, when it became the Colonial Hotel. In 1906 the building was torn down and the Union Trust Company erected in its place.[87]

Wormley's hotel flourished during most of the years of Reconstruction, the era when Africans experienced increased political participation. African emancipation and election to political office was interpreted as enough of a threat to White America to foster increased activity of the Ku Klux Klan and other terrorist organizations in southern states. It was because of this campaign of incessant injustice and violence that the Great Exodus took place during the winter of 1878–1879. As many as forty thousand Blacks migrated from the South into Kansas and other states hoping to escape the intolerable conditions and terrorist mindset of Whites in the South. Hundreds of thousands of African Americans followed suit, a great majority putting down roots in the North, in what became known as the Great Migration of the late nineteenth and early twentieth centuries. They took with them their myriad culinary talents and traditions, implanting them in their new lands of opportunity and continuing challenges.[88]

EPILOGUE

One of the most famous African American chefs was the late Edna Lewis, who received recognition and accolades for her four cookbooks, *The Edna Lewis Cookbook*, *The Taste of Country Cooking*, *In Pursuit of Flavor*, and *The Gift of Southern Cooking*, as well as from the many restaurant kitchens over which she reigned. Her culinary career spanned more than seventy-five years. She began her culinary career at about age sixteen, cooking at the Brazilian embassy in Washington, DC. She became popular as a chef at the Café Nicholson in 1948 in New York and was eventually hired at Gage & Tollner in Brooklyn. She later taught cooking classes, worked as a caterer, and was a visiting consulting restaurant chef. She appeared as a guest chef at a Robert Mondavi Vineyards Great Chefs of France series, and Beringer's Vineyard honored her as one of twelve in their Great Women Chefs Series. Chef Lewis made guest appearances at Bloomingdales Great New York Restaurant series and Macy's DeGustibus Lecture Series. She was also a guest speaker at the Smithsonian Institute in a series on creativity and American cooking.[1]

Chef Lewis did not hedge nor hesitate when asked about the roots of "Southern" cooking. In an interview conducted in 1994 in Washington, DC, she spoke very effectively, offering historical insight on the subject:

> In the beginning Blacks were really the only cooks and they're the ones who developed the food of the South which they called Southern hospitality. . . . There were many Black men in home kitchens. They were in the hotels, they were on the railroads, they were on boats, they were in boarding houses. And through their cooking they developed techniques and flavor and they called it great Southern food. They truly produced the only regional cuisine in this country. In my research I came across a book. On the back of the book it said of course Blacks developed the recipes but the Whites [wrote] them down. So the early recorded history of food was put down by Whites but Blacks had a hand in developing which is really most important because the more they cooked the more ideas came to them and they incorporated what they [saw] their parents do and that's why we have such a great Southern cuisine.[2]

Chef Lewis has spelled it out correctly. Aspects of so-called Soul Food may have been conceived in the economics of survival, using resourcefulness and ingenuity to extract the maximum from what was available; however, "Southern Cuisine" is what Black cooks and chefs in the American South created for themselves and everybody else. Both are the products of African and Native American culinary cultural methods. Chef Lewis obviously understood what has taken place with regard to pushing almost all Black cooks to peripheral or nonexistence status.

Peripheral reference, at best, is given to the African cook's contribution to cuisine in almost all books on Louisiana and American cookery in general. The situation deteriorates daily. Now gumbo and jambalaya have been denied their African roots and are attributed to European culinary "evolution." One example of this attribution can be found in Marcelle Bienvenu, Carl A. Brasseaux, and Ryan A. Brasseaux's *Stir the Pot: The History of Cajun Cuisine*, where it is claimed that "Gumbo has become a symbol of Cajun cuisine throughout the world," although, the authors state, "New Orleans jambalaya is possibly an offshoot of jollof rice, a West African delicacy." Jollof rice is then compared to Spanish paella, which I guess they are telling us came first.[3]

Another such case is John D. Folse's comments on the development of Cajun and "Creole" cuisine. According to Folse the influences of

France, Spain, Germany, and Italy are readily apparent in Louisiana's cuisine. After all, Folse says, the Creoles were European-born aristocrats whose sons brought their wealth and education, along with the "grand cuisines of Europe," which accompanied their cooks and chefs. French bouillabaisse, he states, was integral to the creation of gumbo; Spain gave Creole food its spice; and paella, he continues, was the forefather of jambalaya. Germans brought fine sausage making, he adds, while the Italians had pastry and ice-cream-making skills. The West Indies and Haiti were given credit for exotic vegetables, mirlitons, sauce piquante, and tomatoes, along with the cooking technique of braising, which Folse states, "contributed to the development of *our gumbos* [italics added]." Native Americans are attributed with corn and sassafras leaves (filé powder).[4]

Lastly (and Africa is always mentioned last), Folse decides to throw Africa a bone. "I would be remiss," he laments, "if I failed to mention the tremendous influence of 'the black hand in the pot' in Creole cooking. The Africans brought with them the 'gumbo' or okra plant from their native soil which not only gave name to our premier soup but introduced a new vegetable to South Louisiana. Even more importantly, they have maintained a significant role in development of Creole cuisine in the home as well as the professional kitchen."[5]

"The black hand in the pot"? It was the black hand that made the pot, carried the pot, emptied the pot, cleaned the pot, filled, cooked, and served from the pot in the first and last place. When I read his lines it made me think of a comment made concerning Black men who worked as Pullman porters, waiters, and chefs on the railroads: "Whites used to like to toss them a silver dollar [as a tip], like they thought they were doing them a favor." Clearly, Folse and the authors of *Stir the Pot* as well think they are doing Black folks a favor by mentioning that okra came over on the slave ship with them (okra was only one of many vegetables from Africa that became part of the larder of the Americas), as well as treating the African contribution to Louisiana's cookery as peripheral to a cuisine already created and established by "the grand cuisines of Europe."[6]

Since African Americans are viewed as both culturally and intellectually inferior, it was easy to suggest they had little to no prior history, culinary or otherwise, and therefore no transference of African foodways to the Americas could ever have taken place. White America has constantly denied ever having learned anything of value from Africans, whether Africans were in front of the stove, in the fields, or in the classroom. Africanisms, or African cultural retention and continuity, can be observed in, and permeate, not only African America's culture but White America's as well by virtue of the black hand in virtually every aspect of American culture.

Melville Herskovits had this in mind when he wrote an article in 1935 titled, "What Has Africa Given America?" He concludes that Africanisms are present in many aspects of life of the White population of this country, particularly in American music, speech, manners, religious expression, and certainly cooking. Regarding the African contribution to the cuisine of the South, Herskovits states, "it may be objected that there is no such thing as a Southern cuisine," because, he continues, "*it must nevertheless be realized that the cuisine of Richmond is no more merely a modification and adaptation of that of England than the dishes served at New Orleans are those of France* [italics added]."[7]

The examples presented in this treatise leave no doubt as to the extent to which the cultural elements of descendants of Africans brought to the Americas—North America, South America, Central America, and the Caribbean—have retained Africanisms varying in intensity. Nor is there any doubt regarding the dependence of White America's rich and powerful, and of America in general, on the cooking and cuisine of Black cooks. Fortunately, over the years there have been a few authors who have responded to the gross neglect of celebrating African American culinary achievements. Their work and efforts have been most welcome and are assuredly commendable. In spite of these efforts, however, a false master narrative continues to dominate America's culinary story.

Why bulldoze the African culinary contribution? Why continue to create and honor the dishonest culinary master narrative? In pursuing the goal of an "Africanless"—or Africans only on the periphery—culinary master narrative, writers and numerous so-called culinary historians embark on a relentless policy of "forced removals." African connections are destroyed, and whatever is left is, as "De Jure Housing Segregation in the United States and South Africa" eloquently points out, "expropriated with inadequate compensation in order to force [Blacks] into the designated [Black] areas"—just like residential apartheid in South Africa—and the designated Black area in this case is "soul food." A "sophisticated system of *control* over [African culinary traditions is thereby created] that serves the political, economic, [and] ideological . . . objectives" (italics added) of those who have decided that they are in charge of *all* culinary history, especially African/African American.[8]

John Henrik Clarke, J. C. deGraft-Johnson, Yosef Ben-Jochannan, Chancellor Williams, Cheik Anta Diop, and Basil Davidson, long ago wrote and spoke about the attempt by Europeans to make Africans disappear from world history—to quote John Henrik Clarke, to have "Africa removed from the respectful commentary of history." Gwendolyn Midlo Hall, in more recent years, has written that "it is part of the process of making Africans and their descendants invisible in the history of Louisiana. . . . Their creations and contributions to culture and politics, including resistance to slavery, have been largely ignored. All they created is attributed to outsiders."[9]

The culinary master narrative boldly continues to uphold that anything attributed to Africans had to have started with, or was improved upon, by Europeans. I do agree that "Culinary history is, as all history typically has been, the story of the conquerors." The agenda of writers on the subject does truly represent "colonial objectives" and a colonial mentality that "serves to falsely justify the right of colonial powers to dominate historical accounts." Make no mistake, African/African American culinary history has been as thoroughly colonized as African/African American history.[10]

Clearly, these accounts, these master narratives, encourage the marginalization of Native American and African cultures because the authors writing these narratives need to disavow this country's history of oppression and violence against Native Americans and Africans. The relationship of the United States to the African people dragged to these shores in chains is the history of forcibly exacted free labor, of the raping of African women, of the wholesale destruction of families, of beatings, of lynchings and murders of every sort, of disfranchisement and disenfranchisement, theft, and the destruction of entire Black communities resulting in, or more correctly stated, both creating and producing, a legacy of wholesale poverty, all under the order and sanction of this country's laws, statutes, and legislation. Owing to such a relationship, I think Lynn Houston is justified in stating that the account "seeks to whitewash history by erasing it of conflict." If Blacks are not represented as part of the picture, these things never happened, never have to be mentioned, and certainly then, no credit is due.[11]

Europe's greed for land, labor, and resources unleashed phenomenal violence on a scale tantamount to genocide. And please note, genocide takes numerous forms. Those who survived faced the European dual level of humanity—masters and slaves/colonizers and colonized. The "remarkable arsenal" used to produce these conditions included the Bible, guns, liquor, and social science such as anthropology. Well, we can add culinary history to the social science category.[12]

At the same, exact moment when Africans implanted their culinary traditions in the farm, plantation, hotel, ship, private club, and restaurant kitchens of America, a vital process of cultural production was taking place that only slaveholders and Whites in power would enjoy and also control. Remember one of the fundamentals of slavocracy: What belongs to the slave ultimately belongs to the slave master, including their culinary creations. In the Supreme Court case *The State v. John Mann*, the Court unanimously held that Blacks were *"doomed in [their] own person and [their] posterity, to live without knowledge and without the capacity to make anything [their] own, and to toil that another may reap the fruits* [italics added]."[13]

What this indicates is that, with regard to what African American chefs, cooks, and caterers produce, slavery never ended. There has always been an unwritten law that allowed theft, with impunity, of African/African American culture. Music and cooking and cuisine have always been among those aspects of African/African American culture most vulnerable to theft and appropriation, and it was never necessary to announce out loud the intent, or the common understanding, that it was alright to take whatever was wanted by those who control. Whether articulated as a formal rule of law or not, there was—and is, right now—a general consensus on principles or precepts that accept, and then enforce, the legitimization of racism. Like residential apartheid, whether in Johannesburg or Baltimore, culinary apartheid is another expression of racism that upholds the "law" of White supremacy by means of "slavery jurisprudence." Illustrative of "slavery jurisprudence" as it applies to the fundamental concept of culinary apartheid—that is, the manner of theft and erasure of African/African American culinary contributions—is the opinion written by Chief Justice Roger Brook Taney in 1857: "they [Blacks] had no rights which the white man was bound to respect."[14]

Judge A. Leon Higginbotham Jr. has written extensively on the premises, precepts, goals, and implicit agreements that formed the legal and moral foundation for American slavery and early race relations law. A number of his Ten Precepts of American Slavery Jurisprudence are entrenched in culinary apartheid: "Inferiority: Presume, preserve, protect and defend the ideal of the superiority of whites and the inferiority of blacks. Property: Define the slave as the master's property, maximize the master's economic interest, disregard the humanity of the slave except when it serves the master's interest, and deny slaves the fruits of their labor. . . . Education and Culture: . . . deny them knowledge of their culture." Now, "Powerlessness," which "constituted the foundation of the legal system of slavery," is third on Judge Higginbotham's list of precepts, but I am placing it here because without knowledge of your own culture, culinary and otherwise, *you are powerless,* and thereby "submissive and dependent in every respect, not only to the master but to whites in general." And then, "By Any Means Possible: Support any practice or doctrine from any source whatsoever that maximizes the profitability of slavery, legitimizes racism, and retaliates, including the use of violence, against those of both races who dare to advocate abolition or who, by their speech or actions, deny the inherent inferiority of blacks."[15]

As Judge Higginbotham asks, "Have we often disregarded our legal history to keep from our full consciousness the extraordinary brutality of our past?" Today's culinary apartheid and the culinary master narrative are supported by laws, written and unwritten, indistinguishable from the slavery jurisprudence that legitimized and sanctioned institutional racism during slavery, and the vestiges of which we are still struggling with today.[16]

In 1999 in *The Peppers, Cracklings, and Knots of Wool Cookbook: The Global Migration of African Cuisine* I began a discussion concerning the neglect of the inclusion of Africa as a major contributor to *world* cuisine, by calling attention to this contribution as having been either overlooked, trivialized, or denied. In the current treatise I expand the discussion of Africanisms and African/African American culinary achievements by examining the ideological consequences of this exclusion, consequences resulting in a legacy of culinary apartheid and a false master narrative in American culinary history. My study shines light on those who have satiated, in every possible venue, America's culinary experience. This expansion includes an unvarnished rendering of key Black contributors and their cuisines in the context of the times and societal obstacles, as they established themselves in front of the stoves they encountered in kitchens across America and *At the Table of Power*.

NOTES

Prologue

1. One can choose from a vast array of cookery books—from antebellum through modern times—that either omit, downplay, or distort African American culinary contributions. For a small sample see Mary Randolph, *The Virginia Housewife* (Washington, DC: Davis and Force, 1824); Sarah Rutledge, *The Carolina Housewife* (Charleston, SC: W. R. Babcock, 1847); Marion Cabell Tyree, *Housekeeping in Old Virginia* (Louisville, KY: John P. Morton, 1879); Marion Flexner, *Out of Kentucky Kitchens* (New York: Franklin Watts, 1949); Evan Jones, *American Food: The Gastronomic Story* (New York: Random House, 1974); Camille Glenn, *The Heritage of Southern Cooking* (New York: Workman Publishing, 1986); Stephen A. McLeod, *Dining with the Washingtons*. For a discussion of African culinary contributions to the Americas, see Diane M. Spivey, *Peppers, Cracklings*. Also see Spivey, "Latin American and Caribbean Food and Cuisine." *Encyclopedia of African-American Culture and History*, vol. 2 (New York: Thomson-Gale, and Macmillan Reference, 2005), 838–44.

2. See *The State v. John Mann.*

3. *Plessy v. Ferguson.*

1: From the Beginning

1. See Ronald Takaki, *A Different Mirror*; Joan Montgomery Halford, "A Different Mirror."

2. Spivey, *Peppers, Cracklings*, 263.

3. *Congressional Record*, Senate, 88th Cong., 1st sess., January 18, 1963, 627

4. *Congressional Record*, Senate, 88th Cong., 1st sess., January 21, 1963, 669; "J Millard Tawes Dies, Was Maryland Governor for 8 Years," *Washington Post*, June 26, 1979, cited in J. Millard Tawes, Biographical Series, MSA SC 3520-1485, Maryland State Archives.

5. *Congressional Record*, Senate, 88th Cong., 1st sess., January 21, 1963, 669. Some of

the recipes in this volume are quoted directly from their original sources. However, minor editorial changes allow the presentation style to be consistent throughout the book. These changes include presenting the ingredients in a list at the beginning, spelling out the measurements, and for clarification, modernizing the spelling of some ingredients.

6. Barbara Jeanne Fields, *Slavery and Freedom*, 72; also see 69–71, 73–80.

7. Helen Avalynne Gibson Tawes (1898–1989), Biographical Series (MSA SC 3520-2292, Maryland State Archives); Helen Avalynne Tawes, *My Favorite Maryland Recipes*, dedication, x.

8. Gwendolyn Midlo Hall, *Africans in Colonial Louisiana*, 3, 5–7.

9. Hall, *Africans in Colonial Louisiana*, 8, 9, 11–12, 14–15.

10. Hall, *Africans in Colonial Louisiana*, 29, 31; Philip D. Curtin, *Economic Change in Precolonial Africa*, 6, cited in Hall, *Africans in Colonial Louisiana*, 29n1.

11. Hall, *Africans in Colonial Louisiana*, 34; Bassey Andah, "Identifying Early Farming Traditions of West Africa," 242.

12. Hall, *Africans in Colonial Louisiana*, 34. Bassey Andah, "Identifying Early Farming Traditions of West Africa," 244, discusses "uniquely African invented techniques" (also 242). See also Diane M. Spivey, "West Africa," 41; P. A. Allison, "Historical Inferences," 248; H. G. Baker, "Comments on the Thesis," 229; Marvin P. Miracle, "Introduction and Spread of Maize," 39–44; and W. B. Morgan, "Forest and Agriculture in West Africa," 235–39.

For discourse on pre-European African contact with America, see Leo Wiener's three-volume treatise, *Africa and the Discovery of America*, and Leo Wiener, *Mayan and Mexican Origins*. For additional discourse on pre-Columbian African contact with the Americas, see also, for example, Ivan Van Sertima, *They Came before Columbus*; Harold G. Lawrence, "African Explorers"; Floyd W. Hayes, "African Presence"; M. D. W. Jeffreys, "Pre-Columbian Negroes in America"; Leo Frobenius, *Voice of Africa*; John G. Jackson, *Introduction to African Civilization*.

13. Hall, *Africans in Colonial Louisiana*, 35 ("excellent tobacco," "grew almost without cultivation"), 36 ("with a marvelous flavor," "very fat," and "one sees regiments"). Also see National Research Council, *Lost Crops of Africa*, 1:7, 17–37.

14. Inspired by and adapted from "Kohkohyeh Potoh Potoh," in Zainabu Kpaka Kallon, *Zainabu's African Cookbook*, 107–8.

15. Spivey, *Peppers, Cracklings*, 129.

16. National Research Council, *Lost Crops of Africa*, 1:127–213; Spivey, "West Africa," 43–44.

17. For metallurgy and iron mining in Africa see, for example, Franz Boas, *Race and Democratic Society*; Nino Del Grande, "Prehistoric Iron Smelting in Africa"; Tendai Mutunhu, "Africa"; Hall, *Africans in Colonial Louisiana*, 37; Spivey, *Peppers, Cracklings*, 14.

18. Spivey, *Peppers, Cracklings*, 88–89, 90–91. See also J. F. Ade Ajayi and Michael Crowder, *History of West Africa*; J. F. Ade Ajayi and Ian Espie, *Thousand Years of West African History*; F. A. Chijioke, *Ancient Africa*; Daniel Chu and Elliott Skinner, *Glorious Age in Africa*; Basil Davidson, *Lost Cities of Africa*; Basil Davidson, *African Civilization Revisited*; Basil Davidson and F. K. Buah, *History of West Africa*; Chancellor Williams, *Destruction of Black Civilization*; J. C. deGraft-Johnson, *African Glory*; Leo Africanus, *History and Description of Africa*; Cheikh Anta Diop, *Precolonial Black Africa*; T. A. Osae, S. N. Nwabara, and A. T. O. Odunsi, *Short History of West Africa*; Edward William Bovill, *Golden Trade of the Moors*; Edward William Bovill, *Caravans of the Old Sahara*. See also Melville J. Herskovits, *Myth of the Negro Past*, 296–97.

19. Hall, *Africans in Colonial Louisiana*, 122 (also 10, 34–35, 120–21, 123).

20. Hall, *Africans in Colonial Louisiana*, 126.

21. Hall, *Africans in Colonial Louisiana*, 277 (also 160, 276).

22. Henri Eugene Sée, *Economic and Social Conditions*, 24. See also John D. Folse, *Cajun and Creole Cuisine*, 9.

23. Sée, *Economic and Social Conditions*, 24–25.

24. Sée, *Economic and Social Conditions*, 25, 26.

25. Sée, *Economic and Social Conditions*, 27 ("still quite miserable"), 28 ("often wretched").

26. Sée, *Economic and Social Conditions*, 20 ("peasant meals"), 27–28 ("The food"), 28 ("It is a fact" and "practically no peasants").

27. Sée, *Economic and Social Conditions*, 20, 29, 30.

28. Sée, *Economic and Social Conditions*, 36 (also 7–8).

29. Melvin Kranzberg, *Siege of Paris*, 63 ("pride of Paris"), also 44–46, 62, 64–66; Kenneth James, *King of Chefs*, 63 ("cat embellished" and "bad rye bread"), also 61–62, 251; Auguste Escoffier, *Memories*, 34, 40; "Food and Drink in Paris," *New York Times*, December 11, 1870, 4; "Rats in Paris," *New York Times*, December 4, 1873, 3.

Paris was plagued with rats well into the twentieth century. See, for example, *New York Times* articles "Rat-Killing in Paris," October 14, 1876, 10; "Rats Plague Paris," August 28, 1910, C2; "Paris Votes Funds for War on Rats," September 8, 1920, 12; "War against Rats of Paris," September 26, 1920, 85; "Pack of Rat-Hunting Cats Will Be Trained in Paris," July 30, 1933, 46; "Reports 10,000,000 Rats in Paris," February 22, 1941, 6; "Paris Telephone Wires Partly Devoured by Rats," August 27, 1945, 5.

30. Escoffier, *Memories*, 28; James, *King of Chefs*, 31, 34, 36,192.

31. Kevin Shillington, *History of Africa*, 1; George P. Murdock, *Africa*, 64. See also National Research Council, *Lost Crops of Africa, Volume 1: Grains*; *Volume 2: Vegetables*; and *Volume 3: Fruits*.

32. Francois Mignon and Clementine Hunter, *Melrose Plantation Cookbook*, 2–3 ("skill

and imaginative"); Hall, *Africans in Colonial Louisiana*, 34 ("it is relevant"), 31 ("African nations"), also 9, 37, 159.

33. Hall, *Africans in Colonial Louisiana*, 158–59.

34. Folse, *Cajun and Creole Cuisine*, 9. See also Kathleen Flinn, "Savor the Flavor."

35. Edna Jordan Smith, interview with author, June 12, 2007 (as for all interviews with the author, records are in the form of written notes in author's possession).

36. Marcel Giraud, *History of French Louisiana*, 2:130, 131. Regarding the "prospect of progress" of Louisiana, W. E. B. Du Bois states, "black refugees from San Domingo [Haiti] saved Louisiana from economic ruin," when Etienne de Bore, a colored San Dominican, enlisted the services of other San Dominican refugees and turned a failing sugar, rum-, and syrup-manufacturing enterprise begun by two Spaniards into a great commercial success in agriculture in the Delta. See W. E. B. Du Bois, *Gift of Black Folk*, 68–69.

37. Marcel Giraud, *History of French Louisiana*, 5:325, 327.

38. Donald Spivey, *Fire from the Soul*, 121 ("dedicated"), 27.

39. Dr. Donald Spivey, interview, October 1, 2012. See also Donald Spivey, *If You Were Only White*, xvii, 29; Edward Hotaling, *Great Black Jockeys*, 251–52, 254–55, 273, 282–83. R. Gerald Alvey, *Kentucky Bluegrass Country*, 146, 148, contains discourse lacking in both good taste and historical awareness.

40. *Steele v. Louisville & Nashville Railroad Co*. The case of the L&N fireman William Steele and his lawsuit, *Steele v. The Louisville & Nashville and Brotherhood of Locomotive Firemen and Enginemen* (1944), is mentioned in Spivey, *If You Were Only White*, 20; "Widely Known Chef Dies," *Louisville and Nashville Employees Magazine* 20–21 (1944): 17.

41. "The Man Who Cooks," *New York Times*, November 23, 1902.

42. "Where Are the Black Chefs?" *Chicago Tribune*, March 15, 2012; Psyche Williams-Forson, "African American Food Business," 12.

43. See, for example, "Founding Father of New World Cuisine Norman Van Aken to Guest Judge Culinary Competition" (Association for Healthcare Food Service press release, May 24, 2012). See also "Fabulous Norman's Is Always an Adventure," *Miami Herald*, December 7, 2001, 37G; "Horseman Recovers after 'Pilot Error' Humane Society Exec Vows to Ride Again" / "Food for Thought," *Miami Herald*, June 28, 2000, 4A; "A Columbus of Chefs among the Papayas," *New York Times*, July 8, 1998, F1; "Cooking," *New York Times*, June 1, 2003, A12; "News and Events: Miami Dade College in the News," Miami Culinary Institute, September 27, 2013; "Meet the Authors," *Forum: The Magazine of the Florida Humanities Council* (Fall 2018), 36. There is also biographical material on Norman Van Aken at StarChefs.com, The Magazine for Culinary Insiders.

44. For examples of the contribution of African foodways to Latin American and Caribbean cuisine, see Diane M. Spivey, "Latin American and Caribbean Food"; Spivey,

Peppers, Cracklings, 87–226. See also "Black Chefs' Struggle for the Top," *New York Times*, April 5, 2006; "Where Are the Black Chefs?" *Chicago Tribune*, March 15, 2012.

45. Joe Randall, interview, Southern Foodways Alliance Founders Oral History Project, March 9, 2005; Chef Tanya Holland, interview, *Black Culture Connection*, PBS, 2013. See also Chef Joe Randall interview, *Black Culture Connection*, PBS, 2013; Chef Joe Randall interview, "A Tale of Two Chefs: Marcus Samuelsson and Roble Ali," *In America*, CNN.

46. Nathaniel Burton and Rudy Lombard, *Creole Feast*, xvii.

47. Burton and Lombard, *Creole Feast*, xix, also 15–16, 17–21, 43–44, 55, 57.

48. Burton and Lombard, *Creole Feast*, xix; Lena Richard Exhibit.

49. Lena Richard, *Lena Richard's Cook Book*, preface ("for generations"); Lena Richard, *New Orleans Cook Book*, preface (all other quotes).

50. See also Flyer, advertising lecture at Newcomb College Center for Research on Women (Newcomb Institute of Tulane University, Archives and Special Collections).

51. Lena Richard Exhibit.

52. "Colonial Williamsburg Notebook, 1943" (folder 1, box 1, Lena Richard Papers, Newcomb Institute of Tulane University). See also Lena Richard Exhibit.

53. Lena Richard Exhibit.

54. Profile of Leah Chase, Chef Joe Randall's African American Chefs Hall of Fame (http://africanamericanchefshalloffame.org). Chef Chase died in June 2019, but her restaurant remains a culinary landmark; Burton and Lombard, *Creole Feast*, 15–16.

55. Burton and Lombard, *Creole Feast*, 2–13, 22–41, 45–54, 58–63.

56. Burton and Lombard, *Creole Feast*, xx, offers a brief profile of Mrs. Christine Warren. See also Ms. Lucy Ater, interview with Dorothy Schlesinger, June 13, 1974; Ms. Shirley Bateman, interview with Dorothy Schlesinger, no date (both in Friends of the Cabildo Project, Oral History Program, New Orleans Public Library, Louisiana Division, City Archives and Special Collections, New Orleans, Louisiana).

57. Ms. Lucy Ater, interview; Shirley Bateman, interview.

58. Shirley Bateman, interview.

59. Shirley Bateman, interview.

60. Shirley Bateman, interview.

61. Profile of Chef Robert W. Lee, Chef Joe Randall's African American Chefs Hall of Fame (http://africanamericanchefshalloffame.org).

62. Profile of Chef Robert W. Lee.

63. Profile of Chef Robert W. Lee.

64. Profile of Chef Leon West, and profile of Chef Stanley Jackson, Chef Joe Randall's African American Chefs Hall of Fame (http://africanamericanchefshalloffame.org).

65. "Chef Joe Randall's Cooking School," profile (http://www.linkedin.com>chef-joe-randall-2a781530). See also Profile of Chef Patrick Clark, Chef Joe Randall's African American Chefs Hall of Fame; Chef Joe Randall, interview, *Black Culture Connection*, PBS; "Chef Joseph Randall: A Legendary Top Chef," *Cuisine Noir Magazine*, August 31, 2010; "A Culinary Journey of Color," *Harrisburg Magazine* (February 2011).

2: Sustenance for Sustaining American Liberty

1. A. Leon Higginbotham Jr., *In the Matter of Color*, 116, 117, 118, 119–123, 131.

2. Certificate from Thomas Falconer (Bustill-Bowser-Asbury Collection, Moorland-Spingarn Research Center); pamphlet titled "Philadelphia African Americans: Color, Class and Style, 1840–1940," 5 (folder 11, series 3, Lloyd A. Trent Jr. Family Papers, W. E. B. Du Bois Library, University of Massachusetts; hereafter cited as Trent Family Papers); Anna Bustill Smith, "Bustill Family"; Carter G. Woodson, "Bustill Family"; William Douglass, *Annals of the First African Church*; "Bustill," reel 10, Daniel Murray Papers (State Historical Society of Wisconsin, microfilm edition, 1977; hereafter cited as Daniel Murray Papers [Wisconsin]); "Mossell, Nathan, Autobiography," 18 (no date, folder titled Mossell, Nathan, Alumni Records Collection, University of Pennsylvania Archives).

3. "Receipts from long, long years of housekeeping—1867–1919," 67 (MS. N-384, Carton 2, SH-13-DQ2, Hartwell-Clark Family Papers, Massachusetts Historical Society; hereafter MHS).

4. See Haskin, "The Romance of Fraunces' Tavern," for "Black Sam's" description as "a cook and caterer of talent." Also see Frederic J. Haskin, handwritten file copy, "Culinary Wizard Black Sam" (folder 14, box 454, Walter White Papers, NAACP Records, Administrative File, part 8, Library of Congress); Frederic J. Haskin, "Romance of Fraunces' Tavern." Note: Fraunces's African racial heritage has been denied for many years by a number of people associated with either the tavern itself or keepers of Revolutionary War history. I visited Fraunces Tavern in New York many years ago. I stood next to another visitor who asked one of the museum guides, "Fraunces was Black, wasn't he?" The guide, in a firm and irritated voice responded, "No. He wasn't. He was NOT a Black man!"

5. Haskin, "Romance of Fraunces' Tavern."

6. Haskin, "Romance of Fraunces' Tavern." See also Frederic J. Haskin to Walter White, October 21, 1933 (folder 14, box 454, Walter White Papers, NAACP, Administrative File, part 8, Library of Congress); Frederic J. Haskin, handwritten file copy, "Culinary Wizard Black Sam," sent in response to Walter White's request for a copy of his "Haskin Letter" on Fraunces' Tavern (folder 14, box 454, Walter White Papers, NAACP, Administrative File, part 8, Library of Congress).

7. Haskin, "Romance of Fraunces' Tavern." See also Benson J. Lossing, *Recollections and Private Memoirs*, 411, 420n. A bill for this "entertainment" was made out and dated November 26, 1783, and appears in Vouchers, and Receipted Accounts 2 (series 5, Financial Papers, George Washington Papers, Revolutionary War Accounts, Library of Congress). George Washington to the Legislature of New Jersey, December 6, 1783, in John C. Fitzpatrick, *Writings of George Washington*, vol. 27. (The bill is also mentioned in the author's [John C. Fitzpatrick] notes.)

8. Lossing, *Recollections and Private Memoirs*, 411n; Phoebe is also mentioned in Haskin, "Romance of Fraunces' Tavern." Although George Washington's adopted son tells the same story, the tale of Phoebe has been discounted by some. It has been suggested that Fraunces did not have a daughter named Phoebe, but "Phoebe" may have been a nickname.

9. George Washington to Samuel Fraunces, September 7, 1785, in Fitzpatrick, *Writings of George Washington*. vol. 28.

10. George Washington to Tobias Lear, September 20, 1790, March 27, 1791, in Fitzpatrick, *Writings of George Washington*. vol. 31.

11. Tobias Lear to George Augustine Washington, May 3, 1789, in Dorothy Twohig, *Papers of George Washington*, 247, 248.

12. Washington to Fraunces, August 18, 1783, in Fitzpatrick, *Writings of George Washington*, 27:112 ("suffered in our cause"), 111 ("I am happy to find"). The suggestion that Fraunces was a spy for the Patriots is in George Washington's "Accounts of Expenses While Commander-in-Chief of the Continental Army, 1775–1783," annotation following the debit entry for November 26, 1783 (George Washington Papers, Library of Congress). See also Michael Batterberry and Ariane Batterberry, *On the Town*, 4–8, 11; Charles L. Blockson, *Liberty Bell Era*, 156–58; James Weldon Johnson, *Black Manhattan*, 44–45; pamphlets titled "Sons of the Revolution in the State of New York" and "The Original Structure of Fraunces Tavern Museum, Manhattan's Oldest Building" (both in folder 3, series 1, Trent Family Papers); Herman D. Bloch, *Circle of Discrimination*, 223; John Whiteclay Chambers, "Of Palates and Politics," 224; *1866 Guide to New York City*, 7; "Restaurants," reel 19, and "Caterers. New York Guild," reel 10, both Daniel Murray Papers (Wisconsin); Lossing, *Recollections and Private Memoirs*, 411, 420; Spivey, *Peppers, Cracklings*, 227–29.

13. George Washington to Alexander White, July 14, 1785, in Fitzpatrick, *Writings of George Washington*, vol. 28.

14. Higginbotham, *In the Matter of Color*, 37, 38.

15. Higginbotham, *In the Matter of Color*, 38–39.

16. Lossing, *Recollections and Private Memoirs*, 422. Also see "Memorandum List of Tithables," June 14, 1771 (George Washington Papers, National Archives); "1786 Mount

Vernon Slave Census," in Donald Jackson and Dorothy Twohig, *Diaries of George Washington*, 4:277–83; Fritz Hirschfeld, *George Washington and Slavery*, 70.

17. Washington to Lear, September 9, 1790, in Fitzpatrick, *Writings of George Washington*, 37:570–71.

18. Lossing, *Recollections and Private Memoirs*, 422–23.

19. Lossing, *Recollections and Private Memoirs*, 423; George Washington's Mount Vernon (Digital Encyclopedia, Fred W. Smith National Library for the Study of George Washington).

20. See Stephen A. McLeod, *Dining with the Washingtons*, 28–31; also see, for example, Hirschfeld, *George Washington and Slavery*, 61. In his observation of African women preparing "pots," J. B. Moreton states, "a [pepper] pot is . . . made of a [s]mall piece of [s]alt pork or beef [s]liced, with a fowl di[ss]ected, [s]ome ocras, yams, plaintains, caliloo, and plenty of fire-balls, or red pepper." Moreton, *West India Customs and Manners*, 110. Also, note that a recipe for hoecakes is brazenly described (in *Dining with the Washingtons*, 200) as a family member's (Nelly Custis Lewis's) method for preparing them. In late August/early September 2014, I spoke by telephone with Stephen McLeod, editor of the volume *Dining with the Washingtons*. I asked him which recipes were associated with Hercules. He responded that the only surviving recipes were for "Martha's" Great Cake (merely a fruitcake, one that enslaved cooks in the West Indies were known to prepare; a recipe for a "modern" version is on pages 187–188) and the alcoholic libation Cherry Bounce (on page 205 you can see that the original recipe is written out on a piece of paper in someone's handwriting which present-day archivists say they cannot identify). I then stated to McLeod that we know Hercules did the cooking, so there must be recipes. McLeod responded, *"We don't know how much cooking he actually did at either residence."* My final remark was, "Well, we know Martha didn't do it. So who else would it have been?" There was complete silence.

21. For hot peppers cultivated in Washington's garden, see diary entries dated June 13 and 29, 1785, in Jackson and Twohig, *Diaries of George Washington*, 4:152–53n, 157.

22. Lossing, *Recollections and Private Memoirs*, 421–22.

23. Fugitive Slave Act, February 12, 1793. This act, and the subsequent enactment of the Fugitive Slave Law of 1850, rendered all Black people in America "slaves until proven free" and facilitated the kidnapping and enslavement of thousands.

24. Garry Wills, *"Negro President,"* 209, mentions Washington's reluctance to pursue escaped bondspeople "north of Viginia." Joseph E. Fields, *"Worthy Partner,"* 307, records Martha's remarks.

Oney Judge's frustration at being a slave made her even more "sadly plaiged" than Martha, owing to Martha Washington's characterization of Blacks as "so bad in th[e]ir nature that they have not the least grat[i]tude for the kindness that may be sh[o] wed to them." See Fields, *"Worthy Partner,"* 287. Ms. Judge, Martha's husband commented, "was handy and useful . . . the ingratitude of the girl, who was brought up and treated more like a child than a Servant." See George Washington to Oliver Wolcott Jr., Philadelphia, September 1, 1796, in Fitzpatrick, *Writings of George Washington,* 35:201–2. The Washingtons' letters are also mentioned in Hirschfeld, *George Washington and Slavery,* 64, 65.

25. George Washington to Frederick Kitt, January 10, 1798, in Fitzpatrick, *Writings of George Washington,* 36:123–24.

26. Washington to Kitt, January 29, 1798, in Fitzpatrick, *Writings of George Washington,* 36:148.

27. Wills, *"Negro President,"* 211 ("a bad neighborhood"). Washington's scheme is outlined in George Washington to Tobias Lear, April 12, 1791, in Fitzpatrick, *Writings of George Washington,* 37:573–74, and is also recorded in Wills, *"Negro President,"* 209–10.

28. Haskin, "The Romance of Fraunces' Tavern."

3: Sustenance for Maintaining the Legality of Slavery

1. Edwin Morris Betts, *Jefferson's Farm Book,* 15. See also Wills, *"Negro President,"* 210–11.

2. Betts, *Jefferson's Farm Book,* 15–16.

3. Thomas Jefferson to Martha Jefferson, November 2, 1802, in Barbara B. Oberg, *Papers of Thomas Jefferson,* 622–23.

4. "Randolph/Meikleham Manuscript Cookbook" (accession no. 1975-4-5, Curatorial Department, Thomas Jefferson Foundation).

5. "FOSSETT, Once Slave of Jefferson" ("one of the best known"); Betts, *Jefferson's Farm Book,* 460 ("could do any thing"), also 27–28.

6. Damon Lee Fowler, *Dining at Monticello,* 39, 41–42 ("French trained"), 44 ("In freedom"), 45 ("passed them on"), 34 ("time-consuming"), 35 ("through collaboration"). Published in 2005, this book is not an old text.

7. Fowler, *Dining at Monticello,* 40 (quote), also 42.

8. Leonard L. Richards, *"Gentlemen of Property,"* 34.

9. Richards, *"Gentlemen of Property,"* 123 ("white fanatics," "crowding out," "negro stealing," "could not come," and "impudent wretches"), 126 ("were well armed"), also 122, 124–25, 127–29, 137, 141–42, 149. Mrs. Sarah Fossett, Peter's wife, dedicated her life to Underground Railroad activity. The Fossetts' involvement in the UR placed them in close association with Levi Coffin, a Quaker abolitionist who moved to Cincinnati in 1847. He is credited with helping between two and three thousand Africans escape to freedom in Canada. See Levi Coffin, *Reminiscences.*

10. "FOSSETT, Once Slave of Jefferson"; Richards, *"Gentlemen of Property,"* 34, 122–29, 137, 141–42, 149; Wendell P. Dabney, *Cincinnati's Colored Citizens,* 180, 349–51.

11. Dabney, *Cincinnati's Colored Citizens,* 180. The *Cincinnati Enquirer* obituary article for William B. Fossett has Edith Miller listed as William's daughter. "FOSSETT, Once Slave of Jefferson."

12. Sharron E. Wilkins, "The President's Kitchen," 57. Also see William Seale, "Upstairs and Downstairs," 19.

13. Allan Nevins, *Polk,* 397–98.

14. Carl Bridenbaugh, *Cities in the Wilderness,* 30.

15. Bridenbaugh, *Cities in the Wilderness,* 402–3; La Rouchefoucault-Liancourt, *Travels Through the United States of America,* 595, cited in Marina Wikramanayake, *World in Shadow,* 34; "The Scar on the African's Arm," *Hippocrates: The Magazine of Health and Medicine* (March–April 1989). See also William D. Piersen, *Black Yankees;* Thomas Bailey, *American Pageant.*

16. Dorothy Burnett Porter, "Remonds of Salem," 259, 260; Barbara M. Solomon, "Growth of the Population."

17. Porter, "Remonds of Salem," 262, also 263. See *Naval Documents Related to the Quasi War;* Rayford W. Logan, "Negro in the Quasi War," 128; "Ship out of New York Celebrates St. Eustatius Bicentennial Event," *New York Times,* January 2, 1977; "Miscellaneous" (folder 5, box 1, Remond Family Papers, 1823–1869, Phillips Library, Peabody Essex Museum; hereafter cited as Remond Family Papers).

18. Porter, "Remonds of Salem," 263–64; *Salem Directory and City Register,* 116–17.

19. Porter, "Remonds of Salem," 264–65; Mary Harrod Northend, *Memories of Old Salem,* 243; Marie E. Fabens, *Hamilton Hall,* title page, 4, 6; Shirley J. Yee, *Black Women Abolitionists,* 15–16, 161n14; Dorothy Sterling, *We Are Your Sisters,* 96.

20. Fabens, *Hamilton Hall,* 5, 6; Northend, *Memories of Old Salem,* 248; Porter, "Remonds of Salem," 266.

21. Francis Jackson, *Early Settlement of Newton County,* 363; S. F. Smith, *History of Newton,* 312; Porter, "Remonds of Salem," 267; Sterling, *We Are Your Sisters,* 96.

22. Fabens, *Hamilton Hall,* 6, 7; Porter, "Remonds of Salem," 268.

23. Adelaide M. Cromwell, *Other Brahmins,* 37. Also see Robert Roberts, *House Servant's Directory;* John Daniels, *In Freedom's Birthplace,* 46, 46n3; William C. Nell, *Colored Patriots;* James Oliver Horton and Lois E. Horton, *Black Bostonians,* 25.

24. Daniels, *In Freedom's Birthplace,* 46; Nell, *Colored Patriots;* Horton, *Black Bostonians,* 25; Cromwell, *Other Brahmins,* 37; Porter, "Remonds of Salem," 269; George M. Whipple, *Salem Light Infantry,* 1, 39–40.

25. Menus (folder 3, box 1, series 1, Remond Family Papers).

26. "Dinner on the Two Hundredth Anniversary of the First Settlement of Salem"

Menus (folder 3, box 1, series 1.C, Remond Family Papers). The doebird or Eskimo curlew was considered a delicacy. Now mainly extinct, at one time they arrived in large numbers on the uplands of Cape Cod during the end of August and early September each year. After being shot, the birds were hung with feathers on, in a shady breezy place for four or five days before being cleaned and roasted on a spit over a fire. See nineteenth-century Tremont House hotel (Boston) special dinner menus in "American Menus, the Doe-Birds," January 14, 2011 (www.theamericanmenu.com), and Cornell Lab of Ornithology (www.birds.cornell.edu).

27. Remond Family Papers; Fabens, *Hamilton Hall*, 13. Chief Justice Joseph Story served on the US Supreme Court from 1811 to 1845. He was born at Marblehead, Massachusetts, to Elisha Story and Mehitable Pedrick. His father, Elisha, was a member of the Sons of Liberty and took part in the Boston Tea Party in 1773. Joseph graduated from Harvard University in 1798, second in his class. In November 1811, at the age of thirty-two, he was appointed by President Madison as the youngest associate justice of the US Supreme Court. Soon after Story's appointment, the Court began to exercise the powers that the US Constitution had given it over state courts and state legislation. Joseph Story attended his duties as associate justice and professor of law, but some of the work for which he became famous was his building up the department of admiralty law in the US federal courts; he devoted a great deal of attention to equity jurisprudence and rendered services to the department of patent law. It is interesting to note that in 1819 he caused quite a stir by his vigorous charges to grand juries denouncing the slave trade—interesting because his son William Wetmore Story authored the two-volume *The Life and Letters of Joseph Story* (1851), in which William edited out correspondence concerning his father's suggestions on how to adopt a new fugitive slave law.

28. Agreement, February 8, 1830 (Agreements, folder 1, box 1, series 1, Remond Family Papers).

29. Agreement, February 22, 1832 (Agreements, folder 1, box 1, series 1, Remond Family Papers).

30. Agreement, June 20, 1833 (Agreements, folder 1, box 1, series 1, Remond Family Papers).

31. "Potato Puff," 116 (MS. N-384, Hartwell-Clark Family Papers, Massachusetts Historical Society; hereafter MHS).

32. Undated agreement (Agreements, folder 1, box 1, series 1, Remond Family Papers).

33. Remond Family Papers.

34. Northend, *Memories of Old Salem*, 249.

35. Invoice dated October 14, 1825; Committee for reception of General Lafayette, August 31, 1824; Lafayette Dinner, August 30, 1824; Undated invoice, Settlement be-

tween John Remond and Joseph S. Leavitt for Lafayette Dinner (all from Invoices, series 1, folder 4, box 1, Remond Family Papers).

36. Porter, "Remonds of Salem," 268, mentions the "pivotal occasion of a social life." Also see Miscellaneous (folder 5, box 1, series 1, Remond Family Papers); Correspondence (folder 2, box 1, Remond Family Papers); Martin Robison Delany, *Condition, Elevation, Emigration, and Destiny*, 102; Arnett G. Lindsay, "Economic Condition of the Negroes," 197; Invoices dated July 31, 1824–August 6, 1825, and September 8, 1825–February 17, 1826, Account with David Pingree (both from Invoices, folder 4, box 1, series 1, Remond Family Papers); Miscellaneous (folder 5, box 1, series 1, Remond Family Papers); Philip S. Foner, *History of Black Americans*, 2:264; Bill of Lading dated August 23, 1831 (folder 1, box 4, series 1, Bills of Lading, Remond Family Papers). See also handwritten note, dated August 24, 1831, from Thomas Downing on the back of the bill of lading. Remond is listed as a wine merchant in Salem for 1856 and 1857. See *Salem Directory, Containing the Names*, 210.

37. *Catalogue of Very Choice, and Very Old Wines, Liquors, Cordials*, Remond Family Papers.

38. Advertisements from *Salem Gazette* 41, new series 5, no 97 (December 11, 1827), and no. 69 (September 4, 1827). Also see *Salem Gazette* 41, new series 5, no. 66 (August 24, 1827), no. 67 (August 28, 1827); and Fabens, *Hamilton Hall*, 12.

39. Fabens, *Hamilton Hall*, 14–15; Marianne Cabot Devereaux Silsbee, *Half Century in Salem*, 88–94.

40. *Salem Observer*, December 9, 1848. See also *Salem Advertiser*, February 3, 1847.

41. *Salem Gazette*, October 19, 1849; Silsbee, *Half Century in Salem*, 94. See also Gloria C. Oden, "Journal of Charlotte L. Forten," 131.

42. Fabens, *Hamilton Hall*, 12. Also see Northend, *Memories of Old Salem*, 249; Maritcha R. Lyons, "Memories of Yesterdays," 57, 58, 62; Yee, *Black Women Abolitionists*, 16, 87; Sterling, *We Are Your Sisters*, 175; Porter, "Remonds of Salem," 272–73, 290, 294.

43. Porter, "Remonds of Salem," 280 (quote), also 272–73, 281, 290, 294. See also *Salem Register*, June 26, 1857; Lyons, "Memories of Yesterdays," 57, 58. For examples of Charles Lenox Remond's oratory and writings, see *Black Abolitionist Papers*, 3:314–19, 368–74, 416–24, 442–45, 4:382–90.

44. *Essex County Freeman*, February 4, 1852; Porter, "Remonds of Salem," 289.

45. Lyons, "Memories of Yesterdays," 59 ("substantial desserts," "none were eligible," "Susan's kitchen"), 60 ("Her kitchen," "courted friendliness"). Also see Porter, "Remonds of Salem," 289–90.

46. Porter, "Remonds of Salem," 290–91 (quote), 264–65, 292. Also see Lyons, "Memories of Yesterdays," 10, 59. Cecelia Babcock advertised with her sister Caroline Remond in the *Salem Observer*, August 18, 1849, and the *Salem Gazette*, June 15, 1849. See

also *Salem Directory, Containing the Names*, 54, 157, 201, 202, 254, and especially ad no. 59 in the advertising section of the directory. *Salem Observer*, August 18, 1849; *The Liberator* 29, no. 4 (January 28, 1859): 15; also *The Liberator* 23, no. 10 (March 11, 1853): 39.

4: Triangular Trading and the "Colored" Cooks of Rhode Island

1. "God's Little Acre," *Newport This Week*, December 22, 2004; Richard C. Youngken, *African Americans in Newport*, 3; John Michael Ray, "Newport's Golden Age," 51, 56; Newport Historical Society, "Some Old Papers," 10–31. See also Bridenbaugh, *Cities in the Wilderness*; Du Bois, *Gift of Black Folk*, 57.

2. Ambrose Knox to David S. [L.?] Barnes, January 16, 1793 (MSS 9004, vol. 6, pp. 41–48, Rhode Island Manuscripts, Rhode Island Historical Society; hereafter cited as RIHS). See also Lynne Withey, *Urban Growth*, 72–73;

3. Lerone Bennett Jr., "Black & Green," 36

4. Youngken, *African Americans in Newport*, 3; Withey, *Urban Growth*, 71–72; Ray, "Newport's Golden Age," 51, 54, 55, 56; Robert A. Selig, "German Soldier in New England," 56; Newport Historical Society, "Some Old Papers," 10–31; Edith Ballinger Price, "Court End of Town," 7; Du Bois, *Gift of Black Folk*, 58.

5. Newport Historical Society, "Some Old Papers," 10–31; Ray, "Newport's Golden Age," 51, 52, 56; Withey, *Urban Growth*, 34, 35; Youngken, *African Americans in Newport*, 3, 12; Jay Coughtry, *Notorious Triangle*, 110–11; Du Bois, *Gift of Black Folk*, 58.

6. George Gibbs Channing, *Early Recollections*, 24–26. For discourse on a description of the Blacks encountered at Newport's port area during the Revolutionary War era, see Robert A. Selig's translation of Georg Daniel Flohr's manuscript (located under Ms f 15 in the Bibliothèque Municipale of Strasbourg, France), in Selig, "German Soldier in New England," 49, 55; "God's Little Acre," *Newport This Week*, December 22, 2004.

7. Some ingredients adapted from "Elisabeth's Birds nest pudding," C. Dyer Recipe Collection, 1827 and 1837 (MS. SBd-125, MHS).

8. Channing, *Early Recollections*, 33, 46–47. See also Mrs. John King (May) Van Rensselaer, *Our Social Capital*, 345. Note that Violet's kindness was rewarded by this verbal familiarity with the shopkeeper. Children calling her by her first name was a habit taught by their parents and society.

9. Channing, *Early Recollections*, 158 (quote), 159–61 (for how cooks preserved certain fruits and roasted poultry).

10. Van Rensselaer, *Our Social Capital*, 342 (quotes). See also Youngken, *African Americans in Newport*, 14. Cuffy Cockroach is identified as a cook, and a "noted turtle cook," in the household of Jahleel Brenton in Mason's Newport Narrative (MSS 554, vol. 2, pp. 101–2); and there is an entry for Cuffee Cockroach as "Waiter," in Brigantine

Yankee Account Book, 1814–1816, MSS 382, vol. 6, p. 76, DeWolf Family Papers (all in RIHS Library).

11. Van Rensselaer, *Our Social Capital*, 345; Youngken, *African Americans in Newport*, 50; Charles A. Battle, *Negroes on the Island*, 36–37.

12. Youngken, *African Americans in Newport*, 49–50, 61, 71; "Duchess Quamino: The Pastry Queen of RI," *Newport This Week*, February 17, 2005; "God's Little Acre," *Newport This Week*, December 22, 2004; Battle, *Negroes on the Island*, 7, 28; George E. Brooks Jr., "Providence African Society," 185, 186; Oliver Wendell Elsbree, "Samuel Hopkins," 542; Samuel Hopkins, Edwards Amasa Park, and Sewall Harding, *Works of Samuel Hopkins*, 130–31, 133, 134–35, 138, also 139–56; Franklin Bowditch Dexter, *Literary Diary of Ezra Stiles*, 1:207, 363–66, 2:16, 376, 378; Edmund S. Morgan, *Gentle Puritan*, 125, 309–10, 451–52; John Ferguson, *Memoir*, 83, 89–91, 175–86. Note that the child John Quamino was said to subsequently become a slave of Captain Benjamin Church.

13. "Aunt Hannah's Cookies," MS. SBd-125; "Aunt Julia's Sponge Cake," MS. SBd-125 (both from C. Dyer Dessert Recipe Collection, 1827, 1837, MHS).

14. Channing, *Early Recollections*, 170–71. See also "Duchess Quamino: The Pastry Queen of RI," *Newport This Week*, February 17, 2005.

15. Channing, *Early Recollections*, 170–71; "God's Little Acre," *Newport This Week*, December 22, 2004.

16. "Duchess Quamino: The Pastry Queen of Rhode Island," *Newport This Week*, February 17, 2005; Youngken, *African Americans in Newport*, 24, 68; Battle, *Negroes on the Island*, 29–30.

17. Rice Family Papers (Rhode Island Black Heritage Society); Youngken, *African Americans in Newport*, 24, 55; Myra Beth Young Armstead, "Blacks in Resort Towns," 59–60; Battle, *Negroes on the Island*, 29–30.

18. Rice Family Papers (Rhode Island Black Heritage Society); Youngken, *African Americans in Newport*, 38, 55, 74–75; Battle, *Negroes on the Island*, 29–30.

19. Depositions of William Jordan, Richard Johnson, and also John Gardner involving the riots in Providence in 1831 (MSS 452, folder 124, box 134, Albert Collins Greene Papers, 1804–1863, RIHS Library). See also William J. Brown, *Life of William J. Brown*, 88–96; Richards, *"Gentlemen of Property,"* 34.

20. George F. Jencks Diary, entries for Hardscrabble Riots, February 7, October 19, 1824 (MSS 9001-J, RIHS Library); Richards, *"Gentlemen of Property,"* 34 ("furniture"). See also Youngken, *African Americans in Newport*, 23; Brown, *Life of William J. Brown*, 89–90.

21. Elisha Dyer, "Reminiscences of the South Side" (MSS 677, RIHS Library), 5 ("extended reputation"); "Memorandum," entry for January 21, 1891 (MSS 483, series SG 13, folder 6, box 2, Joseph P. Hazard Collection, RIHS Library). See also Bennett, "Black & Green." Joseph P. Hazard's father, Rowland Hazard, paid wages to his servants "of

colour" and intervened on behalf of illegally enslaved Africans. But, indirectly, he made his living by way of slavery—his business had him traveling extensively throughout the South from the 1820s through the 1840s, selling "Negro cloth" to southern plantation owners and to a primarily southern market. The coarse cloth was used to make clothes for southern bondspeople as well as prison inmates. See Rowland G. Hazard Correspondence (MSS 483, SG 5, RIHS Library) for correspondence between Hazard and southern plantation owners negotiating purchase prices.

22. "Bills Paid to William H. Williams, 1895–1896" (MSS 647, folder 8, box 2, Providence Marine Society, RIHS Library).

23. Youngken, *African Americans in Newport*, 41–43, 55, 64, 68, 78.

24. Youngken, *African Americans in Newport*, 42, 43, 52, 70, 75, 76.

25. Youngken, *African Americans in Newport*, 31, 70; *City Atlas of Newport*; *Atlas of the City of Newport, 1883*; Rhode Island Historical Preservation Commission, "Kay Street"; Armstead, "Blacks in Resort Towns," 66.

26. Erick Taylor, interviewed by Rowena Stewart, July 13, 1977, Rhode Island Black Heritage Society, Providence. See also "The 'Providence' and 'Bristol' in the Seventies: Extracts from the Diary of a Contemporary Traveler," *Fall River Line Journal* (January 1921): 7 (Harvard Business School, Historical Collections Department); Richard C. Youngken, *African Americans in Newport*, 29–30; Armstead, "Blacks in Resort Towns," 160–61.

27. Roger Williams McAdam, *Priscilla of Fall River*, 36.

28. McAdam, *Priscilla of Fall River*, 36 ("the listin's in this menu"). See also Youngken, *African Americans in Newport*, 40; "Armstead, Blacks in Resort Towns," 164–65. George A. Rice was listed as living in Newport, Rhode Island. See George A. Rice listed as steward on the steamer *Pilgrim*, in the Fall River, Massachusetts, directories for 1888. Fall River directories for 1891 through 1894 list him as steward of the steamer *Puritan* (Fall River Historical Society Archives). For a partial list of the steamers' culinary provisions loaded on board each trip, see Roger Williams McAdam, *Old Fall River Line*, 85–86.

29. *Newport Mercury*, June 8, 1872, 2 (Newport Historical Society Newspaper Collection); *Newport Mercury*, July 23, 1892, 1 (Rivera Library, University of California, Riverside); "Local Notes," *Newport Daily News*, July 21, 1892, 5 (Newport Public Library).

30. Fall River Line Menu, 1925 (Fall River Historical Society Archives).

31. Tunis G. Campbell, *Hotel Keepers*, 164.

32. Youngken, *African Americans in Newport*, 29, 47, 55; Armstead, "Blacks in Resort Towns," 165; McAdam, *Priscilla of Fall River*, 36.

33. Youngken, *African Americans in Newport*, 30, 31, 34; Rhode Island Historical

Preservation Commission, "Kay Street," 14, 16, 17, 40; Armstead, "Blacks in Resort Towns," 59.

34. Youngken, *African Americans in Newport*, 31, 34, 52; "Downing, George Thos.," reel 4 (Sterling Memorial Library, Yale University); Battle, *Negroes on the Island*, 32; Henry B. Hoff, "Frans Abramse Van Salee," 207; S. A. M. Washington, *George Thomas Downing*, 3–4; Henry B. Hoff, "Frans Abramse Van Salee," 209–11; "Mr. and Mrs. George T. Downing: Preparations for Their Golden Wedding in Newport," *New York Tribune*, November 22, 1891; Booker T. Washington, "Negro Disfranchisement," 312; US Census Bureau, Eighth Census of the United States, 1860, Newport, Rhode Island (Roll: M653_1204, 282).

35. "Colored Enterprise," Frederick Douglass' Paper, July 27, 1855, 1; "Restaurants," reel 19, Daniel Murray Papers (Wisconsin); "Downing," reel 12, Daniel Murray Papers (Sterling Memorial Library, Yale University, New Haven, Connecticut; hereafter cited as Daniel Murray Papers [Yale]).

36. "Local News Items. Another Incendiary Fire! Downing's 'Sea-Girt House' in Ruins!!" *Newport Daily News*, December 17, 1860; "Local News Items," *Newport Daily News*, December 18, 1860; "Fire," *Newport Mercury*, December 22, 1860; "The Union Telegraph Company" (telegram), folder 39, box 152-1, George T. Downing Papers, Moorland-Spingarn Research Center). The date printed on the Union Telegraph Company stationery is "1861." It was December 1860, and they had apparently already switched over to 1861 stationery. Also see *City Atlas of Newport, 1876*, which shows "Downing Street," and *Atlas of the City of Newport, 1883*, which shows "Downing Street" and "Downing Block."

37. *Public Laws*, 483; Edgar J. McManus, *Negro Slavery in New York*, 184.

38. George T. Downing to Charles Sumner, May 28, 1855 (letter no. 113, folder 1912, Charles Sumner Correspondence Collection, Houghton Library, Harvard University); Sumner to Downing, May 29, 1855 (folder 18–19, box 1, DeGrasse-Howard Family Papers, MHS). See also George T. Downing, "Will the General Assembly Put Down Caste Schools?"; Lawrence Grossman, "George T. Downing"; "Equal School Privileges in Rhode Island," *The Liberator* 30, no. 8 (February 24, 1860); Ichabod Northup, "An appeal from a colored man whose Father fought in the Revolution," broadside, February 1859 (folder 34, box 152-2, George T. Downing Papers, Moorland-Spingarn Research Center); Irving H. Bartlett, *From Slave to Citizen*, 51, 58; J. Stanley Lemons and Michael A. McKenna, "Re-enfranchisement"; "The Colored Man's Future," *New York Times*, November 23, 1877, 3; Maud L. Stevens, "Colonel Higginson and His Friends," 4, 5–6; S. A. M. Washington, *George Thomas Downing*, 19–20.

39. Downing, letter to the editors, in "Personal," *The Independent*, November 11,

1869; Downing to John Jay, March 5, 1877 (Jay Family Papers, Butler Library, Rare Books and Manuscripts, Columbia University).

40. Youngken, *African Americans in Newport*, 52; Armstead, "Blacks in Resort Towns," 67, 168–69, 170.

5: Philadelphia

1. Roger Lane, *William Dorsey's Philadelphia*, 72 (peanut vendor). See also Willard B. Gatewood, *Aristocrats of Color*, 237; Julie Winch, *Elite of Our People*, 11–12, 13; Mary Anne Hines, Gordon Marshall, and William Woys Weaver, *Larder Invaded*, 23; Esther M. Douty, *Forten the Sailmaker*, 100; Roger Lane, *William Dorsey's Philadelphia*, 72; Blockson, *Liberty Bell Era*, 54–56, 152, 153, 154–55.

2. Hines, *Larder Invaded*, 22, 25, 65, 83, 85, 91; William Woys Weaver, *Thirty-Five Receipts*, 71–72.

3. Hines, *Larder Invaded*, 22, 25, 65, 83, 85, 91; Weaver, *Thirty-Five Receipts*, 71–72.

4. G. James Fleming and Bernice Dutrieuille Shelton, "Fine Food for Philadelphia," 107, 114.

5. St. John Appo appears in the *Philadelphia Directory for 1804*, Philadelphia, 18. See also *Census Directory for 1811, Containing the Names, Occupations, & Residence of the Inhabitants of the City, A Separate Division Being Allotted to Persons of Colour*, Philadelphia, 366; reel 9, Daniel Murray Papers (Wisconsin); Blockson, *Liberty Bell Era*, 158; Russell F. Weigley, *Philadelphia*, 265.

6. W. E. B. Du Bois, *Philadelphia Negro*, 18–20. See also Winch, *Elite of Our People*; Spivey, *Peppers, Cracklings*, 286–87, 288, 289.

7. Henry M. Minton, *Negroes in Business*, 11. See also William Woys Weaver, "Those Amazing Augustins"; Weigley, *Philadelphia*, 255.

8. For discourse on Black female caterers in New York, see Booker T. Washington, *Negro in Business*, 38–39.

9. Nicholas Biddle, "Ode to Bogle," 360–61. See also Du Bois, *Philadelphia Negro*, 18–20, 25n16; Minton, *Negroes in Business*, 12–14. Robert Bogle and other Philadelphia caterers are referenced in "Philadelphia Not Keeping Pace in Business," *Chicago Defender*, February 28, 1914, 6; "Bogle," reel 10, Daniel Murray Papers (Wisconsin); Gatewood, *Aristocrats of Color*, 97–98; Lerone Bennett Jr., "Black & Green"; Hines, *Larder Invaded*, 65; *Philadelphia Times*, October 19, 1896; Winch, *Elite of Our People*, 21, 172n119 (and references in this note to the will of Robert Bogle, Philadelphia City Archives, Philadelphia County Deeds); Blockson, *Liberty Bell Era*, 159; Weigley, *Philadelphia*, 255, 264–65. For background on Nicholas Biddle, see Weigley, *Philadelphia*, 258–65.

10. For discussion and examples of Black businesses not serving their own people, and of Whites not patronizing Black businesses unless they were racially restricted, see

Michael E. Lomax, *Black Baseball Entrepreneurs*, 7; Henry Bradshaw Fearon, *Sketches of America*, 59–60; and Quincy T. Mills, *Cutting along the Color Line*. See also "Robert Bogle," reel 10, Daniel Murray Papers (Wisconsin); Winch, *Elite of Our People*, 21; Du Bois, *Philadelphia Negro*, 18–20.

11. Weaver, "Those Amazing Augustins"; Fleming, "Fine Food for Philadelphia," 107; "Augustin, Pierre (Peter)," reel 9, Daniel Murray Papers (Wisconsin). A descendant family member, Bernice Dutrieuille Shelton, writes that Peter Augustin's arrival date was about 1815.

12. *Register of Trades*, 5; "Augustin, Pierre (Peter)," reel 9, Daniel Murray Papers (Wisconsin).

13. "Augustin, Pierre (Peter)," reel 9, and "Robert Bogle," reel 10, both in Daniel Murray Papers (Wisconsin); Du Bois, *Philadelphia Negro*, 19–20; Fleming, "Fine Food for Philadelphia," 107.

14. Fleming, "Fine Food for Philadelphia," 107. Also see Weaver, "Those Amazing Augustins"; Weigley, *Philadelphia*, 255; Du Bois, *Philadelphia Negro*, 20; Spivey, *Peppers, Cracklings*, 287.

15. Lane, *William Dorsey's Philadelphia and Ours*, 112.

16. Weaver, "Those Amazing Augustins"; Lane, *William Dorsey's Philadelphia*, 75. For a look at this printed menu, see "Menu Collection" (box 1, Historical Society of Pennsylvania). See also Hines, *Larder Invaded*, 85; *Philadelphia Colored Directory*, 57.

17. Mrs. Bernice D. Shelton to Mrs. Robyn I. Stone, [no date], page 2 of letter, and Biography, 6–7 (both in folder 1, box 1, Albert E. Dutrieuille Catering Records); Receipts (folders 5–8, box 1, Dutrieuille Catering Records); Weaver, "Those Amazing Augustins"; Fleming, "Fine Food for Philadelphia"; Mr. Peter Shelton, interview, April 8, 2008; *Philadelphia Colored Directory*, 57, 59; Minton, *Negroes in Business*, 11.

18. Biography, 7–8 (folder 1, box 1, Albert Dutrieuille Catering Records).

19. Mr. Peter Shelton, interview, April 8, 2008.

20. Weaver, "Those Amazing Augustins"; "Augustin, Pierre (Peter)," reel 9, Daniel Murray Papers (Wisconsin); Lane, *William Dorsey's Philadelphia*, 112.

21. John W. Forney, "Terrapin," 32. See also Weaver, *Thirty-Five Receipts*, 71; Weaver, "Those Amazing Augustins."

22. Lizzie Martin Recipe Book, 73, Philadelphia, PA, ca. 1890, Recipe of Peter Augustin, Philadelphia Caterer, Library Company of Philadelphia, cited in Weaver, *Thirty-Five Receipts*, 71–72.

23. Prescott Family Cookbook (box L 2005, MHS), 26.

24. Roger Lane, *Roots of Violence*, 68. See also Weaver, "Those Amazing Augustins"; Peter Shelton, interview, April 8, 2008. The Knights of St. Peter Claver organization was founded for Black Catholics in 1909 in Mobile, Alabama, as an answer to continued

discrimination and segregation against Blacks wishing to join the Knights of Columbus. Named after St. Peter Claver, a Spanish Jesuit priest of African descent who ministered to African slaves in Cartagena, Colombia, in the sixteenth century, it is now reportedly the largest African American Catholic lay organization in the United States. By 1910 the group had branches in Norfolk and Richmond, Virginia, Nashville, Tennessee, and several towns in Mississippi. Branches were later opened in northern cities. For additional information, see Nina Mjagkij, *Organizing Black America*; Charles D. Lowry and John F. Marszalek, *Encyclopedia of African-American Civil Rights*.

25. For information on sailmaker James Forten, see Esther M. Douty, *Forten the Sailmaker: Pioneer Champion of Negro Rights*.

26. Folders 5–6, box 127-1, series B, Bustill-Bowser-Asbury Collection, Moorland-Spingarn Research Center; pamphlet titled "Philadelphia African Americans: Color, Class and Style, 1840–1940," 5 (folder 11, series 3, Trent Family Papers); Smith, "Bustill Family"; Woodson, "Bustill Family"; Douglass, *Annals of the First African Church*; "Bustill, Cyrus," reel 10, Daniel Murray Papers (Wisconsin); Nathan Mossell Autobiography, no date, 18 (folder titled Mossell, Nathan, Bustill-Mossell Family Papers, Alumni Records Collection, University of Pennsylvania Archives). Although Cyrus Bustill was encouraged in his business by the people of Burlington, some residents made it clear that if he wanted to maintain their patronage he would have to maintain an African's place by walking humbly and softly and remembering to keep behind Whites on the road. Bustill might have walked softly around his loaves of bread, but he did not believe in moving his wagon aside for Whites. Bustill's residence in Burlington ended when one day he was delivering his bread and he "overtook" the Philadelphia stage in which a certain squire was riding. Enraged, the squire thrust his head through the window of his stage and angrily yelled to Bustill to forget about bringing him any more bread. Cyrus was also said to have refused thereafter to sell to the squire or his family the breads and cakes they normally purchased.

27. Du Bois, *Philadelphia Negro*, 18–20; "Prosser, James," reel 18, Daniel Murray Papers (Yale); Minton, *Negroes in Business*, 11, 12.

28. Martin Robison Delany, *Condition, Elevation, Emigration, and Destiny*, 100 ("The name of James Prosser"). See also "Prosser, James," reel 18, Daniel Murray Papers (Yale); Winch, *Elite of Our People*, 21; Bennett, "Black & Green."

29. Delany, *Condition, Elevation, Emigration, and Destiny*, 100 ("a most gentlemanly man"); Hines, *Larder Invaded*, 25 ("legendary"). See also Blockson, *Liberty Bell Era*, 160; James Prosser Account Receipts for Dinners Served at Board Meetings of The Library Company of Philadelphia (Library Company of Philadelphia Archives).

30. Partially from Clam Soup recipe, "Receipts from long, long years of housekeeping," 33 (Hartwell-Clark Family Papers, MHS).

31. "Prosser, James," reel 18, Daniel Murray Papers (Yale); "McKee, John," and "Minton, Henry," both from reel 16, Daniel Murray Papers (Yale). Booker T. Washington mentions that "John McKee, of Philadelphia, was reputed to be a millionaire, but his estate in Philadelphia, when he died, amounted to but $342,832." Washington, "Negro Disfranchisement," 316. According to Mr. Washington, "Colonel McKee gave directions in his will that the rents and incomes of his estate should accumulate until the death of all his children and grandchildren. The fund was to be used to establish a college for the education of fatherless boys, white and colored" (316). However, on page 39 of a report titled *Efforts for Social Betterment Among Negro Americans, A Social Study made by Atlanta University, Under the Patronage of the Trustees of the John F. Slater Fund*, edited by W. E. B. Du Bois, Colonel John McKee is said to have left an estate, in 1896, of upward of one million dollars in real estate. The study provides an outline of the terms of his will with regard to his real estate, which include erection of "The Colonel John McKee College," so that "a number of poor colored male orphan children and poor white male orphan children born in Philadelphia County . . . may receive a better education, as well as more comfortable maintenance than they usually receive from application of public funds." Du Bois, *Efforts for Social Betterment Among Negro Americans*, 39.

32. Lane, *William Dorsey's Philadelphia*, 111, 115; Minton, *Negroes in Business*; Spivey, *Peppers, Cracklings*, 291, 292; Blockson, *Liberty Bell Era*, 144.

33. Both recipes from "Receipts from long, long years of housekeeping," 220.

34. *Philadelphia Times*, October 17, 1896 (State Library of Pennsylvania), 4. See also Du Bois, *Philadelphia Negro*, 19–20, 25n17; Spivey, *Peppers, Cracklings*, 288–89; Gatewood, *Aristocrats of Color*, 99, 216; "Caterers," reel 10, Daniel Murray Papers (Wisconsin); Lane, *William Dorsey's Philadelphia*, 111; Weigley, *Philadelphia*, 353.

35. "Jones, Henry," reel 15, Daniel Murray Papers (Yale); Minton, *Negroes in Business*, 11; Civil Rights Act of 1875 [18 Stat.335]; Du Bois, *Philadelphia Negro*, 18–20, 25n18, 84, 102n11; Lane, *William Dorsey's Philadelphia*, 168, 170.

36. Delany, *Condition, Elevation, Emigration, and Destiny*, 100–101. See also "Minton, Henry," reel 16, Daniel Murray Papers (Yale); Du Bois, *Philadelphia Negro*, 18–20, 25n19; Gatewood, *Aristocrats of Color*, 98, 216; Winch, *Elite of Our People*, 21; Minton, *Negroes in Business*, 11.

37. *Prigg v. Pennsylvania*, 41 U.S. 539 (1842); Spivey, *Fire from the Soul*, 89–90, 92–94; Akhil Reed Amar, *America's Constitution*, 262; Ripley, *Black Abolitionist Papers*, 3:49, 179n14, 317–18, 382n2, 383; also Joseph Nogee, "Prigg Case"; *United States v. The Amistad*, 40 U.S.(15 Pet.)518 (1841); Howard Jones, *Mutiny on the Amistad*, 193.

38. Lomax, *Black Baseball Entrepreneurs*, 8–9; folder 1 (box 132-1, Thomas and William Dorsey Collection, Moorland-Spingarn Research Center); Robert Clemens Smed-

ley, *Underground Railroad in Chester*, 356–57; Du Bois, *Philadelphia Negro*, 10, 25n17; Winch, *Elite of Our People*, 165; Blockson, *Liberty Bell Era*, 160.

39. *Register of Trades of the Colored People*, 3; *McElroy's Philadelphia Directory for 1844*, 81; *Present State and Condition of the Free People of Color*. See also Sharron Wilkins Conrad, "Philadelphia Caterer Thomas J. Dorsey," 37–38, for information on Dorsey's life and mention of the Augustins listing themselves in the category of caterers in 1865.

40. *Philadelphia Times*, October 17, 1896 (State Library of Pennsylvania), 4. Also see Du Bois, *Philadelphia Negro*, 19, 20, 25n17; Winch, *Elite of Our People*, 21; "Dorsey, Thomas J.," reel 12, Daniel Murray Papers (Yale); Lane, *Roots of Violence*, 151; Conrad, "Philadelphia Caterer Thomas J. Dorsey"; Minton, *Negroes in Business*, 11.

41. Charles Sumner, thank you note to Thomas Dorsey, no date (box 132-1, Thomas and William Dorsey Collection, Moorland Spingarn Research Center). See also Conrad, "Philadelphia Caterer Thomas J. Dorsey."

42. MS. SBd-125 (C. Dyer Recipe Collection, 1827, 1837, MHS).

43. Folder 30 (box 132-2, Thomas and William Dorsey Collection, Moorland-Spingarn Research Center); "Dorsey, Thomas," reel 3, and "Brown, John," reel 10, both in Daniel Murray Papers (Wisconsin); "Pencil Pusher Points," *Philadelphia Tribune*, February 20, 1897.

44. *New York World*, December 11, 1871. See also letter dated July 17, 1864 (folder and box # for hospital letter unknown), and letter dated October 31, 1876 (folder 22, box 132-1, both in Thomas and William Dorsey Collection, Moorland-Spingarn Research Center); *Philadelphia Times*, October 17, 1896 (State Library of Pennsylvania), 4; Du Bois, *Philadelphia Negro*, 93.

45. The *Commonwealth* piece was picked up by *Pacific Appeal (San Francisco)*, March 13, 1875; *Public Ledger*, February 19, 1875 (obituary news clippings, box 132-1, Thomas and William Dorsey Collection, Moorland-Spingarn Research Center). See also *Philadelphia Times*, October 17, 1896 (State Library of Pennsylvania), 4; *The Press*, March 6, 1875; *The Press*, February 20, 1875; Adelaide M. Cromwell, *Other Brahmins*, 219.

46. Lane, *William Dorsey's Philadelphia*, 126, 418; Gatewood, *Aristocrats of Color*, 98, 234–35; Weigley, *Philadelphia*, 589.

47. "Cromwell, Levi," reel 11, Daniel Murray Papers (Yale); Lane, *William Dorsey's Philadelphia*, 111, 112, 417; Lane, *Roots of Violence*, 67; Gatewood, *Aristocrats of Color*, 99.

48. "Trower, John S.," reel 21, Daniel Murray Papers (Yale); Washington, *Negro in Business*, 47–53.

49. Washington, *Negro in Business*, 47–53; "Trower, John S.," reel 21, Daniel Murray Papers (Yale).

50. "Trower, John S.," reel 21. Daniel Murray Papers (Yale); Washington, *Negro in Business*, 47–53; Lane, *William Dorsey's Philadelphia*, 113; *Philadelphia Colored Directory*, 59,

62; Blockson, *Liberty Bell Era*, 161. Fleming, "Fine Food for Philadelphia," 114, mentions Trower's merger with Thomas James. Also see Washington, *Negro Disfranchisement*, 312.

51. Lane, *William Dorsey's Philadelphia*, 125–26; "Trower, John S.," reel 21, Daniel Murray Papers (Yale).

52. "Trower, John S.," reel 21, and "Hotels," reel 14, card #5, both in Daniel Murray Papers (Yale); Washington, *Negro in Business*, 47–53. Also, I was fortunate enough to speak with Mr. Peter Shelton (Albert Eugene Dutrieuille's grandson), in a telephone interview on April 8, 2008, during which he spoke about Mr. Trower and his ice creams. Roger Lane's, *William Dorsey's Philadelphia*, describes John Trower as never having married or ever having had children. Reel 21 of the Daniel Murray Papers (Yale), however, offers a biographical sketch, which states that Mr. Trower left a widow, Miss Matild[a] Daniels of Virginia and *five* children. Booker T. Washington states that John Trower's wife, Matilda Daniels, of Haymarket, Virginia, reared their family of *six* children. Washington, *Negro in Business*, 52.

53. Fleming, "Fine Food for Philadelphia," 114; "Trower, John S.," reel 21, Daniel Murray Papers (Yale); Washington, *Negro in Business*, 47–53; "C. H. Smiley's Friend Dies: John S. Trower, Caterer, Reputed Wealthiest of Race in America, Succumbs," *Chicago Defender*, April 8, 1911, 3.

54. "Receipts from long, long years of housekeeping," 221.

55. "Receipts from long, long years of housekeeping," 219.

56. "Delmonico Club," reel 12, Daniel Murray Papers (Yale).

57. "Stevens, Andrew," reel 8, Daniel Murray Papers (Wisconsin).

58. "Ugly Club," reel 22, Daniel Murray Papers (Yale).

59. "The Ugly Club at Dinner," *New York Freeman*, May 16, 1885.

60. *Sentinel*, June 11, 1881. See also "Ugly Club Jr. Entertained," *Philadelphia Tribune*, May 25, 1912; "Pencil Pusher Points," *Philadelphia Tribune*, December 14, 1912. The Ugly Club Jr. was still garnering headlines during World War I; see "Ugly Club Jr., Royally Entertained by Geo. J. Cole," *Philadelphia Tribune*, January 16, 1915.

61. "The Ugly Club: Celebration of Their Twenty-First Anniversary," *New York Freeman*, May 15, 1886.

62. "Stevens, Andrew," reel 21, Daniel Murray Papers (Yale). Also see Charles Ashley Hardy, "Race and Opportunity," 28; Lane, *Roots of Violence*, 68, 69; "Andrew Stevens," reels 8 and 21, and "Ugly Club," reel 22, in Daniel Murray Papers (Yale); Daniel R. Biddle and Murray Dubin, *Tasting Freedom*, ix, 449.

63. Robinson's "home cooking," advertisement in Soap Box Minstrel souvenir program in Stevens-Cogdell/Sanders-Venning Collection, Library Company of Philadelphia. Also see Hardy, "Race and Opportunity, 28.

64. See Soap Box Minstrel and Jitney Social restaurant and cabaret advertisements

in souvenir programs for Venetian Tea Garden's "good music," Attucks "With all the best," Green's "the restaurant renowned," and Green Dragon, "the popular café," and Soap Box Social Testimonial Banquet program, June 14, 1912 (all in Stevens-Cogdell/ Sanders-Venning Collection, Library Company of Philadelphia). Also see Hardy, "Race and Opportunity, 444–45.

65. Soap Box Social Testimonial Banquet program, June 14, 1912 (Stevens-Cogdell/ Sanders-Venning Collection, Library Company of Philadelphia).

66. Soap Box Social Testimonial Banquet program, June 14, 1912, Menu (Stevens-Cogdell/Sanders-Venning Collection, Library Company of Philadelphia).

67. "Stevens, Andrew," reel 21, Daniel Murray Papers (Yale).

68. Lane, William Dorsey's Philadelphia, 113.

69. Du Bois, *Philadelphia Negro*, 18 ("guild of the caterers"), also 83–84, 85.

70. "Ye Olde Philadelphia Catering Family," 2 (MSS 52, folder 1, box 1, Dutrieuille Catering Records, 1873–1975, Historical Society of Pennsylvania); Fleming, "Fine Food for Philadelphia," 114; Lane, *William Dorsey's Philadelphia*, 111, 112, 113–14; Lane, *Roots of Violence*, 34–35, 114; Hardy, "Race and Opportunity," 15–16, 20, 443. See also the racist diatribe by Jno. Gilmer Speed, "The Negro in New York: A Study of the Social and Industrial Condition of the Colored People in the Metropolis," *Harper's Weekly* 44, no. 2296 (December 22, 1900): 1249–50.

6: "Them Pious Eats Tremendous!"

1. Dutrieuille, Book 1, May 1920–June 1924 (box 2), Book 2, December 1924–June 1928 (box 2), and Book 3, August 1933–May 1939 (box 3) (all in Dutrieuille Catering Records, Historical Society of Pennsylvania).

2. "Ye Olde Philadelphia Catering Family," Biography, 1, 2, 8, and Mrs. Bernice Shelton to Mrs. Robyn I. Stone, no date, 2 (both in folder 1, box 1, Albert E. Dutrieuille Catering Records).

3. "Ye Olde," Biography, 1. Also see Mrs. Bernice Shelton to Mrs. Robyn I. Stone, 2.

4. "Ye Olde," Biography, 2, for "Waste not, want not," and "Oh, you must."

5. "Ye Olde," Biography, 3 ("one of the best,"), and *Commercial Journal*, December 31, 1910 ("We have in this city") in Dutrieuille Catering Records. Also see J. N. Ingham and L. B. Feldman, *African American Business Leaders*, 225, 227; "Dutrieuille, P. Albert," reel 12, Daniel Murray Papers (Yale); Fleming and Shelton, "Fine Food for Philadelphia," 114; *Philadelphia Colored Directory*, 58; Charles Fred White, *Who's Who in Philadelphia*, 48–50. See also photographs of Peter Albert Dutrieuille and kitchen staff, in pamphlet titled "Philadelphia African Americans: Color, Class and Style, 1840–1940," 68–70 (folder 11, series 3, Trent Family Papers).

6. Mrs. Bernice Shelton to Mrs. Robyn I. Stone, 2; "Ye Olde," Biography, 5; Ingham and Feldman, *African American Business Leaders*, 227.

7. "Ye Olde," Biography, 6, 8; Ingham and Feldman, *African American Business Leaders*, 227–28; Mr. Peter Shelton, interview, April 8, 2008; *Philadelphia Colored Directory*, 58.

8. Dutrieuille, Book 1, May 1920–June 1924 (box 2), Book 2, December 1924–June 1928 (box 2), and Book 3, August 1933–May 1939 (box 3) (all in Dutrieuille Catering Records).

9. Jos. Doran to Albert E. Dutrieuille, February 23, 1915. See also Doran to Dutrieuille, March 26, 1915, both in "Correspondence" (folder 2, box 1, Dutrieuille Catering Records).

10. Dutrieuille, Book 1, May 1920–June 1924 (box 2), Book 2, December 1924–June 1928 (box 2), and Book 3, August 1933–May 1939 (box 3) (all in Dutrieuille Catering Records). Note: most of A. E. Dutrieuille's catering records for this period have survived. They do not take into account Library Company of Philadelphia orders before and after these dates.

11. Forney, "Terrapin," 32. See also Weaver, *Thirty-Five Receipts*, 37.

12. Mr. Peter Shelton, interviews, April 8, May 20, 2008.

13. See "Abstract" and "Biography Note," under collection description; also "A History of Black Catholics in the Archdiocese of Philadelphia, 1985" (folder 15, box 10, series 9, St. Peter Claver Roman Catholic Church Records, Collection I.D. BC-035-PC, Charles L. Blockson Afro-American Collection, Temple University Libraries); Winch, *Elite of Our People*, 31; Dennis Clark, *Irish in Philadelphia*, 167, 168, 169, 175; Weigley, *Philadelphia*, 296.

14. "Them Pious," *New York Times*, August 25, 1889, 11 (reprinted from *Blackwood's Magazine*).

15. Mrs. Bernice D. Shelton to Mrs. Robyn I. Stone, no date (folder 1, box 1, Dutrieuille Catering Records). See also "Biography" (folder 1, box 1, Dutrieuille Catering Records); Ingham and Feldman, *African American Business Leaders*, 228.

16. "Menus" (folder 9), "Receipts" and "Invoices" (folder 7), and "Correspondence" (folder 2) (all in box 1, Dutrieuille Catering Records); handwritten menu by Albert Eugene Dutrieuille, in possession of Peter Shelton.

17. Dutrieuille, Book 1, May 1920–June 1924, 3 (box 2, Dutrieuille Catering Records).

18. Dutrieuille, Book 1, May 1920–June 1924, 36 (box 2, Dutrieuille Catering Records).

19. Dutrieuille, Book 1, May 1920–June 1924, 8–10 (box 2, Dutrieuille Catering Records).

20. Dutrieuille, Book 1, May 1920–June 1924, 110–11 (box 2, Dutrieuille Catering Records).

21. Dutrieuille, Book 1, May 1920–June 1924, 113, 357, 455 (box 2, Dutrieuille Catering Records). See also Book 2, December 1924–June 1928, 281 (box 2, Dutrieuille Catering Records).

22. Dutrieuille, Book 3, August 1933–May 1939, 91 (box 3, Dutrieuille Catering Records). See also Weigley, *Philadelphia*, 609–13.

23. Clark, *Irish in Philadelphia*, 170. See also Dutrieuille, Book 3, August 1933–May 1939, 159, 161 (box 3, Dutrieuille Catering Records).

24. Mr. Peter Shelton, interviews with author, April 8, May 20, 2008; "Receipts" (folders 5–8, box 1, Dutrieuille Catering Records); "Abbott's Alderney Dairies," Archivist John Petitt (Urban Archives Department, Samuel L. Paley Library, Temple University).

25. Charles Ashley Hardy, "Race and Opportunity," 3, 4; Matthew Josephson, *Union House, Union Bar*, 17; Douglas Henry Daniels, *Pioneer Urbanites*, 35–40; Myra Beth Young Armstead, "The History of Blacks in Resort Towns," 134–35.

26. Bernice Shelton to Mrs. Robyn I. Stone, no date (folder 1, box 1). See also "Biography" (folder 1, box 1), Dutrieuille, Book 1, May 1920–June 1924, 438 (box 2), and Book 3, August 1933–May 1939, 115, 136, 138, 176, 239 (box 3) (all in Dutrieuille Catering Records).

27. Dutrieuille, Book 3, August 1933–May 1939, 117 (box 3, Dutrieuille Catering Records).

28. "It's Hard Out Here for a Pimp," Three 6 Mafia, Atlantic, Grand Hustle Label, Academy Award, Best Original Song, 2006; "Biography," folder 1, 5 ("I'd rather give") (box 1, Dutrieuille Catering Records); Dutrieuille, Book 1, May 1920–June 1924, 5 (box 1, Dutrieuille Catering Records).

29. Mr. Peter Shelton, interview with author, April 8, 2008.

30. The Prescott Family Cookbook (box L 2005, MHS), 7.

31. Mrs. Bernice Shelton to Mrs. Robyn I. Stone, no date, Dutrieuille, Book 1, May 1920–June 1924, 1, and "Obituary" (all in box 1, Dutrieuille Catering Records); Ingham and Feldman, *African American Business Leaders*, 228; Hardy, "Race and Opportunity," 15; Clora Powell, "Black Owned Businesses."

32. Charles L. Blockson, *Underground Railroad in Pennsylvania*, i, 3, 74, 75, 76, 77; Charles L. Blockson, *Underground Railroad*, 239; William J. Switala, *Underground Railroad in Pennsylvania*, 112.

33. R. J. M. Blackett, *Thomas Morris Chester*, 5 ("public holidays," "principal caterer"), also, *Chester*, 4; *Pennsylvania Daily Telegraph (Harrisburg)*, January 16, 1862 ("terrapins, oysters") and July 3, 1862 ("all the other delicacies"). For background information on George and Jane Marie Chester, see Blockson, *Underground Railroad in Pennsylvania*, 76; Luther Reily Kelker, *History of Dauphin County*, 128–29; *Commemorative Biographical*

Encyclopedia, 256. The Chesters' son Thomas Morris Chester was an Underground Railroad agent, lecturer, a writer who produced pamphlets, and an African correspondent during the Civil War. See "Civil War Reporter: Thomas Chester Kept Philadelphia Informed about Negro Troops in Battle," *Ebony* (November 1959): 132. The article states that Jane Marie Chester "was born in slavery . . . , later escaped to York, Pa., at the age of 17, where she met George Chester, who persuaded her to come to Harrisburg and marry him." The article also mentions the Chesters' restaurant and their support of Underground Railroad activities. See also Yee, *Black Women Abolitionists*, 16–17; US Census Bureau, Seventh Census of the United States, 1850, Harrisburg East Ward, Dauphin County, Pennsylvania (Roll: M432_774), 89A; Blockson, *Underground Railroad*, 239; Switala, *Underground Railroad in Pennsylvania*, 112; "Died," *Pennsylvania Daily Telegraph (Harrisburg)*, October 17, 1859; "Died," *Harrisburg Patriot and Union*, October 18, 1859; US Census Bureau, Eighth Census of the United States, 1860, Harrisburg Ward 2, Dauphin County, Pennsylvania (Roll: M653_1104), 967; "Soft Shell, and devilled crabs," *Pennsylvania Daily Telegraph (Harrisburg)*, July 3, 1862; first column, *State Journal (Harrisburg, Pa.)*, January 24, 1885, 1.

34. "Excellent Breakfast Cakes," and "Oyster Cakes" recipes in the column titled "The Housekeeper's Department," *State Journal (Harrisburg, Pa.)*, October 11, 1884.

35. "Rubber Cookies" recipe in the column titled "Hints for the Housewife," *State Journal (Harrisburg, Pa.)*, January 24, 1885.

36. "Cough Syrup" remedy in the column titled "Hints for the Housewife," *State Journal (Harrisburg, Pa.)*, December 20, 1884.

37. See advertisements for the United States Hotel Restaurant in December 6, 1884, and various other issues of the *State Journal (Harrisburg, Pa.)*; *The Afro-American Ledger*, June 6, 1903, 1; Mr. Peter Shelton, interview, May 20, 2008.

38. "Served Banquet for General Grant, "*Philadelphia Tribune*, May 18, 1912, cited in *Chicago Defender*, May 25, 1912, 1.

39. Rhoda Golden Freeman, *Free Negro in New York City*, 209.

7: "Outcasts and Indigent Sons of Africa"

1. Booker T. Washington, *Negro in Business*, 38–39; Booker T. Washington, *Up from Slavery*, 3, 4. A small excerpt of this chapter appeared in theblackscholar.org on February 4, 2019.

2. "One Hundred and Sixty Years of the Music of Francis (Frank) Johnson (1792–1844)" (Historical Society of Pennsylvania, and Saratoga Springs History Museum and Society, 1977), 6, 7, 8, 11, 12, 13, 19, 20; Armstead, "Blacks in Resort Towns, 39–40; Weigley, Philadelphia, 264, 265. See also William A. Shack, *Harlem in Montmartre*, 8,

for discourse on Frank Johnson and early African musical groups touring Europe; and Evelyn Barrett Britten, *Chronicles of Saratoga*, 475.

3. Solomon Northup, *Twelve Years a Slave*, 24–28, 289; "From Washington. . . . The Kidnapping Case," *New York Daily Times*, January 19, 1853, 8; "The Kidnapping Case: Narrative of the Seizure and Recovery of Solomon Northrup," *New York Daily Times*, January 20, 1853, 1; "The Case of Mr. Northrup," *New York Daily Times*, January 21, 1853, 7; Armstead, "Blacks in Resort Towns," 40. The kidnapping and selling of free Africans became a cottage industry. Northup was not the only free person sold into slavery in 1841. See, for example, the Rowland G. Hazard Papers in the Rhode Island Historical Society Library, which contain three folders relating to several illegally enslaved free Africans in New Orleans. Three letters are from illegally enslaved Rufus Kinsman, dated June 18, 1841, and Charles Delisle, dated April 1 and April 10, 1841 (MSS 483, SG-5, folder 82, box 24, Rowland G. Hazard Papers, RIHS Library). See also E. S. Abdy, *Journal of a Residence*, 2:49–50, 91–93, 94, 98–100 (in which Abdy presents discourse on cases of the kidnapping and selling of Africans), 2:96–97 (in which he describes a Washington slave pen that he saw in 1835). See also "Kidnapped Freemen—High Handed Cruelty," *Colored American*, January 2, 1841.

4. Armstead, "Blacks in Resort Towns," 125 (quote), also 39, 40, 44, 79. Also see Hugh Bradley, *Such Was Saratoga*, 130–31; Britten, *Chronicles of Saratoga*, 475, 479–80. Wealthy slaveowners had to think twice about bringing enslaved servants to New York. An Act More Effectually to Protect the Free Citizens of This State from Being Kidnapped passed on May 14, 1840. As with Northup, many enslaved persons were free, kidnapped blacks. See Northup, *Twelve Years a Slave*, 323–24, for the written statement pertaining to that legislation.

5. Cornelius E. Durkee, *"Reminiscences of Saratoga,"* 65 ("remember Crum's"), 250 ("few prominent men"); "Crum's: The Famous Eating-House on Saratoga Lake," *New-York Daily Tribune*, December 27, 1891, 26 ("king bird," "the only fit bird," and "even Delmonico's").

6. *New-York Daily Tribune*, "Crum's: The Famous Eating-House on Saratoga Lake," December 27, 1891, 26. See also Hugh Bradley, *Such Was Saratoga*, 123.

7. *New-York Daily Tribune*, "Crum's: The Famous Eating-House on Saratoga Lake," December 27, 1891, 26. Also see "This Man Cooked for Commodore Vanderbilt and Jay Gould, and Created a Billion Dollar Business to Boot," *Fortune* (June 1973): 63; Bradley, *Such Was Saratoga*, 122.

8. "Crum's: The Famous Eating-House on Saratoga Lake," *New-York Daily Tribune*, December 27, 1891, 26. *New York Times*, September 1, 1888, 5; *New York Times*, September 3, 1888, 8; Armstead, "Blacks in Resort Towns," 42; Cornelius E. Durkee, *Reminiscences*

of Saratoga, 250; Bradley, *Such Was Saratoga*, 121, 122; William S. Fox and Mae G. Banner, "Folklore Variants,"15, 16, 17.

9. *The Saratogian*, July 5, 1908, 5; *The Saratogian*, July 24, 1918, 2; *Saratoga Springs Directory, 1925*, 46–47; Armstead, "Blacks in Resort Towns," 154–55, 213.

10. Lionel M. Yard, "Blacks in Brooklyn," 289; Craig Steven Wilder, *Covenant with Color*, 145.

11. Hotaling, *Great Black Jockeys*, 112 ("famous five or six miles"), 113 (Tyrone Power quotes), also 111. See also "Restaurants, Taverns," reel 9, Daniel Murray Papers (Wisconsin); Batterberry and Batterberry, *On the Town*, 43, 45; Leslie M. Harris, *In the Shadow of Slavery*, 77.

12. Johnson, *Black Manhattan*, 44 (quotes), also 43.

13. Rhoda Golden Freeman, *The Free Negro in New York City*, 209.

14. See Lyons, "Memories of Yesterdays," 26 ("every thinking man"); Delany, *Condition, Elevation, Emigration, and Destiny*, 102. See also Henry Scott's editorial "To the Public," in the *Colored American*, January 12, 1839, 1; George E. Walker, *Afro-American in New York City*, 36, 37 (also 36–37n22), 56n30; Manual of the Board of Education of the City and County of New York, 1848 (Municipal Archives, City of New York), 84; Manual of the Board of Education, 1849, 99.

15. Freeman, *Free Negro in New York City*, 210. See also *The Emancipator*, May 11, 1837, 7.

16. "Mars, James W." reel 16, Daniel Murray Papers (Yale).

17. Yard, "Blacks in Brooklyn," 289; *1866 Guide to New York City*, 93; Earl of Carlisle, *Travels in America*, 29. See also Batterberry and Batterberry, *On the Town*, 99.

18. "The S.I. Soul Survivors: Descendants & Museum Vibrant in Sandy Ground, Nation's Oldest Existing Community of Free Blacks," *New York Daily News*, March 7, 2007, "Little Africa." Also see Minna C. Wilkins, "Sandy Ground," 3.

19. Lois A. H. Mosley, *Sandy Ground Memories*, 12 ("delighted the palate"), 16 (quote from *Staten Island World*). Also see Clyde L. MacKenzie Jr., "Biographic Memoir of Ernest Ingersoll," 26; Fields, *Slavery and Freedom*, 169; Wilkins, "Sandy Ground," 7; and Mosley, *Sandy Ground Memories*, 15, 17. Oysters were of such economic importance in some of the lower counties of Maryland by the latter nineteenth century that "oysters often pass current as money, and in one town there is a weekly paper . . . about 50 of the subscribers to which annually pay in oysters." See Fields, *Slavery and Freedom*, 182; also Ingersoll, *Report on the Oyster Industry*, 170; and *Report on the Fisheries and Water-Fowl of Maryland*, 31.

20. Mosley, *Sandy Ground Memories*, 196 ("Golden Age"); William Askins, "Oysters and Equality," 9 ("the New York State").

21. Askins, "Oysters and Equality," 9 ("property-based"), and 10. "Natural

growthers" were having similar problems in 1893. See "Battling the Oyster Planters: 'Natural Growthers' Claim the Right to Bivalves in the Sound," *New York Times*, June 12, 1893.

22. Askins, "Oysters and Equality," 10.

23. Mosley, *Sandy Ground Memories*, 75 ("competition with the whites"), also 27–28. See also Askins, "Oysters and Equality," 10. See also "The S.I. Soul Survivors: Descendants & Museum Vibrant in Sandy Ground, Nation's Oldest Existing Community of Free Blacks," *New York Daily News*, March 7, 2007.

24. *Longworth's New York Directory, 1834–1835; Longworth's American Almanac, 1835–1836*, 193. See also Wilson Jeremiah Moses, *Alexander Crummell*, 11–12, 16, 17; Washington, *Negro in Business*, 39.

25. Batterberry and Batterberry, *On the Town*, 98 ("Canal Street Plan," "bad oyster"), 99 ("generous slab").

26. Batterberry and Batterberry, *On the Town*, 99 Abram C. Dayton, *Last Days of Knickerbocker Life*, 128; John H. Hewitt, "Mr. Downing," 229.

27. "Nat's Receipt" (Means Family Recipe Book, MS. 0208.03, [Misc] 01–07 Means Family Papers 1860s, South Carolina Historical Society); "Receipt for Pickling Oysters" (MS. 1035.00, Recipes Pre 1850, folder 11/151/25, Gibbes-Gilchrist Family Papers, South Carolina Historical Society); "Roast Turkey with Oyster Dressing" (MS. 1035.00, folder 11/152/1, page 56, Gibbes-Gilchrist Family Papers, South Carolina Historical Society); "Scalloped Oysters" (Julia Frink Loper Receipt Book, MS. 34/0765-01, pages 84–85, South Carolina Historical Society); "Oyster Sauce," in "Receipts from long, long years of housekeeping," 57 (Hartwell-Clark Family Papers, MS. N-384, Carton 2, SH 13 DQ2, MHS).

28. Dayton, *Last Days of Knickerbocker Life*, 128; Bloch, *Circle of Discrimination*, 223; Johnson, *Black Manhattan*, 44; Lindsay, "Economic Condition of the Negroes," 197; Harmon, "Negro as a Local Business Man," 120; Osofsky, *Harlem*, 5, 11; Freeman, *Free Negro in New York City*, 210, 215; George T. Downing, "Life and Times," 405; Delany, *Condition, Elevation, Emigration, and Destiny*, 103–4; Hewitt, "Mr. Downing," 229; Walker, *Afro-American in New York City*, 37; Daniel Alexander Payne, *Recollections of Seventy Years*, 46; "Restaurants," reel 19, Daniel Murray Papers (Wisconsin); Washington, "Negro Disfranchisement," 312.

29. Batterberry and Batterberry, *On the Town*, 99 ("the only house"); Dayton, *Last Days of Knickerbocker Life*, 101 ("believed"). See also *Longworth's American Almanac, 1835*, 224; Hewitt, "Mr. Downing," 229–30; Harris, *In the Shadow of Slavery*, 77.

30. The quotation is from remarks made by Samuel J. Tilden at a dinner for Senator Casserly. Letter and printed remarks; letter dated February 19, 1869 (both in box 7, 1869, January–September, Samuel J. Tilden Papers, Manuscripts and Archives Division, Hu-

manities & Social Sciences Library, New York Public Library). Tilden's remarks are accompanied by a handwritten cover letter from Nelson Waterbury, apparently someone associated with the dinner for Casserly. The letter simply asks Tilden to edit, if desired, his own remarks, as the intention is to publish them in book form.

31. Hewitt, "Mr. Downing," 230; Walter Barrett, *Old Merchants of New York City*, 73–74.

32. Downing, "Life and Times," 404 (quote), also 402, 403. For more on Thomas Downing see "Downing, Thomas," reel 12, and also "George Thos. Downing," reel 4, both in Daniel Murray Papers (Yale). For a brief discourse on Joseph Head, see James M. Willcox *A History of the Philadelphia Saving Fund Society*, 69, and Downing, "Life and Times," 404.

33. Downing, "Life and Times," 405. See also "Downing, Thomas," reel 12, Daniel Murray Papers (Yale); Washington, *George Thomas Downing*, 5.

34. Downing, "Life and Times," 406.

35. Downing, "Life and Times," 407; folder 20, box 1, DeGrasse-Howard Papers, MHS; Lyons, "Memories of Yesterdays," 45–46; "Downing, Thomas," reel 12, Daniel Murray Papers (Yale); Washington, *George Thomas Downing*, 6.

36. Downing, "Life and Times," 408.

37. "Oysters," *New York Herald*, December 29, 1844, and "Oysters," *New York Herald*, December 31, 1844, 8, for both quotes.

38. "Steam Ship Great Western—The late Dinner on Board—A Mistake Corrected," *New York Herald*, November 9, 1844, 2.

39. Thomas Downing invoice letterhead from the 1850s and Thomas Downing business card (both in folder 10, box 152-1, George T. Downing Papers, Moorland-Spingarn Research Center).

40. Philip Hone, diary entry for February 15, 1842, in Bayard Tuckerman, *Diary of Philip Hone*, 2:117–18. See also Batterberry and Batterberry, *On the Town*, 84; Richards, *"Gentlemen of Property,"* 50; Hewitt, "Mr. Downing," 232.

41. George Templeton Strong, diary entries for December 30, 1859, and April 13, 1860 (holograph, vol. 3, George Templeton Strong Diary, New York Historical Society; hereafter cited at Diary holograph with volume number). Please note that the George Templeton Strong Diary is also available as a book edition. See Allan Nevins and Milton Halsey Thomas, *Diary of George Templeton Strong*, vols. 1–4.

42. Strong, entries for July 10, 1868, and July 18, 1871 (Diary holograph, vol. 4). For Strong's diary entries relating to representation at the conventions for St. Philip's, see Strong, diary entry for September 30, 1853 (Diary holograph, vol. 2); Hewitt, "Mr. Downing," 232, 243–46; Strong, entry for October 12, 1856 (Diary holograph, vol. 3).

Note that these diary entries were written after the death of Thomas Downing. Downing's sons carried on the business for some years.

43. Strong, entry for October 31, 1854 (also October 25, 27, 1854), in Nevins and Thomas, *Diary*, 2:194; Hewitt, "Mr. Downing," 232.

44. Delany, *Condition, Elevation, Emigration and Destiny*, 103 ("leading," "benevolent"), also 104; *Frederick Douglass' Paper*, October 5, 1855 ("most respected").

45. News clipping, in folder 1, box 152-1, George T. Downing Papers (Moorland-Spingarn). See also folder 20, box 1, DeGrasse-Howard Papers; Downing, "Life and Times," 409; Hewitt, "Mr. Downing," 249 and picture on 250 and picture facing 298, in Nevins and Thomas, *Diary, Volume 1*.

46. "Negroes that conducted themselves decently," *Town Topics*, June 27, 1895, 15; Washington, "George Thomas Downing," 18. For brief discourse on Downing loan to owner of *New York Herald*, see typescript in folder 20, box 1, DeGrasse-Howard Papers.

47. John H. Hewitt, "Search for Elizabeth Jennings," 397–98; McManus, *Negro Slavery in New York*, 188.

48. John H. Hewitt, "Sacking of St. Philip's Church," 16. See also George E. Wibecan, "New York Negro Clubs" (folder 10, series 3, Trent Family Papers). Written in 1915, Wibecan's statement on "Jim Crow" in New York is accurate for both time periods. Walker, *Afro-American in New York City*, 20; *Colored American*, January 16, February 20, 1841; news clipping (folder 1, box 152-1, George T. Downing Papers); Hewitt, "Mr. Downing," 246.

49. News clipping (folder 1, box 152-1, George T. Downing Papers).

50. *Colored American*, February 20, 1841. For the account of New York City transportation's second attempt to eject Thomas Downing from a streetcar, see "'One More Unfortunate' Attempt of the Sixth-avenue Railroaders to eject a Colored Man—Thomas Downing abused, but sticks it out," *New York Times*, September 26, 1855, 8; *Frederick Douglass' Paper*, October 5, 1855; Hewitt, "Mr. Downing," 246–47. Note that racial profiling on public transportation was an ongoing practice. The year before, on July 16, 1854, Elizabeth Jennings, a teacher who early in her career taught at a school conducted by the New York Society for the Promotion of Education Among Colored Children, and her companion, Sara E. Adams, were violently ejected from a moving public conveyance operated by the Third Avenue Railroad Company. A delegation led by her father—a New York clothier and tailor and patented inventor of the original dry-cleaning method, Thomas L. Jennings, who was active in the abolitionist movement, suffrage rights struggle, and other reform activities with the Downings—asked the law firm of Culver, Parker and Arthur to take her case. It was the future president twenty-four-year-old Chester A. Arthur, the newest and youngest partner, who was assigned the case. Even though they won the case, their court victory did not prevent the same

acts of violence and discrimination against Africans on public transportation from recurring. See Manual of the Board of Education of the City and County of New York, 1849 (Municipal Archives, City of New York), 100; "Outrage Upon Colored Persons," *New-York Tribune*, July 19, 1854; *Frederick Douglass' Paper*, September 22, 1854; Hewitt, "Search for Elizabeth Jennings," 389, 390–92, 393–94, 399, 400, 401; Ripley, *Black Abolitionist Papers*, 4:230–33; Freeman, *Free Negro in New York City*, 72–74. Also worth mentioning is that New York City custom tailor Thomas L. Jennings was born in 1791. In 1821, at the age of thirty, he is said to have become the first Black person to be granted a patent in the United States (US Patent 3306x). His invention, a dry-cleaning process called "dry scouring," was the forerunner to today's modern dry cleaning. However, most of the money Jennings earned was spent on abolitionist activities. See "Thomas L. Jennings," *Douglass' Monthly* (March 1859): 36; "Thomas L. Jennings," *Anglo-African Magazine* (April 1859): 126–28; "Frederick Douglass Describes the Life of a Negro Tailor, 1859," in Herbert Aptheker, *Documentary History*, 420–22.

51. Hewitt, "Search for Elizabeth Jennings, " 398. Also see Henry Scott's editorial "To the Public, and Particularly to the Citizens of the town of Worcester," *Colored American*, January 12, 1839; *The Emancipator*, March 9, 1837; Freeman, *Free Negro in New York City*, 68–75; Phyllis Frances Field, "Struggle for Black Suffrage," 1–28.

52. "African Colonization," *African Repository and Colonial Journal* 27, no. 9 (September 1851): 263; W. Chambers, *Things as They Are in America*, 354. See also *Report and the Debates and Proceedings*, 790; W. Chambers, *American Slavery and Color*, 37; Nathaniel H. Carter and William L. Stone, *Reports of the Proceedings and Debates*, 180; *Pennsylvania Constitutional Debates of 1837–1838*, 3:91, 9:321, 364–65, 10:24, 104; Leon F. Litwack, *North of Slavery*, 76; Lindsay, "Economic Condition," 194, 196; Bloch, *Circle of Discrimination*, 153–68 (particularly 153, 158, 160, 161, 164); Rhoda G. Freeman, "Free Negro in New York," 2, 127–33; Field, "Struggle for Black Suffrage."

53. Phyllis Frances Field, *Politics of Race*, 30, 32, 33, 34.

54. Hone, entries for August 26, 27, 1835, in Tuckerman, *Diary of Philip Hone*, 1:156–57; Hone, entry for March 25, 1842, in Nevins, *Diary of Philip Hone*, 2:592–93. See also Field, *Politics of Race*, 39; Richards, "Gentlemen of Property," 5, 26–28, 62n23, 63, 69, 84, 87, 88–89, 113–22; Hewitt, "Sacking of St. Philip's Church," 17; Hewitt, "Search for Elizabeth Jennings," 408.

55. Lyons, "Memories of Yesterdays," 26 (quotes), 46.

56. Folder 20, box 1, DeGrasse-Howard Papers; Lloyd A. Trent Jr. to Gilbert Millstein, December 4, 1975 (folder 1, series 1, Trent Family Papers); biography of George Thomas Downing, 7 (folder 20, box 1, DeGrasse-Howard Papers); handwritten notes (folder 1, series 1, Trent Family Papers); *Longworth's American Almanac, 1835*, 224; "Downing," reel 4, Daniel Murray Papers (Yale); Washington, *George Thomas Down-*

ing, 3, 6–7; Moses, *Alexander Crummell*, 17. George T. attended the Mulberry Street School where he met and became lasting friends with James McCune Smith, Philip Bell, Alexander Crummell, and Henry Highland Garnet. In later years he developed an antagonism against Garnet because of Garnet's African Civilization Society, which sought to repatriate Africans back to the Motherland. He was adamantly against all emigration schemes, and at a public meeting of African citizens in New York at Zion Church on April 12, 1860, Downing and Garnet went toe-to-toe on the issue. See *The Liberator*, May 4, 1860.

57. American and Foreign Anti-Slavery Society, *Fugitive Slave Bill*, 31–32; Herbert Aptheker, "Negro in the Abolitionist Movement," 19; Ripley, *Black Abolitionist Papers*, 2:9–11, 25–28, 193; Ripley, *Black Abolitionist Papers*, 3:54–56; "Downing," reel 4, Daniel Murray Papers (Yale); Walker, *Afro-American in New York City*, 156; Ripley, *Black Abolitionist Papers*, 3:337–38; Delany, *Condition, Elevation, Emigration, and Destiny*, 34; Washington, *George Thomas Downing*, 8; Howard Brotz, *African-American Social and Political Thought*, 48; *Manual of the Board of Education, 1848*, 58. Maritcha Lyons records her views of the Committee of Thirteen in Lyons, "Memories of Yesterdays," 26. There was another Committee of Thirteen created by the Senate in Washington on April 18, 1850. The Senate's committee made various resolutions relating to the newly acquired territories of California, Utah, and New Mexico, as well as to the pending Fugitive Slave Act, and (ironically) "A bill to suppress the slave trade in the District of Columbia." The committee made its report on May 8, 1850. Two days after Millard Fillmore signed the Fugitive Slave Act into law and after a long and bitter fight, on September 20, 1850, Fillmore took steps to finally abolish the slave trade (but not slavery) in the District of Columbia. See *Proceedings of the United States Senate*, 18. For a list of the members of the Senate's Committee of Thirteen, see *Journal of the Senate*, April 19, 1850, 301. For the committee's report, see US Senate, *31st Congress, 1st sess. Rep Com. No. 123*.

58. For discourse on the schools set up for Black children by Downing and other Black leaders, see Manual of the Board of Education, 1849, 99–100 (Municipal Archives, City of New York, New York); Hewitt, "Search for Elizabeth Jennings," 399, 400, 401; Manual of the Board of Education, 1848, 84–86, 163–70 (Municipal Archives, City of New York, New York). With regard to assets or taxable income, see W. H. Boyd, *New York City Tax Book, 1856 and 1857*, which contains an alphabetical list of taxpayers that includes George T. Downing, Henry Scott, and other Africans who paid taxes on real estate and personal property in the City. Downing is listed as having $6,800 in real estate, Henry Scott with $9,125, William M. Lively with $5,500 in real estate, S. Porter with $1,000, C. B. Ray with $3,000, and Dr. James McCune Smith as having $7,734 in property. Dr. Smith noted in 1859 that he was deriving an income of $400 out of $1,600 annually from his real estate holdings. Charles L. Reason's annual income was $2,000,

and $400 or $500 of that amount came from property ownership. See Boyd, *New York City Tax Book, 1856 and 1857*; Freeman, *Free Negro in New York City*, 207–8. See also Ripley, *Black Abolitionist Papers*, 2:188–89n6 (for biographical material on Dr. James McCune Smith), 2:79–80n1 (for biographical material on Charles B. Ray).

59. For the story carried on the beating of Fanny Belkizer, see "A Policeman's Brutality," *New York Times*, December 29, 1886, 5.

60. Dr. Evelyn Brooks Higginbotham, "African-American Women's History," 263–64; *The State v. John Mann*, 13 NC 263 [North Carolina Supreme Court, 1829]. See also A. Leon Higginbotham Jr., "Racism," 8–9. The story of a White policeman accusing May Enoch, who was standing on a corner in New York waiting for her boyfriend, of "soliciting," is in *The World*, August 17, 1900, cited in Osofsky, *Harlem*, 46–47. At the time of his appointment to the Supreme Court, Ruffin was president of the State Bank of North Carolina, where "two-thirds of the funds of the bank of North Carolina were invested in loans to slave merchants." See Guion Johnson, *Ante-bellum North Carolina*, 473–74; and Julius Yanuck, "Thomas Ruffin," 460–61. In *The State v. John Mann*, the defendant, John Mann of Chowan County, had rented the slave Lydia from Elizabeth Jones for a year. For whatever reason (and we have only Mann's version), he was in the process of whipping her for a "trifling offense" when Lydia tried to escape. Mann shot and gravely wounded her. Authorities in North Carolina charged Mann with assault and battery for meting out "punishment" disproportionate to the "offense." Mann was found guilty, but he appealed to the US Supreme Court, claiming that assault on a slave, even by a temporary master, should not be indictable. The Supreme Court overturned the conviction, thereby declining legal protection to a female or any other bondsperson.

61. *State of Missouri vs. Celia, A Slave*. The 1850 census lists Newsom as sixty years of age, with an estimated birth year of 1790. See US Census Bureau, Seventh Census of the United States, 1850, District 12, Callaway, Missouri (Roll: M432_393), 197A. For the two statutes regarding protection of women, see Missouri Rev. Stat. ch. 47, section 29, 1845, and Missouri Rev. Stat. ch. 47, section 4, 1845. A. Leon Higginbotham Jr., "Race, Sex, Education," 680–85; Hugh Williamson, "State against Celia"; A. Leon Higginbotham Jr., *Shades of Freedom*, 99–101, 237–39nn; Higginbotham, "African-American Women's History," 257–58; Spivey, *Fire from the Soul*, 25–26. Section 29 of the Missouri criminal statutes states, "Every person who shall take *any* woman, unlawfully, against her will, with intent to compel her by force, menace or duress . . . to defile [her] upon conviction thereof shall be punished by imprisonment." Another statute actually stated, "Homicide shall be deemed justifiable when committed by any person [who is] resisting [attempts] to commit any felony upon . . . her." Note, this last statute clearly states that "justifiable homicide" is not a crime even if death was intentional. Celia's counsel merely asked, therefore, that the court give Celia the same recognition, or right,

to resist sexual assault as did White women, despite her involuntary servitude. See *State of Missouri vs. Celia, A Slave* for the list of the judge's illegal instructions given to the jury; Williamson, "The State against Celia, a Slave," 417–18, for discussion of these illegal instructions.

62. A. Leon Higginbotham Jr. and Anne F. Jacobs, "Law Only as an Enemy," 971n3, 972n5. For another example, see *United States v. Amy*, 24 F. Cas. 792, At 809, 810 [C.C.D. Va. 1859], [NO. 14, 445]. Amy was a slave imprisoned for supposedly pilfering from a post office. Her slaveholder went to court stating that under the Fifth Amendment, "her status as his property made her imprisonment a deprivation of his ownership claim." None other than Chief Justice Roger Brook Taney (of *Dred Scott v. Sandford* fame) decided this case. Taney ruled that "slaves were regarded as legal persons for purposes of enforcing criminal law against them," and thereby the protection of property under the Fifth Amendment did not apply. His decision on *Amy* was made while sitting as a circuit judge in Virginia, which Supreme Court justices were allowed to do until the Circuit Court of Appeals Act of 1891, ch. 517, 26 Stat. 826. Also see Jedediah S. Purdy, "People as Resources," 1061nn27, 30, 31; Higginbotham, *Shades of Freedom*, 29.

63. Frederick Douglass to Thomas Van Rensselaer, May 18, 1847, in Philip S. Foner, *Frederick Douglass*, 83–85; "Anti Slavery Society," *New York Sun*, May 13, 1847. The *Ram's Horn*, published in New York between January 1, 1847, and June 1848. It came out sporadically for about another year, garnering twenty-five hundred subscribers. Restaurateur T. Van Rensselaer, edited the paper together with Willis Augustus Hodges, a free African from Virginia who arrived in Brooklyn in 1836. Hodges went to work as a whitewasher to earn money to keep the paper going. Frederick Douglass also assisted as editor for a while. See Ripley, *Black Abolitionist Papers*, 3:482–83n11.

64. Strong, entry for October 19, 1856 (Diary holograph, vol. 3).

65. Higginbotham, *Shades of Freedom*, 61 (quote), and 62–67. See also *Dred Scott v. Sandford*, 60 US [19 How.] 393 [1857]; and editorial in *Augusta Constitutionalist*, March 15, 1857.

66. Higginbotham, *Shades of Freedom*, 28, 64, 65, 66; Higginbotham, "Race, Sex, Education," 679–80; also Don Edward Fehrenbacher, *Dred Scott Case*; Walker, *Afro-American in New York City*, 37; Payne, *Recollections of Seventy Years*, 46; Delany, *Condition, Elevation, Emigration, and Destiny*, 103; *New-York Daily Tribune*, March 19, 1860; *The Principia*, March 24, 1860, 147; Higginbotham and Jacobs, "Law Only as an Enemy," 971; Purdy, "People as Resources," 1061n31. In 1846 Dred Scott filed suit against his owner, Mrs. Emerson, seeking freedom for himself and his family. The Missouri Supreme Court, reversing a long line of its prior cases, held in a two-to-one decision that Scott and his family were still slaves, according to both the Missouri Compromise of 1820 and the Northwest Ordinance of 1787, even though they had been residing in free territories.

The US Supreme Court upheld the Missouri decision. Benjamin Quarles mentions this incident and has George T. Downing, not his father, Thomas, as the person summoned to court. Quarles, however, does not provide a source for this information. Both father and son were outspoken, so it could have been either one of them. I must say, however, that it sounds more like George T., because he was always said to be more confrontational. Quarles, *Lincoln and the Negro*, 41.

67. Walker, *Afro-American in New York City*, 35–36, and 35–36n19; Harris, *In the Shadow of Slavery*, 39; Philip S. Foner, "William P. Powell," 102–3; Bloch, *Circle of Discrimination*, 31, 41; Frederick Douglass, *My Bondage and My Freedom*, 454–55. George T. Downing continued to work on behalf of Black labor. See Charles H. Wesley, *Negro Labor*, 177, 180.

68. Harris, *In the Shadow of Slavery*, 244, 280; Walker, *Afro-American in New York City*, 166; Field, *Politics of Race*, 150; Johnson, *Black Manhattan*, 45; Albon Man Jr., "Labor Competition," 376–77, 392, 393, 394–98, 400, 402; Field, *Politics of Race*, 154–55; Harris, *In the Shadow of Slavery*, 281, 283; Freeman, *Free Negro*, 212–13; Bloch, *Circle of Discrimination*, 30–37. The Phoenix Society was founded in 1833 by free Africans in New York City who were involved in abolitionist activities. Boston Crummell—caterer, oysterman, and father of Alexander Crummell—served on its board of directors. The Phoenix Society was said to have had the largest membership and widest influence among organizations of Africans in New York. The organization sought to "protect against discrimination in public places and to 'promote the improvement of the colored people in morals, literature, and the mechanical arts.'" The society also sponsored a series of scientific lectures as well as activities promoting cultural, social, and intellectual pursuits. The society founded "Ward Societies," which kept a registry of Africans in the city. Members also established a reading room, which was open Monday, Wednesday, and Friday evenings. The librarian was Samuel Cornish, one of the editors of *Freedom's Journal*; Cornish also organized the scientific lectures. Arthur Tappan, White abolitionist, was also a member. See Moses, *Alexander Crummell*, 13, 14.

69. Man, "Labor Competition and the New York Draft Riots of 1863," 375; Harris, *In the Shadow of Slavery*, 279; Bloch, *The Circle of Discrimination*, 35. Also see *New York Times*, May 14, 1976 article, "Dungeon-Like Subbasement Yields Dusty Municipal Past," which presents the discovery of an old document which records a $10 payment from a man who paid another to enlist in the Union Army in his place. Article also found in *Lloyd A. Trent, Jr. Family Papers*.

70. For literature pertaining to the Draft Riots see, for example, *Report of the Committee of Merchants*, 20, 21, 22, 23; Man, "Labor Competition," 400–401, 402; Harris, *In the Shadow of Slavery*, 280, 283–84, 285; Field, *Politics of Race*, 154; David M. Barnes, *Draft Riots*, 16, 24, 32, 33, 34, 36, 37, 39, 40, 54, 55, 104; story relating to Thomas Downing during

the Draft Riots (folder 20, box 1, DeGrasse-Howard Papers); Williamson, "Folks in Old New York," 5 (typescript, Harry A. Williamson Papers), in which Williamson states that his grandfather Albro A. Lyons, who was a resident in New York at the time, told him about Africans being hung from lampposts along Broadway and near the cemetery of Trinity Church; Johnson, *Black Manhattan*, 51–53; Yard, "Blacks in Brooklyn," 290; Batterberry and Batterberry, *On the Town*, 116–17; Bloch, *Circle of Discrimination*, 35; Ella Bunner Graff, "Reminiscences of Old Harlem," 8; "Reminiscences" also cited partially in Osofsky, *Harlem*, 83; Higginbotham, *Shades of Freedom*, 28; Douglass, *My Bondage and My Freedom*, 454.

71. Lyons, "Memories of Yesterdays," 1, 2, 3, 8; Williamson, "Folks in Old New York," typescript, 5; Walker, *Afro-American in New York City*, 24; "Boarding House for Seamen, Under the Direction of the American Seamen's Friend Society, Colored Seamen's Home, Kept by William Powell," *Colored American*, March 21, 1840; "Results of the Sailor's Home," *Colored American*, April 11, 1840; Foner, "William P. Powell," 89; Freeman, *Free Negro in New York*, 217; Harris, *In the Shadow of Slavery*, 285–86.

72. Lyons, "Memories of Yesterdays," typescript, 9–11a, 12; Williamson, "Folks in Old New York," typescript, 4, 5; Harris, *In the Shadow of Slavery*, 286.

8: Running the Kitchen and Running for Office

1. Charles Sumner to Joshua B. Smith, December 25, 1862 (Charles Sumner Correspondence Collection, The Papers of Charles Sumner, microfilm; hereafter cited as Charles Sumner Correspondence Collection); George T. Downing to Sumner, February 19, 1863 (folder 1912, Charles Sumner Correspondence Collection, Houghton Library, Harvard University). See also Quarles, *Lincoln and the Negro*, 154, 160; Manisha Sinha, "Caning of Charles Sumner," 258.

2. Quarles, *Lincoln and the Negro*, 160.

3. Frederick Douglass to Secretary of War Edwin M. Stanton, July 13, 1863 (Tracy Collection, Connecticut Historical Society); Downing to Sumner, July 24, 1863 (folder 1912, Charles Sumner Correspondence Collection, Harvard). Regarding the letter of recommendation for George T. Downing "for the post of Quartermaster, in our colored forces, as a *commissary*," July 26, 1863 (folder 35, box 152-1, George T. Downing Papers, Moorland-Spingarn Research Center), the letter does not contain an addressee. It is handwritten and signed "Charles Sumner." However, after having read numerous letters written and signed by Charles Sumner on his Senate letterhead, I can state emphatically that the handwriting on this document is not Sumner's. I can offer only that perhaps the original letter was fragile, and a copy of the original was written out and placed in the file at Moorland-Spingarn. Or, perhaps Sumner dictated it to someone who wrote it for him.

4. "Butter, John Sidney," reel 10, Daniel Murray Papers (Wisconsin); Washington, "George Thomas Downing: Sketch of His Life and Times," 11. Also see newspaper clipping (folder 20, box 1, DeGrasse-Howard Collection, MHS); folders 6–7, box 152-1, George T. Downing Papers; "George Thos. Downing," reel 4, Daniel Murray Papers (Yale), 3; Johnson, *Black Manhattan*, 49, 50. See also Quartermaster General's Office, State of Rhode Island, document/letter dated May 2, 1864, sent to George T. Downing, asking Downing to return all arms and equipment (folders 18–19, box 1, DeGrasse-Howard Collection). John Sidney Butter was born a slave in Port Tobacco, Charles County, Maryland, in 1834. He moved to DC in 1855. In 1880, as a "confidential messenger," he was sent to Paris by the State Department during the formation of a treaty between England, Germany, and the United States over the sovereignty of the Samoan Islands. In 1905 Butter was sent to assist diplomats at Portsmouth, New Hampshire, where negotiations were held that led to the Treaty of Portsmouth, ending the Russian Japanese War. Butter died at his home in Washington on April 26, 1916, leaving a daughter and a son.

5. "Negro Casualties in the Civil War," in Herbert Aptheker, *To Be Free*, 101. Also see Douglass to Stanton, July 13, 1863 (Tracy Collection, Connecticut Historical Society); Aptheker, *To Be Free*, 100, 102–3, 104, 105, 112, 219n109.

6. Harris, *In the Shadow of Slavery*, 244. See also Campbell, *Hotel Keepers, Head Waiters*; articles from *New York Herald*, April 13, March 31, April 5, 14, 16, 1853, all cited in Philip S. Foner and Ronald L. Lewis, *Black Worker*, 1:190–96.

7. Tunis G. Campbell, *Sufferings of the Rev. T. G. Campbell*, 5–6; Harris, *In the Shadow of Slavery*, 243.

8. Harris, *In the Shadow of Slavery*, 243–44; Campbell, *Hotel Keepers, Head Waiters*, 5–19, 48.

9. Campbell, *Hotel Keepers, Head Waiters*, 122–23.

10. Campbell, *Hotel Keepers, Head Waiters*, 123.

11. Campbell, *Hotel Keepers, Head Waiters*, 107.

12. Campbell, *Hotel Keepers, Head Waiters*, 163–64.

13. Campbell, *Hotel Keepers, Head Waiters*, 162.

14. Harris, *In the Shadow of Slavery*, 244 (quote), 280. See also Walker, *Afro-American in New York City*, 166; Field, *Politics of Race*, 150; Johnson, *Black Manhattan*, 48.

15. Campbell, *Sufferings of the Rev. T. G. Campbell*, 6, 7.

16. Russell Duncan, *Freedom's Shore*, 20 (quote), 16, 19. Also see Campbell, *Sufferings of the Rev. T. G. Campbell*, 7.

17. Duncan, *Freedom's Shore*, 22–23.

18. Duncan, *Freedom's Shore*, 20, 21, 24, 26–27, 30.

19. Duncan, *Freedom's Shore*, 27–28.

20. Duncan, *Freedom's Shore*, 30–33, 34–36, 37, 41. For a description of some of the exploitation, see Affidavit from Toby Maxwell (Tunis Campbell-Black Legislator, 110 Tunis Campbell: Black Reconstructionist, 1544-0103, Georgia Archives; hereafter cited as Tunis Campbell File).

21. Duncan, *Freedom's Shore*, 42–43, 50–51; Campbell, *Sufferings of the Rev. T. G. Campbell*, 10. For discourse on Campbell's work in the Georgia legislature, see Affidavit, "Protest of John Irvine," from Attorney L. E. B. DeLorme, on behalf of John Irvine (Tunis Campbell File); W. E. B. Du Bois, *Black Reconstruction*, 498, 501, 505; Duncan, *Freedom's Shore*, 52, 70–71; "The Radical Conspiracy Against Savannah in the Georgia Senate," *Savannah Morning News*, August 25, 1870; Duncan, *Freedom's Shore*, 46–47, 48–49, 50–51, 52–54, 69–70.

22. For discourse on Campbell counseling Black workers, see Affidavits from Constable Hamilton Jackson, seaman Francis Lee, seaman Robert Wing, Anthony Franks, Deputy Sheriff Alonzo Guyton, and Warrant for the arrest of Captain John Irvine (Tunis Campbell File). Also see David Donald, *Rights of Man*, 298–99; Duncan, *Freedom's Shore*, 5, 58–59; Buddy Sullivan, *Darien Journal*, 13, 116n26, 118n32, 119n36; Affidavits from William R. Gignilliat, William A. Burney, Charles H. Hopkins Jr., Frank Clayton, James R. Bennett, L. E. B. DeLorme, and others (Tunis Campbell File).

23. For discourse relating to "Campbell exercising great influence" in Black McIntosh County, see sworn statements and affidavits from S. W. Wilson, Alonzo B. Guyton, Hamilton Jackson, Ossian Hanks, William R. Gignilliat, and others (Tunis Campbell File). Hamilton Jackson's and Ossian Hanks's sworn statements suggest that much trouble would follow "if they [authorities] had put him in jail." For discourse on Campbell, if he did not receive help from President Grant and supposedly resorts "to act" because there is only "one resource left," George E. Atwood, W. R. Pritchard, and J. Epping offered sworn statements (Pritchard and Epping provided a "joint" statement) as well. "Another Negro Outrage at Darien," *Savannah Morning News*, August 31, 1871, 3 ("wherever they are in the majority"). Also suggesting that Blacks defend themselves with guns, see Duncan, *Freedom's Shore*, 87–89; James H. Bradley to J. H. Taylor, June 13, 1870 (Tunis Campbell File); Affidavits from James R. Bennett, George E. Atwood, Wm. A. Burney, Alonzo Guyton, S. W. Wilson, E. Champney, and others (Tunis Campbell File). Also see "Tunis G. Campbell Black, of Darien, on the Rampage—He Holds Indignation Meetings, and Proposes to Defy the Law," *Savannah Morning News*, January 11, 1872; "Senator Campbell at His Mischief," *Savannah Daily Republican*, January 11, 1872, 2. E. Merton Coulter, in his two articles "Tunis G. Campbell, Negro Reconstructionist in Georgia," parts 1 and 2, published in the *Georgia Historical Quarterly*, shamelessly ridicules Campbell, using Coulter's own racist commentary and racist articles he chose from newspaper sources to express details of events throughout both pieces. Both ar-

ticles contain some of the same information that I collected from my research, but his commentary viciously lies about or distorts the facts, and I choose, therefore, not to reference any pages from this material.

24. Lieutenant James H. Bradley to Colonel J. H. Taylor, June 13, 1870 (Tunis Campbell File); Campbell, *Sufferings of the Rev. T. G. Campbell*, 14; Affidavits from R. Elliott and Sheriff and Jailor James R. Bennett, also a twelve-page statement on "unjust" incarceration of John M. Fisher, January 17, 1871 (all in Tunis Campbell File); Duncan, *Freedom's Shore*, 89–92; "A Visit to the Jail—Tunis G. Campbell," *Savannah Morning News*, June 28, 1872. For details on Campbell's arrest, see two Declarations of Protest, plus an affidavit, and statements against the Black seamen, with whom Campbell was arrested (Tunis Campbell file); Duncan, *Freedom's Shore*, 78–79; "The Darien Outrage," *Savannah Morning News*, August 15, 1871, 3. For discourse on the harassment and persecution of Huey Newton and the Black Panther Party by the FBI and the Justice Department, see Huey Newton, *War against the Panthers*; Huey Newton, *Revolutionary Suicide*; Samuel F. Yette, *Choice*, 210, 287; also see Ward Churchill and Jim Vander Wall, *Agents of Repression*, 63–99, 397n2; Ward Churchill and Jim Vander Wall, *Cointelpro Papers*, 123, 125–26, 356n64; David Hilliard and Donald Weise, *Huey P. Newton Reader*. See also O'Reilly, "The Only Good Panther: The Pursuit of the Black Panther Party for Self-Defense," in Kenneth O'Reilly, *"Racial Matters."* I disagree with some aspects of O'Reilly's discourse; however, he does discuss the government's behavior in going after Newton and the Black Panthers.

25. Mrs. St. Julien Ravenel, *Charleston*, 91. Also see A. S. Salley Jr., "The Introduction of Rice Culture into South Carolina," *Bulletins of the Historical Commission of South Carolina*, no. 6 (Columbia, SC, 1919), 16; Margaret Washington Creel, *"Peculiar People,"* 36, 37, 44; Daniel C. Littlefield, *Rice and Slaves: Ethnicity and the Slave Trade in Colonial South Carolina* (Chicago: University of Illinois Press, 1991), 6. Regarding rice production: "the culture of rice engross[es] [planters'] whole strength and attention." Bartholomew Rivers Carroll, *Historical Collections of South Carolina*, 1:141. Carroll offers a detailed description of the labor involved in producing rice and ends the description by stating, "much care and great strength are requisite, and many thousands of lives from Africa have been sacrificed, in order to furnish the world with this commodity." Carroll, *Historical Collections of South Carolina*, 1:142.

26. Creel, *"Peculiar People,"* 43–44.

27. The recipe has no title, but it begins "One Quart of Rice Flour" (MS.#1035.00, "Recipes," folder 11/151/25, Gibbes-Gilchrist Family Papers, South Carolina Historical Society).

28. Frederic Mauro, *L'Expansion européenne*, 217–18; also cited in Littlefield, *Rice and Slaves*, 6.

29. Wikramanayake, *World in Shadow*, 106 (quote), 66–68, 70, 79, 103. See also Du Bois, *Black Reconstruction*, 383; Harmon, "Negro as a Local Business Man," 118, 126; *Register of the Mesne Conveyance Office: Book B8*, 202–3, Book X7, 262–64, Book M8, 399–403, Book L7, 1, Book F7, 187–188, Book R7, 196; F. C. Adams, *Manuel Pereira*, 88–89; Jehu Jones Pamphlet, "Jehu Jones: Free Black Entrepreneur" (document no. 2,920, Jones, 1997, South Carolina Historical Society); *Directory and Stranger's Guide*; "Hotels," reel 14, Daniel Murray Papers (Yale); E. Horace Fitchett, "Traditions of the Free Negro," 143–44. For comments on the importance of Charleston's Broad Street, see also Charles Fraser, *Reminiscences of Charleston*, 12–13, as cited by E. Horace Fitchett, "Free Negro in Charleston," 99. One source states that Jehu Jones was once a slave of tailor Christopher Rogers, and that Jones became an expert tailor himself, opening his own business, when Rogers freed him in 1798.

30. Bernard E. Powers Jr, *Black Charlestonians*, 43 ("antique and mixed"); Mrs. St. Julien Ravenel, *Charleston, The Place and the People*, 459 ("luxuries of the table"); Fitchett, "Free Negro in Charleston," 100 ("His house"); Wikramanayake, *World in Shadow*, 110–11 ("Every Englishman"), 106. Also see Jehu Jones Pamphlet, "Jehu Jones: Free Black Entrepreneur"; Adams, *Manuel Pereira*, 88–89; Thomas Hamilton, *Men and Manners*, 347–48; Karl Bernhard, *Travels Through North America*, 2:4–5; Ravenel, *Charleston*, 460–61; Powers, Black Charlestonians, 44.

31. Fitchett, "Free Negro in Charleston," 100; *City Gazette*, August 21, 1822, cited in Fitchett, "Free Negro in Charleston," 100; advertisement, "A First Rate Man Cook for Sale," *Charleston Courier*, August 8, 1844.

32. Recipe Book, 23 (MS #1285.02.01, folder 1285.02.13, container 28/639/10, Mary Mott Pringle Papers, South Carolina Historical Society).

33. Recipe Book, 25 (MS #1285.02.01, folder 1285.02.13, container 28/639/10, Mary Mott Pringle Papers, South Carolina Historical Society).

34. Wikramanayake, *World in Shadow*, 58n33, 103, 106, 110, 177–78; Adams, *Manuel Pereira*, 88–89, 90, 94; Fitchett, "Free Negro in Charleston," 68–69, 101, 102; *Charleston Mercury*, September 27, 1822. See also Petition to the Senate of South Carolina, December 6, 1823, authored by John L. Wilson, governor of South Carolina (from December 1822 to December 1824), on behalf of Jehu Jones, to be allowed to return to South Carolina (Document V, Petition to State, General Assembly Papers, Petitions, no. 138, South Carolina Department of Archives and History). Fitchett, "Free Negro in Charleston," 101, table 9, lists some of Jehu Jones's real estate transactions between 1801 and 1816. The law was retroactive—Ordinance Passed December 19, 1835, Sec. V: "That it shall not be lawful for any free Negro or Person of Color, who has left the State at any time previous to the passing of this Act, or for those who may hereafter leave the State, ever to return again into the same, without being subject to the penalties of the first section

of this Act as fully as if they had never resided therein." See *Digest of the Ordinances of the City Council of Charleston from the Year 1783 to October 1844.*

35. Powers, *Black Charlestonians,* 44. See amended appraisal of Jehu Jones's personal estate after his death, September 13, 1833, where Ann Deas is mentioned as having a bill of sale for Jones's furniture (page 1, document 6, South Carolina Department of Archives and History). See also Larry Koger, *Black Slaveowners,* 38, 154–55. "A room taken out of the 'Mansion House' is installed in the Henry Francis Du Pont Winterthur Museum, near Wilmington, Delaware, where it is still used as a dining room for entertaining guests." Wikramanayake, *World in Shadow,* 111 and n42. The 1848 census for Charleston lists a "free colored female" hotelkeeper, as cited in Fitchett, "Free Negro in Charleston," 75, table 6; Ravenel, *Charleston,* 460–61.

36. Recipe Book, ca. 1840, "Created by Maria Louisa Poyas Gibbs," 1 (MS #34/0702, South Carolina Historical Society).

37. Recipe Book, ca. 1840, "Created by Maria Louisa Poyas Gibbs," 6 (MS #34/0702, South Carolina Historical Society).

38. Powers, *Black Charlestonians,* 166 (quote), 167. See also David S. Shields, *Southern Provisions,* 125, 126.

39. Powers, *Black Charlestonians,* 166–67; David S. Shields, *Southern Provisions,* 122–25. For Fuller versus Gatewood, see *Simons & Simons Case Records,* 1835–1873 (Call No. 0431.02 [F]06: Fuller vs. Gatewood, Box 19, South Carolina Historical Society). Nat Fuller sued Madeleine Gatewood, and Fuller's wife, Diana, continued the suit after her husband's death.

40. Sullivan, *Darien Journal,* 1 (quote), 5, 9. See also Joseph C. G. Kennedy, *Agriculture of the United States in 1860; Compiled from the Original Returns of the Eighth Census* (Washington, DC, 1864), xciv, xcv, 26–27, 128–129, 196.

41. Sullivan, *Darien Journal,* 3, 4, 123n67; Duncan, *Freedom's Shore,* 55. Darien was almost totally destroyed on June 11, 1863, by two all-Black units, the Second South Carolina Volunteers, and the reluctant participation of Colonel Robert Gould Shaw and his Fifty-Fourth Massachusetts Volunteer Infantry Regiment. Then, "both industries, timber and rice, died hard and expired quickly in and around Darien. In a ten-year period from 1901 to 1911 the town rapidly went from peak to valley in terms of commercial shipments of lumber, naval stores and agricultural products. It had long been understood that since the end of slavery the cultivation of rice was no longer a profitable venture on the tidewater. The lumber industry died when the pine timber ran out upriver—along the Altamaha, the primary conveyor of millions of board feet of pine to the active sawmills of Darien." Sullivan, *Darien Journal,* 3.

42. Campbell, *Hotel Keepers, Head Waiters,* 153–54.

43. Campbell, *Hotel Keepers, Head Waiters,* 176–77.

44. Campbell, *Sufferings of the Rev. T. G. Campbell*, 17, 19–20, 21, 23–24; Duncan, *Freedom's Shore*, 93, 94–96, 105–8. See also Du Bois, *Black Reconstruction*, 506, for a discussion of the penitentiary system and convict leasing system in Georgia and how it began to characterize the convict lease system in the entire South.

45. Campbell, *Sufferings of the Rev. T. G. Campbell*, 26, 22. There is an order for "Executive Clemency for Tunis Campbell" (Tunis Campbell File). Note, however, that the clemency order is dated January 25, 1875; Duncan, *Freedom's Shore*, 109.

46. Duncan, *Freedom's Shore*, 109–10. For an example of how Tunis Campbell's legacy remained a part of McIntosh County when one of its Black residents was falsely accused of rape by a White woman, see also W. Fitzhugh Brundage, "Darien 'Insurrection' of 1899"; and Sullivan, diary entries for August 23, 25, and September 18, 1899, in Sullivan, *Darien Journal*, 58, 59.

47. "Smith, John J.," reel 20, Daniel Murray Papers (Wisconsin); Daniels, *In Freedom's Birthplace*, 57. Also see Cromwell, *Other Brahmins*, 49–51; Sinha, "Caning of Charles Sumner," 238.

48. "Bay State Republicans: Delegates for Edmunds as First Choice—The Majority Then for Grant," *New York Times*, April 23, 1880, 1. See also "Smith, John J.," reel 20, Daniel Murray Papers (Wisconsin); Records of the Massachusetts State House of Representatives (Office of the Clerk, Massachusetts State House of Representatives, Boston, Massachusetts); Daniels, *In Freedom's Birthplace*, 100–101, 188; Cromwell, *Other Brahmins*, 51.

49. *Proceedings of the One Hundredth Anniversary*, 37 ("He resembled"). See also Horton and Horton, *Black Bostonians*, 109; "Smith, Joshua B.," reel 20, Daniel Murray Papers (Wisconsin); Daniels, *In Freedom's Birthplace*, 449, 453; Rayford W. Logan and Michael R. Winston, *American Negro Biography*, 565.

50. Daniels, *In Freedom's Birthplace*, 101, 454. See also Martin H. Blatt, Thomas J. Brown, and Donald Yacovone, *Hope and Glory*; also chapters Marilyn Richardson, "Taken from Life," 95; Kathryn Greenthal, "Augustus Saint-Gaudens," 116; Kirk Savage, "Uncommon Soldiers," 163. Smith is mentioned as "not only one of the most prominent black abolitionists in Boston but also a personal friend of the Shaw family." Thomas J. Brown, "Reconstructing Boston," 146. See also "Smith, Joshua B.," reel 20, Daniel Murray Papers (Wisconsin).

51. Sumner referred to as a "bitter pill" in Joshua B. Smith to Charles Sumner, May 18, 1869; Smith to Sumner, dated June 7, 1860 (both in Charles Sumner Correspondence Collection, microfilm). See also Austin Bearse, *Fugitive-Slave Law Days*; Horton and Horton, *Black Bostonians*, 109; Logan and Winston, *American Negro Biography*, 565; Richardson, "Taken from Life," 95. Notably, Lewis Hayden was one of the five Black members of the 207-member Boston Vigilance Committee, organized on October 14, 1850,

to resist the new Fugitive Slave Act. Hayden's home became the chief Boston "station" of the Underground Railroad. See Bearse, *Fugitive-Slave Law Days*, which contains the list of Vigilance Committee members, and also Logan and Winston, *American Negro Biography*, 295–97.

52. Bill of Fare, Dinner of The City Council of Boston, July 4, 1846, Furnished by J. B. Smith (American Broadsides and Ephemera, series 1, no. 16671, Boston Public Library; hereafter cited as American Broadsides, with series number).

53. *Black Entrepreneurs*, 18. See also Bill of Fare, Dinner for the City Council of Boston, in Celebration of the Seventy-Third Anniversary of American Independence, July 4, 1848, Furnished by J. B. Smith (American Broadsides, series 1, no. 16678); Bill of Fare, Dinner for the City Council of Boston, July 4, 1849, Furnished by Joshua B. Smith (American Broadsides, series 1, no. 16681); Bill of Fare, Seventy-Seventh Anniversary of American Independence, July 4, 1853, Dinner for the City Council of Boston, Furnished by Joshua B. Smith (American Broadsides, series 1, no. 16735).

54. "Harriett's" Washington Pie," Prescott Family Cookbook, 17 (box L 2005, MHS).

55. Sumner to Smith, May 19, 1867 (Charles Sumner Correspondence Collection, microfilm). For Sumner's personal thoughts, confided to Joshua Smith, regarding his civil rights bill and what Sumner felt was a lack of support from Black politicians, see Donald, *Rights of Man*, 579; Sumner to Smith, February 25, 1872 (Charles E. French Autograph Collection, MHS); Sumner to Smith, January 1, 1874 (Rare Book, Manuscript, and Special Collections Library, William R. Perkins Library, Duke University). James Wormley was a famous African caterer, restaurateur, and hotelkeeper in Washington, DC.

56. Sumner to Smith, January 3, 1868 (Rare Book, Manuscript, and Special Collections Library, William R. Perkins Library, Duke University).

57. Smith to Sumner, February 12, 1869 (Charles Sumner Correspondence Collection, microfilm).

58. Sumner to Smith, February 25, 1872 (Charles E. French Autograph Collection, MHS). See also Edward L. Pierce, *Memoir and Letters*, 4:337, 338, 566, 591; Smith to Sumner, February 12, May 18, 1869 (Charles Sumner Correspondence Collection, microfilm); "Smith, Joshua B.," reel 20, Daniel Murray Papers (Wisconsin); Logan and Winston, *American Negro Biography*, 566; Donald, *Rights of Man*, 326–27, 327n2. Sumner writes, "why have you not sent me my bill? I shall need you very soon but how can I ask you if you do not send me a bill? We shall be in Boston for a little while at the beginning of June, at the 'old stand' in Hancock St. and I shall be obliged to look to you for help." Sumner to Smith, May 19, 1867. Sumner's family's home was on Hancock Street in Boston. Note: I have theorized that Joshua B. Smith loved Charles Sumner for his work on behalf of Smith's Black brethren and did not want to send him a bill.

59. Smith to Sumner, March 17, 1870 (Charles Sumner Correspondence Collection, microfilm).

60. Smith to Sumner, March 17, 1870, February 4, April 23, 1871, January 7, June 2, 1873 (Charles Sumner Correspondence Collection, microfilm); Lucius R. Paige, *Cambridge, Massachusetts*, 462; "Smith, Joshua B.," reel 20, Daniel Murray Papers (Wisconsin); Daniels, *In Freedom's Birthplace*, 101; *Records of the Massachusetts State House of Representatives*; "Recent Deaths," *Boston Evening Transcript*, July 7, 1879.

61. Pierce, *Memoir and Letters*, 4:550 ("good-will"), 4:551 ("insult to the loyal," "meeting"); "Smith, Joshua B.," reel 20, Daniel Murray Papers (Wisconsin). See also Pierce, *Memoir and Letters*, 4:590; W. G. Constable, "Cranach from the Sumner Collection," 64; Smith to Sumner, telegram, February 11, 1874 (Charles Sumner Correspondence Collection, microfilm); Donald, *Rights of Man*, 584.

62. John Langdon Sibley, entry for October 19, 1860, Diary (Sibley's Private Journal, Harvard University Archives). See also Logan and Winston, *American Negro Biography*, 565; "All Boston Cruelly Deceived for Years," *New York Times*, August 26, 1894, 13 (reprinted from the *Boston Transcript*), which gives an account of the chinaware purchased by Smith for that celebrated banquet during the royal visit. It seems that the chinaware was not imported from France as everyone thought; according to a former Smith employee it was "imported" from Norwich, Connecticut. Note, however, that the former employee, Paul Romer, was in hot water for "pilfering" chinaware originally considered very expensive and rare. Perhaps Romer was trying to garner a lighter sentence by stating that the dishes were not so rare after all.

63. Logan and Winston, *American Negro Biography*, 565; "Declaration of Sentiments of the Colored Citizens of Boston on the Fugitive Slave Bill," *The Liberator*, October 11, 1850, 162.

64. Entries for June 1861 and June 26, 1861, in Benjamin F. Cook, *Twelfth Massachusetts Volunteers*, 14, 15 (also 142). After Joshua Smith's death, his wife prepared handwritten petitions to try to obtain reimbursement for her husband's services. One is a three-page petition, no date, addressed to the Senate and House of Representatives of the Commonwealth of Massachusetts, that offers a plea for "a suitable allowance" for herself and also recounts in detail regiment recruitment, which ended because it "was afterwards filled to the full number required," 1 (in Massachusetts Supreme Judicial Court Archives and Records Preservation). See also information on Fletcher Webster in Appendix and Roster of the Officers, in Cook, *Twelfth Massachusetts Volunteers*; Logan and Winston, *American Negro Biography*, 565.

65. "Receipts from long, long years of housekeeping," 26 (Hartwell-Clark Family Papers, MHS).

66. The following schedule is the breakdown of charges:

April 22 to May 3 [12 days], 4,340 rations—$2,170

May 4 to June 26 [53 days], 42,400 rations—$21,200

May 4 to June 26 [53 days], 32 officers @ 75 cents each—$1,272

June 26 to July 23 [28 days], 28,000 rations @ 50 cents each—$14,000

June 26 to July 23 [28 days], 32 officers @ 75 cents each—$672

In addition, $1,064 was spent, as "Smith provided as above upon the marching of said regiment four days rations for 1,000 men and 32 officers for which he charged 25 cents per day for each private and 50 cents per day for each officer." All from three-page Petition of Emeline I. Smith, Widow of Joshua B. Smith, 1 (Massachusetts Supreme Judicial Court Archives and Records Preservation). Also see Logan and Winston, *American Negro Biography*, 565.

67. Handwritten petition and statement from Joshua Bowen Smith, regarding his claim for reimbursement, to the Senate and House of Representatives and General Court assembled, January 18, 1879. See also "Petition.—House" claim form. "Mr. Hale of Cambridge presents the petition of Joshua B. Smith for payment for Rations furnished to the Twelfth Regiment, January 20, 1879" (Massachusetts Supreme Judicial Court Archives and Records Preservation); Logan and Winston, *American Negro Biography*, 565 ("he was the only caterer"). Also, handwritten three-page petition and statement from Emeline I. Smith, no date, but clearly following her husband's death, in which she asks the Commonwealth for "a suitable allowance" for herself, and also recounts the agreement or contract made between her husband and the governor. She writes that the state's government considered "that the prices charged by said Smith. . . were just, fair and reasonable," 2 (Massachusetts Supreme Judicial Court Archives and Records Preservation).

68. Logan and Winston, *American Negro Biography*, 565 ("no funds"); three-page Petition of Emeline I. Smith, Widow of Joshua B. Smith, 2 ("other military organizations were, during the same time covered . . . and that subsistence therefor[e] was paid for by the State, without regard to the amount"); handwritten petition and statement from Joshua Bowen Smith, regarding his claim for reimbursement, January 18, 1879, in which he mentions being told to take his claim to Washington "in order to obtain payment" (Massachusetts Supreme Judicial Court Archives and Records Preservation). Note, on page 1 of the Petition of Emeline I. Smith, Widow of Joshua B. Smith, Mrs. Smith states that her husband was hired by a recruiting committee, "consisting of William Dehon and others," and that the committee agreed to the $0.50/$0.75 price, and that the agreement was approved by regiment Quarter Master, David Wood, because they all agreed that Smith's price was "reasonable." On page 2 Mrs. Smith states that the governor knew her husband was supplying food to the regiment, and that Mr. Smith "called on His Excellency John A. Andrew Governor of the Commonwealth on or about

June 17, 1861 . . . and asked him whether the State would pay for said subsistence by him [Smith] furnished, and Governor Andrew said to him that of course the State would pay said Smith in the same way that it paid others in like case, . . . and . . . Smith went on and furnished subsistence to said regiment . . . relying upon said promise of Governor Andrew."

69. From March 7 until about April 24, 1879, Smith's petition remained an item for "further consideration." The Journal of the House, for March and April, 1879 has several entries that represent some of the dates that Joshua Smith's case came up for review or discussion: March 11, 351; March 31, 455; page 504 (no date for page); April 15, 508–9; April 16, 515, 517, 521–522; April 17, 530,532; April 18, 533; April 24, 555 (all in Massachusetts Supreme Judicial Court Archives and Records Preservation).

70. Savage, "Uncommon Soldiers," 116, 163, 164; Richardson, "Taken from Life," 95–96; Greenthal, "Augustus Saint-Gaudens, " 116–17; "Topics of the Times. Current Notes. To the late Joshua B. Smith," *New York Times*, June 12, 1897, 6; Logan and Winston, *American Negro Biography*, 565; "Smith, Joshua B.," reel 20, Daniel Murray Papers (Wisconsin). Kirk Savage writes that for many the monument began as a memorial to Shaw only. Also, on March 5, 1851, Smith—along with Charles Remond, William C. Nell, Lewis Hayden, and others—petitioned the state legislature for fifteen hundred dollars to erect a monument for Crispus Attucks. Thirty-seven years later, in 1888, the monument was erected.

71. "Recent Deaths," *Boston Evening Transcript*, July 7, 1879; Brian Sullivan, interview, July 13, 2010; Internments, Archives and Records, Mount Auburn Cemetery; Logan and Winston, *American Negro Biography*, 565; Commonwealth of Massachusetts, Probate Court. Middlesex County, File #10197, Schedule of Personal Estate in Detail, of Joshua B. Smith, September 2, 1879: Oil painting, "The Miracle of the Slave," $100.00 (Massachusetts Supreme Judicial Court Archives and Records).

72. Commonwealth of Massachusetts, Probate Court. Middlesex County, September 14, 1879. Administrator of the Estate of Joshua B. Smith, requesting license to sell real estate of said deceased, "for the payment of his debts, and charges of administration." Also, Commonwealth of Massachusetts, Probate Court. Middlesex County, September 30, 1879. Petition of Emeline I. Smith, widow of Joshua B. Smith, requesting the court to "allow her some parts of the personal estate of said deceased, as necessaries for herself" (both in Massachusetts Supreme Judicial Court Archives and Records Preservation).

73. Commonwealth of Massachusetts. Resolve in favor of Emeline I. Smith, "that there be allowed and paid . . . the sum of five thousand dollars, as a gratuity." Also see handwritten three-page petition from Emeline I. Smith requesting from the Commonwealth of Massachusetts a "suitable allowance" (both in Massachusetts Supreme Judicial Court Archives and Records Preservation).

74. Logan and Winston, *American Negro Biography*, 565

9: Hoteliers, Dining Rooms, and Culinary Diplomacy in the Nation's Capital

1. Dorothy S. Provine, "Economic Position," 61–62, 65.

2. Washington Ordinance of October 28, 1802 (Acts of the Corporation of the City of Washington Passed by the First Council, Washington, 1803), 25; Washington Ordinance of May 25, 1803 (Act of the Corporation of the City of Washington Passed by the First Council), 45–47; Registers of Licenses, 1818–1876 (RG 351, National Archives); Provine, "Economic Position," 65.

3. Sandra Fitzpatrick and Maria R. Goodwin, *Black Washington*, 17, 35; Washington Ordinance of October 29, 1836 (James W. Sheahan, Corporation Laws of the City of Washington, Washington, 1853), 249; Provine, "Economic Position," 66; "Restaurants," reel 19, Daniel Murray Papers (Wisconsin). See also Wormley Family Papers, 1773–1991 (Library of Virginia, Richmond; hereafter cited as Wormley Family Papers). The section on "Lynch Wormley" contains a page from the *Union League Directory*, with an entry titled "Eating Houses. Caterers and Hotel Keepers," listing Snow's first name as Benjamin.

4. See both "Gray, John Andrew," reel 13, Daniel Murray Papers (Yale), and Wilhelmus Bogart Bryan, *History of the National Capital*, 2:583, for discussions of uninvited guests not only crashing social gatherings but eating voraciously, cutting up the furnishings, and taking garments belonging to others as well.

5. "Eating Houses. Caterers and Hotel Keepers," in Andrew Hillyard, *Hillyard's Twentieth Century Union League Directory*, "Lynch Wormley" (Wormley Family Papers). See also Fitzpatrick and Goodwin, *Black Washington*, 25; Ingham and Feldman, *African American Business Leaders*, 130; "Hotels," reel 14, Daniel Murray Papers (Yale), also "Gray, John Andrew," reel 13, Daniel Murray Papers (Yale); James H. Whyte, *Uncivil War*, 29, 258–59; Smithsonian, *Black Washingtonians*, 105.

6. For all quotes, see newspaper clipping (folder E, box 1, Isaac Bassett Manuscript Collection, US Senate Commission on Art, Center for Legislative Archives, NARA), 176A (hereafter Isaac Bassett Manuscript Collection). Also see "Caterers," reel 10, Daniel Murray Papers (Yale), and mention of Hancock's in "Restaurants," reel 19, Daniel Murray Papers (Wisconsin).

7. Newspaper clipping (folder E, box 1, Isaac Bassett Manuscript Collection), 176A.

8. Newspaper clipping (folder E, box 1, Isaac Bassett Manuscript Collection), 176A.

9. Adapted from recipe in Stout Family Papers (MHS), 181.

10. Martini cocktail recipe in "Receipts from long, long years of housekeeping," 25 (Hartwell-Clark Family Papers, MHS).

11. Provine, "Economic Position," 66–67.

12. "Slade, William Andrew," reel 20, Daniel Murray Papers (Wisconsin). Also see "Catering" and "Restaurants," reels 10, 19, Daniel Murray Papers (Wisconsin); Seale, "Upstairs and Downstairs," 20. Andrew Foote Slade was "the first and last colored . . . appointed to the position of Page in the United States Senate" (folder E, box 34, Isaac Bassett Manuscript Collection), 130. A. F. Slade was born on July 4, 1857. He was appointed Senate page on December 1, 1869, riding page on December 1, 1873, and Senate mail carrier sometime later.

13. Downing to Sumner, May 5, 1866 (folder 1912, Charles Sumner Correspondence Collection, Houghton Library, Harvard University). See also Whyte, *Uncivil War*, 36. Whyte is also cited in "James Wormley," (Wormley Family Papers; hereafter cited as "James Wormley," with volume number), vol. 3; Smithsonian, *Black Washingtonians*, 95.

14. Proctor's catering arrangements for Abraham Lincoln and subsequent takeover of the Hole in the Wall is presented in "Procter [Proctor], Samuel," reel 18;, and the "Hole in the Wall" and Andrew Johnson's drinking is the subject of "Hole in the Wall," reel 14, both in Daniel Murray Papers (Yale). See also Margaret Leech, *Reveille in Washington*, 335, where she mentions "conscripted Negroes," one of whom was "George Washington, 'the gorgeous headwaiter' at Willard's [Hotel]."

15. "Wild Cherry Bounce" (MS. N-66, Stout Family Papers, MHS).

16. "The Hole in the Wall," 157–59 (folder F, box 20, Isaac Bassett Manuscript Collection). For other comments on Andrew Johnson's drinking, see folder F (box 20, Isaac Bassett Manuscript Collection), 123 and 134.

17. "Hole in the Wall" and "Procter [Proctor], Samuel," reels 14, 18, both in Daniel Murray Papers (Yale); advertisement "The Senate Saloon," *The Critic*, November 25, 1869.

18. "Uncle Jim Gardner's" receipts," 27 (Hartwell-Clark Family Papers), "Receipts from long, long years of housekeeping."

19. "The Hole in the Wall," 158 (handwritten narrative, folder F, box 20, Isaac Bassett Manuscript Collection).

20. Robert L. Harris Jr., "Daniel Murray," 271; David Rapp, "Man in the Library," 11. See also Sylvia Lyons Render, "Black Presence," 64; "Has A Great Memory: Feats of a Negro in the Congressional Library," *Morning Herald (Baltimore, MD)*, April 10, 1899.

21. John B. Ellis, *Sights and Secrets*, 112.

22. *Guide to the Capitol, 1834*, 6.

23. Felicia Wivchar, conversation, curatorial assistant, Office of History and Preservation, Office of the Clerk, US House of Representatives, January 8, 2007.

24. Paul Sluby handwritten notes ("James Wormley," 1:1). See also "Lynch Wormley" (Wormley Family Papers); Charles E. Wynes, "Wormley Hotel Agreement," 397; Provine, "Economic Position," 66–67; Summons, dated March 2, 1820, "Lynch Worm-

ley" (Wormley Family Papers); C. G. Woodson, "Wormley Family," 75; Fitzpatrick and Goodwin, *Black Washington*, 25.

25. Biographical typescript ("James Wormley," vol. 1); Wynes, "Wormley Hotel Agreement," 397.

26. "James Wormley," vols. 1, 3; Wynes, "Wormley Hotel Agreement," 397–98; Ingham and Feldman, *African American Business Leaders*, 708.

27. "James Wormley," vols. 1, 3; Ingham and Feldman, *African American Business Leaders*, 708; Wynes, "Wormley Hotel Agreement," 398; Bryan, *History of the National Capital*, 2:608.

28. "Lynch Wormley" (Wormley Family Papers), 1; "James Wormley," vols. 1, 3; Ingham and Feldman, *African American Business Leaders*, 708, 709; Leech, *Reveille in Washington*, 128; Leech, also cited in "James Wormley," vol. 3; Wynes, "Wormley Hotel Agreement," 398.

29. George Templeton Strong, entry for July 15, 1861 (Diary holograph, vol. 3).

30. "To make Asparagus Soup," in Campbell, *Hotel Keepers, Head Waiters*, 145–46.

31. "To make a baked Bread Pudding," Campbell, *Hotel Keepers, Head Waiters*, 176.

32. Fehrenbacher, *Slavery, Law, and Politics*, 148. See also "Johnson, Reverdy, Statesman" (biographical sketch, Reverdy Johnson Papers, Library of Congress). See praise for Reverdy Johnson: "It is no marvel for him to walk on the Senate Chamber across the corridor to the Supreme Court and there argue a case of monster intricacies, and then returning to the Senate, take up the discussion of Civil Rights Bills or Constitutional Amendments with more vim than that drowsy body had shown during his absence." News clipping, "Johnson and Howe. A Senatorial Tilt" (Reverdy Johnson Papers).

33. Ingham and Feldman, *African American Business Leaders*, 709. *Washington Star*, December 18, 1938, news clipping ("James Wormley," vol. 2); "Fifty Years Ago in The Star," *Washington Star*, October 21, 1934, D2, news clipping ("James Wormley," vol. 2). See also Andrew Johnson's signed document, dated June 12, 1868, officially appointing Reverdy Johnson "Minister Plenipotentiary of the United States of America to England" (Reverdy Johnson Papers); Leech, *Reveille in Washington*, 436; Leech, also cited in "James Wormley," vol. 3; biographical typescript, "Johnson, Reverdy, Statesman" ("James Wormley," vols. 1 and 3), and James Wormley passport documents ("James Wormley," vol. 3); Don Edward Fehrenbacher, *Dred Scott Case*, 282, 474, 515, 569, 576, 578, 580, 710; Wynes, "Wormley Hotel Agreement," 398; Whyte, *Uncivil War*, 29.

34. List of vintage wines in Washington Morton to Reverdy Johnson, March 26, 1869 (Reverdy Johnson Papers). Note: Supplement to *Congressional Globe*, Senate, 40th Congress, 2nd sess., "Proceedings of the Senate Sitting for the Trial of Andrew Johnson, President of the United States, On Articles of Impeachment Exhibited by the House of Representatives," 22; Reverdy Johnson gives address of support to the president,

August 18, 1866; president's message announcing suspension of Secretary of War Stanton and General Grant as Secretary of War ad interim, 51; Senate resolution of nonconcurrence with Stanton suspension and president's order, removing Stanton from office, 53; Senate resolution stating president has no power to remove secretary of war and to designate any other officer to perform duties, 54; president's instructions on January 29, 1868, to General Grant not to obey orders from the War Department, 80; Reverdy Johnson's opinion on the case, 428–31.

35. Woolley's arrest is documented in Contingent Expenses House of Representatives. "Letter from the Clerk of the House of Representatives," 40th Congress, 3rd sess., misc. doc. No. 25, January 19, 1869 (US House of Representatives, Washington, DC). Detailed statement of contingent expenses and disbursements, etc., p.77; "G.L. [G.T.] Downing," May 25 to June 11, 1868 (US House of Representatives). For all other quotes, see "Impeachment Managers' Investigation," 40th Congress, 2nd sess., Report No. 44, May 25, 1868 (US House of Representatives), 2, 3.

36. James Wormley to Charles Sumner, June 23, 1869 (folder 7012, Charles Sumner Correspondence Collection, Harvard). See also Rayford W. Logan, four-page biographical typescript (no title) and Melvin Roscoe Williams, biographical typescript titled "Blacks in Washington, D.C., 1860–1870" ("James Wormley," vols. 1, 3); Whyte, *Uncivil War*, 36.

37. Entry 49, General Term Minutes, 1863–1903 (RG 21, Records of the District Courts of the United States, National Archives and Records Administration, District of Columbia), vol. 1 (May 4, 1863–October 9, 1871). This entry is dated October 9, 1871, and is quoted in "Minutes General Term 1" ("James Wormley," vol. 3). See also Whyte, *Uncivil War*, 264–65, 294n4, citing Henry E. Davis: "The Safe Robbery Case," *Columbia Historical Society* 25:151.

38. "Excitement Among Playgoers—Rights of Negroes in Theatres—The Question to Be Carried Before the Supreme Court," *New York Herald*, October 5, 1869, 7 (all quotes). See also Williams, "Blacks in Washington, D.C., 1860–1870," by Melvin Williams ("James Wormley," vol. 3); "The Color Question, Civil Rights in Theaters and Restaurants—The Theater Case," *Evening Star*, October 6, 1869, cited in the Historical Society of Washington, DC, commemorative brochure, "Measure of a Man," 13–14.

39. "Personal," *The Independent*, November 11, 1869.

40. Downing, "Personal," *The Independent*, November 11, 1869 ("to the detriment"); Washington, *George Thomas Downing*, 17 ("everywhere his plume"), 11 ("some colored people" and "serve them and send to me"). Also see "Downing, George Thos.," reel 4, Daniel Murray Papers (Yale), 4; "Scope Note," George T. Downing Papers; Ripley, *Black Abolitionist Papers*, 4:317–18.

41. US Census Bureau, Ninth Census of the United States, 1870, Washington, Dis-

trict of Columbia. See also news clipping (folder 1, box 152-1, George T. Downing Papers); "George Thos. Downing," 3, reel 4, Daniel Murray Papers (Yale); Washington, *George Thomas Downing*, 4.

42. Washington, *George Thomas Downing*, 16–17.

43. News clipping (folder 18–19, box 1, DeGrasse Howard Papers, MHS); Washington, *George Thomas Downing*, 16; "George Thos. Downing," 4, reel 4, Daniel Murray Papers (Yale); Charles E. Wynes, "Ebenezer Don Carlos Bassett," 233.

44. Ebenezer Bassett to George T. Downing, October 12, November 9, 1870 (folder 18–19, box 1, DeGrasse-Howard Papers).

45. C. Edwards Lester, *Life and Public Services*, 388, 508–9; William S. McFeely, *Frederick Douglass*, 276; Donald, *Rights of Man*, 509, 510, 511–15; Charles Sumner to George Wm. Curtis, January 16, 1871 (Charles Sumner Correspondence Collection, The Papers of Charles Sumner, microfilm).

46. Philip S. Foner, *Life and Writings*, 4:65, 67; McFeely, *Frederick Douglass*, 276.

47. Foner, *Life and Writings*, 4:68; Charles Sumner to Andrew Dickson White, August 10, 1872 (Charles Sumner Correspondence Collection, The Papers of Charles Sumner, microfilm). See also "The Right Color for a Steamboat Dinner," and "The Case of Fred. Douglass. Excluded from the First Table and Invited to the Second—Alone," *New National Era*, March 30, 1871; *New York Times* articles from 1872, August 6, August 10, 8, August 12, 5, August 15, 5, and August 22, 4; James M. McPherson, "Abolitionists and the Civil Rights Act," 496; Pierce, *Memoir and Letters*, 4:532, 532n2.

48. Foner, *Life and Writings*, 4:72; Sumner to White, August 10, 1872 (Charles Sumner Correspondence Collection, The Papers of Charles Sumner, microfilm).

49. "Letter from Frederick Douglass," *Bangor Daily Whig & Courier*, August 23, 1872. See also Foner, *Life and Writings*, 4:72–73; *New York Times* articles in 1872, August 6, August 10, 8, August 12, 5, August 15, 5, and August 22, 4.

50. Wormley to Sumner, August 10, 1872 (folder 7012, Charles Sumner Correspondence Collection, Harvard); Sumner to White, August 10, 1872 (Charles Sumner Correspondence Collection, The Papers of Charles Sumner, microfilm). See also "Which Knows Best? Sumner Says Douglass was Insulted, and Douglass Says He was Not—Of Course Mr. Sumner Must be Correct," *New York Times* August 12, 1872, 5.

51. Francis J. Grimke and M. F. Perkins, "Communications," 58–60. Grimke is also cited in "James Wormley," vol. 2. See also Whyte, *Uncivil War*, 253, in which mention is made of Douglass's appointment to the Santo Domingo Commission.

52. Willhelm, *Who Needs the Negro?*

53. Grimke and Perkins, "Communications," 58. See also McFeely, *Frederick Douglass*, 276. Grimke also cited in "James Wormley," vol. 2.

54. "Scalloped Oysters (Entrée)," in "Receipts from long, long years of housekeeping," 59.

55. Sumner to Wormley, September 28, 1871 (Letters Received By James Wormley, 1868–1892, MHS; hereafter cited as Letters Received by James Wormley). See also Logan, biographical typescript, "James Wormley," 1:2; Wynes, "Wormley Hotel Agreement," 398; Ingham and Feldman, *African American Business Leaders*, 709. See also "Beyond the Fireworks of '76" ("James Wormley," 3:354).

56. Sumner to Smith, February 25, 1872 (Charles E. French Autograph Collection, MHS); Xeroxed page from *Illustrated Washington, Our Capitol* (American Publishing and Engraving, New York, 1890), and E. E. Barton's Historical and Commercial Sketches of Washington and Environs (Washington, D.C., 1884), 120 (both in "James Wormley," vol. 1). See also Logan, biographical typescript ("James Wormley," 1:2); Wynes, "Wormley Hotel Agreement," 398; Ingham and Feldman, *African American Business Leaders*, 709; James T. Wormley Biography ("James Wormley," vol. 3); "Beyond the Fireworks of '76" ("James Wormley," 3:354); "The principal hotels" ("James Wormley," vol. 2). In Kathryn Allamong Jacob, *King of the Lobby*, 11, reference is made to Wormley's as an "up-scale restaurant."

57. "The National Telephonic Exchange, Washington, D.C." Washington's first telephone book ("James Wormley," vol. 1); Mrs. Freida Wormley, interview, May 24, 2007.

58. Xeroxed page from *Illustrated Washington, Our Capitol* (American Publishing and Engraving, New York, 1890), and undated news clipping "Fifteenth Street," *Washington Star* (both in "James Wormley," vol. 1). See also "Washington's Black Middle Class," *Potomac Magazine*, 12, cited in *Washington Post*, January 26, 1975; Xeroxed pages from "Beyond the Fireworks of '76" ("James Wormley," 3:354–55). Note that Wormley's House was actually the name of James Wormley's business on I Street, before he opened the hotel on Fifteenth and H. It offered dining, catering, lodging, and a confectioner's shop. See the Historical Society of Washington, DC, "Measure of a Man," 6, 8.

59. Xeroxed picture of Wormley residence on Pierce Mill Road ("James Wormley," vol. 1); Ingham and Feldman, *African American Business Leaders*, 710; Mrs. Freida Wormley, interview, Thursday, May 24, 2007.

60. "Crappo Death Recalls Famous Wormley's Hotel in D.C.," news clipping, no date ("James Wormley," vol. 1). See also *Illustrated Washington, Our Capital*, 1890; "They Had a Dream," *Sacramento Bee*, July 26, 1970; "They Had a Dream: James Wormley—Capital Innkeeper," *Evening Star*, September 19, 1970; news clipping "Fifteenth Street," *Washington Star*, which carries a small biography of Wormley and mentions Roscoe Conkling; page 23 of the 1880 census for Washington, DC, which lists the residents of Wormley's Hotel, and one of those residents is Roscoe Conkling; also see news clipping

pertaining to "coterie of New England statesmen" who made Wormley's Hotel their Washington home (all in "James Wormley," vol. 1). "Beyond the Fireworks of '76" ("James Wormley," 3:355). Vice President Colfax is mentioned staying at Wormley's in Whyte, *Uncivil War*, 180.

61. Leech, *Reveille in Washington*, 1; "Why It's Scott Circle: He Loved the Union, and R. E. Lee," *Washington Daily News*, January 23, 1961 ("James Wormley," vol. 1); Historical Society of Washington, DC, "Measure of a Man," 6, 8.

62. Letitia W. Brown and Elsie M. Lewis, "Washington in the New Era, 1870–1970, 21 ("James Wormley," vol. 2). Also see "Illustrated Washington, Our Capital, 1890" ("James Wormley," vol. 1). See also "The Tragic Era," "James Wormley," 245, and Logan, biographical typescript ("James Wormley," 1:2); "Beyond the Fireworks of '76" ("James Wormley," 3:355); Ingham and Feldman, *African American Business Leaders*, 709–10. Whyte mentions the preference for Wormley's Hotel among foreign diplomats. Whyte, *Uncivil War*, 180.

63. Jacob, *King of the Lobby*, 77; J. W. Forney to James Wormley, April 26, 1877 ("James Wormley," vol. 2).

64. Newspaper clipping "Here's Where We Let . . . Old Washington Days" ("James Wormley," vol. 1).

65. Lester, *Life and Public Services*, 245–56. Sumner was a true statesman and an excellent advocate for Blacks in America, but he was not without his faults. Like all of White America, and the majority of those descendant generations of African people born here in America during that era, Sumner knew nothing about Africa and thereby harbored the same prejudices with regard to the history of the continent as everyone else. On June 4, 1860, he delivered a speech to the Senate, titled, "The Barbarism of Slavery," in which he stated in part, regarding that barbarism: "It comes from Africa, ancient nurse of monsters, —from Guinea, Dahomey, and Congo. There is its origin and fountain." He went on to say, "From its home in Africa, where it is sustained by immemorial usage, this Barbarism, thus derived and thus developed, traversed the ocean to American soil. It entered on board that fatal slave-ship." Lester, *Life and Public Services*, 325–26.

66. Downing to Sumner, May 19, 1873 (folder 1912, Charles Sumner Correspondence Collection, Harvard).

67. Pope, Ballard & Loos, letter dated June 26, 1974, signed "Alex" [Alexander M. Heron] ("James Wormley," vol. 1). See also "Notes from Judy Helm August 1977" ("James Wormley," vol. 1).

68. Grimke cited in "James Wormley," vol. 2. See also Grimke and Perkins, "Communications," 58; Sumner to Wormley, November 14, 1868 (Letters Received by James

Wormley; the envelope that accompanies this letter is addressed to Wormley at "Wormley House, I Street"); Historical Society of Washington, DC, "Measure of a Man," 6, 8.

69. Downing to Sumner, January 20, February 7, 1871 (folder 1912, Charles Sumner Correspondence Collection, Harvard). See also Lester, *Life and Public Services*, 501–2.

70. *Congressional Globe*, 42nd Congress, 2nd sess., January 31, 1872, 728–29, 730 (quotes); Downing to Sumner, January 25, 1872 (folder 1912, Charles Sumner Correspondence Collection, Harvard). See also Washington, *George Thomas Downing*, 17; Downing to Sumner, December 12, 1871 (folder 1912, Charles Sumner Correspondence Collection, Harvard). Sumner's quoting of Downing on the Senate floor is also cited in Washington, *George Thomas Downing*, 11–15.

71. "The Colored Men's Convention. Between Two and Three Hundred Delegates Present," *New York Times*, December 10, 1873; and "Memorial of the National Convention of Colored Persons, Praying to be Protected in Their Civil Rights," 43rd Congress, 1st sess., misc. doc. no. 21, Senate, December 1873, 1 (Law Library of Congress). Also see *Congressional Record*, 43rd Congress, 1st sess., December 1873, 325; "Forty-Third Congress. First Session. House of Representatives. Bills Introduced," *New York Times*, December 9, 1873, 2. Note that Sumner reintroduced the Civil Rights Bill in December 1873. See the following discourse pertaining to the bill: "Serenade to Mr. Sumner. Address to the Colored Serenaders—He Urges Them to Vigorously Insist on Their Rights Being Recognized," *New York Times*, December 2, 1873, 4; "Forty-Third Congress. First Session. The Supplementary Civil Rights Bill," *New York Times*, December 3, 1873, 6; "Congress. The President's Message in the Two Houses. Mr. Sumner and Civil Rights," *New York Times*, December 3, 1873, 1.

72. The account of Sumner's last words to Judge Hoar are recounted in the *Boston Daily Globe* (no date given), and cited in Lester, *Life and Public Services*, 521; also 517–19, 520–22. Also see Pierce, *Memoir and Letters*, 4:598, 599; McPherson, "Abolitionists and the Civil Rights Act," 506; "A Moralist and His Ally Leave a Lasting Message," *Boston Globe*, February 27, 2001.

73. Lester, *Life and Public Services*, picture facing page 521 has a drawing titled *Senator Sumner's Last Moments* depicting both Downing and Wormley at Sumner's bedside. There was also an engraving made titled *Charles Sumner's Deathbed*, Currier and Ives, lithograph, 1874, that depicts at least one of the famous Black caterers at his bedside. Donald, *Rights of Man*, 325–26, 586; "Mr. Sumner's Will," *New York Times*, March 15, 1874, 4; Constable, "Cranach from the Sumner Collection," 64. For the commemoration service, see "Commonwealth of Massachusetts. State House. You are invited to attend the services in commemoration of the life and character of Charles Sumner before the Executive and Legislative branches of the Commonwealth, to be held at the Music Hall on the Ninth of June, 1874. . . . Moody Merrill . . . Joshua B. Smith . . . committee of

Arrangements," Boston, June 1st, 1874 (Invitation, American Broadsides, series 1, no. 16534).

74. Julia S. Hastings to George T. Downing, January 24, 1875 (folder 26, box 152-1, George T. Downing Papers).

75. Pierce, *Memoir and Letters*, 4:570.

76. For discourse on South Carolina riots, the reported "remedy" to prevent Blacks from voting, and attorney general Taft's letter to Rutherford B. Hayes, see Rayford W. Logan, *Betrayal of the Negro*, 25. Also, Charles Sumner's Civil Rights Bill finally did pass—partially. Against the protests of abolitionists and a few congressmen, the House removed the provisions outlawing segregated schools and cemeteries. President Grant signed the Civil Rights Act of 1875 into law on March 1. In spite of the penalties set up for those found guilty of breaking the law, it was reluctantly and only rarely enforced by authorities and mostly ignored. In 1883 the Supreme Court ruled that the law exceeded Congress's constitutional power under the Fourteenth Amendment and thereby declared the Civil Rights Act of 1875 unconstitutional. Africans were again officially banned (there was never a time when they were not banned, officially or otherwise) from White restaurants, theaters, hotels, and barbershops, and by 1885 most of the South by law required segregated education. See McPherson, "Abolitionists and the Civil Rights Act," 493, 505, 507–10; John Hope Franklin and Alfred A. Moss Jr., *From Slavery to Freedom*, 238; John Hope Franklin, "Enforcement of the Civil Rights Act," 228, 232–35; C. Vann Woodward, *Reunion and Reaction*, 266; Higginbotham, *Shades of Freedom*, 90, 95–98. See also letter dated February 19, 1869, and news clipping with remarks of Samuel J. Tilden regarding Downing's Oyster House at dinner for Senator Casserly (Samuel J. Tilden Papers, Manuscripts and Archives Division, New York Public Library).

77. Higginbotham, *Shades of Freedom*, 91, 92; Logan, *Betrayal of the Negro*, 13, 16; Wynes, "Wormley Hotel Agreement," 399, 400; Ingham and Feldman, *African American Business Leaders*, 710; "The Electoral Bargain," *New York Times*, February 15, 1878; Woodward, *Reunion and Reaction*, 7–8, 10–11.

78. Logan, *Betrayal of the Negro*, 23. See also Woodward, *Reunion and Reaction*, 9, 224, 225; Wynes, "Wormley Hotel Agreement," 397, 399; Nicholas E. Hollis, "Infamous Final Scene of the 'Crime of 1876'? The Wormley Agreement," Agribusiness Council, https://www.agribusinesscouncil.org/wormley.htm; Ingham and Feldman, *African American Business Leaders*, 710; "A Hotel for the History Books," *Washington Post*, March 18, 2001, B08; "They Had a Dream" ("James Wormley," vol. 1); Higginbotham, *Shades of Freedom*, 91–93.

79. Seale, "Upstairs and Downstairs," 20.

80. "Simms, John Alex," reel 20, Daniel Murray Papers (Wisconsin).

81. A. Gregory to James Wormley, July 13, 1884 (loan request). In his July 20, 1884, letter Gregory asks Wormley, "if it is difficult for you to find 1000/doll. for 3 months, I shall only ask you to pay some bills for me in town for the amount of 3 or 4 hundred dollars, on the conditions you deem just" (both in Letters Received by James Wormley). In his letter to James Wormley dated June 12, 1878 (Letters Received by James Wormley), Henry Adams states: "I suppose David must have got you to pay for the dogs, and I owe you for the charges on the horse. I am ready to pay up at any time." See also Historical Society of Washington, DC, "Measure of a Man," 8, 11. In Wormley to Sumner, October 8, 1867 (folder 7012, Charles Sumner Correspondence Collection, Harvard), Wormley suggests to Sumner, regarding his house, that he should "fit it up" for his own use (which means Wormley will "fit it up") and offers to get Sumner a good steward, cook, and maid. In Wormley to Sumner, June 23, 1869 (folder 7012, Charles Sumner Correspondence Collection, Harvard), Wormley mentions he is enclosing several bills at Sumner's request. These bills are no doubt for items Wormley purchased for Sumner. In Sumner to Wormley, November 14, 1868 (Letters Received by James Wormley), Sumner mentions a "bill of lading" and the arrival of his chandelier. Sumner has not received word of any other delivery but asks Wormley to keep him informed of every arrival. Sumner adds, "I wish the bills for transportation kept till I reach Washington & I will then pay them together." In Sumner to Wormley, September 28, 1871 (Letters Received by James Wormley), Sumner sheds additional light on Wormley's role in Sumner's household affairs; Pierce, *Memoir and Letters*, 4:610n21.

82. Henry L. Pierce to James Wormley, February 26, 1883 (Letters Received by James Wormley; copy of Pierce letter also in "James Wormley," vol. 2). See also Massachusetts State Senate documents, Commonwealth of Massachusetts, No. 292, Executive Department, April 25, 1884, and No. 323, Senate, May 8, 1884, which formally "on behalf of Mr. James Wormley, of Washington, D.C., and at his request, hereby present to the Commonwealth a portrait of the honorable Charles Sumner." In "James Wormley," vol. 2); Mrs. Freida Wormley, interview Thursday, May 24, 2007 ("James Wormley," vol. 3, *The Massachusetts State House New Guide*, 72, states that Sumner's portrait, presented by James Wormley, hangs in the State Library. It has since been moved to the Massachusetts State House of Representatives (per my conversation with Susan Greendyke, art collections manager, Bureau of State Office Buildings in Boston, Massachusetts). Pierce, *Memoir and Letters*, 4:590, 610n21.

83. Typescript of news article from the *Evening Star* on illness of James Wormley, death certificate of James Wormley, and news clipping from *Sunday Star*, December 18, 1938, on life and death of James Wormley (all in "James Wormley," vol. 2); Paul Sluby's biographical typescript on the life and death of James Wormley, Logan's biographical typescript, and newspaper article "They Had a Dream" (all in "James Wormley," vol.

1); "Beyond the Fireworks of '76," 353–57, and biography of life and death of James Wormley ("James Wormley," vol. 3); Woodson, "Wormley Family," 75–76.

84. Francis B. Carpenter, handwritten narrative titled "A Day With Governor Seward at Auburn," July 1870 (folder 10, box 101, William Henry Seward Papers, Rush Rhees Library, University of Rochester). See also magazine clipping, Sluby's biographical typescript, Logan's biographical typescript, also James Wormley partial bio (no title nor date), 401 ("James Wormley," vol. 1); "Washington in the New Era," 21, and article pages on segregation in the District's schools ("James Wormley," vol. 2); Wynes, "Wormley Hotel Agreement," 399; "A Moralist and His Ally Leave a Lasting Message," *Boston Globe*, February 27, 2001; "An Appeal in Behalf of Our People," *Christian Recorder*, March 14, 1863.

85. "The Late James Wormley," *Christian Recorder*, November 6, 1884.

86. Grimke, "Communications," 57–58.

87. Woodson, "Wormley Family," 77; Ingham and Feldman, *African American Business Leaders*, 710; Wynes, "Wormley Hotel Agreement," 401. Also see "Dr. James T. Wormley," *New National Era*, March 30, 1871, for an article on his new pharmaceutical business.

88. Du Bois, *Black Reconstruction*, 385–86, 440, 455, 474, 494, 507; Logan, *Betrayal of the Negro*, 32.

Epilogue

1. Profile of Chef Edna Lewis, Chef Joe Randall's African American Chef's Hall of Fame. See also Francis Lam, "What Edna Lewis Knew," *New York Times Magazine*, November 1, 2015, MM44–51,MM73, MM75; the web version of this article by Francis Lam is titled, "Edna Lewis and the Black Roots of American Cooking," *New York Times Magazine*, October 28, 2015.

2. Chef Edna Lewis, interview, "Taste of Heritage Dinner" (Grand Hyatt Hotel, Washington, DC, 1994). See also Lam, "What Edna Lewis Knew," MM48, MM75.

3. See Marcelle Bienvenu, Carl A. Brasseaux, and Ryan A. Brasseaux, *Stir the Pot*, 133 ("Gumbo has become"), 131 ("New Orleans jambalaya"), 130, 133.

4. Folse, *Evolution of Cajun and Creole Cuisine*, 7.

5. Folse, *Evolution of Cajun and Creole Cuisine*, 8.

6. Chef Joe Randall, interview with author, September 29, 2013, on Black chefs and the railroad; Folse, *Evolution of Cajun and Creole Cuisine*, 7.

7. Melville Herskovits, "What Has Africa Given America?" For more on culinary Africanisms in the Americas, see also Spivey, "Latin American and Caribbean Food." Jean Suret-Canale offers his opinion on Africanisms in the Americas. He states, "In effect, a whole material civilisation, including nutritional practices, was implanted in

tropical America, not only in the African populations but in many cases among those of European origin. It was an imported African material civilisation." Suret-Canale, *Essays on African History*, 67.

8. A. Leon Higginbotham Jr., F. Michael Higginbotham, and S. Sandile Ngcobo, "De Jure Housing Segregation, 780 ("Africanless," "forced removals"), 780–81 ("expropriated"), 779–80 ("sophisticated system").

9. John Henrik Clarke, "John Henrik Clarke: A Great and Mighty Walk," Videotaped Lecture (Black Dot Media), 1996; Gwendolyn Hall, "Myths about Creole Culture," 88–89. For an example of works by these authors, see John Henrik Clarke, *African People in World History*; J. C. deGraft-Johnson, *African Glory*; Yosef ben-Jochannan, *Africa*; Yosef ben-Jochannan, *Black Man of the Nile*; Williams, *Destruction of Black Civilization*; Cheik Anta Diop, *African Origin of Civilization*; Diop, *Precolonial Black Africa*; Basil Davidson, *African Past*; Basil Davidson, *African Genius*, 1969); Davidson, *Lost Cities of Africa*; Basil Davidson, *Africa in History*. See also Herskovits, *Myth of the Negro Past*, 296–97.

10. Lynn Houston, "Serpent's Teeth in the Kitchen of Meaning," 1 ("Colonial objectives" and "serves to falsely justify"), 3 ("culinary history is, as all history").

11. Houston, "Serpent's Teeth in the Kitchen of Meaning," 1.

12. Bernard Magubane, *South Africa*, 134. Also see William L. Patterson, *We Charge Genocide*, xiv.

13. *State v. John Mann*, cited in Higginbotham, "Racism and the Early American Legal Process," 8.

14. *Dred Scott v. Sandford*. See also Higginbotham, "De Jure Housing Segregation," 820, 821, 822, 823.

15. Higginbotham, *Shades of Freedom*, 195–96. See also Higginbotham, "De Jure Housing Segregation," 820, 821, 822, 823.

16. Higginbotham, "Racism and the Early American Legal Process," 11.

BIBLIOGRAPHY

Repositories, Manuscripts, Personal Papers, Diaries, Menus, Archival, and other Primary Sources

Charles L. Blockson Afro-American Collection, Temple University Libraries, Philadelphia, Pennsylvania.
> St. Peter Claver Roman Catholic Church Records.

Boston Public Library, Rare Books & Manuscripts, and Special Collections, Boston, Massachusetts.
> Commonwealth of Massachusetts. State House. You are invited to attend the services in commemoration of the life and character of Charles Sumner before the Executive and Legislative branches of the Commonwealth, to be held at the Music Hall on the Ninth of June, 1874 . . . Moody Merrill . . . Joshua B. Smith . . . Committee of Arrangements. Boston, June 1st, 1874. American Broadsides and Ephemera, series 1, no. 16534.
> Bill of Fare. Dinner of the City Council of Boston, July 4, 1846. Furnished by J. B. Smith. American Broadsides and Ephemera, series 1, no. 16671.
> Bill of Fare. Dinner for the City Council of Boston, in Celebration of the Seventy-Third Anniversary of American Independence, July 4, 1848. Furnished by J. B. Smith. American Broadsides and Ephemera, series 1, no. 16678.
> Bill of Fare. Dinner for the City Council of Boston, July 4, 1849. Furnished by Joshua B. Smith. American Broadsides and Ephemera, series 1, no. 16681.
> Bill of Fare. Seventy-Seventh Anniversary of American Independence, July 4, 1853, Dinner for the City Council of Boston. Furnished by Joshua B. Smith. American Broadsides and Ephemera, series 1, no. 16735.

Butler Library, Rare Book and Manuscript Library, Columbia University, New York.
> Jay Family Papers.

Connecticut Historical Society, Hartford.
> Frederick Douglass, Letter to Edwin McMasters Stanton, July 13, 1863. Tracy Collection.

W. E. B. Du Bois Library, Special Collections and University Archives, University of Massachusetts, Amherst.
Lloyd A. Trent Jr. Family Papers, folders 1, 3, series 1; folders 10, 11, series 3.

Fall River Historical Society Archives, Fall River, Massachusetts.
Directories, Fall River.
Fall River Line Menu, 1925.

Georgia Archives, Morrow, Georgia.
Tunis Campbell File. Tunis Campbell-Black Legislator, 110 Tunis Campbell: Black Reconstructionist, 1544-0103.

Harvard Business School, Baker Library, Historical Collections Department, Harvard University, Cambridge, Massachusetts.
Fall River Line Journal, January, 1921

Harvard University Archives, Harvard/Radcliffe Online Historical Reference Shelf.
John Langdon Sibley's Diary (Sibley's Private Journal), 1846–1882.

Historical Society of Pennsylvania, Philadelphia.
Albert E. Dutrieuille Catering Records, 1873–1975.
Gratz Collection.
Menu Collection.

Historic Newton. The Jackson Homestead and Museum, Newton, Massachusetts.

Houghton Library, Harvard University, Cambridge, Massachusetts.
Charles Sumner Correspondence Collection.

Jefferson Library, Thomas Jefferson Foundation, Curatorial Department, Charlottesville, Virginia.
"Randolph/Meikleham Manuscript Cookbook. Accession no. 1975-4-5.

Carl A. Kroch Library, Division of Rare and Manuscript Collections, Cornell University, Ithaca, New York.
Samuel J. May Anti-Slavery Manuscript Collection.

Library Company of Philadelphia, Philadelphia, Pennsylvania.
Library Company of Philadelphia Archives.
Library Company of Philadelphia Brochure.
James Prosser Account Receipts for Dinners Served at Board Meetings of Library Company of Philadelphia.
Stevens-Cogdell/Sanders-Venning Collection.

Library of Congress, Law Library, Washington DC
US Senate. *Memorial of the National Convention of Colored Persons, Praying to be Protected in Their Civil Rights.* Misc. doc. 21, 43rd Congress, 1st sess., December, 1873.

Library of Congress, Manuscripts and Rare Documents, Washington, DC.
Frederick Douglass Papers, reel 2.
Reverdy Johnson Papers.

Bibliography

NAACP Records.
   Walter White Papers.
Charles Sumner Papers.
George Washington Papers.
   "Accounts of Expenses While Commander-in-Chief of the Continental Army,
      1775–1783," debit entry, November 26, 1783.
   A Bill for an "Entertainment." Revolutionary War Accounts, Vouchers, and Re-
      ceipted Accounts 2, series 5, in Financial Papers.

Library of Virginia, Richmond, Virginia.
   "James Wormley." Vols. 1–3. Wormley Family Papers, 1773–1991.
      "Beyond the Fireworks of '76: A Study of Historic Sites in the District of Columbia
         of Special Significance to Afro-Americans." Prepared by the Afro-American
         Bicentennial Commission, part 2, May 1974, vol. 3, pages 352–57.
      Rayford W. Logan, four-page biographical typescript (no title), vol. 1.
      Paul Sluby, biographical typescript on the life and death of James Wormley, vol. 1.
      "They Had a Dream: James Wormley—Capital Innkeeper." *[Washington] Evening
         Star*, September 19, 1970, vol. 1.
      Melvin Roscoe Williams, biographical typescript titled "Blacks in Washington,
         D.C., 1860–1870."

]Maryland Historical Society, Baltimore.
   Atkinson and Smith Family Papers.
   Eliza Blow Atkinson Papers.
   Frick Family Papers, Susan Carroll Poultney Recipe and Crochet Book.

Maryland State Archives, Biographical Series, Annapolis.
   Helen Avalynne Gibson Tawes. Biographical Series. MSA SC 3520-2292.
   J. Millard Tawes, Biographical Series. MSA SC 3520-1485

Massachusetts Historical Society, Boston.
   DeGrasse-Howard Papers.
   C. Dyer Recipe Collection, 1827, 1837. Ms. SBd-125.
   Charles E. French Autograph Collection.
   Hartwell-Clark Family Papers.
   Letters Received by James Wormley, 1868–1892.
   Prescott Family Cookbook.
   Stout Family Papers.

Massachusetts State House of Representatives, Office of the Clerk, Boston,
Massachusetts.
   Records of the Massachusetts State House of Representatives, Office of the Clerk,
      Boston, Massachusetts.

Massachusetts Supreme Judicial Court, Archives and Records Preservation,
Boston.
   Petition.—HOUSE. Mr. Hale of Cambridge presents the petition of Joshua B. Smith
      for payment for Rations furnished to the Twelfth Regiment, Mass. Vols. in 1861.

House of Reps. Jan. 20, 1879. Referred to the Committee on Claims . . . In Senate, Jan. 21, 1879. Statement of the Claim of the Late Joshua B. Smith Against the Commonwealth for Subsistence Furnished the 12th Regiment of Massachusetts Volunteers. Petition signed January 18, 1879.

Resolve, in Relation to the Claim of Joshua B. Smith. Resolved, That the Governor and Council be and they are hereby authorized to pay to Joshua B. Smith. . . . Senate No. 141—March 7, 1879.

Resolve, in Relation to the Claim of Joshua B. Smith. Resolved, That the Governor and Council be and they are hereby authorized to pay to Joshua B. Smith. . . . House No. 316—April 17, 1879.

Proposed by Mr. Jennings of Fall River as a substitute for the Resolve in relation to the claim of Joshua B. Smith, Commonwealth of Massachusetts. An Act Relative to the Claim of Joshua B. Smith Against the Commonwealth. House, No. 347, April, 1879.

Petition of Emeline I. Smith, Widow of Joshua B. Smith, for an Allowance in Consideration of Services Rendered to the Commonwealth by Her Husband. Referred to Massachusetts State Senate Committee, February 3, 1880.

Commonwealth of Massachusetts. Resolve in Favor of Emeline I. Smith. Chapter 65, p.261, April 24, 1880.

Moorland-Spingarn Research Center, Howard University, Washington, DC.
Bustill-Bowser-Asbury Collection, series B, box 127-1, folders 5 and 6.
Thomas and William Dorsey Collection.
George T. Downing Papers.
Archibald Grimke Notebooks, no. 6.
William Johnson Jr. Family Papers.
Vertical Files.

Municipal Archives, City of New York, New York.
Manual of the Board of Education of the City and County of New York, 1848.
Manual of the Board of Education of the City and County of New York, 1849.

National Archives and Records Administration, Washington, DC.
Isaac Bassett Manuscript Collection, US Senate Commission on Art, Center for Legislative Archives, RG 46.
Martin R. Delany, letter to Secretary of War, E. M. Stanton, December 15, 1863, in MS. War Records Office.
"Memorandum List of Tithables," 14 June 1771, in George Washington Papers.
Records of the District Courts of the United States, District of the Columbia, RG 21, Entry 49, General term Minutes, 1863–1903, Volume 1 (May 4, 1863–October 9, 1871).
Registers of Licenses, 1818–1876. RG 351.

Newcomb Institute of Tulane University, Archives and Special Collections, New Orleans, Louisiana.
"Colonial Williamsburg Notebook, 1943." Folder 1, box 1, Lena Richard Papers.

Bibliography

New Orleans Public Library, Louisiana Division/City Archives & Special
Collections.
  Friends of the Cabildo Project, Oral History Program.

Newport Historical Society, Newport, Rhode Island.
  Newspaper Collection.

Newport Public Library, Newport Rhode Island

New York Historical Society, New York.
  George Templeton Strong Diary: Holograph, 1835–1875.

New York Public Library, Humanities and Social Sciences Library, Manuscripts
and Archives Division, New York.
  Samuel J. Tilden Papers. Box 7, 1869, Jan.–Sept.

New York State Library, Albany, New York
  New York Sun

Office of Commonwealth Libraries, Bureau of State Library, State Library of
Pennsylvania, Harrisburg, Pennsylvania
  Philadelphia Times

Samuel L. Paley Library, Urban Archives Department, Temple University,
Philadelphia, Pennsylvania.
  Urban Archives Department.

William R. Perkins Library, Rare Book, Manuscript, and Special Collections
Library, Duke University, Durham, North Carolina.
  Charles Sumner Papers.

Phillips Library, Peabody Essex Museum, Salem, Massachusetts.
  Remond Family Papers, 1823–1869.

Rush Rhees Library, Department of Rare Books and Special Collections,
University of Rochester, Rochester, New York.
  William Henry Seward Papers.

Rhode Island Black Heritage Society, Providence, Rhode Island.
  Rice Family Papers.

Rhode Island Historical Society Library, Manuscripts Division, Providence, Rhode
Island.
  African Union Society. Proceedings, November 10, 1796. MSS 9001A.
  William Arnold Papers.
  DeWolf Family Papers, Papers of the Slave Trade. Brigantine Yankee Account Book,
    1814–1816, vol. 6. MSS 382.
  First Congregational Church of Newport Records, 1805–1825, MSS 418.
  Robert W. Foster Papers.
  Albert Collins Greene Papers, 1804–1863.
  Richard Ward Greene Papers.

Joseph P. Hazard Collection, Memorandum.

Rowland G. Hazard Papers.

George F. Jencks Diary.

Mason's Newport, Narrative, vol. 2, 1752. MSS 554.

Providence Marine Society, Bills Paid to William H. Williams, 1895–1896.

Rhode Island Citizens Historical Association, "Reminiscences of the South Side of Westminster St. and the 'Lady of the Lake,'" by Elisha Dyer. N.d. MSS 677.

Rhode Island Manuscripts, Letters.

Richard Waterman Family Papers.

Rivera Library, University of California, Riverside

Newport Mercury

Saratoga Springs History Museum, Saratoga Springs, New York.

"One Hundred and Sixty Years of the Music of Francis (Frank) Johnson (1792–1844)." 1977.

Schomburg Center for Research in Black Culture, Manuscripts, Archives and Rare Books Division, New York Public Library, New York.

Maritcha R. Lyons, "Memories of Yesterdays: All of Which I Saw and Part of Which I Was, An Autobiography." 1928. Harry A. Williamson Papers. Typescript.

Harry A. Williamson, "Folks in Old New York and Brooklyn." 1953. Harry A. Williamson Papers. Typescript.

Shelton, Peter. Personal Collection

Handwritten menu by Albert Eugene Dutrieuille.

Fred W. Smith National Library for the Study of George Washington, Mount Vernon, Virginia.

Digital Encyclopedia.

South Carolina Historical Society, SC Department of Archives and History, Charleston.

Amended Appraisal of Inventory of Furniture Belonging to Jehu Jones, Ann Deas listed as owning bill of sale. Document 6, Page 1, 920 Jones, 1997.

Jehu Jones Pamphlet, "Jehu Jones: Free Black Entrepreneur," 920 Jones, 1997.

Papers, Petitions, 1823, no. 138.

Petition, authored by Governor John L. Wilson, dated December 6, 1823, to the Senate of South Carolina, on behalf of Jehu Jones, to allow him to return to South Carolina, General Assembly.

Mary Motte Alston Pringle Papers.

Recipe Book, Circa 1840.

Simons & Simons Case Records, 1835–1873: *Fuller vs. Gatewood*.

State Historical Society of Wisconsin, Madison, Wisconsin.

Daniel Murray Papers. Microfilm, reels 3, 8, 9, 10, 19, 20.

Sterling Memorial Library, Yale University, New Haven, Connecticut.

Daniel Murray Papers. Microfilm, reels 4, 11, 12, 13, 14, 16, 18, 21, 22.

Bibliography

University of Pennsylvania Archives, Philadelphia.
> Bustill-Mossell Family Papers.
> Nathan Mossell, Autobiography (no date). Alumni Records Collection, folder Mossell, Nathan.

US House of Representatives, Office of History and Preservation, Office of the Clerk, Washington, DC.
> Contingent Expenses House of Representatives. Letter from the Clerk of the House of Representatives, Transmitting A Statement of the Contingent Expenses of the House of Representatives. 40th Congress, 3rd sess., misc. doc. no. 25, January 19, 1869. "G.L. [G.T.] Downing: Meals furnished C. W. Woolley while under arrest for refusing to testify before the board of managers of impeachment, May 25 to June 11, 1868." Detailed statement of disbursements, etc., p. 77.

US House of Representatives, Office of the House Historian
> "Impeachment Managers' Investigation." 40th Congress, 2nd sess., report no. 44, May 25, 1868.

US Senate Historical Office, US Senate, Washington, DC.
> Biographical Directory of the United States Congress.

Herman B. Wells Library, Indiana University, Bloomington, Indiana
> The Philadelphia Colored Directory, 1907.

Interviews

Lucy Ater. Interview with Dorothy Schlesinger, June 13, 1974. Friends of the Cabildo Project, Oral History Program, New Orleans Public Library, Louisiana Division, City Archives and Special Collections, New Orleans, Louisiana. Cassette tape.

Shirley Bateman Interview with Dorothy Schlesinger, no date. Friends of the Cabildo Project, Oral History Program, New Orleans Public Library, Louisiana Division, City Archives and Special Collections, New Orleans, Louisiana. Cassette tape.

Susan Greendyke, art collections manager. Telephone interview, Tuesday, July 6, 2010, regarding location of Charles Sumner painting donated by James Wormley, Bureau of State Office Buildings, Boston, Massachusetts.

Tanya Holland, chef. Interview, PBS *Black Culture Connection*, no date.

Phil Lapsansky, curator of African Americana, Library Company of Philadelphia. Telephone conversation, Monday, November 12, 2007.

Edna Lewis. Interview, "A Taste of Heritage Dinner," Grand Hyatt Hotel, Washington, DC, 1994 (tape).

Mr. Sherman Pyatt, Miller F. Whittaker Library, South Carolina State University. Telephone interviews, Thursday, August 6, and Tuesday, August 25, 2009.

Joe Randall, chef. Interview, PBS *Black Culture Connection*, no date.

Joe Randall, chef. Telephone interviews, September 29, 2013, and July 20, 2014.

Peter Shelton (Bernice Dutrieuille Shelton's son). Telephone interviews, Tuesday, April 8, and Tuesday, May 20, 2008.

Edna Jordan Smith. Telephone interview, June 12, 2007.

Dr. Donald Spivey. Interview with author, October 1, 2012.

Brian Sullivan, archivist, Mount Auburn Cemetery. Telephone interview, July 13, 2010.

"A Tale of Two Chefs: Marcus Samuelsson and Roble Ali," CNN *In America*, February 28, 2012.

Erick Taylor. Interviewed by Rowena Stewart, Rhode Island Black Heritage Society, Providence, July 13, 1977.

Felicia Wivchar, curatorial assistant, Office of History and Preservation, Office of the Clerk, US House of Representatives. Telephone conversation, January 8, 2007.

Mrs. Freida Wormley. Interview, Thursday, May 24, 2007, at her apartment.

Mrs. Freida Wormley. Telephone interview, Monday, February 19, 2007.

First-Person Accounts

Abdy, E. S. *Journal of a Residence and Tour in the United States of North America, From April, 1833, to October, 1834*. 2 vols. London: John Murray, 1835.

Bernhard, Karl, Duke of Saxe-Weimar-Eisenach. *Travels Through North America During the Years 1825 and 1826, Volume II*. Philadelphia, PA: Carey, Lea & Carey, 1828.

Brown, William J. *The Life of William J. Brown, of Providence, R. I.* 1883. Freeport, NY: Books for Libraries Press, 1971.

Campbell, Tunis Gulic. *Sufferings of the Rev. T. G. Campbell and His Family in Georgia*. Washington, DC: Enterprise Publishing, 1877.

Channing, George Gibbs. *Early Recollections of Newport, Rhode Island, From the Year 1793 to 1811*. Boston, MA: Nichols and Noyes, 1868.

Dayton, Abram C. *Last Days of Knickerbocker Life in New York*. New York: George W. Harlan, Publisher, 1882.

Ellis, John B. *The Sights and Secrets of the National Capital: A Work Descriptive of Washington City in All its Various Phases*. New York: United States Publishing, 1869.

Fearon, Henry Bradshaw. *Sketches of America. A Narrative of a Journey of Five Thousand Miles Through the Eastern and Western States of America; Contained in Eight Reports. With Remarks on Mr. Birkbeck's "Notes" and "Letters."* 2nd ed. London: Longman, Hurst, Rees, Orme and Brown, 1818.

Graff, Ella Bunner. "Reminiscences of Old Harlem." New York: New York Public Library, 1933.

Hamilton, Thomas. *Men and Manners in America*. Philadelphia, PA: Carey, Lea & Blanchard, 1833.

Moreton, J. B. *West India Customs and Manners: Containing Strictures on the Soil, Cultivation, Produce, Trade, Officers, and Inhabitants, With the Method of Establishing and Conducting a Sugar Plantation*. London: J. Parsons, Paternoster Row, 1793.

Northend, Mary Harrod. *Memories of Old Salem, Drawn from the Letters of a Great-Grandmother*. New York: Moffatt, Yard, 1917.

Northup, Solomon. *Twelve Years a Slave: Narrative of Solomon Northup, A Citizen of New-York, Kidnapped in Washington City in 1841, and Rescued in 1853, From a Cotton Plantation Near the Red River, in Louisiana*. 1853. Auburn, NY: Derby and Miller, 1856.

Silsbee, Marianne Cabot Devereaux. *A Half Century in Salem*. Cambridge, MA: Riverside Press, 1887.

Sullivan, Buddy, ed. *The Darien Journal of John Girardeau Legare, Ricegrower*. Athens: University of Georgia Press, 2010.

Taylor, Susie King. *A Black Woman's Civil War Memoirs*. Princeton, NJ: Markus Wiener, 1988.

Tuckerman, Bayard, ed. *The Diary of Philip Hone, 1828–1851*. 2 vols. New York: Dodd, Mead, 1889.

Van Rensselaer, Mrs. John King (May). *Newport: Our Social Capital*. Philadelphia, PA: J. B. Lippincott, 1905.

US House of Representative and US Senate Documents, Court Cases, Court Records, and US Census

Commonwealth of Massachusetts. Probate Court. Middlesex County, file no. 10197, Estate of Joshua B. Smith, September 2, 1879.

Congressional Globe, Supplement. Senate, Fortieth Congress, Second Session, "Proceedings of the Senate Sitting for the Trial of Andrew Johnson, President of the United States, On Articles of Impeachment Exhibited by the House of Representatives."

Congressional Globe. Forty-Second Congress, 2nd sess., January 31, 1872.

Congressional Record. Forty-Third Congress, 1st sess., December, 1873.

Congressional Record. US Senate. Eighty-Eighth Congress, 1st sess., January 18, 1963, p. 627, and January 21, 1963, p. 669.

"The Crime Against Kansas." Speech of Hon. Charles Sumner of Massachusetts in the Senate of the United States, May 19, 1856.

Dred Scott v. Sandford, 60 U.S. [19 How.] 393 [1857].

Journal of the Senate. April 19, 1850, p. 301.

Naval Documents Related to the Quasi War between the United States and France. Published under the direction of the Honorable Claude A. Swanson, Secretary of the Navy. Prepared by the Office of Naval Records and Library Navy Department, under the supervision of Capt. Dudley W. Knox. Washington, DC, 1935.

Pennsylvania Constitutional Debates of 1837–1838, vols. 3, 1837; 9, 10, 1838, Harrisburg, PA: Packer, Barrett, and Parke.

Plessy v. Ferguson, 163 U.S. 537, 16 S. Ct. 1138; 41 L. Ed. 256; 1896.

Prigg v. Pennsylvania, 41 U.S. 539, 1842.

Proceedings of the United States Senate, on the Fugitive Slave Bill, — The Abolition of the Slave — Trade in the District of Columbia, — and the Imprisonment of Free Colored Seamen in the Southern Ports: With the Speeches of Messrs. Davis, Winthrop and Others. US Congress, 31st, 1st sess., 1849–1850. Senate.

State of Missouri vs. Celia, A Slave. Records of Callaway County Circuit Court *From the Proceedings in the Matter of Missouri vs. Celia, a Slave*, File No. 4496, 1855.

The State v. John Mann, 13 NC 263, North Carolina Supreme Court, 1829.

Steele v. Louisville & Nashville Railroad Co., 323 U.S. 192 [1944] No. 45.

United States v. Amy, 24 F. Cas. 792, At 809, 810 (C.C.D. Va. 1859) (no. 14,445).

United States v. The Amistad, 40 U.S. (15 Pet.) 518 (1841).

US Census Bureau. Census of Charleston, South Carolina, 1848.

US Census Bureau. Seventh Census of the United States 1850. District 12, Callaway, Missouri. Washington, DC: National Archives and Records Administration. Roll M432_393, p. 197A.

US Census Bureau. Seventh Census of the United States 1850. Harrisburg East Ward, Dauphin County, Pennsylvania. Washington, DC: National Archives and Records Administration. Roll M432_774, p. 89A.

US Census Bureau. Eighth Census of the United States, 1860. Harrisburg Ward 2, Dauphin County, Pennsylvania. Washington, DC: National Archives and Records Administration. Roll M653_1104, p. 967.

US Census Bureau. Eighth Census of the United States, 1860. Newport, Rhode Island. Washington, DC: National Archives and Records Administration, 1860. Roll M653_1204, p. 282.

US Census Bureau. Eighth Census of the United States, 1860. Washington, DC: National Archives and Records Administration. Roll M653.

US Census Bureau. Ninth Census of the United States, 1870. Washington, DC: National Archives and Records Administration. Roll M593, RG29.

US Census Bureau. Tenth Census of the United States, 1880. Washington, DC: National Archives and Records Administration, 1880. Roll T9-123.

US House of Representatives. "Impeachment Managers' Investigation." Fortieth Congress, 2nd sess. Report no. 44, May 25, 1868.

US Senate. *Memorial of the National Convention of Colored Persons, Praying to be Protected in Their Civil Rights.* Misc. doc. 21, 43rd Congress, 1st sess., December, 1873.

US Senate. *31st Congress, 1st sess. Rep Com. No. 123. In Senate of the United States. May 8, 1850. Report: [To accompany bills S. No. 225 and S. No. 226].*

Laws and Statutes

An act more effectually to protect the free citizens of this State from being kidnapped, or reduced to Slavery, New York, May 14, 1840.

Civil Rights Act of 1875 [18 Stat. 335].

Digest of the Ordinances of the City Council of Charleston from the Years 1783 to October 1844. To Which are Annexed the Acts of the Legislature Which Relate Exclusively to the City of Charleston. Charleston, 1844.

Fugitive Slave Act, February 12, 1793, ch.7, 1 Stat. 302, Article IV, Section 2.

Fugitive Slave Act, 1850, 9 Stat. 462.

The Ku Klux Klan Act [ch.22, 17 Stat. 13], also called the Civil Rights Act of 1871, or the Force Act of 1871, and officially titled, "An Act to Enforce the Provisions of the Fourteenth Amendment." April 20, 1871.

Homer A. Plessy v. Ferguson, 163 U.S. 537, 1896.

Mass. Acts and Resolves, I, 606.

Bibliography

Missouri Rev. Stat. ch. 47, Section 4, 1845, and Section 29, 1845.

Pennsylvania Laws, vol. 1, p.13, "An Act for the Better Regulation of Servants in this Province and Territories."

Pennsylvania Laws, vol. 1, p. 838, pp. 839–40, section 4.

The Public Laws of the State of Rhode Island and Providence Plantations. January 1789.

Selections from the Revised Statutes of the State of New York: containing all the Laws of the State Relative to Slaves, and the Laws Relative to the Offence of Kidnapping, which Several Laws Commenced and Took Ef[f]ect Jan[u]yary 1, 1830. Together With Extracts from the Laws of the United States, Respecting Slaves [New York, 1830].

Statutes at Large of South Carolina

US Statutes at Large, IX, Section 1, 11 Bos. Rec. Com., 60,72,158,166

Washington Ordinance, October 28, 1802, p.25, Acts of the Corporation of the City of Washington Passed by the First Council [Washington, 1803].

Washington Ordinance of May 25, 1803, pp. 45–47, Act of the Corporation of the City of Washington Passed by the First Council.

Washington Ordinance of October 29, 1836, James W. Sheahan [comp.], p.249, Corporation Laws of the City of Washington [Washington, 1853].

Atlases and Maps, Brochures, Pamphlets, Catalogues, Reports, Convention Proceedings, County Records, City Directories

Atlas of the City of Newport, Rhode Island. Philadelphia, PA: G. M. Hopkins, C.E., 1883.

Black Entrepreneurs of the Eighteenth and Nineteenth Centuries. Boston and Nantucket: The Federal Reserve Bank of Boston and the Museum of African American History, 2009.

Catalogue of Very Choice, and Very Old Wines, Liquors, Cordiuls, &c., &c. Being the Private Stock of Mr. John Remond, of Salem, Mass., Who Commenced Accumulating This Valuable Stock in 1808. Salem, MA: Salem Gazette, 1866. In Remond Family Papers, Phillips Library, Salem, Massachusetts.

Census Directory for 1811. Containing the Names, Occupations, & Residence of the Inhabitants of the City, Southwark & Northern Liberties, A Separate Division Being Allotted to Persons of Colour, Philadelphia: printed by Jane Aitken, 1811.

City Atlas of Newport, Rhode Island, 1876. Philadelphia, PA: G. M. Hopkins, 1876.

The Directory and Stranger's Guide, for the City of Charleston, For the Year 1794, To Which is added An Almanac; the Tariff Duties on all Good Imported into the United States; Rates of Wharfage, Weighing, and Storage, Cartage and Drayage etc. etc. Charleston, 1794.

Efforts for Social Betterment Among Negro Americans. Report of a Social Study made by Atlanta University under the patronage of the Trustees of the John F. Slater Fund: together with the Proceedings of the 14th Annual Conference for the Study of the Negro Problems, held at Atlanta University on Tuesday, May the 24th, 1909, edited by W. E. Burghardt Du Bois.

The 1866 Guide to New York City: New York As it is, Or, Stranger's Guide-Book to the Cities of New York, Brooklyn and Adjacent Places. New York: Schocken Books, 1975.

Flyer, advertising lecture at Newcomb College Center for Research on Women, Tulane University.

Guide to the Capitol of the United States, 1834. Office of History and Preservation, Office of the Clerk.

Historical Society of Washington, DC. "The Measure of a Man: James Wormley, A Nineteenth-Century, African-American Entrepreneur." Commemorative brochure, 1993.

Ingersoll, Ernest. *A Report on the Oyster-Industry of the United States.* Washington, DC: US Government Printing Office, 1881.

Lena Richard Exhibit and Oral History Project, Southern Food and Beverage Museum New Orleans, Louisiana.

Longworth's American Almanac, New-York Register, and City Directory, for the Sixtieth Year of American Independence, 1835–1836. New York: Thomas Longworth, 1835–1836.

Longworth's New York Directory, 1834–1835. New York: Thomas Longworth, 1834–1835.

McElroy's Philadelphia Directory for 1844: Contains the Names of the Inhabitants, Their Occupations, Places of Business, and Dwelling Houses; also a Business Directory. 7th ed. Philadelphia: Edward C. Biddle, Printed by Isaac Ashmead and Co., 1844.

Newton (Massachusetts) City Directory, 1895.

Philadelphia City Archives, Philadelphia County Deeds.

The Philadelphia Colored Directory. Philadelphia, PA: Philadelphia Colored Directory, 1907.

The Philadelphia Directory for 1804 Containing the Names, Trades and Residence of the Inhabitants of the City. Philadelphia, James Robinson, Printed by John H. Oswald, 1804.

The Present State and Condition of the Free People of Color, of the City of Philadelphia and Adjoining Districts, as Exhibited by the Report of a Committee of the Pennsylvania Society for Promoting the Abolition of Slavery, etc. Philadelphia, PA: The Society, 1838.

Proceedings of the Colored National Labor Convention, Washington, D.C., December 6–10, 1869.

Proceedings of the One Hundredth Anniversary of the Granting of Warrant 459 to African Lodge, at Boston, Mass., Monday, Sept. 29, 1884 . . . Boston, MA: Franklin Press, 1885.

Proceedings of the Pennsylvania Convention, Assembled to Organize a State Anti-Slavery Society, at Harrisburg, on the 31st of January and 1st, 2nd and 3d of February, 1837. Philadelphia, PA: Merrihew and Gunn, 1837.

Register of the Mesne Conveyance Office. Charleston County Register of Deeds Office, Charleston, South Carolina.

Register of Trades of the Colored People in the City of Philadelphia and Districts. Philadelphia, PA: Merrihew and Gunn (printer), 1838.

Report and the Debates and Proceedings in the New York State Convention for Revision of the Constitution, 1846. Albany, New York, 1846.

Report of the Committee of Merchants For the Relief of Colored People, Suffering From the Late Riots in the City of New York. New York: George A. Whitehorne, 1863.

Report on the Fisheries and Water-Fowl of Maryland. 1 January, 1872. Annapolis, 1872.

Bibliography

Rhode Island Historical Preservation Commission. "The Kay Street–Catherine Street–Old Beach Road Neighborhood, Newport, Rhode Island." Statewide Preservation Report. January 1974.

Salem Directory and City Register Containing the Names of the Inhabitants, Their Occupations, Places of Business and Residences. Salem, MA, 1837.

The Salem Directory, Containing the Names of the Citizens City Officers, A Business Directory, General Events of the Years 1856 and 1857, and an Almanac for 1859. Adams, Sampson & Co. Salem, MA: Henry Whipple and Son, 1859.

Senatorial Fare: Recipes by and for the Members of the U. S. Senate. (n.d.)

Statistical Inquiry Into the Condition of the People of Colour, of the City and Districts of Philadelphia. Philadelphia: Kite & Walton, 1849.

Saratoga Springs Directory, 1925. Saratoga Springs, NY: Saratogian, 1925.

Newspapers and Periodicals

African Repository and Colonial Journal

Afro-American Ledger

Anglo-African Magazine

Augusta Constitutionalist

Bangor Daily Whig & Courier

Boston Evening Transcript

Boston Globe

Charleston Mercury

Chicago Defender

Chicago Tribune

Christian Recorder

Cincinnati Enquirer

City Gazette (South Carolina)

Colored American

Commercial Journal

The Critic

Cuisine Noir Magazine

Douglass' Monthly

Ebony

The Emancipator

Essex County Freeman

Evening Star (Washington, DC)

Fall River Line Journal

Fortune

Forum: The Magazine of the Florida Humanities Council

Frederick Douglass' Paper

Harper's Weekly

Harrisburg Magazine

Harrisburg Patriot and Union

Hippocrates: The Magazine of Health and Medicine

The Independent

The Liberator

Louisville and Nashville Employees Magazine

Miami Culinary Institute

Miami Herald

Morning Herald (Baltimore, MD)

New National Era

Newport Daily News

Newport Mercury

Newport This Week

New York Daily News

New York Daily Times (*New York Times*)

New-York Daily Tribune

New York Freeman

New York Herald

New York Sun

New York Times

New York Tribune

New York World

Outlook

Pacific Appeal (San Francisco)

Pennsylvania Daily Telegraph (Harrisburg)

Philadelphia Times

Philadelphia Tribune

The Press

The Principia

Public Ledger

Salem Advertiser

Salem Gazette

Salem Observer

Salem Register

The Saratogian

Savannah Daily Republican

Savannah Morning News

The Sentinel

StarChefs.Com, The Magazine for Culinary Insiders

State Journal (Harrisburg, Pa.)

Bibliography

Staten Island World

St. Louis Globe Democrat

Town Topics

Washington Post

Washington Star

Secondary Sources

The following list of secondary sources was useful in assembling the African and African American culinary and historical tapestry. While it is intended to give the reader an indication of some research involved in this study, it is selective and not an endorsement of content.

Adams, F. C. *Manuel Pereira or The Sovereign Rule of South Carolina, With Views of Southern Laws, Life and Hospitality*. Washington, DC: Buell and Blanchard, 1853.

Africanus, Leo. *The History and Description of Africa of Leo Africanus*. Vol. 2, edited by Dr. Robert Brown. New York: Burt Franklin, 1963.

Ajayi, J. F. Ade, and Michael Crowder, eds. *History of West Africa*. Vol. 1. New York: Columbia University Press, 1972.

Ajayi, J. F. Ade, and Ian Espie, eds. *A Thousand Years of West African History*. New York: Humanities Press, 1972.

Allison, P. A. "Historical Inferences to be Drawn from the Effect of Human Settlement on the Vegetation of Africa." *Journal of African History* 3, no. 2 (1962): 241–49.

Alvey, R. Gerald. *Kentucky Bluegrass Country*. Jackson: University Press of Mississippi, 1992.

Amar, Akhil Reed. *America's Constitution: A Biography*. New York: Random House, 2005.

American and Foreign Anti-Slavery Society. *The Fugitive Slave Bill: Its History and Unconstitutionality, With an Account of the Seizure and Enslavement of James Hamlet, and His Subsequent Restoration to Liberty*. New York: William Harned, 1850.

Andah, Bassey. "Identifying Early Farming Traditions of West Africa." In *The Archaeology of Africa: Food, Metals, and Towns*, edited by Thurstan Shaw, 240–54. London: Routledge, 1993.

Aptheker, Herbert, ed. *A Documentary History of the Negro People in the United States, Volume I: From Colonial Times through the Civil War*. New York: Citadel Press, 1951.

Aptheker, Herbert. "Eighteenth-Century Petition of South Carolina Negroes." *Journal of Negro History* 31, no. 1 (January 1946): 98–99.

Aptheker, Herbert. "The Negro in the Abolitionist Movement." *Science & Society* 5 (Spring 1941): 2–23.

Aptheker, Herbert. "South Carolina Negro Conventions, 1865." *Journal of Negro History* 31, no. 1 (January 1946): 91–97.

Aptheker, Herbert (1968). *To Be Free: Studies in American Negro History*. 1948. New York: International Publishers, 1968.

Armstead, Myra B. Young. *"Lord, Please Don't Take Me in August": African Americans in Newport and Saratoga Springs, 1870–1930*. Urbana and Chicago: University of Illinois Press, 1999.

Armstead, Myra Beth Young. "The History of Blacks in Resort Towns: Newport, Rhode Island, and Saratoga Springs, New York, 1870–1930." PhD dissertation, Department of History, University of Chicago, 1987.

Askins, William. "Oysters and Equality: Nineteenth-Century Cultural Resistance in Sandy Ground, Staten Island, New York." *Anthropology of Work Review* 12, no. 2 (1991): 7–13.

Bailey, Thomas. *The American Pageant*. Lexington, MA: D. C. Heath, 1975.

Baker, H. G. "Comments on the Thesis That There was a Major Centre of Plant Domestication near the Headwaters of the River Niger." *Journal of African History* 3, no. 2 (1962): 229–33.

Barnes, David M. *The Draft Riots in New York, July, 1863. The Metropolitan Police: Their Services During Riot Week. Their Honorable Record*. New York: Baker & Godwin, 1863.

Barrett, Walter. *The Old Merchants of New York City*. Vol. 2. 1863–1870. New York: Greenwood Press, 1968.

Bartlett, Irving H. *From Slave to Citizen: The Story of the Negro in Rhode Island*. Providence, RI: The Urban League of Greater Providence, 1954.

Batterberry, Michael, and Ariane Batterberry. *On the Town in New York: From 1776 to the Present*. New York: Charles Scribner's Sons, 1973.

Battle, Charles A. *Negroes on the Island of Rhode Island*. N.p.: n.p., 1932.

Bayles, Richard Mather. *History of Newport County, Rhode Island From the Year 1638 to the Year 1887, Including the Settlement of its Towns, and Their Subsequent Progress*. New York: L. E. Preston, 1888.

Bearse, Austin. *Reminiscences of Fugitive-Slave Law Days in Boston*. Boston, MA: Warren Richardson, 1880.

Bedasse, Monique A. *Jah Kingdom: Rastafarians, Tanzania, and Pan-Africanism in the Age of Decolonization*. Chapel Hill: University of North Carolina Press, 2017.

Bell, Derrick. "Black Faith in a Racist Land: A Summary Review of Racism in American Law." *Howard Law Journal* 17, no. 2 (1972): 300–318.

Bell, Derrick. *Race, Racism, and American Law*. New York: Aspen, 2004.

ben-Jochannan, Yosef. *Africa: Mother of Western Civilization*. Baltimore, MD: Black Classic Press, 1997.

ben-Jochannan, Yosef. *Black Man of the Nile and His Family*. Baltimore, MD: Black Classic Press, 1989.

Bennett, Lerone Jr. "Black & Green: The Untold Story of the African-American Entrepreneur." *Ebony* 51, no. 4 (February 1996), 36–41.

Bernstein, Iver. *The New York City Draft Riots: Their Significance for American Society and Politics in the Age of the Civil War*. New York: Oxford University Press, 1990.

Betts, Edwin Morris, ed. *Thomas Jefferson's Farm Book*. Princeton, NJ: Princeton University Press, 1953.

Bevier, Isabel. *Nutrition Investigations in Pittsburg, Pa., 1894–1896*. Washington, DC: Government Printing Office, 1898.

Bibliography

Biddle, Daniel R., and Murray Dubin. *Tasting Freedom: Octavius Catto and the Battle for Equality in Civil War America*. Philadelphia, PA: Temple University Press, 2010.

Biddle, Nicholas. "Ode to Bogle." *Littell's Living Age* 3, no. 30 (December 7, 1844): 360–61.

Bienvenu, Marcelle, Carl A. Brasseaux, and Ryan A. Brasseaux. *Stir the Pot: The History of Cajun Cuisine*. New York: Hippocrene Books, 2005.

Billington, Ray Allen. "James Forten: Forgotten Abolitionist." *Negro History Bulletin* (November 1949): 31–36, 45.

Blackett, R. J. M. *Thomas Morris Chester, Black Civil War Correspondent, His Dispatches from the Virginia Front*. Baton Rouge: Louisiana State University Press, 1989.

Blatt, Martin H., Thomas J. Brown, and Donald Yacovone, eds. *Hope & Glory: Essays on the Legacy of the Fifty-Fourth Massachusetts Regiment*. Amherst, MA: University of Massachusetts Press, 2001.

Bloch, Herman D. *The Circle of Discrimination: An Economic and Social Study of the Black Man in New York*. New York: New York University Press, 1969.

Blockson, Charles L. *The Liberty Bell Era: The African American Story*. Harrisburg, PA: RB Books, 2003.

Blockson, Charles L. *The Underground Railroad*. New York: Prentice Hall Press, 1987.

Blockson, Charles L. *The Underground Railroad in Pennsylvania*. Jacksonville, NC: Flame International, 1981.

Boas, Franz. *Race and Democratic Society*. New York: J. J. Augustin, 1945.

Bovill, E. W. *Caravans of the Old Sahara: An Introduction to the History of the Western Sudan*. London: Oxford University Press, for the International Institute of African Languages and Cultures, 1933.

Bovill, Edward William. *The Golden Trade of the Moors: West African Kingdoms in the Fourteenth Century*. 1958. Princeton, NJ: Markus Wiener, 1995.

Boyd, W. H. *New York City Tax Book, Being a List of Persons, Corporations, and Co-Partnerships, Resident and Non-Resident, Who Were Taxed, According to the Assessor's Books, 1856 and 1857*. New York: William H. Boyd, 1857.

Bradley, Hugh. *Such Was Saratoga*. 1940. New York: Arno Press, 1975.

Bridenbaugh, Carl. *Cities in the Wilderness: The First Century of Urban Life in America, 1625–1742*. New York: Ronald Press, 1938.

Britten, Evelyn Barrett. *Chronicles of Saratoga*. Saratoga Springs: Published privately by Evelyn Barrett Britten, 1959.

Brookes, George S. *Friend Anthony Benezet*. Philadelphia: University of Pennsylvania Press, 1937.

Brooks, George E. Jr. "The Providence African Society's Sierra Leone Emigration Scheme, 1794–1795: Prologue to the African Colonization Movement." *International Journal of African Historical Studies* 7, no. 2 (1974): 183–202.

Brooks, Henry M. "Some Localities about Salem." *Essex Institute Historical Collections* 31 (1894–1895): 114–15.

Brotz, Howard, ed. *African-American Social and Political Thought, 1850–1920*. New Brunswick, NJ: Transaction Publishers, 1992.

Brown, Henry Collins, ed. *Valentine's Manual of Old New York*. New York: Valentine's Manual, 1926.

Brown, Letitia Woods, and Elsie M. Lewis. *Washington in the New Era, 1870–1970*. Washington, DC: Washington Education Department, National Portrait Gallery. US Government Printing Office, 1972.

Brown, Thomas J. "Reconstructing Boston, Civic Monuments of the Civil War." In Blatt, Brown, and Yacovone, *Hope & Glory*, 130–55.

Brundage, W. Fitzhugh. "The Darien 'Insurrection' of 1899: Black Protest during the Nadir of Race Relations." *Georgia Historical Quarterly* 74, no. 2 (Summer 1990): 234–53.

Bryan, Wilhelmus Bogart. *A History of the National Capital: From Its Foundation through the Period of the Adoption of the Organic Act*. Vol. 2. New York: Macmillan, 1916.

Burton, Nathaniel, and Rudy Lombard. *Creole Feast: 15 Master Chefs of New Orleans Reveal Their Secrets*. New York: Random House, 1978.

Campbell, Tunis G. *Hotel Keepers, Head Waiters, and Housekeepers' Guide*. Boston, MA: Coolidge and Wiley, 1848.

Carlisle, earl of. *Travels in America: The Poetry of Pope*. New York: G. P. Putnam, 1851.

Carroll, Bartholomew Rivers. *Historical Collections of South Carolina, Volume I*. New York: Harper & Brothers, 1836.

Carter, Nathaniel H., and William L. Stone. *Reports of the Proceedings and Debates of the Convention of 1821*. Albany, NY: E. & E. Horsford, 1821.

Chambers, John Whiteclay. "Of Palates and Politics: New York City as a Case Study." *PS* 11, no. 2 (Spring 1978): 224–27.

Chambers, W. *American Slavery and Color*. London, 1857.

Chambers, W. *Things As They Are in America*. London, 1854.

Chijioke, F. A. *Ancient Africa*. London: Longmans, Green, 1966.

Child, Lydia Maria. *The Freedmen's Book*. 1865. Boston, MA: Ticknor and Fields, 1968.

Christian Woman's Exchange of New Orleans, La. *The Creole Cookery Book*. 1855. New Orleans: Pelican, 2005.

Chu, Daniel, and Elliott Skinner. *A Glorious Age in Africa*. Trenton, NJ: Africa World Press, 1990.

Churchill, Ward, and Jim Vander Wall. *Agents of Repression: The FBI's Secret Wars against the Black Panther Party and the American Indian Movement*. Cambridge, MA: South End Press, 2002.

Churchill, Ward, and Jim Vander Wall. *The Cointelpro Papers: Documents from the FBI's Secret Wars against Dissent in the United States*. 1990. Cambridge, MA: South End Press, 2002.

Clark, Dennis. *The Irish in Philadelphia: Ten Generations of Urban Experience*. Philadelphia, PA: Temple University Press, 1973.

Bibliography

Clark, J. Desmond. "The Spread of Food Production in Sub-Saharan Africa." *Journal of African History* 3, no. 2 (1962): 211–28.

Clarke, John Henrik. *African People in World History*. Lecture, May 1993. Baltimore, MD: Black Classic Press, 1993.

Clarke, John Henrik. "John Henrik Clarke: A Great and Mighty Walk." Videotaped lecture. Black Dot Media, 1996.

Coffin, Levi. *Reminiscences of Levi Coffin, The Reputed President of the Underground Railroad*. Cincinnati, OH: Robert Clarke, 1898. New York: Arno Press and The New York Times, 1968.

Commemorative Biographical Encyclopedia of Dauphin County, Pennsylvania, Containing Sketches of Prominent and Representative Citizens, and Many of the Early Scotch-Irish and German Settlers. Chambersburg, PA: J. M. Runk, 1896.

Connolly, Harold X. "Blacks in Brooklyn, from 1900 to 1960." PhD dissertation, New York University, New York, February 1972.

Conrad, Sharron Wilkins. "Nineteenth-Century Philadelphia Caterer Thomas J. Dorsey." *American Visions* 15, no. 4 (August/September 2000): 36–38.

Constable, W. G. "A Cranach from the Sumner Collection; With Some Notes on Charles Sumner as a Collector." *Bulletin of the Museum of Fine Arts* 41, no. 246 (December 1943): 64–68.

Cook, Benjamin F. *History of the Twelfth Massachusetts Volunteers*. Boston, MA: Twelfth (Webster) Regiment Association, 1882.

Coughtry, Jay. *The Notorious Triangle: Rhode Island and the African Slave Trade, 1700–1807*. Philadelphia, PA: Temple University Press, 1981.

Creel, Margaret Washington. *"A Peculiar People": Slave Religion and Community—Culture among the Gullahs*. New York: New York University Press, 1988.

Cromwell, Adelaide M. *The Other Brahmins: Boston's Black Upper Class, 1750–1950*. Fayetteville: University of Arkansas Press, 1994.

Curry, Leonard P. *The Free Black in Urban America, 1800–1850: The Shadow of the Dream*. Chicago: University of Chicago Press, 1981.

Curtin, Philip D. *Economic Change in Precolonial Africa: Senegambia in the Era of the Slave Trade*. Vol. 1. Madison: University of Wisconsin Press, 1975.

Custis, G. W. Parke. *Recollections and Private Memoirs of Washington, of Arlington*. Washington, DC: William H. Moore, 1859.

Dabney, Wendell P. *Cincinnati's Colored Citizens: Historical, Sociological and Biographical*. Cincinnati, OH: Dabney, 1926.

Daniels, Douglas Henry. *Pioneer Urbanites: A Social and Cultural History of Black San Francisco*. Philadelphia, PA: Temple University Press, 1980.

Daniels, John. *In Freedom's Birthplace: A Study of the Boston Negroes*. New York: Johnson Reprint Corporation, 1968.

Davidson, Basil. *Africa in History*. New York: Macmillan, 1974.

Davidson, Basil. *African Civilization Revisited*. Trenton, NJ: Africa World Press, 1991.

Davidson, Basil. *The African Genius*. Boston, MA: Little, Brown, 1969.

Davidson, Basil. *The African Past: Chronicles from Antiquity to Modern Times*. 1964. New York: Grosset & Dunlap, 1967.

Davidson, Basil. *The Lost Cities of Africa*. Boston, MA: Atlantic–Little Brown, 1959.

Davidson, Basil, and F. K. Buah. *A History of West Africa to the Nineteenth Century*. Garden City, NY: Doubleday, 1966.

Deetz, Keeley Fanto. *Bound to the Fire: How Virginia's Enslaved Cooks Helped Invent American Cuisine*. Lexington: University Press of Kentucky, 2017.

deGraft-Johnson, J. C. *African Glory*. 1954. Baltimore, MD: Black Classic Press, 1986.

Delany, Martin Robison. *The Condition, Elevation, Emigration, and Destiny of the Colored People of the United States. Political Considered*. New York: Arno Press and the New York Times, 1968.

Del Grande, Nino. "Prehistoric Iron Smelting in Africa." *Natural History* (September–October 1932): 531–39.

Dexter, Franklin Bowditch, ed. *The Literary Diary of Ezra Stiles, D.D., LL.D.* 2 vols. New York: Charles Scribner's Sons, 1901.

Diop, Cheikh Anta. *The African Origin of Civilization: Myth or Reality*. New York: Lawrence Hill Books, 1974.

Diop, Cheikh Anta. *Precolonial Black Africa*. Brooklyn, NY: Lawrence Hill Books, 1987.

Donald, David. *Charles Sumner and the Rights of Man*. New York: Alfred A. Knopf, 1970.

Donald, David Herbert. *Charles Sumner and the Coming of the Civil War*. New York: Knopf, 1960.

Douglass, Frederick. *My Bondage and My Freedom*. New York: Miller, Orton & Mulligan, 1855.

Douglass, William. *Annals of the First African Church, in the United States of America: Now Styled the African Episcopal Church of St. Thomas, Philadelphia, in its Connection With the Early Struggles of the Colored People to Improve Their Condition*. Philadelphia, PA: King & Baird, Printers, 1862.

Douty, Esther M. *Forten the Sailmaker: Pioneer Champion of Negro Rights*. Chicago: Rand McNally, 1968.

Downing, George T. "The Africo-American Force in America." *A.M.E. Church Review* 1 (October 1884): 157–62.

Downing, George T. "A Sketch of the Life and Times of Thomas Downing." *A.M.E. Church Review* (April 1887): 402–10.

Downing, George T. "Will the General Assembly Put Down Caste Schools?" Providence, RI: N.p., 1857.

Du Bois, W. E. B. *Black Reconstruction in America: An Essay Toward a History of the Part Which Black Folk Played in the Attempt to Reconstruct Democracy in America, 1860–1880*. 1935. New York: Atheneum, 1977.

Du Bois, W. E. B. *The Gift of Black Folk*. Millwood, NY: Kraus-Thomson, 1975.

Du Bois, W. E. B. *The Philadelphia Negro*. New York: Oxford University Press, 2007.

Duncan, Russell. *Freedom's Shore: Tunis Campbell and the Georgia Freedmen*. Athens: University of Georgia Press, 1986.

Bibliography

Durham, John Stephen. "The Labor Unions and the Negro." *Atlantic Monthly* 81 (January 1989): 222–31.

Durkee, Cornelius E. *Reminiscences of Saratoga.* Saratoga Springs, NY: The Saratogian, 1927–1928.

Elsbree, Oliver Wendell. "Samuel Hopkins and His Doctrine of Benevolence." *New England Quarterly* 8, no. 4 (December 1935): 534–50.

Escoffier, Auguste. *Auguste Escoffier: Memories of My Life.* New York: Van Nostrand Reinhold, 1997.

Evans, Louis. *Louis Evans' Creole Cookbook.* 1991. Gretna, LA: Pelican, 2006.

Fabens, Marie E. *Hamilton Hall.* Salem, MA: The Old Salem Corner Studio, c. 1920.

"Favored Recipes of Some Top Black Chefs." *Ebony* (August 1972): 160–64.

Fehrenbacher, Don E. *Slavery, Law, and Politics: The Dred Scott Case in Historical Perspective.* New York: Oxford University Press, 1981.

Fehrenbacher, Don Edward. *The Dred Scott Case: Its Significance in American Law and Politics.* New York: Oxford University Press, 1978.

Ferguson, John. *Memoir of The Life and Character of Rev. Samuel Hopkins, D.D. Formerly Pastor of the First Congregational Church in Newport, Rhode Island.* Boston, MA: Leonard W. Kimball, 1830.

Field, Phyllis F. *The Politics of Race in New York: The Struggle for Black Suffrage in the Civil War Era.* Ithaca, NY: Cornell University Press, 1982.

Field, Phyllis Frances. "The Struggle for Black Suffrage in New York State, 1846–1869." PhD dissertation, Cornell University, Ithaca, New York, 1974.

Fields, Barbara Jeanne. *Slavery and Freedom on the Middle Ground: Maryland during the Nineteenth Century.* New Haven, CT: Yale University Press, 1985.

Fields, Joseph E., comp. *"Worthy Partner": The Papers of Martha Washington.* Westport, CT: Greenwood Press, 1994.

Fisher, Abby. *What Mrs. Fisher Knows About Old Southern Cooking, Soups, Pickles, Preserves, Etc.* 1881. Bedford, MA: Applewood Books, 1995.

Fitchett, E. Horace. "The Free Negro in Charleston, South Carolina." PhD dissertation, Department of Sociology, University of Chicago, Chicago, June 1950.

Fitchett, E. Horace. "The Status of the Free Negro in Charleston, South Carolina, and His Descendants in Modern Society: Statement of the Problem." *Journal of Negro History* 32, no. 4 (October 1947): 430–51.

Fitchett, E. Horace. "The Traditions of the Free Negro in Charleston, South Carolina." *Journal of Negro History* 25, no. 2 (April 1940): 139–52.

Fitzpatrick, John C., ed. *The Writings of George Washington, from the Original Manuscript Sources, 1745–1799.* Vols. 27–28, 31, 35–37. Washington, DC: US Government Printing Office, 1931–1944.

Fitzpatrick, Sandra, and Maria R. Goodwin. *The Guide to Black Washington: Places and Events of Historical and Cultural Significance in the Nation's Capital.* New York: Hippocrene Books, 1999.

Fleming, G. James, and Bernice Dutrieuille Shelton. "Fine Food for Philadelphia." *The Crisis*. (April 1938): 107, 114.

Flinn, Kathleen. "Savor the Flavor of Louisiana." *AAA Going Places* (March/April 2005): n.p.

Folse, John D. *The Evolution of Cajun and Creole Cuisine*. Gonzales, LA: Chef John Folse, 1989.

Foner, Philip S., ed. *Frederick Douglass: Selected Speeches and Writings*. Chicago: Lawrence Hill Books, 1999.

Foner, Philip S. *History of Black Americans, Volume 2. From the Emergence of the Cotton Kingdom to the Eve of the Compromise of 1850*. Westport, CT: Greenwood Press, 1983.

Foner, Philip S., ed. *The Life and Writings of Frederick Douglass*. Vol. 1. New York: International Publishers, 1950.

Foner, Philip S., ed. *The Life and Writings of Frederick Douglass*. Vol. 4. New York: International Publishers, 1955.

Foner, Philip S. "William P. Powell: Militant Champion of Black Seamen." In *Essays in Afro-American History*, edited by Philip S. Foner, 88–111. Philadelphia, PA: Temple University Press, 1978.

Foner, Philip S., and Ronald L. Lewis, eds. *The Black Worker: A Documentary History from Colonial Times to the Present*. 2 vols. Philadelphia, PA: Temple University Press, 1978.

Forney, Col. John W. "Terrapin." In *The Epicure*, 30, 32. New York: H.K. & F.B. Thurber, 1879.

Forten, James. "Letters From a Man of Colour, On a Late Bill Before the Senate of Pennsylvania." In *Works of D. Augustus Straker, John Fortren [i.e. James Forten] et al.* Philadelphia, PA, 1813.

Forten, James Jr. "An Address Delivered Before the Ladies' Anti-Slavery Society of Philadelphia." In *Works of D. Augustus Straker, John Fortren [i.e. James Forten] et al.* Philadelphia, PA: Merrihew and Gunn, 1836.

"FOSSETT, Once Slave of Jefferson and Prominent Man of the Colored Race, Died at His Home after Life of Activity." *Cincinnati Enquirer*, August 13, 1901.

Fowler, Damon Lee, ed. *Dining at Monticello: In Good Taste and Abundance*. Chapel Hill: University of North Carolina Press, 2005.

Fox, William S., and Mae G. Banner. "Social and Economic Contexts of Folklore Variants: The Case of Potato Chip Legends." *Western Folklore* 42, no. 2 (April 1983): 114–26.

Franklin, John Hope. "The Enforcement of the Civil Rights Act of 1875." *Prologue: The Journal of the National Archives* 6, no. 4 (Winter 1974): 225–35.

Franklin, John Hope, and Alfred A. Moss Jr. *From Slavery to Freedom: A History of Negro Americans*. 1947. 6th ed. New York: Alfred A. Knopf, 1988.

Fraser, Charles. *Reminiscences of Charleston*. Charleston, SC: John Russell, 1854.

Freeman, Rhoda G. "The Free Negro in New York City in the Era before the Civil War." PhD dissertation, Columbia University, New York, 1966.

Bibliography

Freeman, Rhoda Golden. *The Free Negro in New York City in the Era before the Civil War.* New York: Garland Publishing, 1994.

Frobenius, Leo. *The Voice of Africa.* 1913. London: Benjamin Blom, 1968.

Gannon, Fred. *Nicknames and Neighborhoods: An Album of Old Pictures of Old Salem.* Salem, MA: Salem Book, 1940s.

Gantt, Jesse Edward Jr., and Veronica Davis Gerald. *The Ultimate Gullah Cookbook.* Beaufort, SC: Sands Publishing, 2002.

Garrison, William Lloyd. "Spirited Meeting of the Colored Citizens of Philadelphia." *The Liberator* 27, no. 15 (April 10, 1857): 57–60.

Gates, Henry Louis, and Kwame Anthony Appiah, eds. *Africana: The Encyclopedia of the African and African American Experience.* New York: Oxford University Press, 2005.

Gates, Henry Louis, and Evelyn Higginbotham, eds. *The African American National Biography.* New York: Oxford University Press, 2008.

Gatewood, Willard B. *Aristocrats of Color: The Black Elite, 1880–1920.* Bloomington: Indiana University Press, 1990.

Gatewood, Willard B. Jr. "Aristocrats of Color: South and North, the Black Elite, 1880–1920." *Journal of Southern History* 54, no. 1 (February 1988): 3–20.

Geffen, Elizabeth M. "Violence in Philadelphia in the 1840s and 1850s." *Pennsylvania History* 36, no. 4 (October 1969): 381–410.

Giraud, Marcel. *A History of French Louisiana.* Vol.2. Baton Rouge: Louisiana State University Press, 1991.

Giraud, Marcel. *A History of French Louisiana.* Vol. 5. Baton Rouge: Louisiana State University Press, 1991.

Greene, Lorenzo J. *The Negro in Colonial New England.* New York: Columbia University Press, 1942.

Greenthal, Kathryn. "Augustus Saint-Gaudens and the Shaw Memorial." In Blatt, Brown, and Yacovone, *Hope & Glory,* 116–29.

Grimke, Francis J., and M. F. Perkins. "Communications." *Journal of Negro History* 21, no. 1 (January 1936): 56–60.

Grossman, Lawrence. "George T. Downing and Desegregation of Rhode Island Public Schools, 1855–1866." *Rhode Island History* 36, no. 4 (November 1977): 99–105.

Gurney, John Joseph. *A Visit to North America, Described in Familiar Letters to Amelia Opie.* Norwich: Joseph Fletcher, 1841.

Halford, Joan Montgomery. "A Different Mirror: A Conversation with Ronald Takaki." *Educational Leadership* 56, no. 7 (April 1999): 8–13.

Hall, Gwendolyn Midlo. *Africans in Colonial Louisiana: The Development of Afro-Creole Culture in the Eighteenth Century.* Baton Rouge: Louisiana State University Press, 1992.

Hall, Gwendolyn Midlo. "Myths about Creole Culture in Louisiana." *Louisiana Cultural Vistas* (Summer 2001): 79–89.

Hardy, Charles Ashley III. "Race and Opportunity: Black Philadelphia during the Era of the Great Migration, 1916–1930." PhD dissertation, Temple University, Philadelphia, PA, August 1989.

Harmon, J. H. Jr. "The Negro as a Local Business Man." *Journal of Negro History* 14, no. 2 (April 1929): 116–55.

Harris, Leslie M. *In the Shadow of Slavery: African Americans in New York City, 1626–1863.* Chicago: University of Chicago Press, 2003.

Harris, Robert L. Jr. "Daniel Murray and the Encyclopedia of the Colored Race." *Phylon* 37, no. 3 (1976): 270–82.

Haskin, Frederic J. "The Romance of Fraunces' Tavern." *St. Louis Globe Democrat.* August 10, 1916.

Hayes, Floyd W. "The African Presence in America before Columbus." *Black World* 22, no. 9 (July 1973): 4–22.

Herskovits, Melville. "What Has Africa Given America?" *New Republic* 84 (September 4, 1935).

Herskovits, Melville J. *The Myth of the Negro Past.* 1941, 1958. Boston, MA: Beacon Press, 1990.

Hewitt, John H. "Mr. Downing and His Oyster House: The Life and Good Works of an African-American Entrepreneur." *New York History* (July 1993): 229–52.

Hewitt, John H. "The Sacking of St. Philip's Church, New York." *Anglican and Episcopal History: Magazine of the Protestant Episcopal Church* 49 (March 1988): 7–20.

Hewitt, John H. "The Search for Elizabeth Jennings, Heroine of a Sunday Afternoon in New York City." *New York History* (October 1990): 387–415.

Higginbotham, A. Leon Jr. *In the Matter of Color: Race and the American Legal Process, the Colonial Period.* Oxford: Oxford University Press, 1980.

Higginbotham, A. Leon Jr. "Race, Sex, Education and Missouri Jurisprudence: *Shelley v. Kraemer* in a Historical Perspective." *Washington University Law Quarterly* 67 (1989): 673–708.

Higginbotham, A. Leon Jr. "Racism and the Early American Legal Process, 1619–1896." *Annals of the American Academy of Political and Social Science* 407 (May 1973): 1–17.

Higginbotham, A. Leon Jr. *Shades of Freedom: Racial Politics and Presumptions of the American Legal Process.* New York: Oxford University Press, 1996.

Higginbotham, A. Leon Jr., F. Michael Higginbotham, and S. Sandile Ngcobo. "De Jure Housing Segregation in the United States and South Africa: The Difficult Pursuit for Racial Justice." *University of Illinois Law Review* 4 (1990): 763–877.

Higginbotham, A. Leon Jr., and Anne F. Jacobs. "The 'Law Only as an Enemy': The Legitimization of Racial Powerlessness through the Colonial and Antebellum Criminal Laws of Virginia." *North Carolina Law Review* 70, no. 4 (April 1992): 969–1070.

Higginbotham, Evelyn Brooks. "African-American Women's History and the Metalanguage of Race." *Signs: Journal of Women in Culture and Society* 17, no. 2 (Winter 1992): 251–74.

Hilliard, David, and Donald Weise, eds. *The Huey P. Newton Reader.* New York: Seven Stories Press, 2002.

Bibliography

Hines, Mary Anne, Gordon Marshall, and William Woys Weaver. *The Larder Invaded: Reflections on Three Centuries of Philadelphia Food and Drink*. Philadelphia, PA: The Library Company of Philadelphia and the Historical Society of Pennsylvania, 1987.

Hinks, Peter P. *To Awaken My Afflicted Brethren: David Walker and the Problem of Antebellum Slave Resistance*. University Park, PA: Pennsylvania State University Press, 1997.

Hirschfeld, Fritz. *George Washington and Slavery: A Documentary Portrayal*. Columbia: University of Missouri Press, 1997.

Hodges, Graham Russell Gao. *David Ruggles: A Radical Black Abolitionist and the Underground Railroad in New York City*. Chapel Hill: University of North Carolina Press, 2010.

Hoff, Henry B. "Frans Abramse Van Salee and His Descendants: A Colonial Black Family in New York and New Jersey." *New York Genealogical and Biographical Record* 121, no. 2 (April 1990): 65–71; (July 1990): 157–61; (October 1990): 205–11.

Holloway, Joseph E., ed. *Africanisms in American Culture*. Bloomington: Indiana University Press, 1990.

Hopkins, Samuel, Edwards Amasa Park, and Sewall Harding. *The Works of Samuel Hopkins, D.D., First Pastor of The Church in Great Barrington, Mass., Afterwards Pastor of The First Congregational Church in Newport, R.I. With A Memoir of His Life and Character. Volume I*. Boston, MA: Doctrinal Tract and Book Society, 1852.

Horton, James Oliver, and Lois E. Horton. *Black Bostonians: Family Life and Community Struggle in the Antebellum North*. 1979. New York: Holmes and Meier, 1999.

Hotaling, Edward. *The Great Black Jockeys: The Lives and Times of the Men Who Dominated America's First National Sport*. Rocklin, CA: Forum/Prima Publishing, 1999.

Houston, Lynn. "Serpent's Teeth in the Kitchen of Meaning: A Theory of South African Culinary Historiography." *Safundi: The Journal of South African and American Studies* 1, no. 1 (2000): 1–9.

Ingersoll, Ernest. "A Report on the Oyster Industry of the United States." In *The History and Present Condition of the Fishery Industries*, edited by George Brown Goode, 30–42. Washington, DC: US Government Printing Office, 1881.

Ingham, J. N., and L. B. Feldman. *African American Business Leaders: A Biographical Dictionary*. Westport, CT: Greenwood Press, 1994.

Jackson, Donald, and Dorothy Twohig, eds. *The Diaries of George Washington*. Vol. 4. Charlottesville: University Press of Virginia, 1978.

Jackson, Francis. *A History of the Early Settlement of Newton County of Middlesex Massachusetts, From 1639 to 1800*. Boston, MA: Stacy and Richardson, 1854.

Jackson, John G. *Introduction to African Civilization*. Secaucus, NJ: Citadel Press, 1970.

Jacob, Kathryn Allamong. *King of the Lobby: The Life and Times of Sam Ward, Man-About-Washington in the Gilded Age*. Baltimore, MD: Johns Hopkins University Press, 2010.

James, Kenneth. *Escoffier: The King of Chefs*. London: Hambledon and London, 2002.

Jeffreys, M. D. W. "Pre-Columbian Negroes in America." *Scientia* 47, no. 88 (1953): 202–18, and supplement, 113–28.

Johnson, Guion. *Ante-bellum North Carolina: A Social History*. Chapel Hill: University of North Carolina Press, 1937.

Johnson, James Weldon. *Black Manhattan*. New York: Atheneum, 1968.

Johnson, James Weldon. "Harlem: The Culture Capital." In *The New Negro,* edited by Alain Locke, 301–11. New York: Albert and Charles Boni, 1925.

Jones, Howard. *Mutiny on the Amistad: The Saga of a Slave Revolt and Its Impact on American Abolition, Law, and Diplomacy*. New York: Oxford University Press, 1987.

Jones, Jacqueline. *Labor of Love, Labor of Sorrow: Black Women, Work and the Family, from Slavery to the Present*. New York: Basic Books, 1985.

Jordan, Winthrop. *White over Black*. Chapel Hill: University of North Carolina Press, 1968.

Josephson, Matthew. *Union House, Union Bar: The History of the Hotel and Restaurant Employees and Bartenders International Union, AFL-CIO*. New York: Random House, 1956.

Kallon, Zainabu Kpaka. *Zainabu's African Cookbook, with Food and Stories*. New York: Citadel Press, 2004.

Kelker, Luther Reily. *History of Dauphin County, Pennsylvania*. Vol. 1. New York: Lewis, 1907.

Kieran, John. *A Natural History of New York City: A Personal Report after Fifty Years of Study and Enjoyment of Wildlife within the Boundaries of Greater New York*. Boston MA: Houghton Mifflin, 1959.

Kimble-Ellis, Sonya. "Mixing Things Up with Chef Joe Brown." *American Visions* 15, no. 2 (April–May 2000): 36–37.

King, Wilma. "'Mad' Enough to Kill: Enslaved Women, Murder, and Southern Courts." *Journal of African American History* 92, no. 1 (Winter 2007): 37–56.

Koger, Larry. *Black Slaveowners: Free Black Slave Masters in South Carolina, 1790–1860*. Jefferson, NC: McFarland, 1985.

Kranzberg, Melvin. *The Siege of Paris, 1870–1871: A Political and Social History*. Ithaca, NY: Cornell University Press, 1950.

Kurin, Richard, and Marjorie Hunt. "In the Service of the Presidency." *American Visions* 10, no. 1 (February 1995): 48–51.

Lam, Francis. "What Edna Lewis Knew." *New York Times Magazine* (November 1, 2015): MM44–51, MM73, MM75.

Lane, Roger. *Roots of Violence in Black Philadelphia, 1860–1900*. Cambridge, MA: Harvard University Press, 1986.

Lane, Roger. *William Dorsey's Philadelphia and Ours: On the Past and Future of the Black City in America*. New York: Oxford University Press, 1991.

Lawrence, Harold G. "African Explorers of the New World." *The Crisis* (June–July 1962): 321–32.

Leech, Margaret. *Reveille in Washington, 1860–1865*. New York: Time Incorporated, 1962.

Lemons, J. Stanley, and Michael A. McKenna. "Re-enfranchisement of Rhode Island Negroes." *Rhode Island History* 30, no. 1 (February 1971): 3–13.

Bibliography

Lester, C. Edwards. *Life and Public Services of Charles Sumner*. New York: United States Publishing, 1874.

Lewis, Edna. *In Pursuit of Flavor*. New York: Knopf, 1988.

Lewis, Edna. *The Taste of Country Cooking*. New York: Knopf, 1976.

Lindsay, Arnett G. "The Economic Condition of the Negroes of New York prior to 1861." *Journal of Negro History* 6, no. 2 (April 1921): 190–99.

Littlefield, Daniel C. *Rice and Slaves: Ethnicity and the Slave Trade in Colonial South Carolina*. Chicago: University of Illinois Press, 1991.

Litwack, Leon F. *North of Slavery: The Negro in the Free States, 1790–1860*. Chicago: University of Chicago Press, 1961.

Litwack, Leon F. "The White Man's Fear of the Educated Negro: How the Negro Was Fitted for His Natural and Logical Calling." *Journal of Blacks in Higher Education* 20 (Summer 1998): 100–108.

Logan, Rayford W. *The Betrayal of the Negro: From Rutherford B. Hayes to Woodrow Wilson*. New York: Macmillan, 1965.

Logan, Rayford W. "The Negro in the Quasi War, 1798–1800." *Negro History Bulletin* 14, no. 6 (March, 1951): 128–32, 143.

Logan, Rayford W., and Michael R. Winston, eds. *Dictionary of American Negro Biography*. New York: W. W. Norton, 1982.

Logan, Shirley Wilson. *"We Are Coming": The Persuasive Discourse of Nineteenth-Century Black Women*. Carbondale: Southern Illinois University Press, 1999.

Lomax, Michael E. *Black Baseball Entrepreneurs, 1860–1901*. Syracuse, NY: Syracuse University Press, 2003.

Lossing, Benson J. *Recollections and Private Memoirs of Washington, By His Adopted Son, George Washington Parke Custis, With A Memoir of the Author, By His Daughter; and Illustrative and Explanatory Notes*. New York: Derby & Jackson, 1860.

Lowry, Charles D., and John F. Marszalek. *Encyclopedia of African-American Civil Rights: From Emancipation to the Present*. Westport, CT: Greenwood Press, 1992.

Maccannon, E. A. *Commanders of the Dining Room: Biographic Sketches and Portraits of Successful Head Waiters*. New York: Gwendolyn Publishing, 1904.

MacKenzie, Clyde L. Jr. "Biographic Memoir of Ernest Ingersoll: Naturalist, Shellfish Scientist, and Author." *Marine Fisheries Review* 53, no. 3 (1991): 23–29.

Magubane, Bernard. *South Africa: From Soweto to Uitenhage: The Political Economy of the South African Revolution*. Trenton, NJ: Africa World Press, 1989.

Man, Albon P. Jr. "Labor Competition and the New York Draft Riots of 1863." *Journal of Negro History* 36, no. 4 (October 1951): 375–405.

Maryland Heritage Committee. *300 Years of Black Cooking in St. Mary's County Maryland*. St. Mary's County, MD: St. Mary's County Community Affairs and the Maryland Heritage Committees, 1983.

Mauro, Frederic. *L'Expansion européenne, 1600–1870*. Paris: Presses Universitaires de France, 1964.

McAdam, Roger Williams. *The Old Fall River Line*. New York: Stephen Daye Press, 1955.

McAdam, Roger Williams. *Priscilla of Fall River*. New York: Stephen Daye Press, 1956.

McFeely, William S. *Frederick Douglass*. New York: W. W. Norton, 1991.

McKitrick, Eric L. *Andrew Johnson and Reconstruction*. 1964. Chicago: Phoenix Books/The University of Chicago Press, 1960.

McLeod, Stephen A., ed. *Dining with the Washingtons: Historic Recipes, Entertainment, and Hospitality from Mount Vernon*. Mount Vernon, VA: Mount Vernon Ladies' Association, distributed by the University of North Carolina Press at Chapel Hill, 2011.

McManus, Edgar J. *A History of Negro Slavery in New York*. Syracuse, NY: Syracuse University Press, 1966.

McPherson, James M. "Abolitionists and the Civil Rights Act of 1875." *Journal of American History* 52, no. 3 (December 1965): 493–510.

Mignon, Francois, and Clementine Hunter. *Melrose Plantation Cookbook*. Natchitoches, LA: Francois Mignon, 1956.

Miller, Adrian. *The President's Kitchen Cabinet: The Story of the African Americans Who Have Fed Our First Families, from the Washingtons to the Obamas*. Chapel Hill: University of North Carolina Press, 2018.

Mills, Quincy T. *Cutting along the Color Line: Black Barbers and Barber Shops in America*. Philadelphia: University of Pennsylvania Press, 2013.

Minton, Henry M. *Early History of Negroes in Business in Philadelphia*. Read Before the American Historical Society. Nashville, TN: A.M.E.S.S. Union, 1913.

Miracle, Marvin P. "The Introduction and Spread of Maize in Africa." *Journal of African History* 6, no. 1 (1965): 39–55.

Mjagkij, Nina. *Organizing Black America: An Encyclopedia of African American Associations*. New York: Garland Publishing, 2001.

Morgan, Edmund S. *The Gentle Puritan: A Life of Ezra Stiles, 1727–1795*. New Haven, CT: Yale University Press, 1962.

Morgan, W. B. "The Forest and Agriculture in West Africa." *Journal of African History* 3, no. 2 (1962): 235–39.

Moses, Wilson Jeremiah. *Alexander Crummell: A Study of Civilization and Discontent*. New York: Oxford University Press, 1989.

Moses, Wilson Jeremiah. *The Golden Age of Black Nationalism, 1850–1925*. New York: Oxford University Press, 1988.

Mosley, Lois A. H. *Sandy Ground Memories*. Staten Island, NY: The Staten Island Historical Society, 2003.

Murdock, George P. *Africa, Its Peoples, and Their Culture History*. New York: McGraw-Hill Book, 1959.

Murray, Daniel. "Bibliographia-Africania." *Voice of the Negro* 1 (May 1904): 186–91.

Murray, Daniel. "The Overthrow of the Jim Crow Car Laws." *Voice of the Negro* 3 (July 1906): 478, 520–23.

Mutunhu, Tendai. "Africa: The Birthplace of Iron Mining." *Negro History Bulletin* 44, no. 1 (January–March 1981): 5, 20.

Bibliography

Nash, Gary B. *Forging Freedom: The Formation of Philadelphia's Black Community, 1720–1840*. Cambridge, MA: Harvard University Press, 1988.

Nash, June. "The Cost of Violence." *Journal of Black Studies* 4, no. 2 (December 1973): 153–83.

National Research Council. *Lost Crops of Africa. Volume 1: Grains*. Washington, DC: National Academies Press, 1996.

National Research Council. *Lost Crops of Africa. Volume 2: Vegetables*. Washington, DC: National Academies Press, 2006.

National Research Council. *Lost Crops of Africa. Volume 3: Fruits*. Washington, DC: National Academies Press, 2008.

Nell, William C. *The Colored Patriots of the American Revolution*. New York: Arno Press and The New York Times, 1968.

Nevins, Allan, ed. *The Diary of Philip Hone, Volume II, 1828–1851*. New York: Dodd, Mead, 1927.

Nevins, Allan, ed. *Polk: The Diary of a President, 1845–1849*. London: Longmans, Green, 1929.

Nevins, Allan, and Milton Halsey Thomas, eds. *The Diary of George Templeton Strong: Volume I, Young Man in New York, 1835–1849*. New York: Macmillan, 1952.

Nevins, Allan, and Milton Halsey Thomas, eds. *The Diary of George Templeton Strong: Volume II, The Turbulent Fifties, 1850–1859*. New York: Macmillan, 1952.

Nevins, Allan, and Milton Halsey Thomas, eds. *The Diary of George Templeton Strong: Volume III, The Civil War, 1860–1865*. New York: Macmillan, 1952.

Nevins, Allan, and Milton Halsey Thomas, eds. *The Diary of George Templeton Strong. Volume IV, Post War Years, 1865–1875*. New York: Macmillan, 1952.

Newport Historical Society. "Some Old Papers relating to the Newport Slave Trade." *Bulletin of the Newport Historical Society* 62 (July 1927): 10 31.

Newton, Huey P. *Revolutionary Suicide*. 1973. New York: Penguin Books, 2009.

Newton, Huey P. *War against the Panthers: A Study of Repression in America*. New York: Harlem River Press/Writer and Readers Publishing, 1998.

Nogee, Joseph. "The Prigg Case and Fugitive Slavery, 1842–1850: Part I." *Journal of Negro History* 39, no. 3 (July 1954): 185–205.

Norton, Mary Beth, Carol Sheriff, and David M. Katzman. *A People and a Nation: A History of the United States*. Vol. 2. Staten Island: Cengage Learning, 2010.

Oberg, Barbara B., ed. *The Papers of Thomas Jefferson: 1 July to 12 November 1802*. Princeton, NJ: Princeton University Press, 2012.

Oden, Gloria C. "The Journal of Charlotte L. Forten: The Salem-Philadelphia Years (1854–1862) Reexamined." *Essex Institute Historical Collections* 119, no. 2 (April 1983): 119–36.

O'Reilly, Kenneth. *"Racial Matters": The FBI's Secret File on Black America, 1960–1972*. New York: Macmillan, 1989.

Osae, T. A., S. N. Nwabara, and A. T. O. Odunsi. *A Short History of West Africa A.D. 1000 to the Present*. 1968. New York: Hill and Wang, 1973.

Osofsky, Gilbert. *Harlem: The Making of a Ghetto, Negro New York, 1890–1930*. New York: Harper and Row, 1968.

Paige, Lucius R. *History of Cambridge, Massachusetts, 1630–1877, With a Genealogical Register*. Boston, MA: H. O. Houghton, 1877.

Parker, Jane Marsh. "Reminiscences of Frederick Douglass." *Outlook* 51, no. 14 (April 6, 1895): 552.

Parkinson, James W. *American Dishes at the Centennial*. Philadelphia, PA: King & Baird, Printers, 1874.

Patterson, William L., ed. *We Charge Genocide: The Historic Petition to the United Nations for Relief from a Crime of the United States Government Against the Negro People*. Civil Rights Congress, 1951. New York: International Publishers, 1970.

Payne, Daniel Alexander. *Recollections of Seventy Years*. 1888. New York: Arno Press, 1968.

Pennypacker, Samuel W. "The Settlement of Germantown, and the Causes Which Led to It." *Pennsylvania Magazine of History and Biography* 4, no. 1 (1880): 1–41.

Pierce, Edward L. *Memoir and Letters of Charles Sumner*. Vol. 4. Boston, MA: Roberts Brothers, 1893.

Piersen, William D. *Black Yankees: The Development of an Afro-American Subculture in Eighteenth-Century New England*. Amherst: University of Massachusetts Press, 1988.

Porter, Dorothy B. "Early Manuscript Letters Written by Negroes: James Forten; John T. Hilton; William Wells Brown." *Journal of Negro History* 24, no. 2. (April 1939): 199–210.

Porter, Dorothy B. "The Organized Educational Activities of Negro Literary Societies, 1828–1848." *Journal of Negro Education* 4 (October 1936): 555–76.

Porter, Dorothy Burnett. "The Remonds of Salem, Massachusetts: A Nineteenth-Century Family Revisited." *Proceedings of the American Antiquarian Society* 95 (1985): 259–95.

Powell, Clora. "Black-Owned Businesses in Early Philadelphia." *Continuum* (February 1989): 2–3.

Powers, Bernard E. Jr. *Black Charlestonians: A Social History, 1822–1885*. Fayetteville: University of Arkansas Press, 1994.

Price, Edith Ballinger. "The Court End of Town." *Bulletin of the Newport Historical Society* 108 (April 1962): 4–23.

Provine, Dorothy S. "The Economic Position of the Free Blacks in the District of Columbia, 1800–1860." *Journal of Negro History* 58, no. 1 (1973): 61–72.

Puckrein, Gary. "The Science of Service." *American Visions* 13, no. 5 (October–November 1998): 34–35.

Purdy, Jedediah S. "People as Resources: Recruitment and Reciprocity in the Freedom-Promoting Approach to Property." *Duke Law Journal* 56, no. 1047 (February 2007): 1047–117.

Purvis, Robert. *Appeal of Forty Thousand Citizens, Threatened with Disfranchisement, To the People of Pennsylvania*. Philadelphia, PA: Merrihew and Gunn, 1838.

Bibliography

Purvis, Robert. *Remarks on the Life and Character of James Forten, Delivered at Bethel Church, March 30, 1842*. Philadelphia, PA: Merrihew and Thompson, Printers, 1842.

Quarles, Benjamin. *Black Abolitionists*. London: Oxford University Press, 1969.

Quarles, Benjamin. *Frederick Douglass*. New York: Atheneum, 1968.

Quarles, Benjamin. *Lincoln and the Negro*. New York: Da Capo Press, 1990.

Quarles, Benjamin. *The Negro in the Making of America*. New York: Collier Macmillan, 1969.

Randall, Joe, and Toni Tipton-Martin. *A Taste of Heritage: The New African-American Cuisine*. New York: Macmillan, 1998.

Randolph, Mary. *The Virginia Housewife: Or, Methodical Cook*. Baltimore, MD: John Plaskitt, 1836.

Rapp, David. "The Man in the Library." *American Legacy* (Winter/Spring 2010): 11–12.

Ravenel, Mrs. St. Julien. *Charleston, the Place and the People*. New York: Macmillan, 1906.

Ray, John Michael. "Newport's Golden Age." *Negro History Bulletin* (December 1961): 51–57.

Reinders, Robert C. "The Decline of the New Orleans Free Negro in the Decade before the Civil War." *Journal of Mississippi History* 24, no. 2 (April 1962): 88–98.

Reinders, Robert C. "The Free Negro in the New Orleans Economy, 1850–1860." *Louisiana History* 6 (1965): 273–85.

Render, Sylvia Lyons. "The Black Presence in the Library of Congress." *Library Lectures* 27 (March 1, 1974): 63–79.

Richard, Lena. *Lena Richard's Cook Book*. New Orleans, LA: Rogers Printing, 1939.

Richard, Lena. *New Orleans Cook Book*. Boston, MA: Houghton, Mifflin, 1940.

Richards, Leonard L. *"Gentlemen of Property and Standing": Anti-abolition Mobs in Jacksonian America*. New York: Oxford University Press, 1970.

Richardson, Marilyn. "Taken from Life, Edward M. Bannister, Edmonia Lewis, and the Memorialization of the Fifty-Fourth Massachusetts Regiment." In Blatt, Brown, and Yacovone, *Hope & Glory*, 94–115.

Rigsby, Gregory U. *Alexander Crummell: Pioneer in Nineteenth-Century Pan-African Thought*. Westport, CT: Greenwood Press, 1987.

Ripley, C. Peter, ed. *The Black Abolitionist Papers*. Vols. 1–4. Chapel Hill: University of North Carolina Press, 1985, 1986, 1991.

Roberts, Robert. *The House Servant's Directory, or A Monitor for Private Families: Comprising Hints on the Arrangement and Performance of Servants' Work*. Boston, MA: Munroe & Francis, 1827.

Robinson, Cedric J. "The Black Middle Class and the Mulatto Motion Picture." *Race & Class* 47, no. 1 (2005): 14–34.

Robinson, Sallie Ann. *Cooking the Gullah Way, Morning, Noon, and Night*. Chapel Hill: University of North Carolina Press, 2009.

Robinson, Sallie Ann. *Gullah Home Cooking the Daufuskie Way: Smokin' Joe Butter Beans, Ol' 'Fuskie Fried Crab Rice, Sticky-Bush Blackberry Dumpling, and Other Sea Island Favorites*. Chapel Hill: University of North Carolina Press, 2003.

Rochefoucault-Liancourt, François-Alexandre-Frédéric, duc de la. *Travels Through the United States of America, the Country of the Iroquois and Upper Canada in the Years 1795–1796, and 1797*. London: R. Phillips, 1799.

Ruchames, Louis, ed. *The Letters of William Lloyd Garrison: A House Dividing against Itself, 1836–1840*. Vol. 2. Cambridge, MA: The Belknap Press of Harvard University Press, 1971.

Russell, Mrs. Malinda. *A Domestic Cook Book: Containing a Careful Selection of Useful Receipts for the Kitchen*. Paw Paw, MI: Malinda Russell, 1866.

Salvatore, Nick. *We All Got History: The Memory Books of Amos Webber*. New York: Random House, 1996.

Samuelsson, Marcus, and Osayi Endolyn. *The Rise: Black Cooks and the Soul of American Food: A Cookbook*. New York: Voracious, 2020.

Savage, Kirk. "Uncommon Soldiers: Race, Art, and the Shaw Memorial." In Blatt, Brown, and Yacovone, *Hope & Glory*, 156–67.

Schweninger, Loren. "Antebellum Free Persons of Color in Postbellum Louisiana." *Louisiana History: The Journal of the Louisiana Historical Association* 30, no. 4 (Autumn 1989): 345–64.

Seale, William. "Upstairs and Downstairs: The 19th-Century White House." *American Visions* 10, no. 1 (February 1995): 16–20.

Sée, Henri Eugene. *Economic and Social Conditions in France during the Eighteenth Century*. South Kitchener, Ont.: Batoche Books, 2004.

Selig, Robert A. "Georg Daniel Flohr's Journal: A New Perspective." *Colonial Williamsburg: The Journal of the Colonial Williamsburg Foundation* 25, no. 4 (Summer 1993): 47–53.

Selig, Robert A. "A German Soldier in New England during the Revolutionary War: The Account of Georg Daniel Flohr." *Newport History* 65, part 2, no. 223 (1994): 49–65.

Selig, Robert A. "Private Flohr's America." *American Heritage* 43 (December 1992): 64–71.

Shack, William A. *Harlem in Montmartre: A Paris Jazz Story between the Great Wars*. Berkeley and Los Angeles: University of California Press, 2001.

Shannon, F. A. *America's Economic Growth*. New York: Macmillan, 1940.

Sharpless, Rebecca. *Cooking in Other Women's Kitchens: Domestic Workers in the South, 1865–1960*. Chapel Hill: University of North Carolina Press, 2010.

Shields, David S. *Southern Provisions: The Creation and Revival of a Cuisine*. Chicago: University of Chicago Press, 2015.

Shillington, Kevin. *History of Africa*. 1989. London: MacMillan, 1993.

Simkins, Francis B., and Robert H. Woody. *South Carolina during Reconstruction*. Chapel Hill, NC: University of North Carolina Press, c.1932.

Sinha, Manisha. "The Caning of Charles Sumner: Slavery, Race, and Ideology in the Age of the Civil War." *Journal of the Early Republic* 23, no. 2 (Summer 2003): 233–62.

Sinkler, George. *The Racial Attitudes of American Presidents: From Abraham Lincoln to Theodore Roosevelt*. Garden City, NY: Doubleday, 1971.

Bibliography

Smedley, Robert Clemens. *History of the Underground Railroad in Chester and the Neighboring Counties of Pennsylvania*. Lancaster, PA: Office of the Journal, 1883.

Smith, Anna Bustill. "The Bustill Family." *Journal of Negro History* 10, no. 4 (October 1925): 638–44.

Smith, S. F. *History of Newton, Massachusetts: Town and City From Its Earliest Settlement to the Present Time, 1630–1880*. Boston, MA: American Logotype (J. E. Farwell), 1880.

Smithsonian Anacostia Museum and Center for African American History and Culture. *The Black Washingtonians*. Hoboken, NJ: John Wiley and Sons, 2005.

Solomon, Barbara M. "The Growth of the Population in Essex County, 1850–1860." *Essex Institute Historical Collections* 95 (1959): 82–103.

Spivey, Diane M. "Latin American and Caribbean Food and Cuisine." In *Encyclopedia of African-American Culture and History*, 2:838–44. Detroit, MI: Thomson-Gale and Macmillan Reference USA, 2005.

Spivey, Diane M. *The Peppers, Cracklings, and Knots of Wool Cookbook: The Global Migration of African Cuisine*. Albany: State University of New York Press, 1999.

Spivey, Diane M. "West Africa." In *Encyclopedia of Food and Culture*, 1:41–46. New York: Charles Scribner's Sons, 2003. (Information from this article that is used in this text is correct. However, readers of the article should be aware that numerous factual and grammatical errors, beyond this author's control, were introduced into the article by the publisher.)

Spivey, Donald. *Fire from the Soul: A History of the African-American Struggle*. Durham, NC: Carolina Academic Press, 2003.

Spivey, Donald. *If You Were Only White: The Life of Leroy "Satchel" Paige*. Columbia: University of Missouri Press, 2012.

Sprague, Rosetta Douglass. "Anna Murray-Douglass—My Mother as I Recall Her." *Journal of Negro History* 8, no. 1 (January 1923): 93–101.

Sterkx, H. E. *The Free Negro in Ante-bellum Louisiana*. Rutherford, NJ: Fairleigh Dickinson University Press, 1972.

Sterling, Dorothy, ed. *We Are Your Sisters: Black Women in the Nineteenth Century*. New York: W. W. Norton, 1984.

Stevens, Charles Emery. *Anthony Burns: A History*. Boston, MA: J. P. Jewitt, 1856.

Stevens, Maud L. "Colonel Higginson and His Friends in Newport." *Bulletin of the Newport Historical Society* (April 1924): 1–13.

Still, William. *The Underground Railroad*. 1871. Chicago: Johnson Publishing, 1970.

Suret-Canale, Jean. *Essays on African History, from the Slave Trade to Neocolonialism*. Trenton, NJ: Africa World Press, 1988.

Switala, William J. *Underground Railroad in Pennsylvania*. Mechanicsburg, PA: Stackpole Books, 2001.

Takaki, Ronald. *A Different Mirror: A History of Multicultural America*. Boston, MA: Little Brown, 1993.

Tawes, Helen Avalynne. *My Favorite Maryland Recipes*. New York: Random House, 1964.

Taylor, Elizabeth Dowling. *The Original Black Elite: Daniel Murray and the Story of a Forgotten Era*. New York: Amistad, 2017.

Thomas, Lamont D. "Paul Cuffe: Against the Odds in Vienna, Maryland." *Log of Mystic Seaport* 45, no. 4 (Spring 1994): 103–7.

Tipton-Martin, Toni. *The Jemima Code*. Austin: University of Texas Press, 2015.

Titus, Mary. "Groaning Tables and Spit in the Kettles: Food and Race in the 19th-Century South." *Southern Quarterly* 20, no 2–3 (1992): 13–21.

Tocqueville, Alexis de. *Democracy in America*. New York: Doubleday, 1969.

Trefousse, Hans L. *Andrew Johnson: A Biography*. New York: W. W. Norton, 1989.

Truth, Sojourner. "Ar'n't I A Woman." In *Lift Every Voice: African American Oratory, 1787–1900*, edited by Philip S. Foner and Robert James Branham, 226–29. Tuscaloosa: University of Alabama Press, 1998.

Truth, Sojourner. "Snakes and Geese." In *Lift Every Voice: African American Oratory, 1787–1900*, edited by Philip S. Foner and Robert James Branham, 269–71. Tuscaloosa: University of Alabama Press, 1998.

Turner, Edward R. *The Negro in Pennsylvania*. Washington, DC: American Historical Association, 1911.

Tuttleton, James W. *Thomas Wentworth Higginson*. Boston, MA: Twayne Publishers, 1978.

Twohig, Dorothy, ed. *The Papers of George Washington, Presidential Series*. Vol. 2. Charlottesville: University Press of Virginia, 1987.

US Capitol Historical Society. *We, the People: The Story of the United States Capitol, Its Past and Its Promise*. Washington, DC: US Capitol Historical Society, 2002.

Usrey, Miriam L. "Charles Lenox Remond, Garrison's Ebony Echo World Anti-Slavery Convention, 1840." *Essex Institute Historical Collections* 106 (April 1970): 112–25.

Van Sertima, Ivan. *They Came before Columbus*. New York: Random House, 1976.

Walker, Billie E. "Daniel Alexander Payne Murray (1852–1925), Forgotten Librarian, Bibliographer, and Historian." *Libraries and Culture* 40, no. 1 (Winter 2005): 25–37.

Walker, David. *David Walker's Appeal, In Four Articles, Together With a Preamble, to the Coloured Citizens of the World, But in Particular, and Very Expressly, to Those of The United States of America*. New York: Hill and Wang, 1965.

Walker, George E. *The Afro-American in New York City, 1827–1860*. New York: Garland Publishing, 1993.

Washington, Booker T. "Negro Disfranchisement and the Negro in Business." *Outlook* 93, no. 6 (October 9, 1909): 310–16.

Washington, Booker T. *The Negro in Business*. Boston, MA: Hertel, Jenkins, 1907.

Washington, Booker T. *Up from Slavery: An Autobiography*. New York: Doubleday, Page, 1907.

Washington, S. A. M. *George Thomas Downing: Sketch of His Life and Times*. Newport, RI: The Milne Printery, 1910.

Watkins, Mel, ed. *African American Humor: The Best Black Comedy from Slavery to Today*. Chicago: Lawrence Hill Books, 2002.

Watson, John F. *Annals of Philadelphia and Pennsylvania in the Olden Time; Being a Collec-*

tion of Memoirs, Anecdote, and Incidents of the City and Its Inhabitants. Philadelphia, PA: Elijah Thomas, 1857.

Weaver, William Woys. Thirty-Five Receipts from "The Larder Invaded." Philadelphia, PA: The Library Company of Philadelphia and the Historical Society of Pennsylvania, 1986.

Weaver, William Woys. "Those Amazing Augustins." American Visions 5, no. 5 (October 1990): 52–53.

Weigley, Russell F. Philadelphia: A 300-Year History. New York: W. W. Norton, 1982.

Werstein, Irving. July, 1863. New York: Julian Messner, 1957.

Wesley, Charles H. "The Negroes of New York in the Emancipation Movement." Journal of Negro History 24, no. 1 (January 1939): 65–103.

Wesley, Charles H. Negro Labor in the United States, 1850–1925. New York: Vanguard Press, 1927.

Wesley, Charles H. "Negro Suffrage in the Period of Constitution-Making, 1787–1865." Journal of Negro History 32, no. 2 (April 1947): 143–68.

West, Cornel. Race Matters. Boston, MA: Beacon Press, 2001.

Whipple, George M. History of the Salem Light Infantry from 1805 to 1890. Salem, MA: Essex Institute, 1890.

White, Charles Frederick. Who's Who in Philadelphia: A Collection of Thirty Biographical Sketches of Philadelphia Colored People, Selected from among the Most Useful and Practical, Illustrating What Is Being Done among Them in the City, Together with Cuts and Information on Some of Their Leading Institutions and Organizations. Philadelphia, PA: AME Book Concern, 1912.

Whyte, James H. The Uncivil War: Washington during the Reconstruction, 1865–1878. New York: Twayne Publishers, 1958.

Wiener, Leo. Africa and the Discovery of America. 3 vols. Philadelphia, PA: Innes and Sons, 1920, 1922.

Wiener, Leo. Mayan and Mexican Origins. Cambridge, MA: Privately printed, 1926.

Wikramanayake, Marina. A World in Shadow: The Free Black in Antebellum South Carolina. Columbia: University of South Carolina Press, 1973.

Wilder, Craig Steven. A Covenant with Color: Race and Social Power in Brooklyn. New York: Columbia University Press, 2000.

Wilk, Daniel L. "The Phoenix Riot and the Memories of Greenwood County." Southern Cultures 8, no.4 (Winter 2002): 29–55.

Wilkins, Minna C. "Sandy Ground: A Tiny Racial Island." Staten Island Historian 6, no. 1 (January–March 1943): 1, 3, 7.

Wilkins, Sharron E. "The President's Kitchen." American Visions 10, no. 1 (February 1995): 56–58.

Willcox, James M. A History of the Philadelphia Saving Fund Society, 1816–1916. Philadelphia, PA: J. B. Lippincott Company, 1916.

Willhelm, Sidney M. Who Needs the Negro? New York: Anchor Books, 1971.

Williams, Chancellor. *The Destruction of Black Civilization*. Dubuque, IA: Kendall/Hunt Publishing, 1971.

Williams-Forson, Psyche. "African American Food Business" In *The Business of Food: Encyclopedia of the Food and Drink Industries*, edited by Gary Allen and Ken Albala, 8–13. Westport, CT: Greenwood Press, 2007.

Williams-Forson, Psyche A. *Building Houses out of Chicken Legs: Black Women, Food, and Power*. Chapel Hill: University of North Carolina Press, 2006.

Williamson, Hugh P. "The State against Celia, a Slave." *Midwest Journal* 409, no. 3 (1956): 408–20.

Wills, Garry. *"Negro President": Jefferson and the Slave Power*. Boston, MA: Houghton Mifflin, 2003.

Winch, Julie, ed. *The Elite of Our People: Joseph Willson's Sketches of Black Upper-Class Life in Antebellum Philadelphia*. University Park: The Pennsylvania State University Press, 2000.

Withey, Lynne. *Urban Growth in Colonial Rhode Island: Newport and Providence in the Eighteenth Century*. Albany: State University of New York Press, 1984.

Woodson, C. G. "The Wormley Family." *Negro History Bulletin* (January 1948): 75–84.

Woodson, Carter G. "The Bustill Family." *Negro History Bulletin* (April 1948): 143–50.

Woodson, Carter G. *The Mind of the Negro as Reflected in Letters Written during the Crisis, 1800–1860*. New York: Russell and Russell, 1969.

Woodson, Carter G., ed. *Negro Orators and Their Orations*. New York: Russell and Russell, 1969.

Woodward, C. Vann. *Reunion and Reaction: The Compromise of 1877 and the End of Reconstruction*. Garden City, NY: Doubleday Anchor Books, 1956.

Wynes, Charles E. "Ebenezer Don Carlos Bassett, America's First Black Diplomat." *Pennsylvania History* 51 (July 1984): 232–40.

Wynes, Charles E. "James Wormley of the Wormley Hotel Agreement." *Centennial Review* (Winter 1975): 397–401.

Yanuck, Julius. "Thomas Ruffin and North Carolina Slave Law." *Journal of Southern History* 21, no. 4 (November 1955): 456–75.

Yard, Lionel M. "Blacks in Brooklyn, N.Y." *Negro History Bulletin* 37 (August–September 1974): 289–93.

Yee, Shirley J. *Black Women Abolitionists: A Study in Activism, 1828–1860*. Knoxville: University of Tennessee Press, 1992.

Yette, Samuel F. *The Choice: The Issue of Black Survival in America*. New York: Berkley Medallion Books, 1971.

Youngken, Richard C. *African Americans in Newport: An Introduction to the Heritage of African Americans in Newport, Rhode Island, 1700–1945*. Newport: Rhode Island Historical Preservation & Heritage Commission, Rhode Island Black Heritage Society, 1995.

RECIPE INDEX

Chapter 5

Chapter 6

Chapter 7

Recipe Index

INDEX

Index

Index

Index

Index

Index

Shrimp Soup Louisiane, Lena Richard famous dish, 28

Sibley, John Langdon, 209

Sickles Brigade (Staten Island), 189

Silver's Ice Cream Parlor and Confectionery, 125

Simmons, Stephen (owned eating house), 164

Simms, John Alex, 249–50

Slade, William Andrew, 220, 222

slavery jurisprudence, xii, 260, 261

"slaves without masters," free Africans considered as, xiv, 41, 45, 179

Smallwood, John, 220

Smith John J., 202–3

Smith, Daniel Arthur, 81

Smith, Dr. James McCune, 175, 295n56, 295n58

Smith, Edna Jordan, 21

Smith, Emeline, 213–14

Smith, Joshua Bowen, "prince of caterers" (Massachusetts), xiv, 183, 203–5, 206, 207–14, 239, 246, 306n58, 307n64, 307–8nn66–67, 308–9nn68–73, 317–18n73

Smith, Milton H., 22

Smith, Reverend Stephen, 116

Smith, William H. (caterer), 122

Smithsonian, Boston branch, 207

Smithsonian Institute (Washington, D.C.), 223, 255

Snow Riot, 217–18

Snow Street, 80

Snow, Mr. Beverly, 217

Snow's Epicurean Eating House, 217

Snowden, Gurden, 220

Soap Box Minstrel performances. *See* Citizens' Republican Club

Society of Sons of Liberty, 54

sorghum (guinea corn), 11, 12

soul food: as a cultural and culinary shackle, xi; Blacks pigeonholed as purveyors of, xi, 3, 24, 25, 256, 258

South Carolina: free Africans regarded as bottomless fund for taxation in, 195; heritage of rice agriculture transplanted

and reinforced in, 193–94; rice culture and production in, 302n25; "race riot" in, 248

southern Black cooks, foundation of America's cuisine formulated by, xi

Southern Cuisine, 33, 256, 258

southern White women, cookbooks published by, 4, 43

Speck, Abe, 154

Spofford, Ainsworth R., 226

Squalls, Chef Annie Laura, 26

St. Catherines (sea island, Georgia), 190, 192

St. Cecilia Ball, 200

St. Domingue (Haiti), 19

St. Peter Claver, 106, 133, 136, 280–81n24

St. Philip's African Episcopal Church (New York), 169

St. Thomas African Episcopal Church, 107

Stanton, Secretary of War Edwin McMasters, 184, 185, 231, 238

State Journal (Harrisburg), 146

State of Missouri vs. Celia, A Slave, 177, 296–97n61

State v. John Mann, xii, 176, 260, 296n60

Stearns, George Luther, 210

Steele, William, 22

Stevens, Andrew F., 101, 111, 122, 123, 124, 125, 127, 128, 130

Stevens, Thaddeus, 192, 231

Stiles, Reverend Ezra, 76

Stir the Pot: The History of Cajun Cuisine, 256, 257

"stolen themselves" (escaped from slavery), 71, 113, 114, 210

Storrs, Emory, 242–43

Story, Supreme Court Justice Joseph, 62, 213, 273n27

Strong, George Templeton, 169–70, 178, 228–29

subordinate race, status of Africans as a, 173, 177, 178

suffrage bill passed by Congress, 1866, 222–23

Sullivan, Brian (Mount Auburn Cemetery archivist), 213

Sumner, Senator Charles, 90, 114, 115, 171, 183, 184, 192, 202–3, 204, 207–8, 209, 210,

Index